All Things Darwin

All Things Darwin

An Encyclopedia of Darwin's World

VOLUME 1
A–I

Patrick H. Armstrong

GREENWOOD PRESS
Westport, Connecticut • London

Library of Congress Cataloging-in-Publication Data

Armstrong, Patrick, 1941–

    All things Darwin : an encyclopedia of Darwin's world / Patrick H. Armstrong.

       p. cm.

    Includes bibliographical references and index.

    ISBN 978–0–313–33492–4 (set : alk. paper) — ISBN 978–0–313–33493–1 (v.1 : alk. paper) — ISBN 978–0–313–33494–8 (v.2 : alk. paper)

    1. Darwin, Charles, 1809–1882—Encyclopedias. 2. Naturalists—England—Biography—Encyclopedias. 3. Natural history—Encyclopedias. 4. Evolution (Biology)—Encyclopedias. I. Title.

    QH31.D2A7894 2007

    576.8'2092—dc22

    [B]   2007026482

British Library Cataloguing in Publication Data is available.

Library of Congress Catalog Card Number: 2007026482
ISBN-13: 978–0–313–33492–4 (set)
         978–0–313–33493–1 (vol. 1)
         978–0–313–33494–8 (vol. 2)

First published in 2007

Greenwood Press, 88 Post Road West, Westport, CT 06881
An imprint of Greenwood Publishing Group, Inc.
www.greenwood.com

Printed in the United States of America

The paper used in this book complies with the Permanent Paper Standard issued by the National Information Standards Organization (Z39.48–1984).

10 9 8 7 6 5 4 3 2 1

Contents

List of Entries   vii

Guide to Related Topics   xi

Preface   xv

Acknowledgments   xix

Introduction   xxi

The Encyclopedia   1

Appendix: Introduction to the Extracts from Darwin's Works   487

General Bibliography   545

Index   547

List of Entries

Anemones, Sea
Animal Behavior
Archaeopteryx
Ascension Island
Australia
Autobiography
Azores

Barlow, Norah (1885–1989)
Barnacles
Bay of Islands, New Zealand
Beagle, HMS
Beagle Diary
Beech, Southern or Antarctic
Beetles
Botany
Brazil
British Association for the
    Advancement of Science
Buckland, William (1784–1856)
Button, Jemmy

Cambrian Big Bang
Cambridge University
Cape of Good Hope
Cape Verde Islands
Catastrophism

Chambers, Robert (1802–1871)
Child Development
Chile and Peru
Chiloé
Climbing Plants
Cocos (Keeling) Islands
Coevolution
Corals and Coral Reefs
Correspondence of Charles Darwin
Covington, Syms (1816–1861)
Crabs
Creationism
Cuvier, Georges (1769–1832)

Dana, James Dwight (1813–1895)
Darwin, Annie (Anne Elizabeth
    Darwin) (1841–1851)
Darwin, Bernard (1876–1961)
Darwin, Charles Galton (1887–1962)
Darwin, Charles Robert (1809–1882)
Darwin, City of
Darwin, Emma (née Wedgwood)
    (1808–1896)
Darwin, Erasmus (junior) (Erasmus
    Alvey Darwin) (1804–1881)
Darwin, Erasmus (senior)
    (1731–1801)

Darwin, Francis (1848–1925)
Darwin, George Howard
  (1845–1912)
Darwin, Horace (1851–1928)
Darwin, Robert Waring (1766–1848)
Darwin College, Cambridge
Darwinism and Literature
Darwinism and Theology
Darwin's Death and Westminster
  Abbey Funeral
Darwin's Fungus
Dawkins, Richard (1941–)
Descent of Man
DNA
Domestic Animals
Down House

Earthworms
Ecology
Edinburgh
Eight Stones
Essay of 1844
Evolution, Convergent
Evolution, History of the Concept
Evolution, Saltatory
Evolutionary Ideas after *On the Origin*
Evolution of the Horse
Evolution through Natural Selection
Expression of Emotions

Falkland Islands
Fernando Noronha
Fertilisation of Orchids
Fieldwork and Collecting Methods
  of Charles Darwin
Fishes
FitzRoy, Robert (1805–1865)
Forms of Flowers
Fossils
Fox, William Darwin (1805–1880)
Frankland, George (1800–1838)

Galapagos Finches
Galapagos Islands
Geological Society of London
Geological Time Scale
Geology of the Voyage of the Beagle
Glaciation

Gladstone, William Ewart
  (1809–1898)
Glen Roy
Gould, John (1804–1881)
Gould, Stephen Jay (1941–2002)
Gradualism
Gray, Asa (1810–1888)

Hardy, Thomas (1840–1928)
Henslow, John Stevens (1796–1861)
Herschel, John F. W. (1792–1871)
Hooker, Joseph Dalton (1817–1911)
Human Evolution
Humboldt, Alexander von
  (1769–1859)
Huxley, Thomas (1825–1895)
Hydrography

Igneous Rocks
Ill Health and Diseases of Charles
  Darwin
Insectivorous Plants
Instinct
Intellectual Aristocracy
Islands

Jenyns, Leonard (later Blomefield)
  (1800–1893)

Kelp and Kelp Beds
King, Philip Gidley (junior)
  (1817–1904)
King, Phillip Parker (1791–1856)
Kingsley, Charles (1819–1875)
Kirby, William (1759–1850)

Lamarck, Jean-Baptiste (1744–1829)
Linnaeus, Carolus (Carl von Linné)
  (1707–1778)
Linnean Society of London
Long-Distance Dispersal
Lyell, Charles (1797–1875)

Malthus, Thomas Robert
  (1766–1834)
Mantell, Gideon Algernon
  (1790–1852)
Maori

Marsupials
Marx, Karl Heinrich (1818–1883)
Mauritius
Megatherium
Mendel, Gregor (1822–1884)
Metamorphic Rocks
Morris, Francis Orpen (1810–1893)
Mutations

Native Peoples
New South Wales
New Zealand
North Wales
Notes and Notebooks

On the Origin of Species
Origin of Life
Origin of the *Beagle* Voyage
Owen, Fanny Mostyn (later
    Biddulph) (1807–1886)
Owen, Richard (1804–1892)

Pacific Ocean
Paley, William (1743–1805)
Patagonia
Peppered Moth
Planaria
Punctuated Equilibrium

Raverat, Gwen (1885–1957)
Ray, John (1627–1705)
Recapitulation
Reconciliation
Red Notebook
Religion in the Life of Charles Darwin
Rheas
River Plate
Royal Navy in the Nineteenth Century
Royal Society

Sedgwick, Adam (1785–1873)
Sedimentary Rocks
Shrewsbury
Sketch of 1842
Smith, Adam (1723–1790)
Spencer, Herbert (1820–1903)
St. Helena and Ascension Island
St. Paul's Rocks
Sulivan, Bartholomew James
    (1810–1890)

Tahiti
Tasmania
Teilhard de Chardin, Pierre
    (1881–1955)
Tenerife
Tierra del Fuego
Tiktaalik
Toponyms
Transitional Forms
Tristram, Henry Baker (1822–1906)

Uniformitarianism

Vestiges
Victoria (1819–1901; sovereign
    1837–1901)
Voyage of the Beagle

Wallace, Alfred Russel
    (1823–1913)
Warrah
Waterhouse, George Robert
    (1810–1888)
Wedgwood, Josiah I (1730–1795)
Wedgwood, Josiah II (1769–1841)
Wilberforce, Samuel (1805–1873)

Zoology of the Voyage of the Beagle

Guide to Related Topics

Darwin's Contemporaries

Buckland, William
Button, Jemmy
Covington, Syms
Cuvier, Georges
Dana, James Dwight
FitzRoy, Robert
Frankland, George
Gladstone, William Ewart
Gould, John
Gray, Asa
Hardy, Thomas
Henslow, John Stevens
Herschel, John
Hooker, Joseph
Humboldt, Alexander von
Huxley, Thomas
Jenyns, Leonard (later Blomefield)
King, Philip Gidley
King, Phillip Parker
Kingsley, Charles
Lyell, Charles
Malthus, Thomas
Mantell, Gideon Algernon
Marx, Karl
Morris, Francis Orpen

Owen, Fanny Middleton
Owen, Richard
Sedgwick, Adam
Spencer, Herbert
Sulivan, Bartholomew James
Tristram, Henry Baker
Victoria, Queen
Wallace, Alfred Russel
Waterhouse, George
Wilberforce, Samuel

Darwin's Travels

Australia
Azores
Bay of Islands
Beagle, HMS
Brazil
Cape of Good Hope
Cape Verde Islands
Chile and Peru
Chiloé
Cocos (Keeling) Islands
Edinburgh
Eight Stones
Falkland Islands
Fernando Noronha

Fieldwork and Collecting Methods
  of Charles Darwin
Galapagos Islands
Glen Roy
Mauritius
New South Wales
New Zealand
North Wales
Origins and Route of the *Beagle*
  Voyage
Pacific Ocean
Patagonia
River Plate
St. Helena and Ascension Island
St. Paul's Rocks
Tahiti
Tasmania
Tenerife
Tierra del Fuego

Concepts and Ideas

Animal Behavior
Botany
Cambrian Big Bang
Catastrophism
Child Development
Coevolution
Creationism
Darwinism and Literature
Darwinism and Theology
DNA
Ecology
Evolutionary Ideas after Darwin
Evolution, Convergent
Evolution, History of
Evolution, Saltatory
Evolution through Natural Selection
Geological Time Scale
Glaciation
Gradualism
Human Evolution
Hydrography
Instinct
Intellectual Aristocracy
Islands
Long-Distance Dispersal
Mutations
Origin of Life

Punctuated Equilibrium
Recapitulation
Reconciliation
Religion in the Life of Charles Darwin
Transitional Forms
Toponyms
Uniformitarianism

Organisms

Anemones, Sea
Archaeopteryx
Barnacles
Beech, Southern or Antarctic
Beetles
Corals and Coral Reefs
Crabs
Darwin's Fungus
Domestic Animals
Earthworms
Evolution of the Horse
Fishes
Fossils
Galapagos Finches
Kelp and Kelp Beds
Marsupials
Megatherium
Peppered Moth
Planaria
Rheas
Tiktaalik
Warrah

Darwin's Family

Barlow, Norah
Darwin, Annie
Darwin, Bernard
Darwin, Charles Dalton
Darwin, Charles Robert
Darwin, Emma
Darwin, Francis
Darwin, George
Darwin, Horace
Darwin, Robert Waring
Down House
Fox, William Darwin
Raverat, Gwen
Wedgwood, Josiah I
Wedgwood, Josiah II

Darwin's Writings

Autobiography
Beagle Diary
Climbing Plants
Correspondence of Charles Darwin
Descent of Man
Essay of 1844
Expression of Emotions
Forms of Flowers
Geology of the Voyage of the Beagle
Insectivorous Plants
Notes and Notebooks
On the Origin of Species
Red Notebook
Sketch of 1842
Voyage of the Beagle
Zoology of the Voyage of the Beagle

Institutions

British Association for the
  Advancement of Science
Cambridge University
Darwin, City of
Darwin College
Geological Society of London
Linnean Society of London
Royal Navy in the Nineteenth
  Century
Royal Society

Modern Darwinians

Dawkins, Richard
Gould, Stephen Jay
Teilhard de Chardin

Darwin's Predecessors

Chambers, Robert
Kirby, William
Lamarck, Jean-Baptiste
Linneaus, Carolus
Mendel, Gregor
Paley, William
Ray, John
Smith, Adam

Geology

Geological Time Scale
Igneous Rocks
Metamorphic Rocks
Sedimentary Rocks

Miscellaneous

Darwin's Death and Westminster Abbey
  Funeral
Ill Health and Diseases of Darwin
Maori
Native Peoples
Vestiges

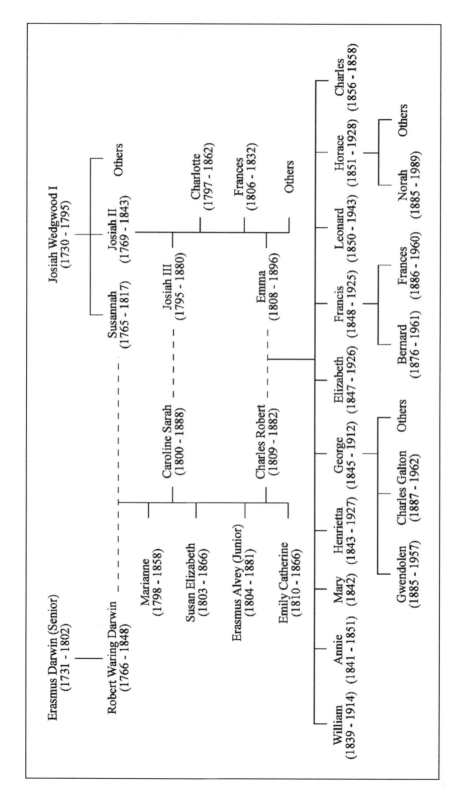

Simplified family tree of the Darwin and Wedgwood families. Note the close connections: three marriages in two generations.

Preface

"All Things Darwin?" An impossible aspiration! It is estimated that Charles Robert Darwin (1809–1882) wrote some six million words including about thirty books (depending on how one defines "book," since he sometimes revised his text so thoroughly that later editions might be appreciably different publications with subtly different emphases). He also published hundreds of scientific papers and articles on a wide variety of topics (botany, zoology, anthropology, psychology, and geology). With his massive network of friends, correspondents, and extended family, he wrote, and had written to him, thousands of letters, many of which still exist. During the voyage of the *Beagle* (1831–1836), he visited three continents, traveling extensively in two of them (South America and Australia), less so in the third (Africa), and set foot on about forty islands in the Atlantic, Indian, and Pacific Oceans, collecting thousands of specimens (plants, mammals, birds, reptiles, amphibians, invertebrates, rocks, fossils) en route. His ideas had a profound effect, not only on most branches of science, but also on theology, literature, and social thought. It is impossible to do justice to such a life in a single work; thus, it has been necessary to be selective. Inevitably, the selection has been personal and will not please all. I have attempted to highlight those parts of Darwin's life and work that, in my opinion, have captured the imagination: the *Beagle* voyage, his most important publications, and those who influenced and were influenced by him. I have included a selection of the places he visited and some of the plants and animals important to his work. This is not a work on evolution as such, and my treatment of evolutionary topics is therefore relatively brief, although I have attempted to carry some of Darwin's ideas forward to the present century. I have tried to make each article reasonably complete in itself, while avoiding excessive duplication, but this middle way inevitably resulted in a measure of overlap between entries on related topics.

This has been something of a personal journey for me. I had the good fortune to grow up in the ancient university city of Cambridge, with its long association with the Darwin family. Among my recollections from early childhood is a memory of Gwen Raverat (Charles Darwin's grand-daughter) painting pictures with an easel fixed to her invalid chair beside the River Cam; I have ever after had an interest in Charles Darwin and the Darwins. Many decades later, I spent two periods of sabbatical leave from the University of Western Australia at Darwin College, Cambridge, which now occupies buildings lived in by the Darwin family (including Gwen Raverat) from the latter part of nineteenth century until the 1960s.

There is another significant personal point of contact. My father, Edward Armstrong, proud to have been born during the reign of Queen Victoria, maintained the great English parson-naturalist tradition (although he was Irish); he was a polymath—an authority on an enormous variety of subjects from Shakespeare's sonnets to birdsong (very Victorian). One of his enthu-siasms was the folklore of birds. On his death in 1978, I inherited part of my father's library. On opening his copy of *The Voyage of the Beagle* (it is beside my laptop as I write), I saw the annotation "emu dance, page 434." On turning to this page, I was interested to see that Darwin's description of the emu dance formed part of his description of Western Australia, where I was then living with my family. Evidently, Darwin disliked Western Aus-tralia and left its shores "without sorrow or regret": I felt I had to inquire further. Those inquiries have taken me around the world several times (thankfully, mainly by modern jet aircraft rather than 1820s-built sailing craft), in Darwin's footsteps and in the *Beagle*'s wake. To pick up fossils from the cliff face in the Falklands and chip at coral rock on the Cocos Is-lands where the great naturalist collected, and with photocopies of his notes in hand, have been sublime experiences. Other special moments have been working through the notes from the *Beagle* period in Cambridge; handling the correspondence concerning Alfred Russel Wallace's "bolt from the blue" (now held in Philadelphia) that told Darwin that another mind was reaching similar conclusions; standing in his study at Down House imagin-ing the great man working on his papers; and visiting the grave of John Stevens Henslow, Darwin's great friend and mentor, in a wildflower-filled churchyard at Hitcham in Suffolk. It was all good fun—even skirting mine-fields warily on East Falkland and kicking small sharks in the head as, like Darwin, I waded across the coral reefs at Cocos. (There were no minefields in the Falklands in 1833–1834, although the place was not without its dan-gers even then.)

What was Darwin's secret? He had the most extraordinary good fortune to be born into a reasonably prosperous, educated family; he was well con-nected through his family background and his time at Cambridge; he visited the right places on the *Beagle* voyage (and in the right order); and he was extraordinarily able. Perhaps most importantly, he embodied the notion that "The habit of comparison leads to generalization": he not only visited about forty islands, but he knew how to *compare* them—their plants, animals, rocks, and people—and extract themes, ideas, and generalizations from these comparisons. At attempt is made to convey this comparative approach in this volume.

With regard to bibliographic sources, there are so many editions and printings of many of Darwin's books that it would be useless to attempt page references to these, so I have usually only provided chapter numbers. For Darwin's *Diary,* I have given date references using the 1933 Cambridge edition of *Charles Darwin's Diary of the Voyage of H.M.S. Beagle* edited by Norah Barlow, another of his granddaughters. References to *Correspondence* refer to the monumental *Correspondence of Charles Darwin,* of which Cambridge University Press has at the time of this writing (early 2007) produced 15 volumes. Although I have avoided giving Web-based sources, which change frequently, readers may nevertheless find it useful to know that many of Darwin's works are available online—some of them at more than one site.

Acknowledgments

I acknowledge first, with gratitude, members of my family: my late father and mother who chose to live in Cambridge in the formative years of my youth; the importance of my inheritance of a part of my father's library is mentioned in the preface. Also my dear, tolerant, wife Moyra, who has from time to time found Charles Darwin to be almost part of the family, but found he was absolutely no help at all when she needed the garden shed to be cleared out.

Grants for my work on Darwin and his influence have, over the years, come from the University of Western Australia, the National Geographic Society (Washington, DC), the Centre for Indian Ocean Studies (Perth, Western Australia), University College Durham, St. Deiniol's Library (Hawarden, North Wales), and the Australian Foundation for Theological Research.

Libraries, archival deposits, and museums that have assisted include:

In Australia: the Reid Library at the University of Western Australia; the Mitchell Library, New South Wales; and the Battye Library, Perth, Western Australia.

In Britain: Cambridge University Library, particularly the Manuscripts Room to which I was introduced by its then curator, Peter Gautrey; the Cambridge University Zoological Museum; the Durham University Libraries, particularly the Palace Green Library; the Bath Royal Literary and Philosophical Institution; the Ipswich and East Suffolk Record Office; Shrewsbury School; and the Natural History Museum (London).

Acknowledgments

In the United States: Yale University Libraries and the American Philosophical Society Library, Philadelphia.

The following institutions have provided hospitality while I was on study leave from the University of Western Australia: Darwin College, Cambridge; St. Deiniol's Library, Hawarden, North Wales; University College Durham; and Southern Connecticut State University.

The following individuals were among the many who assisted during fieldwork, read drafts of my material, and encouraged or supported me in a host of other ways: José and Piedade Azcue (I thank the latter particularly for the benefit of her medical knowledge), Pauline Bunce, Alan and Robyn Cadwallader, Kevin and Ros Cahill, Viv Forbes, Peter Francis, Bob and Marion Keegan, Sarah Lumley, Geof Martin, Jim Moore, Michael and Andrea Roberts (and Holly the border collie), Shannon Rogers (especially for her knowledge of nineteenth-century literature), Mark and Vanessa Seaward, Brian Shaw, and Alison and John Underwood.

I thank them all.

Introduction

Charles Darwin is known as the Great Victorian Naturalist. It is as though the nineteenth century, Queen Victoria's reign, and the scientific revolution of which Darwin's ideas were a part were different ways of considering the same time frame. Darwin's life (1809–1882) spanned much of the nineteenth century, which itself coincided closely with the life of Queen Victoria (1819–1901) (although while Darwin was aboard HMS *Beagle*, King William IV was on the throne; Victoria actually reigned 1837–1901).

Although the American colonies had been lost a few decades before the century opened, the nineteenth century was a period in which Great Britain had unprecedented influence, wealth, and power. As the result of colonization, political influence, trade, and military conquest, England was the center of an empire that extended to all the then-known continents, from the Arctic to the Southern Ocean. The Indian Ocean, with British possessions in Africa, India, and Australia, as well as islands such as Mauritius could have been envisaged as a "British lake." Vessels of the Royal Navy could have been encountered in almost every port (among their other tasks was the stamping out of slavery, which the Westminster Parliament had outlawed throughout the British Empire in March 1807).

Fueled by indigenous supplies of coal, iron ore, and limestone, the industrial revolution in Britain was continuing apace. Manufactured goods were available for export, especially to the Empire, and raw materials (such as cotton and wool) and food for the expanding populations of Britain's industrial cities were imported (again, particularly from the countries of the

Empire). Another of the Royal Navy's roles, therefore, was to protect the trade routes and also, incidentally, to prepare hydrographic charts on which expanding navigation and trade depended. Industrial enterprise, international trade, the development of an empire, and the rise of naval power can therefore be seen as tightly interconnected. This, then, was part of the context of the *Beagle*'s voyage of hydrographic survey and exploration. Darwin was tolerant and open and happy to be on good terms with those of any country, class, and creed; yet he was fully committed to Britain's imperial role. When he visited the "little Englands" of the Southern Hemisphere—in New South Wales, Tasmania, King George's Sound, and at the Cape of Good Hope—he saw them, with approval, as manifesting the strength of the mother country.

The development of industry and trade allowed great fortunes to be amassed. The Darwins and Wedgwoods intermarried over several generations, and thus their combined prosperity was partly based on the enterprise of the Wedgwood pottery business. The growing affluence, together with the demands of industry, also favored scientific endeavors. For example, the need for raw materials contributed to an increasing understanding of geology, and the cutting of canals and the construction of railways provided geological knowledge. The Geological Society of London was founded in 1807. Initially, it tended to be somewhat dominated by a clique of wealthy dilettantes, but this changed, and practical men became involved. Charles Darwin served as secretary for a while shortly after his return from the sea, and he regularly presented papers and published in the pages of its journal.

Other scientific bodies, such as the Royal Geographical Society (RGS) and the British Association for the Advancement of Science (BAAS), had their origins in the first few decades of the century: the RGS in 1830 and the BAAS in 1831.

Yet despite this spirit of adventure, enterprise, and innovation, at the start of the nineteenth century, much in Britain (particularly England; Scotland has always had a radical streak) was as it had been for centuries. The countryside was still dominated by the landed families. There were two universities—Oxford and Cambridge—both firmly within the grip of the Anglican Church, the legally established Church of England. Although even here there was movement in the early decades of the century: Durham University was founded partly to counteract Oxbridge in the north of England in 1832, King's College, London having just preceded it in 1829. The universities were all-male affairs—interestingly, it was London and Durham that opened up university education for women. And Westminster, the Mother of Parliaments, until the passing of the Representation of the People Act of 1832—commonly known as the Great Reform Act (or Bill) of 1832—was anything but a democratic institution. This act was designed to "take effectual Measures for correcting diverse Abuses that have long prevailed in the Choice of Members to serve in the Commons House of Parliament." The statute granted seats in the House of Commons to large cities that sprang up during the industrial revolution, taking seats away from towns that had become depopulated during the preceding centuries (these towns were sometimes called "rotten boroughs" because the seat in Parliament was effectively controlled by a small number of individuals). Furthermore, the act greatly increased the number of those entitled to vote, approximately doubling the size of the electorate. Nevertheless, even after the passing of this act, the vast majority of citizens were unable to vote. The Reform Act also specifically disqualified women, triggering the movement toward women's suffrage.

The struggles for the passing of the Reform Bill typify the political rivalries of the era. The act was proposed by the Whigs, the more radical party led by the prime minister, Lord Grey. The legislation met with significant opposition from the Tories (conservatives) particularly in the House of Lords (the members of which inherited their seats). The Tory party and the members of the House of Lords (who included the bishops of the Church of England) were often among those who were, or were aligned with, the landed interests who benefited from the status quo. The Darwin and Wedgwood families, in the Whig radical tradition, were firmly in support of these developments. Robert FitzRoy, captain of HMS *Beagle,* with his aristocratic connections, and a High Tory, would not have been in favor.

The preeminence of the Church of England was associated with religious discrimination of various kinds, some of it trivial, some more serious—in the universities and in Parliament. Another oddity was that, until the later decades of the nineteenth century, teachers at the universities other than the masters of colleges and professors were not permitted to continue in office and to marry—harking back to an ancient monastic tradition. Many of the professors (including, for example, Darwin's teachers Adam Sedgwick and John Stevens Henslow) were clergy of the Church of England.

Among the most important developments in the nineteenth century were those in communications. When Darwin went ashore from the *Beagle* at Falmouth on the stormy night of October 2, 1836, he traveled to his home in Shrewsbury by stagecoach. A few years later, he and his family were traveling around the country by train: the expansion of the railways between the 1820s and 1860s was both encouraged by and encouraged industrial expansion. The penny postage came in 1840, the first telegraph entering use in April 1839. These administrative and technological developments greatly assisted communication and, therefore, the ease with which scientists such as Darwin could maintain contact with one another. Darwin, Charles Lyell, Joseph Hooker, and other members of their circle wrote hundreds of letters to one another in the 1840s, 1850s, and 1860s, to the enormous advantage of their work. This would have been quite impossible just a few decades earlier.

The life and work of Charles Darwin needs to be seen in the context of his times. He (and his wife Emma) came from the expanding, increasingly affluent middle classes—the products of industrial enterprise. The expanding Empire and the importance of the Royal Navy provided him with the opportunity for the *Beagle* voyage. His ideas formed a part, admittedly a leading part, of the surge of interest in science and technology that was linked to the commercial development of the middle and later years of the century. Yet despite his revolutionary ideas and the Whiggish, somewhat radical tradition of the family (he strongly supported the abolition of slavery and Parliamentary reform), he was in some ways a conservative man. He believed it was his duty to have as many children as possible for the country and for the Empire (he and Emma had 10, 7 of whom survived to adulthood). He adopted the life-style of a country squire, living in the small village of Downe in the heart of the Kent countryside. He became a local magistrate and supported local activities (religious and secular). Despite pressure, he refused to take a militant, antireligious posture, perceiving that religion was a force for stability. He was a landowner in a small way and loved the countryside. Progressive in some ways, deeply traditional in others, Charles Darwin typifies the Victorian era.

Anemones, Sea

Marine-living Coelenterata—that is, animals having a coelenteron or single body cavity into which there is only one opening, the mouth, through which everything passes in and out. The mouth is surrounded by a number of tentacles.

Since his days in **Edinburgh,** beachcombing along the Firth of Forth, examining the varieties of marine life, Charles Darwin had an interest in these organisms. He encountered them many times on his voyage on the *Beagle*—for example, in the **kelp beds** of the **Falkland Islands** and in the **coral reefs** of the islands of the Pacific and Indian Oceans.

Always interested in the associations between organisms, he was struck by the tripartite ecological link between mollusks, hermit crabs, and sea anemones (*Actinia*) on the shores of the **Cocos (Keeling) Islands:**

> *Actinia:* The specimen which I found was adhering to old shells which were inhabited by hermit crabs; they lay beneath the large stones on the outer reef. (*Zoological Diary,* Cambridge University Library, Darwin Archive)

Darwin was also, throughout the voyage and afterward, interested in the behavior of organisms and their capacity to respond to stimuli, and he performed experiments to test this. He experimented with the octopus in the **Cape Verde Islands,** and the **planaria** (flatworms) he found in Tasmania. Here Darwin describes a "purplish red" sea anemone:

The animal has the remarkable power when irritated of emitting from its mouth . . . bunches of viscous threads. These threads are colored "Peach & Aurora Red," they can be drawn out when in contact with any object to the length of some inches, & are emitted with considerable force. The pores near the part most irritated only affected this substance. (*Zoological Diary*, Cambridge University Library, Darwin Archive)

Darwin added the note of the "viscous threads": "I know not their nature or use." They were, in fact, cnidoblasts, the stinging structures containing toxin used for defense and the capture of food by coelenterates. The threads spring out when a bristlelike trigger or cnidril is touched—hence the modern name of the phylum (major biological group) Cnidaria, which includes anemones, corals, jellyfish, and hydras. These stinging cells can inflict a painful sting, as Darwin found to his cost during his experiments.

Animal Behavior

The term now used for the scientific study of animal behavior is *ethology*. The behavior of animals, both vertebrates and invertebrates, was of special interest to Darwin throughout much of his career. He believed (rightly) that its study could provide evidence for his evolutionary theories.

Darwin was an enthusiastic collector of beetles as a schoolboy and undergraduate and, from an early date, occasionally noted the activities as well the appearance of these creatures. An anecdote he recalled in later life involved his finding two fine specimens, and then a third. Unable to hold three at once, he put one beetle into his mouth, where it expelled an unpleasant fluid and the young Charles spat it out.

From the earliest days on the *Beagle*, Darwin was making detailed observations about the creatures he encountered, often comparing the behavior of one organism with that another, or comparing the same organism at different times. Less than a month after leaving England, on January 28, 1832, poking around in the rock pools of Quail Island in the **Cape Verde Islands** at low tide, he encountered an octopus. The account from his *Zoological Diary* is worth quoting at some length.

Found amongst the rocks West of Quail Island at low water. . . . When first discovered he was in a hole & it was difficult to perceive what it was. As soon as I drove him from his den he *shot with great rapidity* across the pool of water, leaving in his train a large quantity of ink. Even when in a shallow place it was difficult to catch him, for he twisted his body with great ease between the stones & by his suckers stuck very fast to them. When in the water the animal was of a brownish purple, but immediately on the beach the colour changed to a yellowish green. When I had the animal in a basin of Salt water on board this fact was explained by its having the Chamaelion like power of changing the colour of its body. The general colour of the animal was French grey, with numerous spots of bright yellow. The former of these colours varied in intensity, the other entirely disappeared and then returned. Over the whole body there were continually passing clouds, varying in colour from a "hyacinth red" to a "Chestnut brown." [There was a color chart aboard the *Beagle*, and Darwin often used it in his descriptions.] As seen under a lens these clouds consisted of minute points apparently injected with a coloured fluid. The whole animal presented a most extraordinary mottled appearance, & much surprised every body who saw it. The edges of the sheath were orange, this likewise varied in tint. The animal seemed susceptible to small shocks of galvanism [electricity]: contracting itself & the parts between the points of contact of the wires, [and] became almost black. This in a lesser degree followed the scratching [of] the animal with a needle. . . . The animal was slightly phosphorescent at night. (*Zoological Diary*, Cambridge University Library, Darwin Archive)

Darwin compared these observations with others made a few days later (February 3):

Another upon seeing me instantly changed its colour. When in a deep hole being of a dark, but [when it was] in shallow of a much paler colour. From this cause & the stealthy way in which it creeps along, occasionally darting forward had much difficulty in watching it. (*Zoological Diary*, Cambridge University Library, Darwin Archive)

Darwin also later noted that **Georges Cuvier** had commented on the ability of octopi to change color and noted this on the blank page opposite the original annotations in his *Zoological Diary*. He was constantly comparing, not only his own observations at different times and places, but his own with those of others.

Darwin's zoological notes from the *Beagle* years are full of comparable observations. He collected nests made by insects and birds; he detailed the complexity of the bird calls and songs of some of the species he encountered in South America; and he commented on the display of whales, as they leapt and then flopped into the sea in the waters off Tierra del Fuego with a sound "like a great gun."

Many of Darwin's observations on animal behavior are remarkably integrative. He attempts to relate the organism's behavior to its appearance and structure, and sometimes also to its environment and way of life. Here is his account of the Falklands flightless steamer duck (modern scientific name *Tachyeres brachydactyla*) on East Falkland in April 1834:

A logger-headed duck called by former navigators race-horses, & now steamers has been described from its extraordinary manner of splashing & paddling along; in large flocks; In the evening when preening themselves make the very same mixture of noises which bull-frogs do in the Tropics: their head is remarkably strong (my big geological hammer can hardly break it) & their beak likewise; this must fit them well for their mode of subsistence: which from their dung must chiefly be shell-fish obtained at low water & from kelp—They can dive but little, are very tenacious to life, so as to be (as all our sportsmen have experienced) very difficult to kill; They build amongst bushes & grass near the sea. (*Zoological Diary,* Cambridge University Library, Darwin Archive)

The account describes many aspects of behavior: locomotion, feeding, nesting, and communicating. Darwin describes how the organism "slots into its habitat"—that is, its behavior, food, habitat, and structure are all related to one another. The heavy head and beak "fit them well for their mode of subsistence"; they seldom dive but feed from the "shell fish obtained at low water and the kelp." They are very social, abounding in large flocks; they are thus very vocal with a vigorous "splashing and paddling" display. The young naturalist does not link their seashore (rather than inland) nesting to their lack of capacity for flight or suggest that the ducks' robust tenacity to life might be a compensation for flightlessness, but there is a remarkably integrative approach in the manner in which Darwin noted his observations.

Yet, of course, Darwin is a man of his time. Many of his accounts are very anthropomorphic (i.e., he gives animals human characteristics) to an extent that would be an anathema to a modern ethologist. The octopus was "stealthy"; other creatures were described as "cunning," "quarrelsome," "patient," or "crafty." Nevertheless, even at this early stage, there are signs that he was arranging information in ways that were important later when he was developing his evolutionary ideas. Here, he is still in the Falklands, suggesting that behavior as well as structure and appearance might be used to show relationships between bird species.

Mr Mellersch [a shipmate on the *Beagle*] having wounded a cormorant, it went on shore & immediately these birds [caracaras, *Phalconoenus australis*] attacked & by blows tried to kill it.—Connection in habit as well as structure with true Hawkes. (*Zoological Diary,* Cambridge University Library, Darwin Archive)

Darwin clearly appreciated that behavioral attributes might be inherited. He compared the extreme tameness of birds in the Falklands (and other remote island groups he visited) with that at mainland locations and at Tierra del Fuego, where for generations birds had been persecuted. The idea of the inheritance of behavioral traits and the related notion that these could be used as a basis for taxonomy have considerable evolutionary significance.

Throughout his career, Darwin was fascinated by **instinct** (innate or inbuilt behavior); he thought that its study in animals and humans might assist in him in establishing his idea that humans had evolved from other species of animals, and it could show the interconnectedness of animal groups. He studied the development of his own children in an attempt to gain insights to these phenomena. He showed how "wild" instincts were inherited by domesticated animals. There is a long chapter on instinct in

On the Origin of Species (chapter 7) in which he develops the idea that instincts are subject to natural selection pressures as well as morphology: "[N]atural selection acts only by the accumulation of slight modifications of structure or instinct, each profitable to the individual under its conditions of life." Later he developed his ideas on behavior in general and instinctive behavior in particular in *The Expression of Emotions in Man and Animals* (1872), in which he applied similar approaches to the study of behavior in animals and humans, aiming to demonstrate similarities in their patterns of behavior, and therefore their relatedness.

See also: Child Development.

Archaeopteryx

From immediately after the publication of **On the Origin of Species,** scientists have sought to find evidence for Darwin's theories in the form of transitional forms between the major groups. One of the earliest candidates was *Archaeopteryx lithographica* (literally, ancient wing from the printing stone). The fossil of this somewhat birdlike and somewhat reptilian organism, approximately the size of a crow, has become the subject of much controversy.

The limestone in which it was discovered is a smooth, fine-grained stone, which was formerly used in printing and quarried from workings in and near Solnhofen in Germany. The rock was probably formed on the bed of a very saline lagoon of late Jurassic age, about 150 million years ago.

Eight specimens of *Archaeopteryx* have been found: seven reasonably complete specimens and one single feather. The feather was the first to be found, near Solnhofen, in 1860. The first complete specimen was found in 1861, near Langenaltheim. This is probably the best known; it was bought by the British Museum of Natural History in London, as the result of the enthusiasm of **Richard Owen,** for what was, at the time, the very high price of £700. (Although the lot included over a thousand other fossils from Solnhofen. The fossil was sold by a local doctor who had received it in lieu of payment for medical treatment.) Owen produced a detailed scientific description of the specimen in 1863, recognizing that it represented a **transitional form**—although not in the Darwinian, evolutionary sense, as Owen was a fierce opponent of Darwin's ideas.

Another specimen appeared in 1877 near Blumenberg. This was a better specimen than the London fossil, having a complete, although crushed, head. It was acquired by the Berlin museum, coincidentally having been sold by the son of the doctor who passed the 1861 specimen to Owen. Several other specimens of *Archaeopteryx* have been found since (one early find was originally described as a pterodactyl and was correctly identified only in the 1970s). An incomplete specimen was found close to the site from which the London specimen came in 1958; it was scientifically described the following year. However, in 1992, after the death of its original finder and owner, the specimen was found to be missing and it is thought that it was secretly sold. Its present location is unknown.

Archaeopteryx has two characteristics that are virtually confined to birds and three characteristics that are typical of birds but occasionally are found in certain groups of reptiles.

1. The possession of feathers, which are characteristic of all modern birds and are found on no other living vertebrates. (However, 1998 discoveries in China suggest that birds may not be quite unique in this. Dinosaur species *Protoarchaeopteryx robusta* and *Caudipteryx zoui* appear to have feathers.)
2. An opposable big toe (hallux). This also is a characteristic of birds and not of dinosaurs.
3. A wishbone (furcula) formed of two collar bones (clavicles) fused together. Indeed, until recently, even clavicles were almost unknown in the theropod dinosaurs (the group of reptiles from which the birds are thought to have evolved). It has recently been discovered that some theropod dinosaurs did indeed have clavicles (e.g., *Segisaurus, Velociraptor, Euparkeria, Ornithosuchus*).
4. An elongate and backward-directed pubis (a paired cartilage-bone forming the front lower part of the pelvic girdle of some vertebrates). This is a feature of birds, but it is also a feature of some theropod dinosaurs and so is not diagnostic of birds. However, the pubic shafts of *Archaeopteryx* and one of a group of theropod dinosaurs, which are thought to be closely related to birds, are somewhat similar.
5. Bones that are pneumatic (air-containing). *Archaeopteryx* bones appear to have air sacs, as do those of birds and some dinosaurs.

Archaeopteryx has many characteristics typical of reptiles:

1. No bill or beak; all birds have a keratinized or horn-covered bill.
2. In the abdomen or trunk region, the vertebrae (the small bones that make up the backbone) are free. In birds, the trunk vertebrae are always fused together.
3. The cerebral (brain) hemispheres are elongate and slender, and the cerebellum (a part of the hindbrain) is situated behind the midbrain and does not overlap it from behind or press down on it. This is a strongly reptilian feature. In birds, the cerebral hemispheres are stout, and the cerebellum is much enlarged, so that it spreads forward over the midbrain and compresses it downward. Thus, the shape of the brain of *Archaeopteryx* is not like that of modern birds, but rather intermediate between dinosaurs and birds.
4. The neck is attached to the rear of the skull, as in dinosaurs, and not from below, as in modern birds.
5. A long, bony tail with many free vertebrae all the way up to the tip. Birds have a short, bony tail (in contradistinction to the tail of feathers), and the caudal or tail vertebrae are fused together.

6. Possession of teeth. No modern birds have teeth, although bird embryos form tooth buds.
7. The ribs are slender, without bracing structures between them and do not articulate with (hinge onto) the sternum (breastbone). Birds have stout, strong ribs with uncinate processes (braces linking them) and that articulate with the sternum.
8. The sacrum (the structure formed from the fusion of vertebrae developed for the attachment of the pelvic girdle) occupies 6 vertebrae. This is the same number as in reptiles and some dinosaurs. The bird sacrum covers between 11 and 23 vertebrae. So, while the range of variation seen in modern birds is considerable, it is much greater than the number found in *Archaeopteryx*.

There are a number of other reptilian characteristics, such as the possession of claws and the form of the skull and the limb bones, but a discussion of these would be repetitious and rather technical.

There are those who argue that *Archaeopteryx* could not be transitional between the reptiles and birds, because some of the reptilian features are present in some birds. For example, claws are present (on the forelimbs or wings) in the juvenile hoatzin (a South American species), and the touracos (African) have two claws but lose them as they mature. However, many birds have claws when in the egg; to some extent, the life history of an organism recapitulates the evolutionary history. Thus, the possession of clawlike structures on the wings of *Archaeopteryx* tends to confirm the reptilian affinities rather than contradict them.

Others who argue against the transitional form of *Archaeopteryx* maintain that the earliest bird fossils predate *Archaeopteryx;* but there is some uncertainty about whether these fossils (from the Trias) are, in fact, birds; they are much damaged. And even if it were proved that true birds did exist before *Archaeopteryx* was feeding around the salty lakes of southern Germany in the Jurassic period, this does not invalidate the transitional hypothesis. It was probably not the case that *Archaeopteryx lithographica* was the ancestor of *all* birds; it may have been something of a branch on the evolutionary tree that had some similarities to the true ancestral form and that persisted for some time.

In the 1980s, an attack came from a particularly extraordinary source. The famous (and brilliant) English astronomer, Professor Sir Fred Hoyle published an article, and later a book, claiming that the London specimen was a hoax. A dinosaur fossil, it was claimed, had been treated with a paste made from powdered limestone and then, while the paste was still semiliquid, had feathers pressed into it. The staff at the museum were outraged. The British Museum of Natural History (now the Natural History Museum) was dependent on government support, and an attack by such a distinguished scientist (albeit someone with no previous reputation in the field of paleontology—the study of fossils) was extremely damaging. A detailed study of the fossil (which was the pride of the museum's collection) revealed that the allegation was arrant nonsense. For one thing, there were feather imprints *underneath* some of the fossil bones.

So it can be said that *Archaeopteryx* was a bird, had feathers, and could probably fly, if somewhat clumsily; perhaps like the modern grebes on fresh-water lakes, it required a long run for takeoff. It had many reptilian characteristics, and its closest affinities among the reptiles seem to be with a group called the theropod dinosaurs. It can be said that it was a form transitional between the birds and dinosaurs, although it may not have been the ancestor of *all* modern birds. Despite the controversy—the disappearing specimens, the accusations of fraud and the uncertainty about its precise biological position, and the fact that much remains to be found out about this strange creature and its affinities—*Archaeopteryx* does fit into a Darwinian evolutionary model.

Ascension Island

Small volcanic island in the tropical south Atlantic Ocean.

See also: St. Helena and Ascension Island.

Australia

The southern continent covers 2,967,909 square miles (about 7,678,700 square kilometers). It comprises five percent of the world's land area, yet it is the planet's sixth largest country.

Australia is the smallest continental land mass (and the largest island). It is the only country that comprises an entire continent. The main continental mass extends from the northernmost point of Cape York, Queensland (10° 41' 21" S) to South Point, on Wilson's Promontory, Victoria (39° 08' 20" S). South East Cape on the adjacent island of Tasmania penetrates as far south as 43° 38' 40" S. The continent extends from Cape Byron, New South Wales (153° 38' 14" E) to Steep Point, Shark Bay, Western Australia (113° 09' 18" E). It is thus about 3,700 kilometers from north to south and 4,000 kilometers from east to west. The country contains a wide variety of environments, but large areas are arid or semiarid. Although the Australian Aborigines have been present for at least 40,000 years (possibly as long as 100,000 years), European settlement dates from 1788. In 1901, six British colonies federated to form the Commonwealth of Australia, an independent dominion within the British Commonwealth.

Charles Darwin visited three of the Australian colonies (New South Wales, Tasmania, and Western Australia) during the voyage of the *Beagle* in January, February, and March 1836. He had no great liking for any of the places he visited; he disliked the economic dependence of the colonies on convict labor; he thought the country was harsh—the area around King George's

2. *Naturels du Port du Roi George.*

Australian Aborigines at King George's Sound, at about the time of Darwin's visit. From: Dumont d'Urville, *Voyage Pittoresque autour du Monde*, 1835.

Sound was particularly "dull and uninteresting"—and that the people were money-grubbing. Nevertheless, there were many aspects of the continent that fascinated him, and, indeed, the visit may have been quite important in the development of his ideas. He collected many dozens of specimens (insects, shells, rocks, and a few vertebrates) while he was in Australia.

HMS *Beagle* arrived in Port Jackson (now Sydney), New South Wales on January 12, 1836, and Darwin spent 18 days around the port and traveling inland—over the Blue Mountains to Bathurst—and left for Tasmania (which he much preferred) on January 30. During his time at Hobart Town, he made important geological observations before crossing the Great Australian Bight for the then tiny settlement of King George's Sound, Western Australia, leaving "without sorrow or regret" on March 14.

While traveling through the open, sunny forests of inland New South Wales, Darwin noticed the almost ubiquitous effects of fire. Birds were not very abundant, but he saw large flocks of white cockatoos (probably sulfur-crested *Cacatua galerita*) and "a few most beautiful parrots," and there were crows "like our jackdaws" and "another bird something like a magpie." He saw *casurinas*, thinking it odd that they were called oaks (she-oaks)

Australian bushland ecosystem, dominated by *Eucalyptus* (gum trees), similar to that experienced by Charles Darwin. Photo: Patrick Armstrong.

because they did not in the least resemble English oak trees. In the pleasant evening, he took a stroll along a chain of ponds, where he had the good fortune to spot several platypus or *Ornithorhyncus paradoxicus*. In the same dairy entry, he recorded:

I had been lying on a sunny bank & was reflecting on the strange character of the animals of this country compared to the rest of the World. An unbeliever in everything beyond his own reason might exclaim, "Surely two distinct Creators must have been at work; their object is the same & certainly the end in each case is complete". Whilst thus thinking, I observed the conical pitfall of a Lion-Ant:— a fly fell in & immediately disappeared; then came a large but unwary Ant. His struggles to escape being very violent, the little jets of sand described by Kirby (Vol. 1. p. 425) [Kirby's book on insects was the standard work, and a copy was aboard the *Beagle*] were promptly directed against him.— His fate however, was better than that of the fly's. Without doubt the predacious Larva belongs to the same genus but to a different species from the European kind.— Now what would the Disbeliever say to this? Would any two workmen ever hit on so beautiful, so simple, & yet so artificial a contrivance? It cannot be thought so. The one hand has surely worked throughout the universe. A Geologist perhaps would suggest that the periods of Creation have been distinct & remote the one from the other; that the Creator rested from his labor.

The use of the words Creator and Creation (and the use of capitals), the idea of more than one episode of creation, and the sentence "The one hand has surely worked throughout the universe" might signify that Darwin still adopted a Creationist, almost fundamentalist, approach. They clearly echo chapter 1 of the book of Genesis; the final words "the Creator rested in his labor" reflect the words of Genesis 2:2–3. He was certainly writing from a Christian viewpoint just a few weeks earlier, in Tahiti and New Zealand. Although here and there in the notes from the *Beagle* period there are vague hints that the idea of mutability of species went though his mind, all the evidence suggests that it was not until after his return to England, in about March 1837, that his full "conversion" to the evolutionary outlook occurred. Although not particularly religious, at the time of his embarkation on the *Beagle,* he was contemplating a career as a Church of England parson, and he probably accepted much of the Genesis creation narrative as an accurate account of life's origins. These conventional notions had been to some extent reinforced in his undergraduate days by his reading of **William Paley**'s (1802) *Natural Theology*, which argued that the complexity of the living world and level of adaptation of organisms to their environment and way of life provide evidence for the existence of the Deity: design implies a designer.

The "sunny bank" was possibly that of Cox's River, between Blackheath and Bathurst, New South Wales. Darwin had traveled for several days through an open forest of eucalyptus, acacia, and casurina, which were often burnt. He had had been hunting for emu and kangaroo and had seen flocks of cockatoos and parrots. He had encountered groups of hunting Aborigines. He was very conscious of traveling through an environment quite different from any that he had seen before.

But there was much more to his Australian travels. A few hours before he encountered the ant lion, he had dragged a kangaroo rat out of a hollow tree, "as big as a rabbit, but with the figure of a Kangaroo." He had had seen several platypuses playing in a chain of ponds that represented the dry summer remnants of a river; they "might easily have been mistaken for many water rats," although, when his companion shot one, he could see that they were quite different—"a most extraordinary animal." In the gum trees above him were birds "something like the [European] magpie" but, although

Port Jackson (Sydney), at about the time of Darwin's visit. From: Dumont d'Urville, *Voyage Pittoresque autour du Monde*, 1835.

black and white, were very different in structure. He heard tell of "tigers and hyaenas," called such "simply because they are Carnivorous"; they were very different from animals with these names elsewhere. The Australian trees, with their waxy vertically hanging leaves were completely different from the oaks of the English countryside. And the ant lion (the larval form of an insect related to the lacewing, family Myrmeleontidae) was remarkably similar to that described by **William Kirby** from Europe in its appearance and its behavior, and yet also subtly different. Darwin was noticing an environment that was different, with different organisms, isolated from the rest of the world—and yet there were creatures that, even if they belonged to different species, genera, or families, resembled those with which he was familiar. Of the "two distinct Creators"—one of Australia, one of the rest of the world—he mused, "their object has been the same & certainly in each case the end is complete." Today we might argue that the platypus and the water rat, the Australian magpie and its European analogue, the different species of ant lion, and the marsupial carnivores and their placental mammal equivalents filled similar ecological niches and had been subjected to similar selection or adaptation pressures. Darwin was not able to go as far as that while he was in Australia in January 1836, but he was on his way. He was not an evolutionist when he lay on the grassy bank in New South Wales that hot day, but he was already beginning to think ecologically, in terms of whole environments, and to wonder about the manner in which individual organisms relate to their surroundings. The she-oaks and gum trees with their vertical leaves, the climate, the occurrence of fire, the soils, the Aborigines, the parrots and cockatoos, the emus, kangaroos, and kangaroo rats were components of an integrated and highly distinctive system.

In New South Wales, and at King George's Sound in Western Australia, Darwin saw a good deal of Australian Aboriginal society. As did other explorers of the nineteenth century, Darwin shows great interest in the weird, striking, and (to him) bizarre. Here is his account of an Aboriginal corroboree that he witnessed at King George's Sound:

> A large tribe of natives, called the White Cockatoo men, happened to pay the settlement a visit while we were there. These men, as well as those of the tribe belonging to King George's Sound . . . were persuaded to hold a "corrobery" or great dancing party. As soon as it grew dark, small fires were lighted, and the men commenced . . . painting themselves white in spots and lines. As soon as all was ready, large fires were kept blazing, round which the women and children were collected as spectators; the Cockatoo and King George's Men formed two distinct parties, and generally danced in answer to each other. The dancing consisted in their running either sideways or in Indian file into an open space, and stamping on the ground with great force as they marched together. Their heavy footsteps were accompanied by a kind of grunt, by beating their spears together, and by . . . extending their arms and wriggling their bodies. It was a most rude and barbarous scene, and to our ideas without any sort of meaning; but we observed that the black women and children

watched it with the greatest pleasure. Perhaps these dances originally represented actions, such as wars and victories; there was one called the Emu dance, in which each man extended his arm in a bent manner, like the neck of that bird. In another dance, one man imitated the movements of a kangaroo grazing in the woods, whilst a second crawled up, and pretended to spear him. . . . [T]he air resounded with their wild cries. Every one appeared in high spirits, and the group of nearly naked figures, viewed in the light of the blazing fires, all moving in hideous harmony, formed a perfect display of a festival amongst the lowest barbarians. In Tierra del Fuego, we have beheld many curious scenes in savage life, but never, I think, one where the natives were in such high spirits and so perfectly at their ease. (*The Voyage of the Beagle*, chapter 19, based on *Diary* entry for March 6–13, 1836)

This is a typical Darwin account in several ways. We see his great interest in the exotic and strange, but can also appreciate the superb level of detail of his observations. We note his comparative approach—he makes a comparison with the people of **Tierra del Fuego.** We see him venturing tentatively into interpretation, speculating on the possible origins of the dances, as well as an oblique reference to animals, even if there be no *direct* comparison between the behavior of humans and other creatures. Negative words and phrases are common: "rude and barbarous," "lowest barbarians," "wild cries," "hideous harmony." It is clear that the young English gentleman sees Aboriginal society and customs as inferior in many respects to his own.

Throughout his travels, Darwin made observations on what he saw as evidence for changes in the relative levels of the land and the sea. These were important, because his first flirtation with **gradualism**—the idea that what we see in the world today is the result of long periods of gradual change—was the coral atoll theory, which held that coral atolls were formed by the gradual rise in sea level (or submergence of the island). Darwin's understanding of the importance of gradual change brought about by ongoing processes was obtained from **Charles Lyell**'s, *Principles of Geology,* all three volumes of which, by the time of his Australian visits, Darwin possessed. Gradualism can be seen as a stepping stone to the concept of evolution through natural selection. Here is an extract from Darwin's geology notes, made following his visit to **Tasmania:**

I now come to a subject which I have so frequently discussed in my Geological Memoranda, viz recent movements in the level of the land. On both sides of the Bay, & along nearly the whole line of coast broken shells are found on the land to the height of 30 & 40 ft in quantities which make it rather difficult to believe they have all been carried there by the Aborigines. Amongst these shells are found many rounded pebbles and individuals two [*sic*] small to be brought for the purposes of eating; the coast moreover in a few places, by its outline, obscurely shows a small vertical retreat.

Darwin was convinced in his published account "that we must attribute the presence of the greater number [of shell deposits] to a small elevation of the land." He was convinced, also, that the sea had formerly "stood higher" (as he had been in Chiloé, the Falkland Islands, New Zealand, New South Wales, and many places in South America); the long narrow inlet of the Derwent and Storm Bay, now thought to be drowned valleys, did not strike him as evidence of submergence. But he was self-critical:

> On the shore of Ralph Bay (opening into Storm Bay) I observed a continuous beach about fifteen feet above high-water mark, clothed in vegetation, and by digging into it, pebbles encrusted with Serpulae were found: along the banks, also of the river Derwent, I found a bed of broken sea shells above the surface of the river, and at a point where the water is now too fresh for sea shells to live; but in both of these cases, it is just possible, that before certain spits of mud in Storm Bay were accumulated, the tides might have risen to the height where we now find shells. (*Geology of the Voyage of the Beagle,* Vol. 2: *Volcanic Islands*)

In a footnote to these observations, Darwin compares the situation with that on another island:

> It would appear that some changes are now in progress in Ralph Bay, for I was assured by an intelligent farmer, that oysters were formerly abundant in it, but that about the year 1834 they had, without any apparent cause, disappeared. . . . At Chiloé, in South America, I heard of a similar loss, sustained by the inhabitants, in the disappearance from one part of the coast of an edible species of Ascidia [sea-squirt].

Hobart Town, at about the time of Darwin's visit. From: Dumont d'Urville, *Voyage Pittoresque autour du Monde,* 1835.

Darwin seems to have been firmly under the spell of Lyell, understanding that changes can occur relatively gradually in the environment, and indeed are continuing today.

In his three short visits to different parts of Australia, Charles Darwin experienced a variety of environments: the mountains and damp forests of Tasmania, the dry open woodlands of inland New South Wales, and the coastal inlets of King George's Sound and near Hobart Town. He saw something of the distinctiveness of Australian plant and animal communities and the way they were adapted to their surroundings, and he appreciated the ecological importance of fire. He had close contact with Aborigines on several occasions, studying their customs and noticing that Aboriginal society was already in decline. He made a number of observations on the behavior of organisms (such as the ant lion). He found evidence for sea-level change. As elsewhere, he made mistakes—for example, in failing to see that Sydney Harbour, the Derwent Estuary, Tasmania, and King George's Sound were submerged river valleys, focusing on the (relatively trivial) evidence that the sea had "stood higher." (Admittedly, geomorphologists now appreciate that there is evidence for both rises and falls in the level of the sea in relation to the land around Australia's coasts.) All these observations were of immense importance to him later.

Although he supported Britain's imperial mission, strongly approving of the "little Englands" that were growing in the Southern Hemisphere—New Zealand, the Australian colonies, and the Cape of Good Hope—he disliked certain aspects of the manner in which they were governed and of their society. At the conclusion of his visit, he rather presciently wrote:

> Farewell Australia, you are a rising infant & doubtless some day will reign a great princess in the South but you are too great & ambitious for affection, yet not great enough for respect. (*Diary,* March 14, 1836)

FURTHER READING

Armstrong, Patrick. 1985. *Charles Darwin in Western Australia: A Young Scientist's Perception of an Environment.* Nedlands: University of Western Australia Press.

Nichols, F. W. and J. M. Nichols. 1989. *Charles Darwin in Australia.* Cambridge, England: Cambridge University Press.

Autobiography

An account of a life written by the subject. Charles Darwin wrote such an account when he was 67 "for his own amusement and the interest of his children and their descendants."

Darwin wrote this relatively short narrative (121 pages) between May 31 and August 3, 1876, writing for an hour most afternoons. During the remaining six years of his life, he added to this account as further memories occurred to him, inserting another 67 pages into the appropriate places in the earlier manuscript. The original leather-bound volume is held in the Darwin Archive of Cambridge University Library.

There were several editions of the autobiography as a published work. One, edited by his son Francis appeared in 1887, five years after the great naturalist's death. At that time, the family thought it expedient to omit certain portions. The first complete edition was edited by Charles Darwin's granddaughter, **Norah Barlow,** and was published in 1958.

Darwin divided the account as follows: from birth to going to Cambridge; Cambridge life; voyage of the *Beagle;* from his return home to his marriage; from marriage and residence in London to settling at **Down House;** residence at Down; an account of how several books arose; and an estimation of his mental powers. The essay does not precisely follow these headings.

He opened the account by recalling that he would have been most interested to have read a sketch of his grandfather, **Erasmus Darwin,** "written by himself, and what he thought about and did and how he worked." Darwin therefore attempts, now and again, to say something of his "inner life"—his thoughts and concerns at different stages of his life. However, it must be emphasized that the account was prepared when he approached old age, and some of the incidents occurred some 40 or 60 years earlier, and there is good reason to believe that some of his memories are erroneous. Some discrepancies are trivial—for example, his account of the route followed during his field visit to **North Wales** with Professor **Adam Sedgwick** in the summer of 1831 does not square completely with other evidence.

On his visit to the Galapagos he comments:

During the voyage of the Beagle I had been deeply impressed. . . . By the South American character of most of the productions of the Galapagos archipelago, and more especially by the manner in which they differ slightly on each island of the group; none of these islands appearing to be very ancient in a geological sense. It was evident that facts such as these, as well as many others, could be explained on the supposition that species gradually become modified; and the subject haunted me. (*Autobiography of Charles Darwin,* Norah Barlow, ed., 1958, 118–119)

One might get the impression from reading this that there had been a Eureka-like experience while he was on the Galapagos Islands. In fact, he did not particularly like the islands, was rather puzzled by the origins of some organisms while there, and it was not until about March 1837 (after his return to England) that he appreciated the significance of the differences between the islands.

None the less, Darwin's autobiography is extremely interesting and revealing: the account of the effect of his mother's when he was eight on himself and his sisters is short, but perhaps explains aspects of his development. There are also illuminating accounts of the characters of Captain **Robert FitzRoy** and Professor **John Henslow.** He also gives interesting accounts of the way in which he worked and collected material for his books.

His final words on his own mental abilities are worth quoting in full:

[M]y success as a man of science, whatever this may have amounted to, has been determined, as far as I can judge, by complex and diversified mental qualities and conditions. Of these the most important have been—the love of science—unbounded patience in long reflecting over any subject—industry in observing and collecting facts—and a fair share of invention as well as of common-sense. With such moderate abilities as I possess, it is truly surprising that thus I should have influenced to a considerable extent the belief of scientific men on some important points. (*Autobiography of Charles Darwin*, Norah Barlow, ed., 1958, 144–145)

Azores

Archipelago of volcanic islands in the north Atlantic Ocean. The last group of islands visited on the *Beagle* voyage.

The Azores, a group of islands under Portuguese sovereignty about 900 miles (1,450 kilometers) west of Lisbon in the north Atlantic (38° 30' N. 28° W'), were the last port of call of the *Beagle* before the ship called at Falmouth in Cornwall, in the west of England on October 2, 1836. The only island in the Azores upon which Darwin landed was Terceira, an oval-shaped island, about 18.5 miles (30 kilometers) by 10.5 miles (17 kilometers), although he saw, and described, São Miguel from quite close inshore. Darwin was impatient to be home; his observations were somewhat less thorough in the Azores than elsewhere, and he collected few specimens.

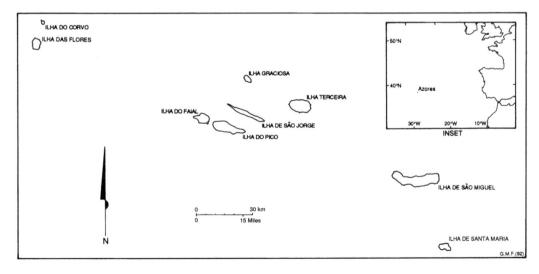

Map of the Islands of the Azores. Darwin landed on Terceira, but sailed close to and described São Miguel. Map drawn at Geography Department, University of Western Australia.

Although, when he looked at the organisms of the Azores, he saw some species of birds, insects, and plants that were familiar to him from the English and Welsh countryside, it was the volcanic rocks and land forms and the geological history of the islands that were of greatest interest to him.

And he was once more able to compare the volcanic features of the island with the many other volcanic islands he had seen. He noted the rounded volcanic hills—some still showing almost complete craters, some much eroded—and the variety of lava types, which confirmed his ideas formed elsewhere (e.g., **Tahiti, St. Helena and Ascension Island**) that there was a sequence of events in the development of volcanic islands, that one type of lava followed another, that the magma perhaps differentiates at a depth, and that as crystals differentiate out from a magma, so its composition changes. Moreover, erosion continues as volcanic activity proceeds, he concluded.

Although Charles Darwin had experienced an earthquake in South America, Terceira was one of the few localities where he got a real sense of active volcanism and earth movement. He heard tell of frequent earthquakes within the last year, and then, as now, there was evidence of seismic activity in the presence of earthquake-damaged buildings. "During a few days a jet of steam issued from a bold precipice . . . not far from the town of Angra," he recorded.

Steam vents, Terceira, Azores. Site visited by Darwin, September 1836. Photo: Patrick Armstrong.

Volcanic lava, Terceira, Azores. Photo: Geography Department, University of Western Australia.

Eroded volcanic islets, off the coast at Terceira, Azores. Photo: Patrick Armstrong.

The steam vents or fumaroles in the center of the island (Furmas do Enxofre) that he visited the day after his arrival provided the geological site of greatest interest. Here is the description from *Volcanic Islands,* which combines material from several of his accounts written at (or very close to) the time of his visit.

> In the central part of the island there is a spot, where steam is constantly issuing in jets from the bottom of a small ravine-like hollow, which has no exit, and which abuts against a range of trachytic mountains. The steam is emitted from several irregular fissures; it is scentless, soon blackens iron, and is much too high a temperature to be endured by hand. The manner in which the solid trachyte is changed on the borders of these orifices is curious: first the base becomes earthy, with red freckles evidently due to the oxidation of the particles of iron; then it becomes soft; and lastly even the crystals of glassy feldspar yield to the dissolving agent.

Clearly, by this time, Darwin was conscious that he was living in a dynamic, changing world, modified alike by processes within the Earth and from without.

B

Barlow, Norah (1885—1989)

Granddaughter of Charles Darwin and editor of her grandfather's works.

Norah was the daughter of **Horace Darwin,** the founder of the Cambridge Scientific Instrument Company. She married Alan, the son of Sir Thomas Barlow, president of the Royal College of Physicians. Sir Alan became a senior civil servant. Norah was a keen plantswoman and gardener and had a variety of columbine named after her. She was also a distinguished Darwin scholar and edited several of her grandfather's works, including *The Autobiography of Charles Darwin* (London: Collins, 1958). She part-owned a house called the Orchard in Cambridge, which had been in the Darwin family for 70 years, until it became the site for New Hall (one of the first colleges for women in Cambridge) in 1954.

FURTHER READING

Barlow, Norah, ed. 1958. *Charles Darwin and the Voyage of the "Beagle."* London: Collins.

Barnacles

Marine crustaceans (similar to crabs, lobsters, and prawns) that have jointed legs and shells of connected overlapping plates. Instead of crawling on the sea floor seeking food, however, they attach themselves to rocks, ships, harbor structures, and sometimes the shells of turtles and the bodies of whales and other marine mammals, extracting their food from the sea water. Darwin devoted about eight years of his life to a careful study of living and fossil barnacles, and the publication of major monographs on the subject established his scientific reputation.

When barnacles are under water or when a wave washes over them, they extend small, feathery, barbed legs to absorb oxygen and catch plankton (small organisms) as food. A barnacle's fertilized eggs hatch into larvae, at which stage they leave the parents' shells. They spend their youth swimming. After a number of molts, they attach themselves to a firm foundation, held in place by one of the strongest known natural adhesives. Barnacles (Cirripedia) are divided into two groups: the acorn barnacles (Balanomorpha), in which the plates attach directly to the rock, and goose barnacles (Lepadomorpha), which are attached on the end of a stalk. A few are parasitic, living in association with crabs or other barnacles. There are several hundred species worldwide, and locally they may be extremely numerous. They may be present in concentrations of 30,000 or more in a square meter, imparting a grayish color to the middle levels of a seashore. It is asserted that male barnacles have proportionately the largest penis in the animal kingdom.

Although the young Charles Darwin probably noticed the barnacles living on the shores of the Firth of Forth while beachcombing with Dr. Robert Edmond Grant in **Edinburgh,** it was in South America that he became seriously interested in this strange biological group. Quite early in the voyage he was closely examining fossil barnacles:

> The cliffs in Sebastian's Bay [Tierra del Fuego] . . . are composed of fine sandstone. . . . In these beds are fragments of wood, legs of crabs, barnacles encrusted with corallines still partially retaining their colour.

Along the shores of **Chiloé,** on the west cost of South America, he collected specimens of acorn barnacles. His zoological notes record:

> Great Balanus (for dissection). Are esteemed very good eating, grow to 5 or 6 times the size of the specimen; sometimes at the lowest spring tides can be seen, generally grow in deeper water. (*Zoological Diary,* Cambridge University Library, Darwin Archive, Notes on Shells in Spirits of Wine)

These massive barnacles—often 8 inches (20 centimeters) across—are something of a delicacy on the island of Chiloé and elsewhere in southern Chile, are locally considered excellent eating, and can be seen in laden crates in local fish markets. This species is mentioned in Darwin's great work on the group, *A Monograph on the Sub-class Cirripedia.* In part one of volume two of this work, he gives a detailed description, although the illustration is poor and rather small. He uses the name *Balanus psittacus.* He noted:

This, which is the largest known species of the genus, ranges from Peru (Arica being the most northern spot, whence I have seen specimens), along the coast of Chile, where it is abundant at a few fathoms' depth, at least as far as southern Chiloé. . . . [T]his Balanus, when cooked, is universally esteemed as a delicious article of food. (pp. 208–209)

In fact the first specimen he ever dissected, when he embarked on his detailed study of the barnacle group, was the smallest. Among the islands of the Chonos Archipelago, to the south of Chiloe, he collected specimens of *Cryptophialus minutus.* In the detailed description of the species in his book on the Balanidae, as well as commenting that it is "the smallest known cirripede [barnacle]," he notes:

This cirripede inhabits, in vast numbers, the shells of the living Concholepas Peruviana [a species of shellfish], among the Chonos islands; the whole outside of the shell being sometimes completely drilled by its cavities. (p. 567)

In describing organisms, Darwin often takes an ecological approach and notes the relationship of the organism with other species. He adds an interesting personal footnote:

I am greatly indebted to Dr Hooker, for having, several years ago, when I examined my first cirripede, aided me in many ways, and shown me how to dissect the more difficult parts, and for having made several very correct drawings, which, with some subsequent alterations are now engraved. (p. 567)

Darwin spent about eight years, following 1846, working on barnacles. He dissected many dozens, establishing their relationships, and he wrote to naturalists and others all over the world seeking specimens. He described many species that were new to science. In his series of monographs on barnacles (which over 150 years later are still revered), he was able to show his grasp of the minutiae of the taxonomy of a complete group of organisms, and he established his scientific reputation beyond doubt, so that his later publications had to be taken seriously. Moreover, in considering the morphology of closely related forms in great detail, he was able to obtain insights to the nature of species and their adaptation to their environments.

FURTHER READING

Darwin, Charles. 1851–1854. *A Monograph on the Sub-class Cirripedia*, Vol. 1: *Lepadidae;* Vol. 2: *Balanidae* (volume 2 is in two parts). London: Ray Society.

Darwin, Charles. 1851–1854. *Monographs of the Fossil Lepadidae and the Fossil Balanidae of Great Britain* (2 vols.). London: Paleontographical Society.

These monographs on barnacles were reprinted by William Pickering, 1988.

Bay of Islands, New Zealand

Large bay, close to the northern tip of North Island, New Zealand.

Darwin was only a week in New Zealand, at the very end of 1835, and did not much care for the place. The colony was barely established; there was a small, rough population of "worthless characters"—the human flotsam and jetsam of the Pacific—in Koroareka (now called Russell). There were "runaway convicts" and a transient population of the crews of whaling ships. He described "the whole population [as being] addicted to drunkenness." There were probably a few prostitutes: words such as "vice," "filth," and "disgusting" color Darwin's account. The local missionaries were building a church (Darwin and the officers of the *Beagle* contributed), and the young Englishman thought they had selected the right spot "to attack vice in her very Citadel." The wooden church still exists—it is the oldest church building in New Zealand.

Across the inlet, at Pahia, things were a little more respectable; although Darwin thought that the settlement hardly deserved the title of a village, he admired the small number of whitewashed missionaries' cottages, with English flowers such as honeysuckle, stocks, and sweetbriar growing outside them. The local administrator—the "British Resident"—had just constructed a small but elegant Residency.

As in Tahiti, Charles Darwin admired the work of the missionaries in Christianizing the local people, the **Maori.** He traveled inland about 15

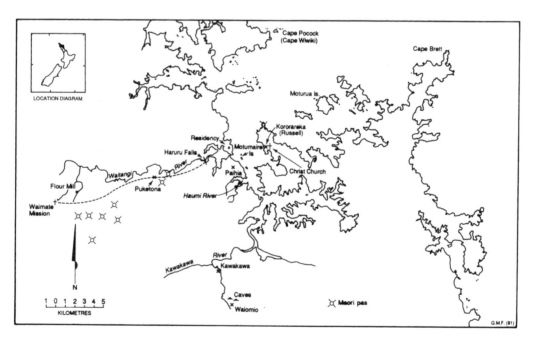

Map of Bay of Islands, North Island, New Zealand, showing some of the places visited by Darwin. Map drawn at Geography Department, University of Western Australia.

The Residency. Visited by Darwin and FitzRoy, Christmas 1835. Photo: Patrick Armstrong.

miles (24 kilometers) to a missionary settlement of Waimate. A farm, barns, and a mill had been constructed; cornfields had been planted; the gardens were established; and some of the Maori children were playing the very English game of cricket.

The impact of European society on the Maoris was paralleled by the effect of introduced plants and animals on the land. Darwin described the forests of the magnificent New Zealand native kauri trees, but noticed that "several sorts of weeds" including gorse and dock as well as rats were invading rapidly. Much land had been cleared using fire, and "tall fern and low bush" covered some of the land.

Indigenous peoples interested Darwin wherever he went. The Maoris (a group descended from the Polynesians who arrived in New Zealand about A.D. 1000) attracted a good deal of his attention. He described the custom of rubbing noses, which he compared with the Western handshake. He noted, correctly, that the Maoris belonged to "the same family of mankind" as the Tahitians. He attended a funeral and mentioned that the Maoris used some limestone caves as burial places.

In addition to the Maoris, the missionaries, and, to some extent, the vegetation, what interested Darwin the most about New Zealand was its geology. He compared the landscape and the rocks with those of other volcanic islands he had visited. Along the road to Waimate, he noted that:

Christ Church, Bay of Islands, New Zealand. Darwin and the officers of HMS *Beagle* contributed to the building of this, the oldest church in New Zealand. Photo: Patrick Armstrong.

the whole surface was covered with shaggy and highly vesicular [air bubble–filled] lavas. In a neighbouring . . . hill, the form of a crater could be traced. . . . Near Waimate, two or three truncated conical hills are said to be surrounded by deep circular cavities, and clearly have at one time existed as active volcanoes. (*Geological Notes*, Cambridge University Library, Darwin Archive)

One of the missionaries told him of the existence of active volcanoes elsewhere in New Zealand and the frequent occurrence of earthquakes. He was close to the mark when, later, aboard the *Beagle*, he wrote:

These volcanic districts in the Northern Island of New Zealand may from its position and direction of its coast, be with propriety described as the SE termination of the great band of volcanic action which contains the parallel lines of New Caledonia, New Hebrides, New Ireland and New Guinea. (*Geological Notes*, Cambridge University Library, Darwin Archive)

Although he does not use the terms, this must be one of the first appearances of the idea of island arcs and the Pacific ring of fire. The mountains, the Maori culture, the volcanoes, the forests, and the hot springs are what bring thousands of visitors to New Zealand in the twenty-first century. In Darwin they have a worthy predecessor.

Beagle, HMS

A Royal Navy 10-gun, square-rigged sailing brig of the Cherokee class (sometimes the term brig-sloop was used), named after the breed of dog used for hunting hares, and made famous by her use in three important surveying voyages, the second of which carried Charles Darwin around the world.

The ship was 90 feet (about 27 meters) in length, had a beam measurement of 24.5 feet (7.5 meters), and a draught of 12.5 feet (3.8 meters). Her displacement was about 235 tons, although additional work done before the second voyage increased this to 242 tons. Other modifications made at this time reduced the number of guns to six and added a mizzenmast (to give the vessel a total of three masts). Her complement on the second voyage was 65 plus 9 "supernumeraries," of which Darwin was one. (The records contain some variations in personnel numbers, the result of deaths, departures, and additions.)

The *Beagle* was launched in May 1820 from the Royal Naval Dockyard at Woolwich, on the Thames. The cost was £7,803. In July of the next year, the ship took part in a naval review held to celebrate the coronation of King George IV. In this, the *Beagle* was the first ship to sail under the newly constructed London Bridge. Thereafter, there seems to have been no immediate need for the ship, and so for several years she was moored afloat but unmanned. It was then that the *Beagle* was adapted as a survey ship and was subsequently used in three major surveying expeditions.

HMS *Beagle* set sail on May 22, 1826, for her first long voyage, under the command of Captain Pringle Stokes. The mission was to accompany the slightly larger ship HMS *Adventure* (380 tons) on her survey of the southernmost part of South America, including the island of **Tierra del Fuego.** The expedition was under the overall command of Captain **Phillip Parker King.**

HMS *Beagle* in full sail at the Mouth of Berkeley Sound, Falkland Islands. From: *Narrative of the Surveying Voyages,* 1839.

THE 'BEAGLE LAID ASHORE, RIVER SANTA CRUZ.

HMS *Beagle* ashore on the coast of South America. From: *Narrative of the Surveying Voyages*, 1839.

Captain Stokes became extremely depressed, perhaps because of the difficulties he faced under the severe weather conditions, and in the waters off Tierra del Fuego, he locked himself in his cabin for 14 days. He then shot himself in the head and died 12 days later. King replaced Stokes with the executive officer of the *Beagle*, Lieutenant W. G. Skyring. They limped northward to Rio de Janeiro, where, in December 1828, Rear Admiral Sir Robert Otway, commander in chief of the Royal Navy's South American station, appointed his personal aide, Lieutenant **Robert FitzRoy** to the command (somewhat against the wishes of King). However, the young FitzRoy (he was 23 years old when he gained his first command) proved to be an able commander and an extremely competent surveyor. Late in the voyage, a group of Fuegians stole one of the ship's boats, and FitzRoy took several individuals on board as hostages, hoping to exchange them for the boat. (See article on **Jemmy Button.**) The ruse failed, and FitzRoy took them to England to educate them and convert them to Christianity. HMS *Beagle* returned from this voyage to Plymouth, on the southwest coast of England on October 14, 1830.

After some uncertainty about how to return the Fuegians, FitzRoy was reappointed as commander in June 1831, along with Lieutenants John Clements Wickham and **Bartholomew James Sulivan.** The *Beagle* underwent extensive rebuilding and refitting. FitzRoy had the upper deck raised by 8 inches (200 millimeters) aft (toward the back of the ship) and 12 inches (300 millimeters) forward. The Cherokee class ships had previously

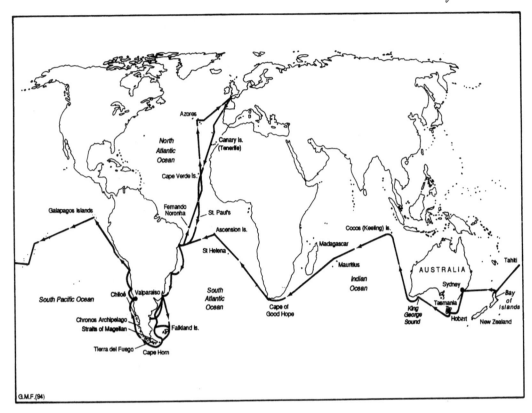

The route of the voyage of the *Beagle*, 1831–1836, showing some of the places and islands visited. Map drawn at Geography Department, University of Western Australia.

had the reputation of handling badly and being prone to sinking. By allowing the decks to drain more rapidly, less water collected in the gunnels and made the *Beagle* less likely to become top heavy and capsize. FitzRoy acquired 22 chronometers and much other navigational and scientific equipment for use on the voyage.

Perhaps partly because of the fate of Captain Stokes (and also the suicide of his own uncle), FitzRoy was concerned about the isolated position of a ship's captain at that time. This, as well as the need to have someone who could concentrate on natural history, possibly explains why Charles Darwin, as a gentleman traveler, a supernumerary unconnected with the navy, was appointed.

The *Beagle* was originally scheduled to leave in October 1831, but, because of delays in her preparations and bad weather, the departure was delayed until December 27. After completing important surveys of South America (and returning the surviving Fuegians—one had died), the ship crossed the **Pacific Ocean,** returning via **New Zealand, Australia,** and the **Cape of Good Hope,** calling in at Falmouth, Cornwall (on the southwest tip of England) on October 2, 1836, before proceeding to the Thames.

Six months later, early in 1837, HMS *Beagle* set off again to survey large parts of the Australian coast under the command of Captain John Clements Wickham, who had been a lieutenant on the second voyage. His assistant surveyor was Lieutenant John Lort Stokes (no relation to Pringle Stokes), who had been a midshipman on the first voyage of the *Beagle*, and then mate and assistant surveyor on the second voyage. They commenced their survey with the west coast between the Swan River (the location of modern Perth and Fremantle) and what they named as the FitzRoy River (after their former captain) on the northwest coast. Then the *Beagle* proceeded to Bass Strait and southeastern Australia. In May 1839, they sailed north to survey the southern shores of the Arafura Sea. Captain Wickham named the Beagle Gulf, and Port Darwin in what is now Australia's Northern Territory (see **Darwin, City of**). In March 1841, command was taken by John Lort Stokes when Wickham fell ill and was invalided. The voyage and the survey continued until October 1843.

After the *Beagle's* illustrious surveying career, she was handed over to the Department of Customs and Excise and was used as a base from which to control smuggling along the maze of quiet waterways of the Essex marshes, on the north coast of the Thames Estuary. In 1851, the vessel had the ignominy of being renamed *Southend Work Vessel Number 7.*

It is often stated that HMS *Beagle* ended her days at Japan, but this seems to be in error. Recent evidence suggests that the ship was sold to nearby traders in Essex in 1870. It is possible that some of her timbers were incorporated into nearby buildings, but that some parts of the hull remain buried in the swampy soil of the Essex marshes. Further investigations are in prospect.

See also: Origin of the *Beagle* Voyage.

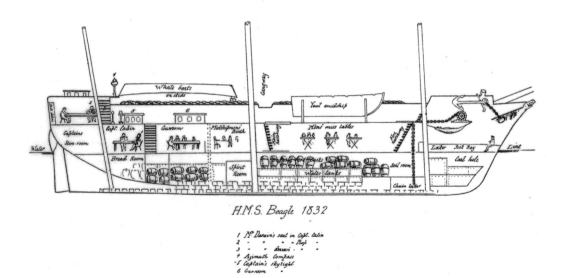

Sketch of HMS *Beagle*, drawn by Philip Gidley King. Mitchell Library, Sydney, New South Wales.

FURTHER READING

Hordern, Marsden. 1989. *Mariners Are Warned! John Lort Stokes and H.M.S. Beagle in Australia 1837–1843*. Melbourne, Australia: Melbourne University Publishing.

Beagle Diary

The record maintained by Charles Darwin of his voyage aboard HMS *Beagle*, 1831–1836. It has been subsequently published several times.

Darwin commenced his diary—or journal, as he often called it—on October 24, 1831, upon his first arrival in Plymouth "after a pleasant drive from London," and continued in almost exactly the same format until the last entry, which records the removal of the *Beagle* (a month after Darwin's departure) to Woolwich on November 7, 1836.

It is written in dark ink on gatherings of paper producing pages approximately 10 inches by 8 inches (25 by 20 centimeters). The manuscript is 751 pages (there are a few errors in pagination). The diary was not always kept on a daily basis (although it often was while he was aboard the *Beagle*), and following long shore journeys, particularly in South America, it was sometimes compiled retrospectively, up to three months after the events described (presumably with the aid of notebooks kept on these journeys); there are occasional errors in date. Despite the generally fluent style, there is evidence in some of his letters home that Darwin sometimes struggled with writing the entries. At times he adopts note form, and at other times his style is almost flowery. He was probably influenced by his reading of **Alexander von Humboldt.** Portions of the diary were sent back to his family in **Shrewsbury,** to whom it gave "lively pleasure."

The diary formed the basis of the book, *The Voyage of the Beagle,* and many passages are almost identical. It was also extensively referred to in some of Darwin's later work.

Horace Darwin, one of Charles's sons, made three typed copies of the original (which is held at Down House) in 1891 "to ensure against the possible loss of the manuscript." Because typing was then in its infancy, these copies contain many errors, although they have been used by some subsequent scholars.

The published *Voyage of the Beagle* omits large sections of the original diary, and thus the full text was published by **Norah Barlow,** Charles Darwin's granddaughter, in 1933. This was reprinted numerous times and is probably the most widely used source. A facsimile edition was published in 1979 (by Genesis Publications of Guildford, United Kingdom). An entirely new version, possibly in some very minor ways more faithful to the original than the Barlow edition, was edited by Richard Darwin Keynes (a distinguished Cambridge University professor of physiology and a descendant of Charles Darwin) in 1988, reappearing in a paperback version in 2001.

FURTHER READING

Barlow, Norah, ed. 1933. *Charles Darwin's Diary of the Voyage of HMS Beagle*. Cambridge, England: Cambridge University Press.

Keynes, R. D. 1988. *Charles Darwin's Beagle Diary*. Cambridge, England: Cambridge University Press.

Beech, Southern or Antarctic

Scientific name: *Nothofagus*. A genus of broad-leaved trees in the same family (Fagaceae) as beech *(Fagus)*; some are deciduous, some are evergreen. There are about 35 species, all of which are native to the Southern Hemisphere. All have small, oval leaves with fine-toothed edges; their fruits are small, bristle-covered, and similar to those of beeches of the Northern Hemisphere.

Deciduous species include the South American noble beech *N. obliqua*, which grows to 115 feet (35 meters), and the antarctic beech *N. antarctica*, which grows to 50 feet (15 meters). Evergreen species include the Australian myrtle beech *N. cunninghamii* and the New Zealand black beech *N. solandri*, which form huge forests of trees that can grow to 80 feet (25 meters). They are important components of temperate forests in Australia (including Tasmania), New Zealand, the southern part of South America, the island of New Caledonia in the Pacific Ocean, and in the mountain forests of New Guinea. Fossil material has been found in Antarctica.

Charles Darwin encountered southern beech, *Nothofagus* forests in **Tierra del Fuego** and **Chiloé** in South America. He found them attractive, although in places difficult to penetrate. On Chiloé, on the west coast of South America, he thought that the forests (of *Nothofagus nitida*) he encountered were stunted and close to their northern limit. The species he describes—and his account of the fern-drooped, tangled, dripping forest—are familiar to modern travelers who have encountered one of the areas of original forest of Chiloé, such as those in the Chiloé National Park, near Cuaco on the west coast. The dead trunks, Darwin thought, gave the forests a "solemnity"; a common feature of old growth forests is the occurrence of dead and near-dead timber.

These beech forests are important in the Darwin story because their study provided examples of the interconnectedness of plant and animal communities. This extract, partly based on his contemporary observations, had been reworked for *The Voyage of the Beagle*.

> There is one vegetable production deserving notice from its importance as an article of food to the Fuegians. It is a globular, bright-yellow fungus, which grows in vast numbers on the beech-trees. When young it is elastic and turgid, with a smooth surface; but when mature, it shrinks, becomes tougher, and has its entire surface deeply pitted or honey-combed. This fungus belongs to a new and curious genus; I found a second species on another species of beech in Chile; and Dr Hooker informs me, that just lately a third species

has been discovered in Van Diemen's Land [Tasmania]. How singular is this relationship between parasitical fungi and the trees on which they grow, in distant parts of the world! In Tierra del Fuego the fungus in its tough and mature state is collected in large quantities by the women and children, and is eaten uncooked. It has a mucilaginous, slightly sweet taste, with a faint smell like that of a mushroom. With the exception of a few berries, chiefly of a dwarf arbutus, the natives eat no vegetable food besides the fungus. (*Voyage of the Beagle,* chapter 11)

The fungus had other species dependent on it. Darwin describes finding large numbers of a small carabid beetle (later identified as *Abropus splendidus*) "flying about sea coast in the evening. These insects live amongst the soft yellow balls which are excrescencies; or rather fungi growing on the Fagus antarcticus, and which are eaten by the Fuegians."

Darwin has some appreciation of the whole complex: the *Nothofagus* trees, the fungus, the insect, the Fuegians. Here is an early example of the young Darwin thinking in an integrated, holistic, ecological manner. This ecological method of thinking was profoundly important in his later work, including the development of the idea of evolution through natural selection. In the extract he compares his own observations with those of others on geographical distribution. Today the Southern Hemisphere distribution of *Nothofagus* is described as Gondwanic: it is seen as evidence for the existence of the former southern supercontinent of Gondwana. Its correlation with the distribution of fungi dependent upon it strengthens the link. Darwin knew nothing about plate tectonics, but he was thinking along the right lines.

Beetles

The largest group of insects; the scientific name for the group is Coleoptera. The collection of beetles was one of Darwin's major activities as a schoolboy and as a young man, and was one of the avenues through which he became interested in natural history.

It is estimated that over 300,000 species of beetles are known, and new species are being described at the rate of about 2,300 per year. They occur in almost every terrestrial and freshwater habitat from the tropics to subantarctic islands and thus constitute a major component of the planet's biodiversity. They vary in length from less than a fraction of an inch to over 6 inches (1 millimeter to over 20 centimeters). They are characterized by elytra—hard, leathery, outer protective wing cases. They undergo metamorphosis, passing through the stages of egg, larva, pupa, and adult. Some are very colorful.

Darwin's near fanaticism in collecting beetles is illustrated by this extract from his *Autobiography*:

[N]o pursuit in Cambridge was followed with nearly so much eagerness or gave me so much pleasure as collecting beetles. It was the mere passion for collecting: for I did not dissect them, and rarely compared their external characters with published descriptions, but got them named anyhow. I will give proof of my zeal: one day, on tearing off some old bark, I saw two rare beetles, and seized one in each hand; then I saw a third one, which I could not bear to lose, so that I popped the one I held in my right hand into my mouth. Alas! It ejected some intensely acrid fluid, which burnt my tongue, so I was forced to spit the beetle out, which was lost, as was the third one. (F. Darwin, ed., *Life and Letters of Charles Darwin, Including an Autobiographical Account*, London: John Murray, 1887, Vol. 1, p. 50)

Darwin collected around Shrewsbury, in Wales, and near Cambridge. Some of his early specimens still exist. Perhaps Darwin was not being entirely fair to his younger self when he maintained he was unsystematic in his studies, for he goes on to state:

I was very successful in collecting and inventing two new methods; I employed during winter a labourer to scrape during the winter, moss off old trees and place it in a large bag, and likewise to collect the rubbish at the bottom of the barges in which reeds are brought from the fens, and thus got some very rare species. No poet ever felt more delighted at seeing his first poem published than I did at seeing, in Stephen's "Illustrations of British Insects," the magic words "Captured by C. Darwin, Esq." (*Autobiography*, chapter 2)

These entries, are, effectively, Charles Darwin's first publication. They consist of very short notes such as: "In great abundance near Cambridge in 1829" opposite the name *Blethisa multipunctata*.

While at Cambridge, Darwin collected beetles with his cousin, **William Darwin Fox** (1805–1880), to whom he used to defer when it came to identifying specimens (although Darwin seems to have been more than competent in this regard). Darwin and Fox visited another beetle collector, the Reverend Samuel Hey of Ockbrook, Derbyshire, to view his "very fine collection . . . [containing] several very rare insects" once or twice. After one visit, Mr. Darwin was described as "a very intelligent man."

Darwin collected many hundreds of beetles on the *Beagle* voyage (using a sweep-net and by examining carrion, decaying fungi, dead wood, and by searching in freshwater bodies); specimens were collected from almost every port of call and small island visited. Most of these were sent to specialists on beetles when he returned to England, particularly **George Robert Waterhouse,** who published descriptions of many of them. A particular interest at many of the locations visited on the voyage was the occurrence of dung beetles (species whose larvae feed on the dung of larger animals, sometimes burying parcels of dung in the soil). He noted their occurrence in Patagonia, on the Chilean island of **Chiloé,** in **Australia** and **Tasmania,** and on the isle of **St. Helena** in the Atlantic. Darwin was interested in and surprised by the fact that in Tasmania there was a quite extensive dung beetle fauna, feeding on the dung of cattle, which had only been introduced some three decades before. Previously, the largest land vertebrates had been kangaroos, which produced a very different type of dung. In describing this network of relationships in *The Voyage of the Beagle,* he refers, in a very ecological way, to "that chain by which so many animals are linked together," which "man had disturbed." In this type of thinking, Darwin was far ahead of his day.

The notion of organisms becoming adapted to their environments would later be of immense importance to him. He also compared the distribution of beetles in the different countries, noting that there were far more in Patagonia than south of the Magellan Strait in **Tierra del Fuego.**

There are few references to beetles in Charles Darwin's major evolutionary texts, but he seems to have reignited his early enthusiasm during the boyhood of some of his sons, encouraging them to collect beetles. Indeed, there appears in the *Entomologist's Weekly Intelligencer* for June 25, 1859, a note recording the capture of several rather rare species, purporting to have been written by three of his sons (**Horace, Francis,** and Leonard). The note commences: "We are three very young collectors having lately taken in the Parish of Down. . . ." As the boys were then aged from about eight to twelve years, it seems unlikely that they had much to do with the writing of the note, although they may have helped by capturing the creatures concerned. All three became scientists, so perhaps history repeated itself with them as with their father: the apparently random collection of beetles in youth led to more systematic studies later.

FURTHER READING

Smith, K.G.V. 1987. "Darwin's Insects." *Bulletin of the British Museum (Natural History)* 14 (1).

Botany

The study of plants; probably less significant to Charles Darwin than zoology or geology early in his career, although he wrote several important books on plants in the latter part of his life.

Despite the influence of the Reverend **John Stevens Henslow,** professor of botany at Cambridge, Darwin did not take a very systematic interest in plants while an undergraduate, although he attended some of Henslow's lectures. At school, and at Cambridge, the collection of **beetles** held many more attractions for him. Even during the voyage of the *Beagle,* his interest in botany was sporadic. He described the *Notofagus* or **southern beech** habitats of South America, noting the fungus (**Darwin's fungus**) associated with the trees and the covering of mosses and lichens that clothed them. He described the **kelp and kelp beds** off the shores of the **Falkland Islands** and the myriad creatures that live in them in a remarkably ecological manner. He also painted a clear picture of the eucalypt forests of New South Wales:

Everywhere we have open woodland, the ground being partially covered with a most thin pasture. The trees nearly all belong to one peculiar family; the foliage is scanty & of a rather peculiar light green tint; it is not periodically shed; the surface of the leaves are placed in a vertical, instead of as in Europe a nearly horizontal position: This fact & their scantiness makes the woods light & shadowless; although under the scorching sun of summer, this is loss of comfort, it is of importance to the farmer, as it allows grass to grow where it otherwise could not. (*Diary,* January 16, 1836)

Darwin goes on to describe the subtle relationships in this plant community among the vegetation, climate, soil, fire, animals, and the Aboriginal population. (See article on **Australia.**) He also includes a good description of grass trees at King George's Sound. He tended to see plants as components in a landscape or habitat (or ecosystem, to use modern terminology). Nevertheless, his identification is often quite good, and he collected enthusiastically from time to time. Considering the interest he had in island environments, and the importance they assumed in his work, it is not surprising that he made fairly thorough collections on the **Cocos (Keeling) Islands** and on the **Galapagos Islands.** He noted that the terrestrial floras of these archipelagoes and those of the **Falkland Islands** and **Tahiti** were depauperate in comparison with continental environments. Accompanying these observations were occasional speculations about how the plants (or their seeds or spores) were dispersed: by the wind, floating on the ocean, and attached to the feathers or feet of birds. **Long-distance dispersal** was later of considerable interest to him, as he realized, after adopting an evolutionary view, that all the plants and animals on remote islands, or their ancestors, must have made their journey via some such dispersal mechanism. Long-distance dispersal is the handmaiden of evolution. Here again it was the big picture rather than the minutiae of the individual plant that interested him.

Later in life, Darwin's focus changed somewhat, and he made more detailed studies of individual plants and plant species, often using a microscope to see minute details and carrying out careful experiments. *On the Origin of Species* contains numerous botanical examples, sometimes based on his own experiments. To investigate hybridization and variation, he raised 233 cabbage seedlings of different varieties close to each other "and of these only 78 were true to their kind." Also emphasizing the advantages of cross-pollination in promoting variation:

In the case of a gigantic tree covered with innumerable flowers, it may be objected that pollen could seldom be carried from tree to tree. [N]ature has . . . provided . . . by giving to trees a strong tendency to bear flowers with separated sexes. . . . [P]ollen must be regularly carried from flower to flower; and this will give a better chance of pollen being occasionally carried from tree to tree. (*On the Origin of Species,* chapter 4, "Natural Selection")

Much of Darwin's work following the publication of *On the Origin* in 1859 represents a further exploration of ideas introduced in the 1859 volume. *Variation in Animals and Plants under Domestication* (1868) was an expansion of the ideas expressed in the first chapter of *On the Origin of Species*. **Descent of Man** (1870) sought to extend the evolutionary principle to humanity. *The Expression of Emotions in Man and Animals* (1872), with its focus on behavior, looked back, to some extent, to the chapter on instinct in *On the Origin*. The title emphasizes the evolutionary theme in confirming the continuity of humanity with the animal kingdom; one of its major themes is a confutation of the notion that the facial muscles of humans were a quite special endowment. His last book with a zoological theme, *Vegetable Mould and Worms*, stresses how minute changes wrought over a long period of time can have substantial results.

The botanical texts illustrate a similar development. Both *On the Origin* and *Descent of Man* emphasize the importance of sexual reproduction in promoting variety, and both *Fertilisation of Orchids* (1862), and **Forms of Flowers** (1877) discuss this theme, illustrating it with many detailed examples from the British flora and plants from overseas. **Climbing Plants** (1865) and **Insectivorous Plants** (1875) stress the idea of adaptation to environment, an important element in natural selection.

The position of *Fertilisation of Orchids* (1862) is particularly interesting. Published just three years after *On the Origin,* the book had an evolutionary message and also was strongly ecological. It was concerned with the details of the relationships between the reproductive structures of orchids

and the insects that pollinate them. Darwin in his early career was much influenced by **William Paley**'s doctrine of natural theology, and it is interesting to note that Darwin's American botanist friend **Asa Gray** stated that, if the orchid volume had appeared before *On the Origin* rather than just after it, "the author would have been canonised rather than ananthematised" by the natural theologians. A journal called the *Literary Churchman* felt that Darwin's detailed description of the "contrivancies" of orchids was an indirect way of saying: "O Lord, how manifold are thy works" (Psalm 104, v. 24). The book was highly praised by botanists, and Darwin himself was much pleased with the work, but it did not sell well: only 6,000 copies were sold in Britain before the end of the century.

It has been suggested that the structure of *On the Origin* presents "one long argument." It could further be stated that the entire cor-

Grass tree (*Kingia australis*), southwestern Australia. Photo: Patrick Armstrong.

pus of Darwin's work, from the later editions of the *Voyage of the Beagle,* via *Coral Reefs* (both of which have evolutionary nuances, although they pre-date On the *Origin of Species*), through to *Worms* represent the development of that "long argument." The several botanical works are important components of the whole edifice.

Brazil

Large South American country, formerly governed by Portugal, visited several times by Darwin on the *Beagle* voyage.

The *Beagle* entered All Saints Bay at Bahia (now Salvador) in Brazil, on February 28, 1832. The bay was "scattered over with large ships" and the view was "one of the finest in the Brazils." The vast country had received its independence from Portugal only 10 years before—it was then an independent kingdom and did not become a republic until 1889. Slavery was still practiced, and Darwin could scarcely believe some of the tales of cruelty he heard. He went ashore on the tropical mainland for the first time, passing through narrow, squalid streets close to the port, but described many tall, whitewashed houses, along with fine "convents, porticos and public buildings." Inland was the luxuriant forest; Darwin wrote in his diary:

> The mind is in a chaos of delight . . . among the multitude it is hard to say what set of objects is the most striking; the general luxuriance of the forest bears the victory, the elegance of the grasses, the novelty of the parasitical plants, the beauty of the flowers, the glossy green of the foliage, all tend to this end. A most paradoxical mixture of sound and silence pervades the shady parts of the wood; the noise from the insects is so loud in the evening it can be heard even on a vessel anchored several hundred yards from the shore; yet in the recesses of the forest a universal stillness appears to reign. (*Diary*, February 28 and 29, 1832)

This was the first of Darwin's experiences of Brazil. On April 4, the *Beagle* anchored at Rio de Janeiro, 800 miles southwest of Bahia "under the Sugar loaf . . . the changing prospect of the mountains . . . enveloped in white clouds" behind. Darwin was impressed by the gridlike rectangular plan of the town, which he compared in certain respects to that of parts of **Edinburgh,** where he had received medical training; the broad streets, the fine palace, the squares, and the bright colors of the houses with their balconies all appealed to him. He also noted the vibrant activity of the streets and the large number of ships in the harbor, "which bespeaks the commercial capital of South America." There were several warships in port, for this was also the base for British naval operations in South America.

Darwin made a number of excursions into the interior and along the coast from Rio, and he gives many details of the forests and mountains: the gaudy butterflies and fireflies, the several species of humming birds, the toucans and bee-eaters, the orchids and cabbage palms, the creepers that covered some trees, the great tree-ferns and the mimosa plants that reacted when touched by a passerby, the "conical ants' nests" 12 feet (3.5 meters) high—termite mounds, which, he said, "injured" a tract of pasture. He noted the red soil. The tropical forest, he wrote, "is a gold mine to a naturalist." He was also most observant of the economic basis of the territory, commenting on the many kinds of fruit grown—pawpaw, breadfruit, mango, banana, and jackfruit; he noted particularly pineapples "planted in rows" in sandy soil. Tapioca was an important product, and sugar cane, then as now, was grown, along with rice "in the swampy parts." Already Brazil was noted for coffee production. At one estate where he stayed, he recorded: "Coffee is the most profitable [crop]: the brother of our host has 100,000 trees, producing an average of 2 lb per tree, many however will bear 8 lb, or even more."

But there was a darker side; Darwin complained of the corruption and criminal violence. And slavery, which was not abolished in Brazil until 1888, was an ever-present abomination. On one estate that he visited, following some petty quarrel:

> Mr Lennon . . . threatened to sell at public auction an illegitimate mulatto child . . .; also he nearly put into execution taking all the women and children from their husbands and selling them separately in Rio. Can two more horrible and flagrant instances be imagined? And yet I will pledge myself that in humanity and good feeling Mr Lennon is above the common run of men. (*Diary*, April 15, 1832)

Another aspect of life in Brazil that troubled the young Englishman was the prevalence of fever and disease generally. Darwin was unwell more than once, suffering from swellings in both his knee and his arm caused by infections following a small injury. Several of his shipmates suffered from fever (perhaps malaria, the insect-born nature of which was not understood for many decades).

The *Beagle* departed from Rio on July 5, 1832; during some of the intervening few months, the crew had been undertaking surveys offshore, leaving Darwin to travel inland and explore on his own or with a small group of friends. But he had not seen the last of "the Brazils"; four years later (on August 1, 1836) the ship again anchored in All Saints Bay, Bahia, on the homeward run. Captain FitzRoy used the opportunities provided by less than favorable winds on leaving Ascension Island to remake certain navigational observations "completing his chain of meridians around the world." The stay was a short one, and less than a week later they departed, calling in to Pernambuco, 400 miles to the northeast. Darwin again went ashore for a few days of exploration. He disliked the place: "The town is in all parts disgusting, the streets narrow, ill-paved, filthy; the houses very tall and gloomy." Nevertheless, it had a good harbor, formed by a reef that ran "in a perfectly straight line parallel to and not far distant from the shore." Inland, and situated at the foot of a range of hills, was the old city of Olinda, which was found to be "sweeter and cleaner" than Pernambuco; it was reached by a creek along which vivid green mangroves "spring like a miniature forest out of the greasy mud banks."

British Association for the Advancement of Science

Founded in 1831 to promote science in Britain, the British Association for the Advancement of Science (BAAS) currently describes itself as "a charity which exists to advance the public understanding, accessibility and account-ability of the sciences and engineering."

The British Association was founded in the year that the *Beagle* left England, somewhat loosely modeled on the German organization Gesellschaft deutscher Naturforscher und Aerzte. It has, in turn, had its own imitators, such as the Australian and New Zealand Association for the Advancement of Science, founded in 1888.

In the early 1830s, the principal scientific organization in Britain was the **Royal Society.** Some maintained that this was a somewhat conservative and elitist organization, and they looked for a forum that would be more open and that would publicize scientific matters toward an increasingly educated public. Among those who were influential at the founding of the BAAS was Sir David Brewster (physicist, 1781–1868) and the Reverend William Vernon Harcourt (1789–1781), who became president in 1839. The first meeting was held in York on September 27, 1831, and the British Association has subsequently met in a different provincial city each year (war years excepted). It has occasionally met outside the British Isles. The yearly meetings became a major forum for the discussion of scientific matters, and also became major social (and especially more recently, media) events. In the nineteenth century, it became one of the main public arenas for the discussion of scientific matters. The yearly meetings are divided into sections for mathematical physics, geology, botany, zoology, geography, anthropology, and so on (the sections have varied over the years). The presidential addresses soon became a significant vehicle for pronouncements on science from what some considered the British "parliament of science." Indeed, the term "Queen's speech" was sometimes used for the presidential address.

There has been considerable discussion of the role and importance of the British Association. Some argue that its powerful influence was unfortunate, even pernicious. It is suggested that, although it was, in the Victorian era, a decentralized organization, meeting outside London, in fact it came under the control of London-based elites who used it to display a particular version of science: orthodox, religiously respectable, and politically on the side of the established order, and thus frustrating the development of new ideas. Darwin's opponent **Richard Owen,** for example, more than once used the Association meetings as a platform for his antitransmutation notions. Another instance of this conservatism occurred in 1878, when a committee of the Association recommended against the construction of an analytical engine devised by Charles Babbage. It has been suggested that this decision may have delayed the computer revolution well over half a century. On the other hand, the Association has done, and continues to do, a remarkable job in bringing the ideas of science into the mainstream of British thought. As a counter to those who emphasize the conservatism of the BAAS, it should be remembered that the meeting at Oxford in 1860 hosted the Great Debate between **Thomas Huxley** and Bishop **Samuel Wilberforce,** chaired by **John Henslow.**

Despite his dislike of travel in later life, and indeed his reluctance to be very far from home and family at Down, Darwin attended the meetings of the British Association a number of times, having important discussions at some of them with the leading scientists of the day. Thus, he was present at the meeting of 1839 (in Birmingham), 1846 (Southampton), 1849 (Birmingham again), and 1855 (Glasgow). Sometimes his wife Emma accompanied him. He often went reluctantly; he attended the 1849 meeting, very much against his preference, partly because he had been elected a vice president. He said of the meeting that he became weary of "all that spouting."

FURTHER READING

Morrell, Jack and Arnold Thackray. 1981. *Gentlemen of Science: Early Years of the British Association for the Advancement of Science.* Oxford, England: Clarendon Press.

Buckland, William (1784—1856)

Oxford geologist and eccentric. The first person to identify and name a dinosaur. Originally a catastrophist and creationist who believed that superficial deposits were laid down by the flood described in Genesis, he was later won over to the glacial theory.

Buckland was something of an eccentric and a larger-than-life figure in the history of geology. Like many nineteenth-century English naturalists and scientists, he was the son of a Church of England clergyman and became a priest himself. His father

The Reverend Professor William Buckland, lecturing in 1823. National Portrait Gallery, London.

was rector of a Devonshire parish, and, as a boy, he used to accompany his father around the Devon countryside, looking at geological exposures in roadsides and finding fossils. He gained a scholarship to Corpus Christi College, Oxford, in 1801, graduating in 1804. He was ordained to the priesthood and became a fellow of his college. While an undergraduate, he attended the lectures of John Kidd in mineralogy, in 1813 succeeding him as reader in mineralogy and being elected to the chair of geology a little later. He was elected a fellow of the **Royal Society** in 1818.

His inaugural address as professor of geology (May 15, 1819) was published the following year as *Vindiciae Geologiae: Or the Connection of Geology with Religion Explained*. This was pure scriptural geology. It sought to justify the relatively young science of geology and reconcile the biblical account of the creation and the flood with geological evidence—to reconcile the "book of nature" with the "book of God." Buckland has been described as an old Earth creationist. He did not maintain that the Earth was a mere 6,000 years old, as had some previous thinkers, but that the word "beginning" in Genesis implied an undefined, but possibly long, period between the creation of the Earth and that of the present inhabitants. During this period, a number of creations and extinctions had occurred. He maintained that superficial or "drift" deposits that covered much of Britain (glacial till or boulder clay, sands, and gravels) were deposited by the biblical flood.

Buckland was extremely energetic and a most enthusiastic field worker. He investigated Kirkdale Cavern in Yorkshire, in northern England, producing some of the bones he found there at a dinner of the **Geological Society of London,** of which he was two-time president (1824–1826 and 1839–1841). He concluded that the caves had been inhabited by hyenas in antediluvian (preflood) times, which had brought in carcasses, rather than the bones there being the remains of creatures that had perished in the flood and being carried by the surging waters from the tropics, as had previously been suggested. He argued, however, that it was the layer of sediment above the animal remains that had been deposited by the flood. These ideas appeared in *Reliquae Diluvianae, or Observations on the Organic Remains Attesting the Action of the Universal Deluge,* which appeared in 1823, was reprinted several times, and became something of a best-seller.

However, following 1840 and the publication of *Étude sur les glaciers (Study on Glaciers)* by Swiss (later American) geologist Louis Agassiz (1807–1873), Buckland became convinced of the reality of the Ice Age and accepted the idea that the superficial deposits in Britain and elsewhere in Europe were deposited by glaciers. Nevertheless, he remained a catastrophist, substituting glaciers for the flood in his schema.

He described the first pterodactyl, found by Mary Anning in 1828. When the same young woman found fossil cephalopods with their ink sacs well preserved, he persuaded the noted artist Sir Frank Chantry to use the ink to draw an ichthyosaurus. He was a vigorous and earnest debater, sometimes vehemently defending his scientific point of view. He seems to have been a bit of a bon vivant, enjoying the Geological Society dinners. It is recorded that he, "when he travelled to London to attend meetings of the Society was accustomed to stay at the Salopian Coffee House and Tavern in Charing Cross, a house noted for good dinners and wines."

Some of his culinary tastes were more unusual. Canon Buckland claimed to have eaten his way through the animal kingdom. Crocodile is known to have been served to visitors, along with mice cooked in batter. He claimed that the most unpleasant-tasting animal he ever ate was the mole.

His method of teaching was equally individual. He sometimes kept his audience roaring with laughter as he imitated the alleged movements of iguanodon or megatherium (extinct animals), or, seizing the tails of his clerical coat, would leap around purporting to show how a pterodactyl flew.

Audiences loved it—in the field as well as in the lecture hall. At the meeting of the **British Association for the Advancement of Science,** held in Birmingham in 1839, he attracted thousands to a lecture at Dudley Caverns, specially lit with thousands of candles for the occasion. After a discussion of the geology, he seems to have become carried away by a stream of patriotic emotion. The mineral wealth of the area, he declaimed, showed that Providence had intended, by these gifts, for Britain to be the richest and most powerful nation. On this announcement, the great crowd, returned toward the entrance to the cave, thundering out the words of "God Save the Queen."

He often added to the incongruity by conducting fieldwork in extraordinarily elaborate formal dress. He roamed the countryside wearing his black frock coat, dark suit, and top hat, carrying an umbrella. Sometimes he would produce specimens "like a conjurer" from a large dark-colored bag.

RELIQUIÆ DILUVIANÆ;

OR,

OBSERVATIONS

ON THE

ORGANIC REMAINS

CONTAINED IN

CAVES, FISSURES, AND DILUVIAL GRAVEL,

AND ON

OTHER GEOLOGICAL PHENOMENA,

ATTESTING THE ACTION OF AN

UNIVERSAL DELUGE.

BY THE REV. WILLIAM BUCKLAND, B.D. F.R.S. F.L.S.

MEMBER OF THE GEOLOGICAL SOCIETY OF LONDON; OF THE IMPERIAL SOCIETIES OF MINERALOGY AND NATURAL HISTORY AT PETERSBURG AND MOSCOW; OF THE NATURAL HISTORY SOCIETY IN THE UNIVERSITY OF BONN, ON THE RHINE; AND OF THE NATURAL HISTORY SOCIETY AT HALLE; HONORARY MEMBER OF THE AMERICAN GEOLOGICAL SOCIETY; CORRESPONDENT OF THE MUSEUM OF NATURAL HISTORY OF FRANCE; FELLOW OF C.C.C. AND PROFESSOR OF MINERALOGY AND GEOLOGY IN THE UNIVERSITY OF OXFORD.

SECOND EDITION.

LONDON:
JOHN MURRAY, ALBEMARLE-STREET.

MDCCCXXIV.

Title page from William Buckland's *Reliquiae Diluvianae.* 1824.

His domestic life seems to have been almost as unique. The staircase in his home was covered with fossils and fragments of rock, "an immense tortoise," and a stuffed wolf. Books, papers, and boxes were piled into a "mass of confusion" in the breakfast room. The room had not "been invaded by a dust cloth" for five years. Living creatures roamed the house. His lively wife attempted to tidy up occasionally but abandoned the attempt because it disturbed Professor Buckland so severely.

Buckland had a considerable effect on the development of science. He was an inspiring, if somewhat eccentric, teacher; he encouraged fieldwork and was an important force in the adoption of the glacial theory. His performances in the lecture hall and in the field captured the imagination. But some found his posturing and histrionic antics graceless. Charles Darwin, despite the dullness of some of the lectures he endured at **Edinburgh,** regarded Buckland as "a vulgar and almost coarse man" concerned more with "a craving for notoriety, which made him behave like a buffoon, than by a love of science."

See also: Catastrophism, Reconciliation.

Button, Jemmy

Native name Orundellico (c. 1815–1864), was a native Fuegian of the Yaghan or Yamana tribe from the islands south of **Tierra del Fuego.** He was taken to England by Captain **Robert FitzRoy,** on HMS *Beagle* during the ship's first surveying voyage to South America.

In 1830, Captain FitzRoy, in an attempt to secure the return of one of the ship's boats that had been taken, took a small number of hostages. The ploy was unsuccessful, but the captain decided to take the four young Fuegians all the way to England "to become useful as interpreters, and be the means of establishing a friendly disposition towards Englishmen on the part of their countrymen." He seems to have shown considerable concern for the four, ensuring they were well fed and intending them to be educated and taught the basics of Christianity in the hope that they could improve the conditions of their people.

The names given to the four Fuegians by the crew were York Minster (after an island from which he came, itself named for its alleged resemblance to the ecclesiastical building), Jemmy Button (so named because he is said to have been bought for a mother-of-pearl button), Fuegia Basket (a young girl of about nine or ten, "as broad as she was high") and Boat Memory. Their original names were, respectively, el'leparu, o'run-del'lico, and yok'cushly. Boat Memory died from smallpox shortly after his arrival to England, and so his name is lost.

The Admiralty was not enthusiastic about the scheme but agreed not to interfere with FitzRoy's plans, to assist with the care of the Fuegians, and afford them passage home. They were provided with medical care in the Royal Naval Hospital in Plymouth, and then given schooling by the Reverend William Wilson of Walthamstow, east of London. They became quite proficient at English. While in England, they became minor celebrities and were presented to King William IV and Queen Adelaide.

A couple of years later, on the voyage on which Darwin accompanied Captain FitzRoy, the *Beagle* returned to Tierra del Fuego, taking the three surviving Fuegians home. Darwin's description of Jemmy at this time was as follows:

Jemmy Button was a universal favourite, but likewise passionate; the expression of his face at once showed his nice disposition. He was merry and often laughed, and was remarkably sympathetic with any one in pain: when the water was rough, I was often a little sea-sick and he used to come to me and say in a plaintive voice, "Poor, poor fellow!" but the notion, after his aquatic life, of a man being sea-sick, was too ludicrous, and he was generally obliged to turn on one side to hide a smile or laugh, and then he would repeat his "Poor, poor fellow!" He was of a patriotic disposition; and he liked to praise his own tribe and country, . . . and he abused all the other tribes: Jemmy was short, thick, and fat, but vain of his personal appearance; he used always to wear gloves, his hair was neatly cut, and he was distressed if his well-polished shoes were dirtied. He was fond of admiring himself in a looking-glass. (*Voyage of the Beagle,* chapter 10)

The plan was to establish a small mission station, to be manned by a young missionary named Richard Matthews.

The place decided upon was close to Jemmy Button's original home, at the junction of the Beagle Channel and Ponsonby Sound; as they camped overnight, they were joined round their fire by Jemmy's relatives. Jemmy had forgotten his own language and attempted to communicate with his compatriots in an almost unintelligible mixture of broken English and Spanish. When the *Beagle* party arrived at "Jemmy's Cove," or Woollya, his relatives and friends began to pour in—120 of them. This place was considered appropriate for the missionary establishment, having suitable flat land on which it was hoped European vegetables would grow. Darwin's journal continues:

Everything went on very peacibly [*sic*] for some days. Three houses were built, & two gardens dug & planted; & what was of more consequence the Fuegians were quiet and peacible. (*Diary,* January 24, 1833)

But after a while, the situation deteriorated.

They asked for everything & stole what they could. . . . suddenly every woman & child & nearly all the men removed themselves & we were watched from a nearby hill. We were all uneasy about this, as neither Jemmy or York understood what it meant . . . it did not promise peace in the establishment. (*Diary,* January 27, 1833)

Darwin, FitzRoy, and a small group of seamen took some small boats further along the channel; after a couple of weeks, they arrived back at the missionary settlement to find the place in chaos.

> From the moment of our leaving, a regular system of plunder commenced, in which not only Matthews, but also York and Jemmy suffered. Matthews had nearly lost all his things; & the constant watching was most harassing & entirely prevented him from doing anything to obtain food &c. Night & day large parties of the natives surrounded his house. . . . One day, having requested an old man to leave the place, he returned with a large stone in his hand. Another day, a whole party advanced with stones & stakes. . . . I think we returned just in time to save his life. (*Diary,* February 6, 1833)

Jemmy's brother was party to some of this, and there were feuds among the Fuegians: Jemmy said, "They were all very bad men." Darwin concluded that the excursion of the three Fuegians to England would "not be conducive to their happiness." Richard Matthews was rescued and taken to New Zealand, where he had relatives who were missionaries. The experiment was at an end. FitzRoy later reluctantly wrote that the whole undertaking had been on far too small a scale.

Many months later, the *Beagle* returned to Woollya. The sight was not particularly encouraging. The houses were empty, and the gardens were neglected. York Minster had left some months before to return to the land of his own people but had denuded Jemmy of most of his belongings. Jemmy looked pitiful: a year before he had been plump and well fed, but he now had lost weight and was pale and ill-kempt. His hair was long and straggly, and he wore little but a blanket. There had been raids by other tribes, and the Woollya folk had been compelled to take refuge on the smaller islands. Despite all this, Jemmy described himself as being in good health. Although he refused to return to England, he still spoke good English and behaved well when dining with the Captain, remembering his old friends with affection. He gave FitzRoy a couple of otter skins and gave Darwin some spearheads. He was loaded down with gifts of clothing and other items. Charles Darwin wrote:

> Every soul on board was sorry to shake hands with poor Jemmy for the last time, as we were glad to have seen him. I hope & have little doubt he will be as happy as if he had never left his country; which is much more than I formerly thought. He lighted a farewell signal fire as the ship stood out of Ponsonby Sound. (*Diary,* March 6, 1834)

Darwin was overoptimistic here—his initial feelings, that the trip to England would not contribute to his long-term contentment, were probably close to the mark. A number of explorers, missionaries, and others made occasional contact with Jemmy (and also with York Minster and Fuegia Basket) in the decades that followed, being surprised to encounter someone "at the end of the earth" who spoke English and knew about London and Plymouth. Jemmy was once taken to the Falkland Islands by the South American Missionary Society; this venture was not a success. Indeed, some sources claim that, in 1859, a group of missionaries was slaughtered by Fuegians, allegedly led by Jemmy and his family.

Several semifictionalized biographies of Jemmy Button have appeared, and he has captured the imagination of readers ever since he was described by Darwin and FitzRoy in the 1830s. His story encapsulates the notion of the clash of cultures. And without the "capture" of Jemmy and his companions, there might not have been a Darwin voyage. And the world would have been very different.

FURTHER READING

Nichols, Peter. 2003. *Evolution's Captain*. London: HarperCollins.

C

Cambrian Big Bang

The burst of evolution that occurred in the Cambrian period, approximately 540 million years ago.

An oft-quoted example of "suddenness" in the fossil record is the apparent abrupt appearance of many different biological groups (phyla) at an early point. Darwin mentions the "grave" difficulty of the manner in which numbers of species of the same group "suddenly appear in the lowest known fossiliferous rocks." He admitted that "the case at present must remain inexplicable." But even he probably underestimated the problem that has been exposed by recent (since about 1990) findings of fossils from the Cambrian rocks in regions as far separated as Namibia in southwest Africa, western Canada, Greenland, and China. Particularly well known (and sometimes misrepresented) are the fossils of the Burgess Shale, British Columbia. These include a sluglike creature covered in sharp spines to which the name *Wiwaxia* has been given (and which was possibly allied to living bristle worms), *Hallucigenia* (a velvet worm with tiny legs and sharp spines; strange name, strange creature), and *Opabinia* (a creature that seems to have no relatives, with five eyes and a long proboscis like that of an elephant). There seems to have been an enormous burst of evolution in the early Cambrian period (perhaps about 543 to 530 million years ago) to which the phrase Big Bang has been applied. In this explosion appeared forms that represented examples of most of the basic designs of modern organisms (phyla).

Two important questions emerge in discussions of the Cambrian Big Bang:

1. Why did this burst of evolution occur at this time?
2. Why has there been nothing comparable during the whole of geological time since?

Perhaps one answer is based on the "empty barren" or "wide open space" theory. Once life had reached a certain critical stage, the biosphere (the part of the Earth in which life was possible) was wide open to exploitation, and there was a tremendous evolutionary search to fill available ecological niches. As herbivores evolved, so predators quickly followed to utilize the new resources. Once ecological spaces were occupied, carving out a new niche became more and more difficult. It has also been suggested that there was a rapid change in the genetic structure of some organisms at this time, allowing greater complexity to arise quickly; but that a little later the genes in organisms—their "genetic software"—became more complex and inflexible. So although, for example, winged flight could develop in several major biological groups and occasion substantial "radiation" (the evolution of many different forms from a common ancestor—for example, in birds), or the marvel of the human brain appeared, with very few exceptions, no totally new types of organisms emerged out of the mix. Later innovation is limited to relatively modest improvements in already reasonably efficient designs. In a similar way, after fairly spectacular initial experimentation, the essential form of aircraft and automobiles have remained much the same for many decades. But some scientists see the causes of the Big Bang as being at least partly environmental. At this time, preexisting continents broke up, allowing coastal margins and shelf seas to become more important habitats, and the chemical composition of the atmosphere changed.

See also: Punctuated Equilibrium.

Cambridge University

England's second oldest university, founded in 1209. Attended by Charles Darwin 1828 to 1831.

There was a settlement of consequence at Cambridge in Roman times, taking advantage of a bridging point on the River Cam or Granta. Well before the establishment of the university, in medieval times, Cambridge was an important trading center and had a vigorous town life. This is evidenced by the number of buildings that have Saxon or Norman elements in their structures.

Although the origins are obscure, Oxford seems to have already been a center for scholarship in the late eleventh century. In 1209, a group of scholars seem to have fled from Oxford as the result of riots. These scholars, mainly clerks (clergy) were numerous enough by 1226 to have established a formal organization, presided over by a chancellor, and to have arranged regular courses of study, taught by their own members. King Henry III provided protection in 1231 and arranged for them to be protected from exploitation by unscrupulous landlords and overcharging by local trades-people. Thus was born a "town versus gown" rivalry that has persisted for 800 years, intermittently rising to real antagonism, when the town (now city) council and local townspeople reveal their resentment of the privileges of the university and its constituent colleges.

Cambridge University has, since its earliest days, been a collegiate or federal university, made up of a number of colleges, each of which is self-governing, has its own traditions, and has a large measure of independence. There were 17 such colleges in Darwin's day; there are now 31. Traditionally, and still to some extent today, much of the university's teaching was done by the colleges, rather than by the university. Over the past century, however, the need for sophisticated laboratories and massive computing resources has meant that more and more teaching is done centrally in departments, but still "supervisions" (tutorials) are often arranged in colleges, of which every undergraduate is a member. Each college is administered by a governing body of fellows (senior faculty or academics), under a master (or in some cases a principal or provost). The titular head of the university remains the chancellor, who holds the position for life (the present holder of the office is the Duke of Edinburgh, the husband of the Queen). The day-to-day administration is performed by a vice chancellor. Today, Cambridge University has some 16,000 full-time students, of whom about a third are postgraduates, along with about 15,000 part-time students. In 1829, the entire university would only have comprised a few hundred.

The oldest college is Peterhouse, founded in 1284. Darwin's own college, Christ's College, was founded in 1505, although it incorporated Godshouse, which had been founded in 1439. St. John's College, the college of Darwin's mentor and friend, the Reverend Professor **John Henslow,** came into existence in 1511.

After his *Beagle* voyage, Darwin lived in Cambridge for some months following December 1836, sorting his collections, distributing some of them to the leading men of science of the day, and discussing them with John Henslow and other naturalists.

Much later, some of Cambridge's clerical academics opposed Darwin's evolutionary ideas vehemently and thus, despite his distinction, for decades Cambridge was reluctant to acknowledge his contribution to science. However, in November 1877, 18 years after the first publication of *On the Origin of Species,* Cambridge University capitulated to overwhelming pressure and awarded Charles Darwin an honorary doctorate of laws. The occasion of the conferment was a spectacular one. His wife Emma and some of his children were in the audience, and undergraduate students filled the galleries, stood in the windows, and even perched on statues, sometimes shouting and laughing. A puppet monkey frolicked above the crowd on a cord strung across the Senate House, the hall in which the ceremony was to be performed. Later, the "missing link," a ring decorated with bright ribbons, appeared. Students cheered. On a more sober note, a speech in Latin was given describing the great naturalist's achievements. Darwin beamed at the crowds.

In 1964, the wheel turned full circle, and **Darwin College** was founded at the university, commemorating both the life and work of Charles Darwin and other distinguished members of the Darwin family, several of whom formerly resided in the building adjoining the River Cam that now forms its core. The college is entirely for postgraduate students.

The colleges and university departments are scattered around the city of Cambridge, giving the place much of its distinctive character.

Cape of Good Hope

The popular name for the southern tip of Africa; originally a Dutch colony, later part of the British Empire, and now part of the Republic of South Africa.

South Africa, in recent decades, has been notable for its ethnic tensions; although majority rule was attained in 1994, stresses remain between the various ethnic groups that make up the population. Such pressures were already apparent at the time of Darwin's visit in June 1836. Darwin noted the strong tensions between the English and the Dutch; he commented on the presence of "Hottentots," "the ill-treated aboriginals of the country," and the "Negroes." There was already an appreciable Asian component in the form of the Malays "descendants of slaves brought from the East Indian archipelago." The ethnic complexity of the Cape of Good Hope is evident through a good deal of Darwin's writings from and about South Africa.

The influence of British India was strong: "several ships from India had arrived at this great inn on the great highway of nations." Some of the people from India who he met in South Africa—merchants and administrators, presumably—he found pretentious, opinionated, and tiresome. He referred to them as "Nabobs" and avoided them as much as possible. The young Darwin, despite his liberal outlook on race, slavery, and many other matters, on the whole was proud of Britain's imperial stance and noted with approval the development of a number of "little Englands" developing in the Southern Hemisphere. He was impressed by the development of agriculture, and in particular sheep farming, the generally well-planned nature of Cape Town (he compared the grid pattern to that of towns in South America), and the rapid development of infrastructure such as the building of roads. He noted that the population of Cape Town was about 15,000 and that of the whole colony about 200,000 and implies that both the economy and the population were expanding quickly. The cultural landscape contrasted favorably with the rather stark environments of Australia through which he had been traveling a few months before. In a letter to his sister, he wrote of the "tidy white houses, gardens, avenues of small oaks and many vineyards . . . pretty well watered" in Paarl and the country nearby, and in a notebook he commented on the scotch firs and shady lanes on the road from Simonstown to Cape Town. Wine production was later to become one of the mainstays of the economy of South Africa.

Darwin made extensive geological observations at the Cape of Good Hope. Perhaps the most interesting were his notes on that characteristic element in the South African landscape, the *kopje*—rounded granite domes formed by spheroidal weathering.

> The granite is subject to extreme decomposition. . . . At the village of Paarle [sic] there are some extraordinary fine examples of loose balls of enormous size lying on the summits of the base mammiform hills of granite. Parallel and vertical fissures cross the mountains in directions at right angles to each other. These may now be seen of various widths and it would appear that the great balls are only the remnants of original vertical masses. Besides the general composition . . . patches of granite yield to the weather much more readily than the adjoining parts. As we see in some granites spherical masses . . . possessing a harder and slightly different structure . . . it appears certain that no cause other than the quiet action of the weather has removed the central parts. (*Geological Notes,* Cambridge University Library, Darwin Archive)

Darwin was perhaps the first to explain the formation of the granite spheres above the settlement of Paarl. (An earlier explorer had noted the sphere-shaped masses atop the mountain and thought they resembled pearls; paarl = pearl.) The features still attract visitors.

Perhaps the most significant event of Darwin's African sojourn was his brief entry into a community or society including several men of science. Darwin, along with Captain **Robert FitzRoy,** visited astronomer Sir **John F. W. Herschel,** who was then visiting the Cape to make observations on Halley's comet; Darwin also seems to have dined with him. Another astronomer then in Cape Town working with Sir John was Thomas Maclear (later Sir Thomas, Astronomer Royal at the Cape of Good Hope 1834–1870). Darwin found him "kind and hospitable." Darwin also went on some geological excursions with Dr. Andrew Smith (also later knighted), who was an army physician, explorer, and naturalist. Darwin mingled with these people and must have discussed his findings with them. Almost for the first time since leaving England, Darwin was part of a reasonably sized group of scientific men; he seems to have reveled in the experience. It must have made him anticipate all the more eagerly the time when he could make his own contribution after his return to England.

Cape Verde Islands

A group of 10 islands, with a total area of 1,577 square miles (4,033 square kilometers), 350 miles (560 kilometers) from the coast of Africa (16° N, 24° W).

Some of Darwin's shipmates had been uncomplimentary about the archipelago, and his initial impression was that it was "sterile" and "desolate" as the result of the recent volcanic activity, and the tropical heat (the vegetation is described as dry forest and scrub, but the vegetation had been damaged by centuries of grazing by goats). Nevertheless, he warmed to the island of St. Jago (San Tiago).

> Here I first saw the glory of tropical vegetation: Tamarinds, Bananas and Palms were flourishing at my feet. . . . It is not only the gracefulness of their forms or the novel richness of their colours, it is the numberless and confused associations that rush together . . . and produce the effect. I returned to the shore, treading on Volcanic rocks, hearing the notes of unknown birds, and seeing new insects fluttering about still newer flowers. It has been for me a glorious day, like giving to a blind man eyes. (*Diary*, January 16, 1832)

Darwin also, for the first time since his excursion to **North Wales** with **Adam Sedgwick,** was able "to make out the geology of the country." He saw volcanic rocks overlying limestone, baking the shells and corals it contained into a "hard white rock." He saw evidence of uplift, but also of subsidence near craters. He compared the corals in the limestone with those living in the sea nearby. He was beginning to see in three dimensions and to see how changes had occurred—both uplift and subsidence had taken place in relatively recent geological time.

> It then first dawned on me that I might perhaps write a book on the geology of the various countries visited, and this made me thrill with delight. (*Autobiography*, 81)

The island of St. Jago (as Darwin referred to it) in the Cape Verde group was important in other ways, too. It was here that Darwin undertook some of his first experiments and observations on **animal behavior.** He found an octopus among the rocks on tiny Quail Island and describes its locomotion, its squirting of ink, and its changing color in remarkable detail; he experimented on its response to stimuli, including small electric shocks (galvinism). We also see Darwin beginning to think ecologically; he is beginning to describe assemblages or organisms—those of the seashore, those of the gorges, and those of the open, volcanic country. He noted "the gay coloured kingfisher and its prey, the less gaudy grasshopper."

If there was a eureka moment for Darwin on the voyage, it was not on the Galapagos Islands, but on the dry, "sterile" Cape Verdes. Here Darwin resolved to write a book, began to understand the complexity and fascination of geology, experienced the heat of the tropics for the first time, and saw a plethora of plants and creatures that were new to him.

See also: Ecology, Geology of the Voyage of the *Beagle*.

Catastrophism

The doctrine that the history of the Earth, and everything in or on it, can be understood with reference to sudden, spectacular events. The term was introduced by William Whewell (1794–1866) and stands in opposition to the notion of **uniformitarianism** or **gradualism,** which maintains that the development of the Earth and life on it are best explained by the long-continued action of very gradual processes.

Before the nineteenth century, much of Western thought accepted that the Bible, and particularly the book of Genesis, provided an accurate account of the origin of the Earth and of living organisms. Quite possibly, the young Darwin was of this view; the notion was compatible with the doctrine of natural theology as set forth by **William Paley** (whose ideas were strongly influenced by the seventeenth-century divine **John Ray**), whose books Darwin had studied at university. Biblical events such as the flood (the deluge), the destruction of Jericho and of Sodom and Gomorrah were seen as historic events for which, if one were to search in the right place, geological evidence might be found. Many late eighteenth- and nineteenth-century geologists, such as **William Buckland** early in his career, had no hesitation in claiming that superficial deposits, now known to be of Quaternary Ice Age origin, were deposited by the biblical deluge. (See article on **Glaciation.**) Baron **Georges Cuvier** (1769–1832) was a leading exponent of catastrophist ideas. He studied the many layers of rock in the Paris Basin, noting that each contained a different assemblage of fossils. He argued that there had been a series of "revolutions"—catastrophic events that caused the extinction of many creatures.

Such views were not universal, however, and the Scottish philosopher James Hutton (1726–1797) was writing of erosion having continued for immensely long periods of time—"no vestige of a beginning, no prospect of an end"—in the eighteenth century.

Darwin, early in his career, was influenced by catastrophist ideas. He had real experience of catastrophic events: for example, at Valdivia, in **Chile** on February 20, 1835, he experienced an earthquake.

> I was on shore and lying down in a wood to rest myself. It came on suddenly and lasted two minutes. . . . The rocking was sensible; the undulation appeared . . . to travel from due East. There was no difficulty in standing upright; but the motion made me giddy. I can compare it to skating on very thin ice or to the motion of a ship in a little cross ripple.
>
> An earthquake like this destroys the oldest associations; the world, the very emblem of all that is solid, moves under our feet like a crust over a fluid. . . . In

the forest, a breeze moved the trees, I felt the earth tremble. . . . At the town . . . the scene was more awful. . . . The houses were violently shaken and creaked much, the nails being particularly drawn. . . . The effect on the tides was very curious; the great shock took place at a time of low water; an old woman on the beach told me that the water flowed quickly but not in big waves to the high-water mark, and as quickly returned to its proper level. She said it flowed like an ordinary tide but a good deal quicker. (*Diary,* February 20, 1835)

A few days later, the *Beagle* reached Concepción: there was not a house left standing, 70 villages had been destroyed and "a great wave" (tsunami, tidal wave) had washed away almost everything that remained.

The whole coast was strewed over with timber and furniture as if a thousand great ships had been wrecked. Besides chairs, tables, bookshelves etc in great numbers, there were several roofs of cottages almost entire. Storehouses were burst open. . . . The force of the wave must have been very great, for in the fort a gun and carriage, which . . . weighed about 4 tons, was removed 15 feet upwards. 200 yards from the beach and well within the town there is now lying a fine schooner, a most strange witness to the height of the wave. . . . The length of the coast which has been much affected is rather less than 400 miles. (*Diary,* March 5, 1835)

Some of the effects of the "great wave" on the coast were permanent. In his notes, Darwin several times used the world "convulsion" to describe features such as the stone runs of the **Falkland Islands.** Even after the end of the voyage he was still able to write:

[I]t seems . . . probable that they [the fragments] have been hurled down from the nearest slopes; and that since, by a vibratory movement of overwhelming force, the fragments have been levelled into one continuous sheet. If during the earthquake which in 1835 overthrew Conception, in Chile, it was thought wonderful that small bodies should have been pitched a few inches from the ground, what must we say to a movement which has caused fragments many tons in weight, to move onwards like such so much sand on a vibrating board, and find their level. (*Voyage of the Beagle,* chapter 9)

However, can we not detect a note of uncertainty in the last sentence? For throughout the voyage, Darwin was coming increasingly under **Charles Lyell's** uniformitarian spell, as he read and reread the *Principles of Geology* in the *Beagle* cabin. Even while he was in the Falklands, Darwin commented on the gradual accumulation of peat and the gradual infilling of some of the long, narrow inlets through deposition. In **Tahiti,** in late 1835, he wrote in his geological notes about the way stream action was very gradually eroding the volcanic rocks of which the island was composed.

Just after leaving Tahiti, Darwin prepared the first draft of the Coral Atoll Theory—the idea that, as result of a rise in sea level (or fall in land level), fringing coral reefs, barrier reefs, and atolls have been gradually transformed into each other. They were members of a series. Here was the young naturalist using Lyell's uniformitarian, gradualist ideas in a systematic way for the first time.

Uniformitarian ideas have largely held their ground in science ever since. Quite apart from Darwin's evolution through natural selection concept, in the late nineteenth century, American geomorphologist W. M. Davis expounded the Cycle of Erosion: landscapes, after uplift, underwent very gradual denudation over millions of years, passing through, he argued, the stages of youth, maturity, and old age. Frederic Clements developed the concept of ecological succession. Plant communities (through hundreds rather than millions of years) passed from a pioneer stage, where a few plants invaded a bare surface (such as a young sand dune or recently solidified lava) and gradually developed through increasingly complex successional stages to an ecological climax.

Nevertheless, catastrophism has always had its devotees. After all, spectacular natural events, sometimes with enormous destructive power, do occur. The volcanic islet of Krakatoa in what was then the Dutch East Indies, exploded in 1883; Mount St. Helens erupted in the northwest United States on May 18, 1980. Some 300,000 people were killed in many countries around the northern Indian Ocean when a tsunami radiated from a point in the sea off the province of Aceh, Indonesia, on December 26, 2004. All these events had spectacular effects on the landscape and on plant and animal life.

In 1980, Walter and Luis Alvarez and some of their colleagues published an important article suggesting that an asteroid (a comet or miniplanet) about 10 kilometers (6 miles) in diameter struck the Earth some sixty-five million years ago, at the end of the Cretaceous period. The resulting impact would have left a crater at least 100 miles (160 kilometers) in diameter. If the impact site had been in the ocean, huge tsunami would have risen several kilometers, sweeping hundreds of kilometers across continents, destroying everything before it. As hot material thrown up from the impact fell back to Earth, huge fires would be ignited. Dust thrown up by the impact and smoke from the fires, would have spread out, shrouding the Earth in darkness. Temperatures would have dropped. Plants would not have received sufficient sunlight for photosynthesis to continue and would perish. As the plants died, the herbivorous animals would die, as would carnivores once their plant-eating prey had disappeared. In the oceans, an accumulation of acid rain would change the chemistry of the water and destroy shell-bearing organisms, disrupting entire food webs. Some 70 percent of all species died out at the end of the Cretaceous period, including the dinosaurs, the group that had dominated life on Earth for tens of millions of years.

Over two decades of research has largely confirmed this theory. In many parts of the world, a clay layer marks the boundary between the Cretaceous and Tertiary periods (the K/T layer), which not only separates rocks with very different fossil assemblages, but contains small quantities of metals such as iridium—rare in the Earth's crust but abundant in some meteorites. Moreover, an apparent site for the impact has been discovered in the sea, just north of the Yucatan Peninsula, Mexico. Drilling has found evidence of the melting of rocks beneath the sea at this place, which has been named the Chicxulub Impact Crater, after a small village on the nearby mainland.

Hundreds of miles away, rocks have been found that were shattered by the explosive impact. The thinking now is that, as the result of the impact, some 200,000 cubic kilometers of material was vaporized, melted, or ejected from the crater—sufficient to cause the biological and physical changes that have been noted.

The truth is that both uniformitarianism and catastrophism are useful ideas in certain circumstances. Most changes on the Earth's crust are gradual; evolution through natural selection must of necessity be slow. But throughout geologic time, occasional dramatic changes wreaked by earthquakes, volcanoes, tidal waves, floods, and meteoritic impact must have had effects far greater than many thousands of years of normal erosion and deposition. Some biologists, such as **Steven Jay Gould,** argue that much the same could be said of evolutionary processes. The doctrine of **punctuated equilibrium** asserts that long periods of slow or negligible change are interrupted by short periods of much more rapid evolution. It is a simple step to suggest that a marked change in the physical environment, causing the extinction of some forms and mutations in others, might trigger major changes in the direction of evolution.

FURTHER READING

Alvarez, L. W., W. Alvarez, F. Asaro, and H. V. Michel. 1980. "Extraterrestrial Cause for the Cretaceous/Tertiary Extinction." *Science* 208: 1095–1108.
Sharpton, Virgil L. 1995. "Impact Crater Provides Clues to Earth's History." *Earth in Space* 8 (4): 7.

Chambers, Robert (1802–1871)

Scottish journalist, publisher, and philosopher. Anonymous author of *Vestiges of the Natural History of Creation,* an early evolutionary text.

Although born in Peebles, in southern Scotland, to a reasonably well-off family, the collapse of Chambers's father's business brought about a reversal of fortunes for the family. In about 1818, Robert Chambers and his brothers took to selling books from a stall in **Edinburgh;** the business prospered, growing into a major publishing concern.

Chambers's main interest was Scottish history and tradition, but he taught himself the rudiments of geology and botany, and, being strongly influenced by Lamarck, he wrote *Vestiges* in part to open up the question of evolution to serious discussion. The book sold well, over 20,000 copies in a decade. U.S. President Abraham Lincoln and Queen Victoria read it (the Queen strongly disapproved); so did poets such as Alfred Lord Tennyson and Elizabeth Barrett Browning, along with politicians such as **William Ewart Gladstone,** and numerous scientists including **Thomas Huxley** and **Adam Sedgwick.**

Vestiges commenced with an explanation of the nebular hypothesis of the formation of the solar system, and went on to present a grand picture of the progressive evolution of life on Earth. Chambers's practical knowledge of science was limited, and he included much in his book that professional scientists found absurd. He accepted, and reported at length about on, the experiments of an eccentric who claimed to have generated living mites (small, spiderlike creatures) by passing electric currents through a chemical solution. He saw organic evolution as steady upward progress governed by unknown, but probably ascertainable, natural laws.

Darwin, who read the book when he was grappling with his own ideas on the transmutability of species, thought the book was "strange" but "capitally written." He described the work as "unphilosophical" (i.e., unscientific). Thomas Huxley, later to be Darwinism's great champion, wrote what has been described as one of most venomous reviews ever written: he said that the author had "dispensed with logic."

Chambers published the book anonymously because he felt, probably on good grounds, that if its authorship were to be revealed, his publishing business might be damaged. Some people—including Darwin—guessed who was responsible, but it was only with the eighth edition in 1884, long after Robert Chambers's death, that the name of the writer was released. There is little in the book that has proved to be of lasting value. But its publication and popularity show that some evolutionary ideas were in circulation before *On the Origin of Species* was published, and also indicated to Darwin the type of opposition his own ideas might eventually face.

Child Development

An aspect of psychology that was a subsidiary, but not unimportant, aspect of Charles Darwin's work.

Darwin's published psychological work included his chapter 7 (on **instinct**) of *On the Origin of Species* (1859), portions of **Descent of Man** (1871), *The Expression of Emotions in Man and Animals* (1872), and an article published in the journal *Mind* in 1877 titled "Biographical Sketch of an Infant." Two distinct but tightly interwoven strands run through his work on animal behavior and the human mind. First, that the activities of animals and humans in many ways resemble one another and can be studied in similar ways, using similar techniques and terminologies. Second, that patterns of behavior (in both man and animals) develop and change over time, both in the long term and in the short term.

An important part of Darwin's thinking on child development arose from a "baby diary" that Darwin wrote following the birth of his eldest son, William, on December 27, 1839. These were reworked and published nearly 40 years later in the "Biographical Sketch" article, the published version being presented in a more scientific or objective style than the original notes, which retain a more personal character.

On the first page of Darwin's diary of the development of his first child, he wrote: "W. Erasmus Darwin born Dec. 27th 1839—During first week, yawned, stretched himself like an old person." He went on to describe how William hiccupped and cried. When the sole of his foot was touched with a spill of paper, when the child was exactly one week old, "it jerked it away very suddenly & curled its toes, like [a] person tickled." Darwin thus tried experiments, just as he had with creatures as varied as planaria, sea anemones, and octopi aboard the *Beagle*. When the surface of a warm hand was placed to William's face, he immediately attempted to suck: "either instinctive or associates knowledge of warm smooth surface of bosom."

As William grew older, between four and a half and seven and a half months, his power of recognition grew. Darwin's experiments grew a little more sophisticated, using mirrors. At four and a half months, Darwin wrote, "Three or four days ago smiled at himself in glass—how does he know his reflection is that of a human being? . . . —Smiled at my image, & seemed surprised at my voice coming from behind him." Increasingly, as the months pass, there is reciprocal interaction and communication. At approaching three years, William was able to obey instructions (bringing a handkerchief from across a room) and displayed sadness when his father was absent. Darwin is displaying his powers of observation, an eye for detail in notetaking, and his experimental approach in a similar manner to those adopted in his zoological work

In *Descent of Man* (chapter 4), Darwin wrote:

> In the next chapter I shall make some few remarks on the probable steps and means by which the several mental and moral faculties of man have been gradually evolved. That such evolution is at least possible, ought not to be denied, for we daily see these faculties developing in every infant; and we may trace a perfect gradation from the mind of an utter idiot, lower than that of an animal low in the scale, to the mind of a Newton.

Ernst Haeckel (1834–1919) developed the notion of **recapitulation,** the idea that "ontogeny repeats phylogeny," or that the life history of an individual organism "recapitulates" the evolutionary history of a biological group. Although Charles Darwin made mention of embryology in *On the Origin of Species,* his emphasis was more on the fact of "embryos of different species within the same class, generally, but not universally resembling one another" and that these similarities might be used as a basis for classification. Nevertheless, he ended his section on embryology thus:

Embryology rises greatly in interest, when we thus look at the embryo as a picture, more or less obscured, of the common parent-form of each great class of animals. (*On the Origin of Species,* chapter 13)

Darwin seems, at least to some extent, to have seen the development of the individual as an *allegory* for the development of the whole biological group through time. His work on child development should perhaps be seen in this way—as an allegory.

Nevertheless, Darwin should not be seen as a strict recapitulationist in regard to child development, along the lines of G. S. Hall and Sigmund Freud, for example. Rather, his work on child development should be seen as a manifestation of the theme of **gradualism,** which runs through much of Darwin's work, including his researches on the crystallization of igneous rocks, coral reefs, and, of course, on evolution through natural selection.

FURTHER READING

Darwin, Charles R. 1877. "A Biographical Sketch of an Infant." *Mind: Quarterly Review of Psychology and Philosophy* 2: 285–294.
Keegan, Robert T. and Howard E. Gruber. 1985. "Charles Darwin's Unpublished 'Diary of an Infant': An Early Phase in His Psychological Work." In *Contributions to a History of Developmental Psychology*, eds. G. Eckhardt, W. G. Bridgemann, and L. Sprung, 127–145. New York: Mouton.

Chile and Peru

Countries on the west coat of South America.

Peru extends from the equator to 18° S, Chile from 17° to 57° S. Peru extends across the Andes, including the northern headwaters of the River Amazon; Chile comprises a long, narrow strip that includes the western sierras of the Andes. Whereas Peru has an area of 496,000 square miles (approximately 1,285,200 square kilometers) and is a relatively compact country, Chile has 292,150 square miles (about 756,700 square kilometers), but has a coast-line of over 2,500 miles (4,000 kilometers) and an average width of only about 100 miles (175 kilometers); in a few places, it is less than 20 miles (30 kilometers) from the Pacific coast to the eastern border with Argentina. The borders, however, were relatively ill-defined at the time of the *Beagle*'s visits. Both were former Spanish colonies and had obtained their independence only a few years before Darwin's journeys—Chile in 1818, Peru in 1824. Evidence of their former colonial status is frequently mentioned in Darwin's writings.

HMS *Beagle* emerged from the Magellan Strait, and from weeks of poor weather and near-destruction, on June 10, 1834, close to South Desolation Island, Darwin wrote in his *Diary:*

Outside the main islands, there are numberless rocks and breakers, on which the long swell of the open Pacific incessantly rages. We passed out between the "East and West Furies". . . . The Captain, from the number of breakers called the sea the "Milky Way." The signs of such a coast is enough to make a landsman dream for a week about death peril and shipwreck.

For many months, the ship zigzagged and doubled back along the west coast of South America, visiting the island of **Chiloé** several times along with several ports of call in Chile and Peru (Valdivia, Valparaiso, Concepción, Lima). Darwin left the ship at several points, sometimes going for long journeys into the Andes, hiring or buying groups of horses and mules for these treks (he was an accomplished horseman until late in life). The first call was at Valparaiso. The vegetation nearby was very different along this central coast of Chile from the forested coasts of **Tierra del Fuego** and Chiloé. It was Mediterranean-type shrubland, which Darwin characterized in the following terms:

> The vegetation has a peculiar aspect . . . owing to the number and variety of bushes . . .: many of them bear very pretty flowers and very commonly the whole shrub has a strong resinous or aromatic smell. In climbing amongst the hills one's hands and even clothes, become strongly scented.

But even more interesting to the naturalist than the living plants and animals was the evidence of past life in the country inland from Valparaiso. His diary account continued:

> I have already found beds of recent shells, yet retaining their colors at an elevation of 1300 feet; and beneath this the country is strewn with them.

In places, these beds were being worked as a source of lime. Clearly there had been changes in sea level along the coast of South America.

Months later, high in the Andes, in a "clay slate," he found "abundant impressions of shells, of which *Gryphaea* is the most abundant . . . *Ostraea, Turritella*, . . . small bivalves" at the height of 12,000 to 13,000 feet (about 4,000 meters). Here was evidence indeed that the great Andean range had been uplifted. Not many days later he encountered:

> in an escarpment of compact greenish sandstone . . . a small wood of petrified trees in a vertical position. The sandstone consists of many layers and is marked by the concentric layers of bark. . . . They are close together within 100 yd.

This was at an elevation of about 7,000 feet (2,150 meters), where the existing landscape was bleak and bare, and again seemed to tell the story of a remarkable rise in the land and a striking change in the conditions.

Darwin had felt the evidence that the landscape of the Andes was unstable when he was at Valdivia. There he experienced an earthquake and an associated tsunami.

Although the destruction was on a smaller scale—Darwin estimated that 100 people had been killed rather than over 300,000—the details that he records of the earthquake and "great wave" are uncannily similar to the tsunami that affected the province of Aceh, Indonesia, and adjacent parts of Southeast Asia on December 26, 2004. (See article on **Catastrophism**.)

Darwin and his captain, **Robert FitzRoy,** noticed that the earthquake seemed to have had an effect on the local sea level. Because changes in the topography of the seabed in the vicinity of ports had implications for navigation, FitzRoy made a special study of this. It was noted that, at the southern end of St. Mary's Island (Isla Santa Maria), in the approaches to Concepción, there had been a rise of eight feet, and to the north nine feet. Extensive beds of mussels and other shellfish, still adhering to the rocks were "upraised above high water mark." In some places, areas of flat rock, now dry but formerly covered by sea water, "exhaled an offensive smell from the many attached and putrefying shells."

But there was other evidence of elevation that suggested that the uplift had been happening for a long time. Inland from Copiapo in northern Chile was a plain estimated to be nearly 300 feet above sea level; on it were abundant shells, many broken and many cemented by "white calcareous matter." Northward again, close to Lima in Peru, Darwin noticed a terrace, about a mile long and 85 feet above high water mark, with a two-foot layer of shells on it.

Not every observation that Darwin made concerning sea level change in South America has been corroborated by more recent studies. It has been argued, for example, that some of the accumulations of shells were the result of the Amerindian inhabitants' food-gathering activities. Nevertheless, it was Darwin's work in Chile and Peru, together with his experience of the earthquake and the tsunami, that convinced him that, in some places at least, both in the high Andes and along the coast, extensive uplift had taken place. Later he argued that this was compensated for by areas of depression or downwarping in the Pacific Ocean.

Although Darwin experienced an enormous variety of environments along the western coast of South America—the temperate forests of Valdivia; the mediterranean scrub around Valparaiso; the fertile, "humanised" landscapes of the irrigated inland valleys; the snowfields, bare screes, and alpine meadows of the high Andes; and the arid deserts of northern Chile—and he collected numerous plant, insect, and vertebrate specimens, it was probably his geological work and speculations on sea level change that was of greatest long-term importance. The world was continually changing, and these changes had implications for living things.

Chiloé

Island off the coast of southern Chile, visited by Darwin several times during 1834 to 1835.

HMS *Beagle* visited Chiloé on three occasions: in June 1834, in November and December the same year, and again early in 1835. By the end of the final visit, Darwin felt that he had "well seen" the island, having circumnavigated it, crossed it from east to west and from north to south, and visited several of the outlying archipelago of small islets that lie between the island and the mainland of South America. The island is approximately rectangular, situated at 42–43° S and 74° W; it is about 100 miles (160 kilometers) long and 25 miles (40 kilometers) wide. The climate is cool and rainy—a fact that Darwin constantly grumbled about (although he experienced a few fine clear days when he was able to view the volcanic cones and snow-capped summits on the mainland). The highest point in the interior of the island is 2,550 feet (777 meters), but the landscape is rolling rather than mountainous. The east coast is deeply indented and scattered with offshore islands, the result of the downing of preexisting valleys due to the postglacial rise in sea level. When Darwin visited, almost the entire isle was forest covered; the exceptions were small areas around the settlements. Darwin describes the thick forests in detail. In places the undergrowth was so thick that it was impossible to cut through. On occasion, he found himself clambering above the tangled scrub that covered the forest floor. In some places, the trees were covered by ferns, lichens, and mosses. **Southern (antarctic) beech** (*Nothofagus*) and winter's green (*Drimys winteri*) were the main trees. He also described the vast rhubarblike leaves of *Gunnera* (used locally as a source of food). (All these species still occur.) Although he did not, of course, use the term biodiversity, Darwin noted both the luxuriance of the forests and the variety of species that make them up. The forests of Chiloé had more kinds of plants

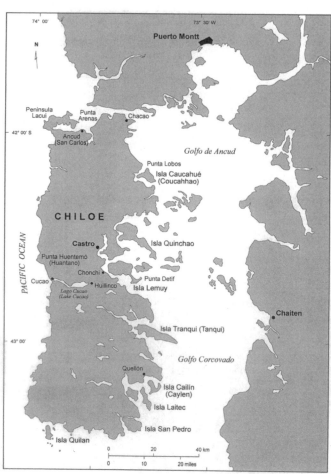

Map of Chiloé, west coast of Chile. Map drawn at Geography Department, University of Western Australia.

and animals than the forests of **Tierra del Fuego,** but less than the tropical forests of **Brazil,** he noticed (he was always comparing). He noted the mammals: coypu, sea otters, and foxes; several species of small forest birds (passerines), and many kinds of insects. The seashore and marine life was also rich, and he described the giant **barnacles** that are still found on the rocks.

Geologically, the rocks of Chiloé are similar to those on the adjacent shores of South America. Darwin described the **igneous rocks** (granites and volcanics), **sedimentary rocks** (mudstones and sandstones), and **metamorphic rocks.** The north-south alignment of the island provides confirmation that the island is a continuation of the trend of the Andes (like parts of Tierra del Fuego, but quite different from the structure of remote volcanic islands).

Although he comments on the politeness and friendliness of the Chilotans (the inhabitants of Chiloé), he gives a picture of poverty, local decline, and near despair. Potatoes, corn, and apples were grown, and stock (especially pigs and sheep) were raised; fishing was locally important. But Darwin describes the economy in these terms:

> no one can be considered to possess a regular income. Each person raises enough for the consumption of his own family and a little more such as hams and potatoes which are . . . exchanged for such articles of clothing as they cannot themselves manufacture. (*Diary,* November 27–28, 1834)

He analyzed the reasons for the poverty. There was no efficient marketing system and very little money in circulation; the people largely resorted

Gunnera growing on the west coast of Chiloé. Photo: Patrick Armstrong.

Temperate rain forest, Chiloé. Photo: Patrick Armstrong.

to barter. The infrastructure was very poor; the roads were sometimes bad and in places built of logs. The administrative burdens and taxes on clearing and developing land discouraged any initiative. The area seems to have been neglected by the "patriot" (i.e., postindependence) government that had displaced the Spaniards 16 years before. Many had been in the Spanish Service (the army) and were looking forward to retirement at half-pay for the remainder of their lives. This expectation was thwarted when Chile obtained independence. Darwin describes the old capital of the island—Castro—as almost deserted with grass growing in the streets and main square and grazed by sheep.

Conditions have improved in the last 180 years. Darwin noted that a recent census had given the population of Chiloé and the adjacent islands as 42,000. In 1999, it was 130,688. Tourism, an expansion of fishing (including fish-farming), and enormous improvements in communications and transport have brought prosperity. Areas of natural forest remain, but land has been reclaimed and a patchwork of green fields contributes to the picturesque nature of the island.

Climbing Plants

From his earliest days on the *Beagle,* Darwin was interested in the behavior of animals, and particularly their responses to stimulation. He performed experiments on **planaria** (flatworms), octopi, **sea anemones, earthworms,** insects, and other creatures, testing their responses to the stimuli of touch, electric shock, sound, and vibration. His interest in two specialized types of plant—climbing plants and insectivorous plants—can be seen as an extension of that work; both types of plants can be said to be able to "perceive" aspects of their environment and to respond to it. Darwin had a large greenhouse at **Down House** and performed experiments in it, besides collecting much information by correspondence. These inquiries can be seen as part of his research on the broad themes of the relationship between organisms and their environments and that of growth and change.

Darwin first published an article on this subject in the *Journal of the Linnean Society* in 1865, but an expanded and corrected form appeared as a monograph published by John Murray (who published many of Darwin's works) with the full title *The Movements and Habits of Climbing Plants* in 1875. A second edition appeared in 1882.

Darwin recognized four classes of climbing plants: (1) twining plants, "those that twine spirally round a support"; (2) "those endowed with irritable organs, which, when they touch any object clasp it" (he accepted that these two classes overlap to some extent); (3) those that climb with hooks; and (4) those that climb by rootlets. However, because neither of the latter two exhibited "any special movements, they present little interest," and Darwin did not discuss them at any length. Darwin discussed a limited number of case studies in great detail. The first was the hop; he described the manner in which the shoot was

> seen to bend to one side and to travel slowly towards all points of the compass, moving, like the hands of a watch, with the sun. (*Climbing Plants,* chapter 1)

He then described the manner in which "leaf climbers" and "tendril bearers" climb, again giving a number of case studies. The extract below, from his account of *Bignonia unguis,* is typical:

> The young shoots revolve. . . . The stems twines imperfectly around a vertical stick some times reversing its direction. . . . Each leaf consists of a petiole bearing a pair of leaflets, and terminates in a tendril. . . . It is curiously like the leg and foot of a small bird, with the hind toe cut off. The straight leg of tarsus is longer than the three toes, which are of equal length, and diverging, lie in the same plane. The toes terminate in sharp, hard claws, much curved downwards, like those on a bird's foot. . . . The whole tendril, namely the tarsus and three toes, are likewise sensitive to contact, especially in their under surfaces. When a shoot grows in the midst of thin branches, the tendrils are soon brought by their revolving movement . . . into contact with them; and then one toe of the tendril, or more, commonly all three, bend, and after several hours seize fast hold of the twigs, like a bird when perched. If the tarsus of the tendril comes in contact with a twig, it goes on slowly bending, until the whole foot is carried quite round, and the toes pass on each size and seize it. (*Climbing Plants,* chapter 3)

Here we see evidence of Darwin's superb, careful observation, his attention to detail, and his experimental approach. We also see interesting aspects of his style: he often uses simile, and indeed metaphor, to get his points across. His description of the movements in plants is similar to the way in which he might describe an element of animal behavior—proof that he saw his work on "movements and habits" of climbing plants as an extension of his work on animal behavior, that led to his book *The Expression of Emotions in Man and Animals* (1872).

The *Climbing Plants* book is also an evolutionary text. He saw twiners, leaf twiners, and tendril climbers as members of a series: "On the view given here leaf-climbers were primordially twiners, and tendril bearers (when formed of modified leaves) were primordially leaf-climbers." He is also at pains to point out in many places the way in which climbing can be seen as an adaptation to environment: in the tropical forests, climbing allows many species to reach the light of the upper layers of the forest canopy.

Cocos (Keeling) Islands

Group of coral atolls in the Indian Ocean.

The rather clumsy name of the Cocos (Keeling) Islands is now used for this extremely small group of coral islets, now under Australian administration, in the Indian Ocean about 1,720 miles (2,770 kilometers) northwest of Perth, Western Australia, and 620 miles (1,000 kilometers) southwest of the most westerly point of Java in Indonesia. There are 27 islands in two separate atolls, with a total area of less than 6 square miles (14 square kilometers). North Keeling is a single, almost circular island—a narrow breach opens into a lagoon—and is about 15 miles (24 kilometers) north of the southern atoll. Only six islands in the southern group are of appreciable size, and only two (Home Island and West Island) are inhabited. The position of the archipelago is latitude 12° 10' S, and 96° 50' E; the highest point is about 20 feet (6 meters) above sea level. Apart from some low sand dunes, the islands are composed entirely of coral. They were extremely important in Darwin's intellectual development.

In many ways, Darwin's brief sojourn in these islands was a high point of his voyage: between April 2 and April 12, 1836, he visited about six of the islands in the southern group, crisscrossed the enclosed lagoon in a ship's boat, and, on departing, glimpsed the northern

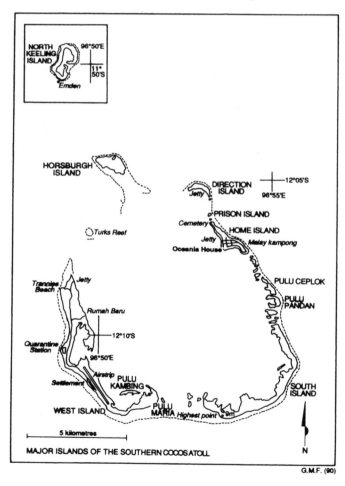

Map of Cocos (Keeling) Islands, Indian Ocean. Map drawn at Geography Department, University of Western Australia.

atoll from a short distance offshore. He had left **Australia** "without sorrow or regret" a fortnight before; although there was much about the Great South Land—the plants, animals, and Aborigines—that fascinated him, he found the landscape "uninviting." The exquisite beauty of unspoiled tropical islands surrounding the aquamarine lagoon, the bright green palm trees standing against the "blue vault of heaven" (as he put it in one of his more lyrical moments), the brilliance of the light, and the unimaginable beauty of some of the corals and other creatures of reef and lagoon presented a striking contrast to the subdued gray-greens of the Australian bush.

Darwin's powers of observation were excellent, and in his notes he described, with accuracy and insight, the overall form of the atoll, its interior lagoon, and surrounding wave-battered beaches. "I was glad that we visited these islands," he wrote as the *Beagle* sailed away. The reason for his enthusiasm was, besides the islands' intrinsic beauty, the fact that he thought that his "Theory of Coral Reefs," on which he had been working for some months, had been confirmed. While crossing the Pacific in late 1835, he had glimpsed, probably from the masthead of the *Beagle,* a couple of tiny coral atolls (low circular or horseshoe-shaped islands or archipelagoes surrounding a shallow lagoon). He then spent a few days in **Tahiti,** where he spent a great deal of time examining coral reefs. Probably while on the passage between Tahiti and the **Bay of Islands, New Zealand,** he wrote out the first draft of his theory; the manuscript is held in the Cambridge University Library. In this document, written on the basis of his experiences in Tahiti, his masthead atoll glimpses, and some notions of sea-level change that had been in his mind since South America, he postulated that fringing reefs (coral reefs adjacent to an island's shore), barrier reefs (those separated by a lagoon), and atolls (where there was no central island) were members of a series.

One form passed into another as the result of the gradual submergence of the (usually volcanic) island or a rise in sea level. This is important, because this notion of **gradualism,** gradual change, is developed in his ideas on **child development,** the development of **igneous rocks** (heat-formed rocks) as different types differentiate out from an original magma (molten rock source), as well, of course, as his theory of evolution through natural selection. The coral atoll theory was his first flirtation with gradualist ideas. Fieldwork at Cocos gave Darwin confirmation that he was on the right track. Here is an extract from Darwin's diary for April 4, 1836:

> I was employed all day in examining the very interesting yet simple structure and origin of these islands. The water being unusually smooth, I waded in as far as the living mounds of coral on which the swell of the open sea breaks. In some of the gullies and hollows, there were beautiful green and other colored fishes, & the forms & tints of many of the Zoophytes [coral organisms] were admirable. It is excusable to grow enthusiastic over the infinite numbers of organic beings with which the sea of the tropics . . . teems.

Elsewhere in his notes he describes a particular species of coral (see article on **Coral and Coral Reefs**).

At the broad scale—the level of the complete island—and at the microscopic level, the young naturalist's observations are perceptive and detailed. He also has an aesthetic sense; here is an extract from his book *The Voyage of the Beagle* (based on notes made at the time):

On entering [the lagoon] the scene was very curious and rather pretty; its beauty, however, entirely depended on the brilliancy of the surrounding colors. The shallow, clear and still water of the lagoon, resting in its greater part on white sand, is, when illuminated by a vertical sun, of the most vivid green. This brilliant expanse, several miles in width, is on all sides divided, either by a line of snow-white breakers from the dark heaving waters of the ocean, or from the blue vault of heaven by strips of land, crowned by the level tops of cocoa-nut trees. As a white cloud here and there affords a pleasing contrast with the azure sky, so in the lagoon, bands of living coral darken the emerald green water.

On some of the smaller islets, nothing could be more elegant than the manner in which the young and full-grown cocoa-nut trees, without destroying each other's symmetry, were mingled into one wood. A beach of glittering white sand formed a border to these fairy spots.

Here is both the scientist's eye for detail and the appreciation of the beauty of a scene.

Coconut palms surrounding lagoon, Cocos (Keeling) Islands, Indian Ocean. Photo: Patrick Armstrong.

He had important ideas circulating in his mind as he walked along the coasts, explored the offshore coral groves, and wandered through the tangled vegetation of the islets. He was particularly aware of the manner in which creatures were "exquisitely adapted" to their environments and the way in which one organism was linked to others. He observed the hermit crabs on Direction Island; these animals have soft hind-parts and protect them in the shells of mollusks:

> The large claw or pincers of some of them are most beautifully adapted when drawn back, to form an operculum [a doorlike structure closing the shell's opening] to the shell, which is as perfect as the proper one which the living molluscous animal formerly possessed. I was assured, & as far as my observation went it was confirmed, that there are certain kinds of these hermits which always use certain kinds of old shells.

But besides the idea of each organism neatly fitting into its own place in the scheme of things—a concept borrowed from the doctrines of natural theology (he had read **William Paley**'s book at Cambridge)—competition and struggle were to be found almost everywhere:

> The aspect and constitution of these islands at once calls up the idea that the land & the ocean are here struggling for mastery; although terra firma has obtained a footing, the denizens of the other think their claim at least equal. In every part one meets Hermit-Crabs of more than one species . . . carrying on their backs the houses they have stolen from the nearby beach.

A few days later, he described the ocean throwing its waters over the reef as "an invincible, all-powerful enemy" did, yet one that is "resisted and even conquered" by the lowly coral creatures. In the words and phrases "struggling for mastery," "obtained a footing," "their claim at least equal," "stolen," "invincible enemy," "resisted," and "conquered," Darwin is using the metaphors of warfare and competition he used later—for example, when he referred to "the struggle for existence."

The contrast between the low diversity of the land and the great diversity of the sea struck him. Although the islands were covered by a thick, almost junglelike vegetation, Darwin was not deceived:

> Besides the Cocoa nut . . . there are five or six other kinds. . . . Besides these trees the number of native plants is exceedingly limited; I suppose it does not exceed a dozen.

He did collect specimens of a "cabbage tree" that grows profusely along the coast. Henslow, when identifying the Cocos plants, gave it the name *Scaevola Koenigii;* the present correct scientific name is *Scaevola taccada.* On animal forms, Darwin wrote:

> There are no true land birds. . . . Insects are very few in number.

Throughout his writings on the animals and birds of islands, words such as "poor," "paucity," "few," and "only" occur. This is important, and of evolutionary significance; he noted the poverty of island biotas on Tahiti, the **Falkland Islands,** and **St. Paul's Rocks,** as well as at Cocos. He did not attach evolutionary significance to this at the time, but he later realized, and emphasized in his writings, that the poverty of the biotas of remote islands provides evidence for evolution. If all life is derived from a common source, the plants and animals of remote islands (or their ancestral forms) must have made the journey from other land masses. There is evidence that in revising his diary for publication, particularly in later editions, he saw the significance of this more clearly; in *The Voyage of the* Beagle he wrote:

> As the islands consist entirely of coral, and must have at one time have existed as mere water-washed reefs, all their productions must have been transported here by the waves of the sea.

Much later he realized that **long-distance dispersal** was the handmaiden of evolution.

Darwin's "habit of comparison" got some exercise; the poverty of terrestrial life forms contrasted strongly with those of the nearby coral reef. He wrote: "Although the productions of the land are thus scanty, if we look at the surrounding sea, the number of organic beings is indeed infinite." Dar-

Exposed outer coast, West Island, Cocos (Keeling) Islands, Indian Ocean. Photo: Patrick Armstrong.

win was coming close here to making a comparison of the biodiversity of contrasting ecosystems.

As at many other ports of call, Darwin showed a profound interest in the human community. A party of Malays had been brought to Cocos from various islands of what is now Indonesia; there was also some African blood in the group, and possibly some European. They were held in something not too far removed from "a state of slavery" to work in the coconut plantations by the proprietor of the islands, a Captain Clunies Ross (who was absent on a trading voyage at the time of the *Beagle*'s visit; Darwin and FitzRoy were shown around by Ross's second-in-command, William Liesk). Darwin describes the Malay people in some detail, mentioning their Muslim religion and their customs, their hunting of turtles in the lagoon, and fishing. He also mentions the native plant fruits that they ate, and their appearance. He thought that in a number of ways they resembled the Tahitians. At this time, Darwin was anticipating his later ideas on the evolution of humanity, by arranging the various human societies he had encountered on a "ladder." The Cocos people, in Darwin's mind, were well above the Fuegians and Australian Aborigines in the scale of development.

Darwin enjoyed himself at Cocos; he appreciated the beauty of the environment as a whole, and of the individual corals; he was able to put the finishing touches to his theory of coral reefs. He thought about competition, struggle, and adaptation; he compared the poverty of island terrestrial biotas with the richness of the surrounding reef. He examined another human society, and he collected specimens. The islands represent one of the most important landfalls of the voyage.

Coevolution

The evolution of two or more species of organisms in an association with each other. It should not be confused with **convergent evolution.**

Two species that live in the same habitat, and have an ecological association with one another, may exert a selection pressure on each other. The two species (or groups of related species) may or may not be dependent on one another.

Parasites are often dependent on a single host. There are species of plants that are dependent on particular insects for pollination or dispersal. There are cases where the extinction of one partner in such a mutualistic relationship has led to the extinction or virtual extinction of the other. Often, however, the relationship is more diffuse: bumblebees, for example, have coevolved with flowers of many species. Possibly the **southern beech** and **Darwin's fungus** coevolved.

In fact, ecosystems are complex networks of ecological relationships, and a species may be dependent on a whole community rather than a party to a one-to-one link. Tropical rainforests have evolved as complex, integrated ecosystems over tens of millions of years.

See also: Ecology.

Corals and Coral Reefs

Corals are marine, colonial, coelenterate animals (i.e., possessing an internal sacklike body cavity or coelenteron) with a hard, calcareous skeleton, occurring particularly in tropical regions. They belong to the class *Anthozoa* which also includes the **sea anemones.** A reef is a ridge, or mass of rocks, close to sea level or protruding just above it. Coral reefs are, therefore, masses of living coral or accumulations of dead coral or coralline limestone, often comprising, or adjacent to, tropical islands and coasts. The largest living reef is the Great Barrier Reef, off the coast of Queensland, Australia.

Corals and coral growth had interested Darwin since he had seen a few tiny coral-like forms along the Scottish coast while a medical student in Edinburgh. How much bigger and more spectacular were the corals growing in the sea at his feet as he sat by the tide line on Quail Island, off St. Jago in the **Cape Verde Islands,** just a few weeks into the voyage of the *Beagle*. The limestones on the shore behind him told the story of uplift of deposits laid down in the geological past. This site seems to have been that of his geological awakening, the point where he began to appreciate, in a vivid way, that he lived in a changing, dynamic world.

A few weeks later he scrambled ashore the little islets of the Abrolhos, off the coast of Brazil, surveyed by the *Beagle* in March 1832. These were apparently composed entirely of coral—he noticed the huge brain corals in the

Coral rock, on the shore of West Island, Cocos. Photo: Patrick Armstrong.

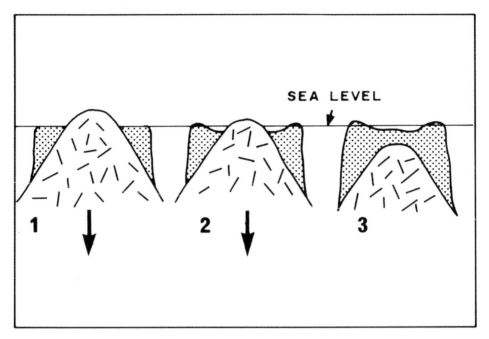

SEA LEVEL

1　2　3

Diagram showing the conversion of a fringing reef into a barrier reef and atoll. Drawn at Geography Department, University of Western Australia.

sea nearby. But although Darwin did not set foot again on a true coral island for over two years, there is evidence in his letters and notes that related ideas concerning changes in the relative level of the land and sea ran through his mind many times—in the **Falkland Islands,** on the Island of **Chiloé,** and around the coast of much of mainland South America (especially Chile).

His letters and notebooks indicate that his interest in a theory of coral islands was reawakened shortly before he left the west coast of South America. **Charles Lyell,** in *Principles of Geology,* which Darwin had had constantly by his side during the voyage, expressed the view that circular coral atolls were the result of the growth of coral around the lip of a volcanic crater; Darwin, at an early stage thought that this was a "monstrous" notion.

On November 13, 1835, the *Beagle* was passing through the main part of the "Low, or Dangerous Archipelago" in the **Pacific Ocean,** and Darwin noted that at first daylight, and again at noon, they had recorded two islands that were not on the charts. Despite his professed hatred of ships and the sea, and frequent bouts of seasickness, Darwin seems to have steeled himself to climb the mast to view the islands. His description is quite detailed:

> a long and brilliantly white beach is capped by a low bright line of green vegetation. This stripe on both hands, rapidly appears to narrow & sinks beneath the horizon. The width of dry land is very trifling; from the Mast-head it was possible to see at Noon Island across the smooth lagoon to the opposite side. This great lake of water was about 10 miles wide. (*Diary,* November 13, 1835)

Glimpses of other distant atolls followed as he crossed the Pacific. A few weeks later from a high point on the Island of **Tahiti,** he was able view the Isle of Eimeo (now called Moorea), where he saw a barrier reef in all its glory. During the same visit, from an outrigger canoe and with a jumping pole, he was able to examine the detailed form of coral reefs; he appreciated that different parts of the reef were associated with different species of corals and that corals only thrived in shallow, disturbed water. FitzRoy's hydrographic surveys showed that offshore from Tahiti, and also at Aituaki—one of the Pacific atolls that they glimpsed but upon which they did not land—the seabed shelved sharply; it became clear that the coral formations were the caps of isolated submarine mountains, probably volcanic (at Tahiti, a volcanic island core was surrounded by a skirt of coral). Between

DATE	PLACE	COMPONENT	DOCUMENTS
Pre-April 1835	South America	Evidence for change in levels of land and sea accumulated.	Miscellaneous notes and letters.
April 1835	South America	First glimmerings of coral island theory.	Entries in "little note-books"
13 November 1835	Low Archipelago	First glimpse of atoll.	Diary entry.
15-26 Nov. 1835	Tahiti	Observations on barrier reefs.	Diary entries Geological Notes.
December 1835 (possibly early January 1836)	On board HMS Beagle	First written draft of theory.	"Coral Islands" DAR. 40:1-22
5-17 February 1836	Hobart Town	Observations on sea level change.	Geological Diary DAR. 38.1
6-14 March 1836	King George Sound	Observations on sea level change.	Geological Diary DAR. 38.1
1-12 April 1836	Cocos Islands	Only visit to atoll. Detailed observations on living corals.	Diary entries Zoological Diary DAR. 31.2
29 April 1836	Mauritius	Satisfaction with theory expressed.	Letter to Caroline DAR 223
29 April - 9 May 1836	Mauritius	Observations on fringing reefs. Evidence of elevation	Entry in "little note book" Geological Diary DAR. 38.1
31 May 1837	Geological Society of London	First formal presentation of theory.	Paper: "On certain areas of elevation and subsidence ...." Proceedings 2, (1838) 552-554
1842	London	Publication of full statement.	Geology of the Voyage of HMS Beagle vol. I The Structure and Distribution of Coral Reefs.

Table showing the development of Darwin's "Theory of Coral Reefs." The documents illustrating each stage of the process are identified. DAR = Documents held in Cambridge University Darwin Archive. Drawn at Geography Department, University of Western Australia.

Tahiti and New Zealand, the first full draft of the "coral atoll theory" was prepared. This manuscript, simply headed "Coral Reefs," was not published until the 1960s. Simply stated, his theory is the notion that fringing coral reefs, barrier reefs, and atolls are members of a series, and that the main vehicle driving the transformation is a rise in sea level or a subsiding land level. This first draft included detailed descriptions of the barrier reef situation he had seen at Moorea and the lagoon islands or atolls he had seen from the masthead.

The **Cocos (Keeling) Islands,** visited after Australia, provided a case study. It was the first true atoll upon which he had set foot, and he was able to study both the gross form of the atoll as a whole, with its many islets, and also the form of individual coral organisms, considering their ecology in relation to the wave-bashed outer reef, the inner reef, and the sheltered lagoon. This account of a coral that he identified as a *Madrepora* is worth quoting in full, because it illustrates his remarkable capacity for detailed observation and his ecological appreciation.

1836 April Keeling Is

Madrepora [specimen number] 3560 This stony branching elegant coral is very abundant in the shallow still waters of the lagoon: it lives in the shoalest [shallowest] parts which are always covered by water to a depth of 15 ft & perhaps more. Its color is nearly white or pale brown. The orifice of the cells is nearly simple or protected by a strong hood: the polypus is closely attached to the edge of the orifice: it cannot be drawn back out of sight; it consists of a narrow fleshy lip which is divided into 12 tentacula [tentacles] or subdivisions of the lip. These tentacula are very short & minute & are flattened vertically; are brown colored, tipped with white. The animal possesses very little irritability on being pricked, the mouth is folded into an elongated figure & partially drawn back. . . . I could see a sort of abdominal sac & attached to the side of this there were intestinal folds of a whitish color. These when separated from the body possessed a sort of peristatic motion. I examined the Madrepora [specimen number] 3584 also common in the lagoon & found the same sort of polypus & from a shorter examination I believe such will be likewise found in kinds 3612, 3586. (*Zoological Notes,* Cambridge University Library, Darwin Archive)

Darwin was convinced that he saw evidence of rising sea level in relation

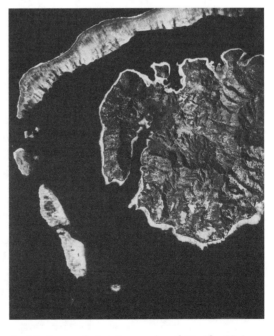

Aerial photo of a barrier coral reef, Pacific. University of Western Australia aerial photo collection.

to the land at Cocos when he noticed the way in which the roots of the palm trees were being eroded. In fact, he probably much overestimated the rate of subsidence of the atoll. Places where the roots of coconut trees have been washed away can be seen today, and there is no evidence that there has been measurable change in over 170 years. The exposure of the roots of the trees as they get older and their eventual collapse seems to be part of their normal life cycle. Not for the only time in his scientific career, Darwin reached the correct conclusion on the basis of erroneous evidence.

He also saw, and collected, specimens of coral rock containing the remains of old, dead coral exposed on the shore, demonstrating that the islands were of some age and composed a solid foundation representing the accumulation of generations of coral organisms. From soundings off the shore of the Cocos archipelago made by FitzRoy, Darwin expressed the view that the limit of growth of coral was 20 fathoms (120 feet or 37 meters); later, comparing (he was always comparing) his observations with those of others, he increased that figure slightly. The limit is now held to be about 110 meters, although there is some variation; nevertheless, bearing in mind the conditions in which he was working, Darwin's estimate was very fair. The fact that coral organisms were not able to grow at great depths confirmed to him that the island must have subsided.

In Darwin's day, the nature and importance of a postglacial rise in sea level (caused by the return to the sea of water locked up in the ice caps of the Pleistocene epoch) was not understood, and Darwin reasoned that, if some parts of the ocean were sinking, other areas must be rising. The Pacific coast of South America might be such an area; he had seen what he perceived to be shell deposits and raised beach features high above the present sea level on the cost of Peru and evidence for very recent changes in level at **Chiloé** along with other parts of the Pacific and perhaps elsewhere. It is perhaps worth remembering that just a few days into the voyage, just after New Year 1832, the *Beagle*'s crew had searched a part of the North Atlantic for the **Eight Stones** in vain. Perhaps this tiny group of islets had been volcanic and had disappeared, maybe subsiding back into the sea from whence they had come. Possibly this incident stuck in the young naturalist's mind. Modern thinking is that the subsidence seen on coral atolls is the combined effects of genuine downward collapse of volcanic islands and the postglacial rise in sea level.

There were clear links between the development of the coral atoll theory and Darwin's work on volcanic islands. While atolls had developed through gradual change as the result of subsidence, time and again Darwin stated that he thought that some volcanic islands were rising; he thought that rises in one part of the ocean floor were compensated for by subsidence elsewhere. Certainly he felt he had seen evidence of rise at St. Jago, where limestones containing the remains of marine organisms that were still around were raised above sea level. On Mauritius, visited a few weeks after Cocos, surrounded by coral reefs, but with a volcanic island core, he had also found coral material raised above the level of the beach.

Darwin continued to think about corals, and the reefs they built, for the rest of his life. In his final book, published in 1881, he compared the slow, steady work of corals in building reefs with that of earthworms in gradually burying objects in the soil. In the same year, he wrote to Louis Agassiz:

> If I am wrong, the sooner I am knocked on the head the better . . . so much the better. . . . I wish that some doubly rich millionaire would take it into his head to have borings made into some of the Pacific and Indian [Oceans] atolls. (*The Life and Letters of Charles Darwin*, Vol. 3, ed. F. Darwin, 1887, 183–184)

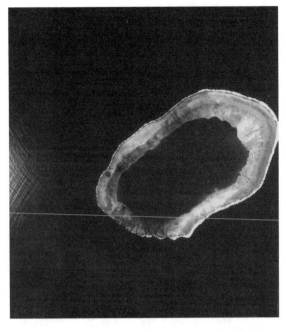

Aerial photo of coral atoll, Pacific. University of Western Australia aerial photo collection.

The "doubly rich millionaire" who proved the truth of Darwin's coral atoll hypothesis beyond all reasonable doubt, was the United States Atomic Energy Commission, which in 1952 drilled on Eniwetak Atoll in the northern Marshall Islands. Volcanic rocks were found beneath 4,158 feet (1,267 meters) and 4,610 feet (1,405 meters) of shallow-water limestones.

Darwin's work on corals and coral reefs shows him, very early in his scientific career, working at his integrative best. He compared evidence from several localities; he combined work at the level of the individual organism (or at least groups of organisms, for corals are colonial); he studied creatures in their natural habitats; and he observed the gross form of the islands and island groups, both onshore and (with the aid of information from Captain Fitz-Roy's hydrographic surveys) offshore. The theory is also profoundly ecological, emphasizing relationships between organisms and their environments—as did the theory of evolution through natural selection. And, again, like this later theory, it emphasized the capacity for gradual change over time to achieve spectacular results.

The theory of coral atolls, originally sketched out while aboard the *Beagle*, was put before the **Geological Society of London** on May 31, 1837, not long after Darwin's return to England, and was published the following year. The ideas were much expanded in the *Coral Reefs* volume of the *Geology of the Voyage of the Beagle*. Thus in notebook, draft, letter, and publication, the accumulation and development of ideas—in fits and starts perhaps and by way of the occasional tangled diversion—can be traced.

FURTHER READING

The original paper was:

Darwin, C. R. 1838. "On Certain Areas of Elevation and Subsidence in the Pacific and Indian Oceans, As Deduced from the Study of Coral Formations." *Proceedings of the Geological Society of London* 2: 552–554.

It is included in:

Barrett, Paul H., ed. 1977. *The Collected Papers of Charles Darwin*. Chicago: University of Chicago Press, 46–48.

See also:

Rosen, Brian. 1982. "Darwin, Coral Reefs and Global Geology." *BioScience* 32 (6): 519–525.

Correspondence of Charles Darwin

Darwin was certainly one of the greatest scientific letter writers of all time. Among the first rank of scientists, in sheer numbers of letters he was probably exceeded only by Einstein. Over 14,000 letters (7,591 sent and 6,530 received) are known, and new letters are continuing to be discovered at the rate of about 60 per year. Sometimes Darwin wrote several letters a day. On each of Christmas Eve and Christmas Day 1859 (the year of the publication of *On the Origin*), he wrote three letters. The record seems to be New Years Day 1874, when he wrote 12 letters. Probably many hundreds of his letters have been destroyed or lost. Several times in the last 30 years of his life he sent and received over 300 letters in a year; he wrote an average of 0.59 letters per day during this period. He typically replied to letters written to him very promptly.

There are a number of reasons for this apparent profligacy. Perhaps the most important were that postal communication became practicable and inexpensive with the introduction of Britain's penny postage in 1840, four years after Darwin's return from the *Beagle* voyage. Originally a teacher, in 1837 Rowland Hill (later Sir Rowland) published *Post-office Reform,* in which he advocated a low and uniform rate of postage to be prepaid by stamps. Previously, postage had been much more expensive and had usually been paid by the person receiving a letter.

Second, Darwin led a reclusive life at Down House, Kent, from 1842 until he died in 1882. This "retired" life, as he called it, was the result of his ill health. Away from the centers of discussion and discourse in Oxford, Cambridge, and London, he had no alternative to conducting many of his scientific inquiries and personal and business affairs by correspondence.

Third, the nature of his work required communication with naturalists all over the world, and from every department of natural history. For example, he wrote to G.H.K. Thwaites in March 1856 about the possibility of obtaining skins of breeds of pigeons from India. "I have concluded it would be better to work carefully at the varieties of a few animals, than compile brief notices on all our domestic animals," he wrote. His work on the development of the varied breeds of **domestic animals** played a part in the formulation of his views on natural selection and led later to his book *Animals and Plants under Domestication.* In May 1860, he wrote to botanist James Drummond in Western Australia about the pollination of a plant called *Lechenaultia,* which was to play a role in experimental work on pollination. He wrote to his old shipmate **Bartholomew James Sulivan** about the animals and plants of the Falklands and their dispersal, and to his former servant **Syms Covington,** who in later life lived in New South Wales, seeking marine specimens. It was the incoming "bolt from the blue" from **Alfred Russel Wallace** in the summer of 1858 that led to the linking together of several manuscript fragments to comprise the first Darwin-Wallace presentation on natural selection to the **Linnean Society of London.** One of the components of this presentation was a part of a letter written to American botanist **Asa Gray.** Subsequent correspondence with the likes of botanist **Joseph Hooker,** geologist **Charles Lyell,** and zoologist **Thomas Huxley** led to a refinement of the ideas presented to the world in 1859. Darwin maintained a lively correspondence with nurserymen and gardeners, diplomats, academics, and clergy—anyone who he felt could provide some small fact or (less frequently) specimens. He contacted army officers, explorers, and colonial administrators throughout the British Empire in the same way, seeking information on the plants, animals, rocks, and peoples of remote lands. The correspondence thus provides an insight into the manner in which Darwin collected, sifted, and compared data, but it also provides evidence of a powerful social and political network, besides a scientific network extending throughout Britain and throughout the world.

But in his correspondence we see Darwin the affectionate husband and family man; we note his devastation on the death of his young daughter **Annie.** Who cannot be affected on reading his letter from Malvern, written on April 23, 1851?

My Dear Dearest Emma

I pray God Fanny's note may have prepared you. She went to her final sleep most tranquily, most sweetly at 12 o'clock today. Our poor dear child has had a very short life but I trust happy, & God only knows what miseries might have been in store for her. She expired without a sigh. How desolate it makes one to think of her frank cordial manners. . . . I cannot remember ever seeing the dear child naughty. God bless her. We must be more & more to each other my dear wife—Do what you can to bear up & think how invariably kind & tender you have been to her. . . . My own poor dear dear wife, C Darwin. (*Correspondence,* Vol. 5, page 24, and Cambridge University Library, Darwin Archive)

Darwin's correspondence also shows him as a typical Victorian country gentleman, preoccupied with the concerns of his class. He worried about the costs of educating his sons; he opposed slavery; he took an interest in politics; he made prudent (but not always successful) investments in land, bonds, and shares. His letters also portray him as a generous friend and as a supporter of local charities and village organizations.

By far the largest collection of letters written and received by Charles Darwin is in the Darwin Archive in the Cambridge University Library (the library also holds most of the naturalist's notes from the *Beagle* and post-*Beagle* periods). The archive holds about 9,000 original letters and some 6,000 photocopies of letters held by private individuals and institutions in over 20 countries, including the United Kingdom, Ireland, Germany, Australia, New Zealand, and the United States. They are being progressively published in a project that started in 1974. Volume 1 (1821–1836)—containing the letters of childhood, student days, and the *Beagle* years—was published in 1985 by Cambridge University. The series had reached volume 15 (1867) by 2006. It will be at least 2020 by the time the series is complete, in about 30 volumes. The library has placed many of the letters on the Internet.

FURTHER READING

Burkhardt, Frederick et al. 1985–2006. *The Correspondence of Charles Darwin*, volumes 1–15. Cambridge, England: Cambridge University Press.
Oliveira, João Gama and Albert-László Barabási. 2005. "Human Dynamics: Darwin and Einstein Correspondence Patterns." *Nature* 437 (October 27): 1251.

Covington, Syms (1816—1861)

Charles Darwin's servant aboard HMS *Beagle* and subsequently. Later emigrated to New South Wales, Australia.

Syms seems to have come from a tradesman's family in Bedford, in England's East Midlands; he was employed on HMS *Beagle* "as fiddler and boy." In 1833, he became Darwin's servant and remained so for the remainder of the voyage and for several years after. There is some evidence of a slightly strained relationship—perhaps no more than the normal stresses and strains that can exist between master and servant—but afterward they seem to have warmed to each other. Covington shot and skinned most of the bird specimens that Darwin collected, assisted with many other specimens, and acted as a secretary and amanuensis. He traveled with Darwin on many of his inland journeys. Covington kept a diary, somewhat sporadically, while aboard the *Beagle*. The original is in the Mitchell Library, Sydney, New South Wales, Australia; a well-edited version is on the Web. The same library holds a number of his paintings. Covington was not a naturalist, but was an extremely competent assistant. He remained in Darwin's service after the return to England, and indeed copied most of the manuscript of *The Structure and Distribution of Coral Reefs*. Shortly after Darwin married in 1839, Covington emigrated to New South Wales, carrying with him fulsome introductions from Darwin, who said "I have the highest opinion of him . . . I have perfect confidence in his scrupulous honesty." In Australia, Covington found a wife, Eliza Twyford, from the small New South Wales town of Stroud, and he prospered in a modest way, working first as a clerk at a coal depot, later running an inn and post office at Pambula, on the south coast of New South Wales. Covington and Darwin maintained a friendly correspondence until the former's death of "paralysis" on February 19, 1861, and indeed Syms sent specimens of barnacles from the Australian coast when Darwin was working on this biological group. Syms Covington's life and times formed the basis of a novel, *Mr Darwin's Shooter,* by Roger McDonald (Transword/Anchor, 1998).

Crabs

Order: Decapoda, in the invertebrate class Crustacea, of the phylum Arthropoda. Crabs are related to lobsters and shrimps. However, they have evolved so that they can walk or run sideways as well as burrow and swim. The body is covered by a chitinous shell or carapace.

Since his days at Edinburgh, beachcombing along the shore of the Firth of Forth, Charles Darwin had an interest in seashore creatures. This interest emerged several times during his days aboard the *Beagle,* notably at the **Cocos Islands,** in the Indian Ocean, visited in April 1836. He saw crabs, particularly hermit crabs (which have no protective shell of their own and appropriate the shell of another organism), as symbols of both the complex of interrelationships that existed in nature and the conflict or competition between land and sea that he observed on that coral atoll. Here is part of his diary entry for his first day ashore on the Cocos Island group, on Direction Island, where he had seen the powerful waves smashing on the reef—he mentions "the violence of the open ocean"—although he noted that the whole of the islands was composed of coral. A battle between land and sea existed:

> The aspect and constitution of these Islands at once calls up the idea that the land & the ocean are here struggling for the mastery: although terra firma has obtained a footing, the denizens of the other think their claim at least equal. In every part [of the land area] one meets Hermit-crabs of more than one species. (*Diary,* April 6, 1836)

A line or two later, he refers to the partly terrestrial hermit crabs "carrying on their backs the houses they have stolen from the neighbouring beach." The notion of competition, or struggle, between land and sea recurs many times—a precursor, perhaps, of the idea of the "struggle for existence" that underpins the notion of natural selection.

Darwin also noted other relationships that were more harmonious. He was struck by the tripartite ecological link between mollusks, hermit crabs, and sea anemones:

Actinia [a type of sea anemone] The specimen which I found was adhering to old shells which were inhabited by hermit crabs; they lay beneath the large stones on the outer reef. (*Zoological Notes,* Cambridge University Library, Darwin Archive)

In his diary he expanded; he had been assured and his own observations confirmed "that there are certain kinds of these hermits which always use certain kinds of old shells." He noted how well some of the hermit crabs were adapted to their curious way of life:

The large claw or pincers of some of them are most beautifully adapted when drawn back, to form an operculum [a closing doorlike structure] to the shell, which is nearly as perfect as the proper one which the molluscous animal formerly possessed.

Darwin saw an animal's behavior as part of its adaptation to environment, and his observations of a creature's behavior often were extremely detailed. Here he writes of the coconut crab of the Cocos Islands:

These monstrous crabs inhabit the low strips of dry coral land; they live entirely on the fruit of the cocoa nut tree, Mr Liesk [a resident of the islands] informs me he has often seen them tearing, fibre by fibre, with their strong forceps, the husks of the nut. This process they always perform at the extremity, where their three eyes are situated. By constant hammering the shell in that soft part is broken & then by the aid of their narrow posterior pincers the food is extracted. I think this is as curious a piece of adaptation and instinct as I ever heard of. The crabs are diurnal in their habits; they live in burrows which frequently lie at the foot of the trees. Within the cavity they collect a pile, sometimes as much as a large bag full of the picked fibre & on this they rest. At night they are said to travel to the sea; there also their young are hatched, & during the early part of their life they remain & probably feed on the beach. Their flesh is very good food: in the tail of a large one there is a lump of fat which when melted down gives a bottle full of oil. They are exceedingly strong. The back is coloured dull brick red: the under side of the body & legs is blue, but the upper side of the legs clouded with dull red. In the "Voyage par un Officier du Roi" to the Isle of France [Mauritius] there is an account of a crab which lives on Cocoa Nuts in a small island North of Madagascar: probably it is the same animal, but the account is very imperfect.

Mr Liesk informs me that the crabs with swimming plates to posterior claw employ this tool in excavating burrows in the fine sand and mud & that he has repeatedly watched the process. (*Zoological Notes,* Cambridge University Library, Darwin Archive)

In this account of the robber, or coconut, crab (the modern scientific name is *Birgus latro*), Darwin shows excellent powers of observation and attention to detail. He enriches the account with material from another observer and from a book that was on the *Beagle*. There are traces of the comparative approach that he often used. But of special interest is that as much attention is given to the behavior of the organism as to its appearance: feeding and burrowing are described in detail, along with the lining of the burrows with fiber; breeding and daily rhythms are touched upon. The account relates the creature to its habitat—coconut palm groves, growing in a sandy soil, close to a beach. The structure of the organism is related to its behavior. Similar to Darwin's observations of other organisms, his descriptions of crabs strikingly integrate the morphology of the animals, their habitat, and their behavior.

Creationism

Strictly speaking, the belief that the universe, the Earth, and all life upon it, had an ultimate Creator or was brought into existence, either at one time, or over a longer period. Now, at least in the popular understanding, creationism is taken to mean that the book of Genesis (particularly Genesis 1) is to be interpreted literally, and that creation took place some six to ten thousand years ago, in the span of six 24-hour days, and that most of the rock strata of the Earth's crust were deposited during the period of Noah's flood, as described in Genesis 6–8. Moreover, creationists (in this narrower sense) maintain that "true" science supports these views and that "orthodox" science—in maintaining the very great age of the Earth and asserting the doctrine of evolution—is completely wrong.

To some extent, such believers are the heirs to ancient doctrines. As one current commentator elegantly states:

> In the year 1550, no educated person doubted that the earth was only a few thousand years old, but by the year 1860, no educated person doubted that the earth was millions of years old. (M. Roberts, 2007, 39)

It is sometimes asserted, both by scientists and by popular writers, that all, or almost all, Christians until the publication of *On the Origin of Species* in 1859 believed that creation had taken took place, as calculated by Archbishop Ussher in the mid-seventeenth century, in 4004 B.C. It is also asserted that there followed a battle between science and religion, which, despite an army of blinkered and bigoted churchmen, science eventually won. Some identified the alleged victory of **Thomas Huxley** over **Samuel Wilberforce,** Bishop of Oxford, at the **British Association for the Advancement of Science** meeting at Oxford in 1860 as a particularly important skirmish in that war.

Much of this is erroneous, or at least oversimplified, for, although Archbishop Ussher's chronology was printed in many Bibles in the eighteenth century, it never formed part of official Anglican doctrine. There were many other estimates of the Earth's age in circulation.

Another misconception is that it was not until **Charles Lyell** published *Principles of Geology* (1831–1833) that the catastrophist doctrine of earlier thinkers (almost an essential companion of the doctrine of independent, sudden, or instant creation) was overthrown, and uniformitarianism, the doctrine of gradual change, was substituted. In fact, the likes of James Hutton (1726–1797) had been proclaiming that "The present is the key to the past" since 1795. Thus, by the early nineteenth century, many geologists and other scientists accepted that Earth was many millions, possibly billions, of years old. **Adam Sedgwick,** although he did not accept the ideas set out in *On the Origin* in later life, certainly believed, as he set out with the young Darwin into the hills of North Wales in the summer of 1831, that the rocks they were studying had accumulated over a long period of time and that the Earth was of great age.

A variety of strategies were employed in attempts to reconcile the accounts of creation in Genesis with the evidence of geology concerning the age of the Earth. One was the "day-age" hypothesis, which was the notion that each day in the biblical account stood for an age of indeterminate, but possibly very lengthy, time. To mention a single example, the Reverend James Douglas, in *A Dissertation on the Antiquity of the Earth* presented to the **Royal Society** in 1785, declared that "Many well-informed persons have therefore been inclined to suppose that the Earth was created in six expanses of time instead of six days."

Another approach was to invoke a long, possibly immensely long, period of chaos before the commencement of the six days, relying on Genesis 1:2:

> And the Earth was without form and void: and darkness was on the face of the deep.

T. Burnet in 1681, wrote in *Sacred Theory of the Earth* of a chaos of indefinite length "so it is understood by the general consent of commentators." Bishop Patrick, in a lengthy 1694 commentary on Genesis that was in use well into the 1850s, argued that the length of chaos "might be a great while." Thomas Chalmers, originally a Scots Presbyterian but later an evangelical, was among the best known proponents of what has become known as the Gap Theory between about 1804 and 1830. So, long before Darwin's *On the Origin of Species* and Lyell's *Principles of Geology,* the notion of immensely long corridors of time has captured the imagination, at least among the educated. And Darwin's evolutionary views received various responses from churchmen in the 1860s and 1870s. **Charles Kingsley** and **Henry Baker Tristram** were enthusiastic, **Francis Orpen Morris** was against; many were somewhere in between, accepting parts of Darwin's thesis and rejecting others. The notion of a battle or war was brought into sharp focus in a book by A. D. White, published in 1896 but reprinted as late as 1955, titled *A History of the Warfare of Science and Religion*. The reality is much more complex.

Although among evangelicals and fundamentalists—particularly but not exclusively in the southern states of the United States—a literalism in relation to creation narratives persisted from the nineteenth century and into the twentieth among a relatively small minority of Christians. The Scopes Monkey Trial (*State of Tennessee versus John Scopes*) found a teacher on trial for teaching evolutionary concepts in Tennessee in 1925.

However, Creation Science or Young Earth Creationism has come to the fore since the publication of *The Genesis Flood,* by J. C. Whitcomb and H. M. Morris in 1961. The origins of this movement are apparently with the Seventh Day Adventist Church, but its influence is growing in many parts of the English-speaking world—including the United Kingdom, Australia, and New Zealand—and elsewhere. Important creationist institutions are the *Institute of Creation Research,* based near San Diego, California. *Creation Ministries International,* formerly *Answers in Genesis,* is an international movement. In Britain, there exist the *Creation Science Movement* and the *Biblical Creation Movement.* Some of these organizations are well funded and produce attractive literature and maintain attractive Web sites.

Young Earth Creationists (YEC) often make a distinction between physics and chemistry, which they describe as empirical or experimental, and what they dub "origins" science (paleontology, geology, and cosmology)—the disciplines that deal with past events, attempting to explain them by theories, which, they argue cannot be verified experimentally.

In particular, they attack the doctrine of uniformitarianism—the idea that the Earth is of great age and has been formed by the long continued action of processes that can be seen today. But even uniformitarian geologists such as Lyell allowed for some catastrophism. When, for example, Stephen Jay Gould advanced ideas that had some neocatastrophic elements in punctuated equilibrium, the creationist groups saw this as a repudiation of the Darwinist approach when, in fact, it was no such thing. Gould was a firm devotee of Darwin's ideas. Polystrate fossils—fossil trees that pass through several feet of strata and that occur in the carboniferous coal measures of northern England and in Yellowstone National Park in the western United States—are stated by creationists to argue against uniformitarianism. If, they argue, sediments do accumulate immensely slowly, in the time that it would take for a meter or so of sediment to accumulate, the tree trunk would have decomposed. In fact, such fossils are rare and occur in sandstone sedimentary layers that accumulated abnormally quickly, possibly under conditions of subsidence.

Modern methods of dating rocks have come under scrutiny by the YEC propagandists. They have suggested, for example, that dates of 160 Ma (million years in age) to many times that figure for the radiometric (isotope) age of a lava in Hawaii formed in an 1802 eruption proved the inaccuracy of this method of dating. In fact, these ancient dates were obtained for inclusions—fragments of included or foreign rock from deep within the Earth—and not the modern solidified lava itself.

Similarly, contamination of very old rocks with pollen from very young or modern material has allowed creationists to argue that paleontological evidence is in error, and that the order that evolution posits for the development of life on Earth is incorrect, or at least that the evidence is unreliable.

The occasional occurrence of catastrophic events such as the eruption of Mount St. Helens in 1980 or the tsunami that affected much of the Indian Ocean basin in late 2004 is seen by creationists to disprove uniformitarianism, and therefore the idea of an old Earth, and, by extension, evolution. The St. Helens eruption caused the cutting of gorge 140 feet (about 45 meters) deep by a mud flow. If this could happen in a short period, it is argued, the Grand Canyon in Arizona could have been carved in a few hundred years.

Creationist groups seize on the discovery of defects in the writing or experimental methods of published scientific work on geology or evolution; criticisms of Kettlewell's methods in his study of the **peppered moth** provided one example. Sometimes quotations from original sources turn out to be misquotations, highly selective, or taken out of context.

Orthodox scientists tend to ignore or ridicule this strand of opinion, but it is, nevertheless, influential. Those who advocate its being taught in schools and universities (and demands have from time to time mounted to a clamor in parts of the United States, Britain, and Australia) are highly creative. The term intelligent design is sometimes used as a substitute for creationism. Equal access is sometimes demanded rather than the entire displacement of evolutionary ideas. Young Earth Creationists, have, however, forced traditional scientists to be careful with their language, to avoid phrases that can be misinterpreted, and to document their methods carefully.

See also: Darwinism and Theology; Geological Time Scale.

FURTHER READING

Roberts, Michael. 2007. "Genesis Chapter 1 and Geological Time from Hugo Grotius and Marin Mersenne to William Conybeare and Thomas Chalmers (1620–1825)." In *Myth and Geology, Geological Society of London Special Publications,* eds. L. Piccardi and W. B. Masse, 39–49. London: Geological Society of London.

Cuvier, Georges (1769—1832)

French paleontologist. Often described as the father of vertebrate paleontology and one of the pioneers in comparative anatomy.

Georges Chrétien Frédéric Dagobert Cuvier was born in Montbéliard, in eastern France, in an area that was under the control of a German duke. After studying in Stuttgart from 1784 to 1788, Cuvier took a post as a tutor to a family in Normandy, thus avoiding much of the violence of the French Revolution. In 1795, he became an assistant to Geoffroy Saint-Hilaire at the Natural History Museum in Paris and was later appointed professor of animal anatomy. Cuvier remained at this post when Napoleon came to power and was appointed to important official positions, including that of inspector general of public education. He retained his positions of influence on the restoration of the monarchy, being appointed chancellor of the University of Paris. He was almost unique in maintaining a position as state councilor under the revolutionary regime, Napoleon's empire, and the restored monarchy. Throughout these turbulent decades of France's history, Cuvier continued to lecture and to carry out important scientific research at the museum. By the time of his death, he had been knighted and created a baron.

He saw organisms as integrated wholes, each species adapted to its particular life-style. He did not believe in evolutionary change, because change would mean that a creature's body was no longer precisely adapted to its environment and would render it less likely to survive. He asserted this on the basis of the study of mummified ibis and cats taken back to France after Napoleon's military venture in Egypt. He found that the remains were no different from their modern, living equivalents.

But this "functional integration" of organisms also meant that each part of an organism bore signs of the whole. Cuvier was, in fact, extremely successful in his attempts to reconstruct the appearance of extinct organisms from small fossil fragments, and some of his reconstitutions were later shown to be very accurate. He claimed he could reconstruct a vertebrate from a single tooth. He was, however, aided in some of his reconstructions by his excellent knowledge of the anatomy of living organisms. The combination of his anatomical knowledge and his functional integration approach led him to revolutionize the classification of living creatures using a "natural system." The were four *embranchements* (branches) in his animal classification, based on the fundamental organization of *Vertebrata*, *Articulata* (arthropods and segmented worms), *Mollusca* (soft, bilaterally symmetrical invertebrates), and *Radiata* (for example, echinoids [sea urchins] and starfish). These branches were so different that, in Cuvier's view, there could not be any evolutionary relationship between them.

Cuvier understood the importance of fossils:

> Why has not anyone seen that fossils alone gave birth to a theory about the formation of the earth, that without them, no one would have ever dreamed that there were successive epochs in the formation of the globe? (*Discourse on the Revolutions of the Surface of the Globe,* English edition, 1831)

He appreciated that the rocks were immensely old and that some of the rocks of the Paris Basin had been laid down in the sea. Based on his studies of fossil elephants in plaster of Paris deposits in Montmartre, he developed the concept of extinction—that some organisms had disappeared entirely. This expression of the concept of extinction was possibly his most important and most lasting contribution. He dismissed the idea suggested by some of his contemporaries that mammoths, for example, might be found in thitherto unexplored parts of North America and other continents. Cuvier stressed that layers of rock contained distinctive assemblages of fossils. From time to time, however, there were revolutions or catastrophic upheavals, each one of which eliminated many species. Cuvier remained a Protestant despite surviving the atheistic revolution and later succeeding in a largely Catholic Paris. Nevertheless, he avoided seeing equivalence between these catastrophic revolutions and biblical and historical events. Some of his English contemporaries, however, were less reticent. **William Buckland** (1784–1856), for example, in the earlier part of his career, saw many Quaternary (Ice Age) deposits as remnants of the biblical flood.

Cuvier's notions of the stability of species were opposed to the ideas of some of his contemporaries, such as **Jean-Baptiste Lamarck** and Geoffroy St. Hillaire, who suggested that animals might change in response to changes in the environment. There existed vestigial, functionless structures in some organisms that might provide clues to the anatomy of the biological group in the past; embryonic development might provide clues to the past history. Cuvier and Geoffroy St. Hillaire had a famous debate at the Paris Académie Royale des Sciences in 1830, which was attended by the young English anatomist, **Richard Owen,** for whom Cuvier was something of a mentor. It was stated at the time that Cuvier won the debate, but Geoffroy St. Hillaire's views conformed with the broad evolutionary sweep of science. Nevertheless, although scientific opinion shifted away from Cuvier's catastrophic ideas, in the last decade or two, the importance of mass extinctions in the fossil record has been appreciated. The elimination of many species (including dinosaurs) at the end of the Mesozoic may have been caused by a meteoritic impact in the Americas. And the integration of form and function is an important theme in modern biology. It might be said that modern evolutionary thought has combined some of the ideas of Cuvier with those of his scientific adversaries.

Georges Cuvier seems to have had a difficult temperament. He was able and knew it; he did not suffer fools gladly, and those who differed from him were often considered fools. He used his enormous scientific reputation to bully and intimidate. Some say he held racist views. But he was one of the greatest naturalists of his time.

See also: Catastrophism.

D

Dana, James Dwight (1813—1895)

American explorer, geologist, zoologist, and longtime correspondent of Charles Darwin.

Comparisons have often been made between the lives and careers of Charles Darwin and James Dana. They were born exactly four years apart, having the same birthday (February 12). Both, early in their scientific careers accompanied important circumnavigational expeditions and undertook important work on the Pacific Islands; both undertook some of the earliest geological studies in Australia; both were particularly associated with a theory on the development of coral reefs and atolls that has come to bear their names. Both were outstanding observers, prolific collectors, and superb integrators. Analogies can be carried to their personal lives as well: both were happily married, had several children, and suffered from ill health. Both became leading scientific figures of their generation: Dana had a long career at Yale University, holding that position for nearly 50 years and becoming a dominating influence in American geological science. Both profoundly influenced ideas on the nature of the earth.

What is less frequently emphasized is that they corresponded with each other for some 30 years, frequently exchanging publications and specimens. Although they never met, a genuine friendship developed between them; they exchanged fragments of family gossip and grumbled about their health. James Dana once wrote asking for a photograph; Darwin obliged and got the reply that its receipt had given "great pleasure." "I thank you warmly for it," Dana wrote, "I value it all the more that it was made by your son." They were important influences on each other.

Dana's family immigrated to Massachusetts in about 1640 from England. The family produced a number of divines, academics, lawyers, and writers. James was born—one of 10 children—in Utica, New York. He attended Utica High School, and, again like Darwin, while a student he was interested in insects. He proceeded to Yale College in 1830, studying science under Professor Benjamin Silliman and also studying Latin and Greek. Unable to find suitable scientific employment, he accepted an appointment as a teacher of mathematics to midshipmen on the U.S. training ship *Delaware* in 1833, later transferring to the *United States*. A training voyage to the Mediterranean lasted over a year. Dana made good use of the time studying crystallography and undertaking geological fieldwork on the Island of Minorca and at Mount Vesuvius. A period of uncertainty without paid employment followed, before he returned to Yale as assistant to his former mentor in 1836. He wrote an article on Vesuvius and the innovative *A System of Mineralogy*.

It was through the support of **Asa Gray** that Dana joined the United States Exploring Expedition as geologist. This expedition, which had the objective of establishing the United States in the first rank in the fields of science and exploration, was commissioned under Lieutenant Charles Wilkes in 1838. The expedition had six vessels and was excellently equipped: Wilkes had visited London in 1836 to purchase equipment and, during the course of that visit, apparently met Darwin.

During the course of his work as geologist to the expedition, Dana worked briefly in South America before crossing the **Pacific Ocean** by way of the Tuamotus, Samoa, and **Tahiti** (September 1839), arriving at Sydney, **New South Wales, Australia** in November 1839. After remaining a while at the **Bay of Islands, New Zealand** (February 1840), the team called at Fiji and Hawaii (1840). The expedition then returned eastward across the Pacific Ocean, arriving at the mouth of the Columbia River in July 1841. Explorations in Oregon and California followed. The vessels then crossed the Pacific for the third time, negotiating through the passages of the East Indies, calling briefly at Cape Town (April 1842), and finally returning to New York in July 1842. Many of these locations had been, of course, visited by Darwin and the *Beagle* just a few years previously, heightening the impression of the parallelism of the lives of Darwin and Dana.

For the next 10 years, the work of publishing the series of the monumental reports of the expedition continued. Just as Darwin produced the *Zoology of the Voyage of the Beagle* (with the involvement of other specialists) and the *Geology of the Voyage* (on his own) in the years that followed 1836, so Dana produced the expedition reports on geology, zoophytes (corals), and crustaceans (two volumes). Associated with each report was an atlas with dozens of plates, often drawn by Dana.

After a period of residence in Washington, DC, he returned to Yale. He married Henrietta Silliman (daughter of his former employer and mentor) in 1844, and in 1850 became Silliman Professor of Natural History at Yale, where he became a well-respected teacher.

From the age of 45, his health deteriorated, and some have asserted that this was partly the result of excessive mental exertion or overwork. Possibly, as has been suggested for Charles Darwin's mysterious illnesses, it was partly psychosomatic. At times his duties at Yale had to be reduced. Yet he revisited Hawaii in 1887, at the age of over seventy, only retiring entirely from Yale in 1890.

Even after retirement, James Dwight Dana's intellectual vigor and productivity remained high. He was honored by universities and scientific organizations in many countries, but chose to accept few of these invitations in person. Thus, the Copley Medal awarded in 1877 (it had been given to Darwin in 1864) was received by Yale graduate Edwards Pierpont, U.S. Minister in London, on Dana's behalf.

His publications, many of them in the *American Journal of Science,* were numerous. While compiling reports on the Exploring Expedition, he also published articles on the influence of temperature in the distribution of corals, the craters of the moon, the classification of crustaceans, crystallography, and mineralogy. He wrote books for general readers as well specialized works. He was a great integrator, often seeking to show how different branches of knowledge bore on a single topic. Here is an extract from the *Geology* report:

> It is obvious that the geology of the Pacific Islands embraces topics of the widest importance. There are extensive rock formations in progress, proceeding from the waters through the agency of animal life; there are other formations, exemplifying on a vast scale the operation of igneous causes in modifying the earth's surface; there are also examples of denudation and disruption commensurate with the magnitude of the mountain elevation. These great sources of change and progress in the earth's history are abundantly illustrated. (U.S. Exploring Expedition, Vol. 10, *Geology,* 1849)

Dana (again like Darwin) enthusiastically embraced **Charles Lyell**'s **uniformitarian** or **gradualist** ideas. The morphology of the Pacific Islands could be explained in terms of the long-continued applications of processes that could be observed today: coral growth, volcanic activity, and denudation. He described in detail how these various processes complemented each other.

He acknowledged his profound debt to Darwin: while in Sydney in December 1839, he read a newspaper article outlining the English naturalist's theory of the origin of coral atolls—the notion that fringing reefs, barrier reefs, and atolls were stages in a single progress, the result of the gradual submergence of a volcanic island. Dana wrote: "The paragraph threw a flood of light on the subject, and called forth feelings of particular satisfaction and gratefulness to Mr Darwin." He just a few months later applied all these ideas to the Fiji island group, finding evidence of all stages of the cycle. He was more successful than Darwin in finding convincing evidence of the subsidence.

He also pointed out that the rocks of the rugged, deeply dissected islands such as Tahiti were similar to those of the domelike structure of Mauna Loa, in Hawaii. The transformation was the result of long periods of denudation (by streams). The extent of the dissection provided an indication of the period that had elapsed since the volcano had originally formed. Moreover, the existence of islands with long narrow inlets provided further evidence of the recent flooding of valleys, and therefore of submergence. The submergence hypothesis has become known as the Darwin-Dana theory of the formation of coral reefs and atolls.

Dana also appreciated that the Islands of the Pacific were arranged in clear patterns:

> There is a system in their [the islands'] arrangement, as regular as in the mountain heights of a continent. . . . Even a cursory glance at a map is sufficient to discover a general linear course in the groups, as was long ago remarked by . . . geographers and a parallelism between those in distant parts of the ocean. (U.S. Exploring Expedition, Vol. 10, *Geology*, 1849, 12)

Further, Dana's study of the extent of denudation on the various islands within groups led him to the theory that volcanic islets became older as one moved along particular chains. Recent datings have confirmed the general accuracy of this hypothesis. Indeed the idea is entirely compatible with the modern theory of plate tectonics. He associated some lines of volcanic islands with major fractures in the ocean floor, another idea that has received modern confirmation. Like Darwin, he sought to locate those great areas of the Pacific Ocean that were subject to submergence and the areas where uplift predominated.

He was, therefore, operating at every level from the internal structure of individual corals, through the morphology of the particular coral reef, and that of the entire island or atoll, through to the major features of and processes occurring on the surface of the whole planet. Here was true integration.

Throughout his studies, Dana was impressed by the role of erosion, particularly subaerial denudation (the effects of streams and rivers), while Darwin was usually prepared to explain features by changes in sea level (in Australia, South America, on coral islands, and, later, in Scotland). Darwin interpreted the deep, steep, gorges of the Blue Mountains in New South Wales, Australia, as inlets cut by a former sea into a cliffed coastline; Dana, more accurately, interpreted these valleys as being the result of the long-continued action of running water. Darwin, after hearing of Dana's explanation, wrote to him in December 1849 that he "would have liked to have fought a friendly battle over the Australian valleys." This was a part of a long correspondence between the two that covered many subjects. The link between the two of the leading scientists in England and America was an important one.

James Dana, while in New South Wales, sketched the first Australian geological map. He also collected the first plant fossils from the Illawara district, to the north of Sydney, including the first specimen of *Glossopteris* (an ancient fernlike plant). This discovery proved significant: Dana appreciated that "the Flora of the southern hemisphere differed from that of the northern at the Carboniferous period." Dana's work, and indeed the fossils themselves, could be said to have laid the groundwork for the development of the idea that there existed during the Paleozoic era a land mass, to which the name of Gondwana has been given, that included Australia, parts of India, and the other southern continents, which later fell apart.

Another idea that was European in origin, but which Dana publicized in North America, was that of the influence of continental ice sheets. The notion that much of Europe was covered by ice was set forth by Louis Agassiz (1807–1873). Agassiz moved from Europe to Harvard and sought to explain features of the northern United States in a similar way. Although this suggestion was opposed in some quarters, Dana enthusiastically embraced the idea and found evidence for the former existence of glaciers in the New England landscape.

James Dwight Dana and Charles Robert Darwin were close contemporaries. They corresponded for many years and indirectly and directly influenced one another. Both were innovators, both worked on coral reefs, and both were interested in remote islands. There are numerous parallels in their lives and in their work. But while Darwin pulled many of his ideas together in the revolutionary *On the Origin of Species* in 1859, the world had to wait until the latter half of the twentieth century, and the enunciation of plate tectonics theory for a comparable paradigm-shifting set of ideas in geology.

See also: Corals and Coral Reefs; Glen Roy; Ill Health and Diseases of Charles Darwin.

FURTHER READING

Appleman, D. E. 1985. "James Dwight Dana and Pacific Geology." In *Magnificent Voyagers: The US Exploring Expedition 1838–1842*, eds. H. J. Viola and C. Margolis, 88–117. Washington, DC: Smithsonian Institution.

Darwin, Annie (Anne Elizabeth Darwin) (1841–1851)

Charles and Emma Darwin's much-loved second child and eldest daughter.

Charles, in a memorial to Annie, described her as "the joy of the household." He mentioned also her "buoyant joyousness" and her sensitivity. She was neat in dress, charming, nimble with her hands, artistic, and musical. Even allowing for the possible exaggeration of a grief-stricken parent, she seems to have been a delightful and model child. She died, possibly of tuberculosis, in Malvern, where she had been sent for medical treatment after some nine months of illness. She is buried at Malvern, and her head-stone carries the words "A dear and good child."

Annie's death profoundly affected the family. The opinion has also been expressed that the death of his dearest child was an important incident in Charles's journey toward evolutionary ideas. It may have shattered what remained of his Christian faith; it demonstrated to him that death was a natural phenomenon—a part of life. He was always concerned that his children might inherit his own ill heath and that marriage to cousins was deleterious, reducing the possibility of the combination of characteristics from different ancestries (this was long before the nature of genes was understood). Heredity was an important component in natural selection, so it may be that the combination of thoughts and feelings that Annie's death triggered nudged him in the direction of his notions of natural selection and the survival of the fittest. Certainly in the months following her death, Charles concentrated on his species theory.

FURTHER READING

Keynes, Randal. 2001. *Annie's Box: Charles Darwin, His Daughter and Human Evolution.* London: Fourth Estate.

Darwin, Bernard (1876–1961)

Charles Darwin's grandson; sportsman, essayist, journalist, and sports writer.

Bernard Darwin was the son of Cambridge botanist **Francis Darwin** and his first wife, Amy Ruck (who died four days after his birth). Educated at Eton College and Cambridge University, he qualified as a lawyer in 1903, but soon opted to become a full-time writer. He played golf for Cambridge University, captained the British golf team in the first Walker Cup match in the United States in 1922, and was captain of the Royal and Ancient Golf Club in 1934. He wrote extensively about golf; he was correspondent for *The Times* (1907–1953) and *Country Life* (1907–1961). His literary prowess is shown by the fact that he was selected to write the introduction to the *Oxford Dictionary of Quotations* (1941).

He provides an example of how the Cambridge Darwin dynasty, in the century following Charles Darwin's death, excelled in many fields.

Darwin, Charles Galton (1887–1962)

Grandson of Charles Robert Darwin; mathematician and physicist, director of the British National Laboratory.

Charles Galton Darwin was one of a long line of Darwin distinguished scientists. He was the first child of **George Howard Darwin** and, like his father and grandfather, was elected a fellow of the **Royal Society**—Britain's leading scientific honor—and was knighted.

With one distinguished physicist as a father and another (Lord Kelvin) as godfather, it might seem that the young Charles Darwin's destiny was predetermined, and, indeed, he did well in mathematics from his schooldays at Marlborough College. Nevertheless, he showed a great range of ability; he retained a great interest in history and archaeology throughout his life, and an anecdote showed that he was an accomplished classicist. While he was an undergraduate at Trinity College, attendance at chapel was compulsory, and all scholars were required to read the lesson. When his turn came, he found a Greek New Testament on the desk instead of the usual English version, and read the lesson of the day in perfectly pronounced Greek, as if it were a matter of course. Soon after graduation in mathematics from Cambridge, Charles took an appointment lecturing in mathematics, commencing work in nuclear physics. At the outbreak of the First World War in 1914 he was shipped to France; he worked initially as a censor but later transferred to the Royal Engineers and applied his knowledge of physics to artillery. He returned to Cambridge in 1919, working on the properties of the atom. He was elected a fellow of the Royal Society in 1922, and then became Tait Professor of Natural Philosophy (Science) at the University of Edinburgh. Two years as master of Christ's College Cambridge followed, but, foreseeing the Second Word War and that science would be even more important than when he was a young officer in World War I, he accepted the position of the director of the National Physical Laboratory. Seconded to Washington for a year in 1941, he did further work connected with the atomic bomb. Interestingly, despite this work, he sounded a cautionary note as early as 1940 as to the legitimacy of using the weapon (at that time, its use against Berlin was envisaged).

He retired to Newnham Grange in Cambridge, the home of some branch of the Darwin family for over 80 years, and displayed his wide range of interests in his 1952 publication *The Next Million Years*. This book attempted to predict the fortunes of the human race, drawing attention to the enormous increases in population already taking place in relation to the finite resources of the Earth. He drew attention to matters now regarded as of the utmost importance. In some ways the book was in the tradition of Malthus and his grandfather. But he made a mistake in suggesting that a period of a million years was critical. Time horizons have now considerably shortened. Nevertheless, it was an important work.

Charles Galton Darwin died at Newnham Grange on the last day of 1962. Within six months, his widow, Lady Katherine Darwin, had agreed to make the property and the adjoining Old Granary available to the Cambridge University for the formation of a new college for graduate students, and **Darwin College** was born.

Darwin, Charles Robert (1809—1882)

English naturalist and originator of the concept of evolution through natural selection.

Charles Darwin was one of the most influential thinkers of all time. A somewhat retiring Victorian naturalist, his influence on science, philosophy, politics, religion, and literature—in short, on the way in which humanity thought about itself in relation to the universe—was incalculable.

Early Life

Charles Darwin was born in **Shrewsbury,** a small city in the county of Shropshire, in the West Midlands of England, not far from the border with Wales. He was the son of **Robert Darwin** (1766–1848), a fashionable and prosperous doctor, and Susannah (née Wedgwood, 1765–1817). He was also the grandson of **Erasmus Darwin (senior)** (1731–1802)—physician, poet, philosopher, polymath, and one who espoused evolutionary concepts long before his grandson developed his integrated theory of evolution through natural selection. The family tended toward nonconformity and the Whig (liberal, progressive) tradition in politics. Charles's mother died when he was eight, and in later life he said he had little recollection of her. Charles's father besides being an eminent physician, must have had a dominating presence; he was over six feet (1.88 meters) tall, and is said to have, at one point, weighed over 330 pounds (about 152 kilograms). The young Charles was extremely fond of him, and later wrote that he was the kindest man he ever knew. However, Dr. Darwin's attempts to influence the direction of Charles's career led, from time to time, to a certain amount of conflict.

After a year at a small school run by a Mr. Case, the young Darwin went to Shrewsbury School, one of England's well-known private schools. He did not perform well academically, and left the school, not unwillingly, at the age of 16. Thereafter, for a few months in the summer of 1825, he served as a sort of apprentice to his father, helping with patients and in the preparation of medicines, before he was dispatched to **Edinburgh** Medical School in Scotland, where his elder brother (**Erasmus Darwin (junior)**) was completing his training. Although he attended a few rather unexciting lectures on geology there, made contact with the freethinking Dr. Robert Grant (1793–1874)—a comparative anatomist and specialist in the zoology of marine life—and enjoyed beachcombing along the coast of the Firth of Forth looking for seashore life, Darwin detested medical training. The sight of operations (performed, of course, in those days, without anesthetic), appalled him, and after two years he left Edinburgh unqualified. Nevertheless, Darwin did gain something from the medical training—some development of the powers of observation perhaps and an interest in his fellow humans. Sometimes in reading through his notes from later life one can perceive the insights of the former medical student.

His father was very disappointed. It was decided that, although it was completely outside the tradition of the family, Charles might make a Church of England parson, so he was sent to Christ's College, **Cambridge University,** to take a general degree in arts. There a modest amount of theology, philosophy, mathematics, and New Testament Greek was studied, good food eaten, wine consumed, and friends made. He collected beetles with his cousin, **William Darwin Fox** (1805–1880). In 1831, he graduated with a bachelor of arts degree. Particularly important influences at Cambridge were his friendships with the Reverend **John Stevens Henslow** (1796–1861), the young professor of botany with whom he used to go for walks in the Cambridgeshire countryside, and with the Reverend **Adam Sedgwick** (1785–1873), a professor of geology. Both men encouraged Charles's interest in natural history. Darwin, Henslow, and some other younger Cambridge dons (academics, faculty members) were, throughout the summer of 1831, planning an expedition to **Tenerife.** During that summer, Sedgwick took the young Darwin on a geological expedition through **North Wales.** Darwin later described the trip as follows:

> As I had come up to Cambridge at Christmas, I was forced to keep two terms after passing my final examination, at the commencement of 1831; and Henslow then persuaded me to begin the study of geology. Therefore on my return to Shropshire I examined sections and coloured a map of parts round Shrewsbury. Professor Sedgwick in the beginning of August intended to visit North Wales to pursue his famous geological investigation amongst the older rocks, and Henslow asked him to allow me to accompany him. Accordingly he came and slept in my Father's house . . .
>
> Next morning we started for Llangollen, Conway, Bangor and Capel Curig. This tour was of decided use in teaching me a little how to make out the geology of a country. Sedgwick often sent me on a line parallel to his, telling me to bring back specimens of the rocks and to mark the stratification on a map. I have little doubt that he did this for my own good, as I was too ignorant to have aided him. . . . At Capel Curig I left Sedgwick and went in a straight line by compass and map across the mountains to Barmouth, never following any track unless it coincided with my course. I thus came on some strange wild places and enjoyed much this manner of travelling. (*Autobiography of Charles Darwin,* Norah Barlow, ed. 1958, 68–71)

Darwin used, in his explorations during the *Beagle* voyage, almost every aspect of what he had learned from Sedgwick and what he had taught himself that summer, in the Welsh borderland and North Wales. These included the direct transect line across country, the inspection of sections and exposures, the marking of stratification on a map, the collection of rock specimens, the use of a clinometer (an instrument for measuring the dip of strata) and compass. Darwin regretted his "incapacity to draw," and certainly some of his geological cross-section drawings and sketch maps are a little crude. They are, however, sufficient, and it is quite clear that he had the knack of "making out the geology of a country" in three dimensions. He had good cause to write to Henslow on April 11, 1833, just after he had left the **Falkland Islands** in the South Atlantic, asking him to tell Sedgwick the he had "never ceased to be thankful for that short tour in Wales."

The *Beagle* Voyage

Charles returned to Shrewsbury from the Welsh excursion to find a letter from Henslow awaiting him, suggesting that he might be interested in accompanying Captain **Robert FitzRoy** on the *Beagle* voyage as a "supernumerary." Darwin's father was not initially in favor of the idea, but with the help of friends (particularly his uncle, **Josiah Wedgwood II (1769–1843)**, Charles managed to persuade him. An interview with FitzRoy in London followed. The next few months were spent in a frantic round of collecting equipment and materials for the voyage, and obtaining instruction in the best methods of preparing specimens. For the last few weeks before the ship departed, the enthusiastic Charles was in residence at Plymouth, in the southwest of England, where the *Beagle* was moored, supervising the taking aboard of some of his equipment and supplies.

There were delays due to poor weather and other difficulties, and indeed a couple of false starts, but on December 27, 1832, the *Beagle* departed on her voyage around the world. Darwin recalled that he and FitzRoy had dined well with some naval notables just before departure, and that his lack of emotion on departing from his native country for a long voyage was perhaps to be blamed on champagne and lamb chops.

From England the ship proceeded, after a brief hesitation at Tenerife (where, to Darwin's intense disappointment, they were not allowed to land because of quarantine restrictions), to the **Cape Verde Islands,** off the African Coast (January 1832). Although Darwin's first impressions were that this was a "miserable place" with a "desolate" landscape, after a day's exploration his idea had quite altered; he had seen "the glory of tropical vegetation" and heard "the notes of unknown birds." This, too, was where Darwin commenced his geological studies in earnest and where it occurred to him that he might write a book about his findings on the voyage. From there, the *Beagle* proceeded to **St. Paul's Rocks**

Darwin as a young man, about 1840. From Norah Barlow (ed.), *Charles Darwin's Diary*, 1933.

and **Fernando Noronha,** tiny islets in the South Atlantic (February 1832). At these, and at many other islands and ports visited, FitzRoy's task was to establish their position precisely: he was charged by the Admiralty with establishing a chain of meridians around the world. He had over 20 chronometers to assist him to determine longitude accurately. From St. Paul's and Fernando Noronha, the *Beagle* proceeded to the mainland of South America, where the main program of hydrographic survey commenced. The *Beagle* visited Bahia, in **Brazil**, and it was here that the young Darwin first described the richness of tropical forests (February–March 1832). A detailed survey of **Tierra del Fuego** followed, visits to the Falklands alternating with the periods in the waters around the myriad of promontories and islands around Tierra del Fuego. FitzRoy had hoped to establish a mission station on this remote island, but this enterprise failed because the missionary FitzRoy had brought with the expedition was attacked by the local people, the Fuegians. Eventually, in mid-1834, the Magellan Strait between Tierra del Fuego and the South American mainland was traversed, and the expedition set out northward, to the Island of **Chiloé** and the scattering of islets that constitute the Chonos archipelago to its south. Surveys along the coast of **Chile and Peru** allowed Darwin the opportunity of making a number of excursions inland in South America, and he was able to climb high into the Andes. In September 1835, the *Beagle* set out across the Pacific, calling first, as is well known, at the **Galapagos Islands** (September–October 1835), which Darwin did not particularly like. Then followed the longest leg of the voyage, from the Galapagos to **Tahiti** (November 1835). Here Darwin made important observations on coral reefs. Tahiti, and especially the missionaries working there, left positive images in his mind, and he was sorry to leave. **New Zealand** (Christmas 1835), where again Charles was impressed by the work of missionaries, he liked less. Mainland **Australia,** with its brashness, the convict presence, and the dry, stark landscape, was not much preferred, although some of the observations he made there were important (in New South Wales and at King George's Sound). He preferred green, mild **Tasmania** (February 1836).

From Australia, perhaps because of some change of plans at a late stage, FitzRoy decided to go to the **Cocos (Keeling) Islands** in the Indian Ocean; he had been instructed to fix their position, if possible (April 1836). Darwin enjoyed his time there, and observations at this atoll were important in the development of his theory of coral reefs. A short visit to **Mauritius** was followed by a brief sojourn at the **Cape of Good Hope.**

Back in the Atlantic, there were visits to **St. Helena and Ascension Island** (July 1836), and then, to "complete the chain of meridians," Bahia in Brazil was visited for a second time (August). A return visit to the Cape Verde Islands was followed by a few days in the **Azores** (September 1836) before Falmouth in Cornwall, the southwestern tip of England was gained on the "stormy night" of October 2, 1836, from whence Darwin took a stagecoach to his anxious family waiting in Shrewsbury.

Many of the scientific enterprises in which Darwin was later engaged can be traced to his days on the *Beagle,* and an important part of his inspiration came from his explorations of remote islands. "The habit of comparison leads to generalization," he wrote toward the end of the voyage. Darwin visited many islands in the Atlantic, Pacific, and Indian Oceans; tropical, semiarid, temperate, and subantarctic; large (Australia, New Zealand, Tasmania) and tiny (St. Paul's Rocks, Cocos) and was constantly comparing them—their geology, natural history, and human inhabitants.

After the *Beagle*

After his return from the voyage, Charles Darwin spent a frantic few years, mainly in London and Cambridge, sorting his specimens, writing up his material for publication, and discussing his observations with the leading scientific men of the day. He edited his diary for publication—it was published in 1839 as the third part of a full account of the voyage, *Narrative of the Surveying Voyages of HMS Beagle,* with major contributions by Captain **Philip Parker King** (the commander of the first *Beagle* exploration voyage to South America, 1826–1830) and Captain FitzRoy. It later became known as *The Voyage of the Beagle.* **Syms Covington,** his servant from the *Beagle* days, assisted him as amanuensis and clerk for some of this time in London and Cambridge. Darwin became secretary of the **Geological Society of London.** It was probably during this period (despite possible occasional glimmerings during the voyage) that he developed an evolutionary outlook. A date of March 1837 has been suggested for this "conversion."

After initial sorting and study following his return from the voyage, many of his specimens were dispersed; they were given to those knowledgeable about particular biological groups for study or to other appropriate experts. Many have been lost, but museum collections in Cambridge, London, Dublin, and elsewhere still contain large numbers of Darwin specimens. Most of his scientific notes from the voyage remain in the Cambridge University Library Manuscripts Collection.

Darwin's first major scientific project (apart from the editing of the diary) was the publication of *The Zoology of the Voyage of HMS Beagle.* The production of this five-volume work, which has been described as "sumptuous," occurred between October 1838 and October 1843. He managed, through the good offices of influential persons such as the Duke of Somerset and the Earl of Derby, to secure substantial government funding. Darwin did not write the whole text of these volumes, although he wrote introductions to some of them, and a lot of material from his notes and specimen labels is included. He collaborated with appropriate experts in each case for the volumes on fossil mammals (volume 1), mammals (volume 2), birds (volume 3), fish (volume 4), and reptiles (volume 5). Excellent illustrations accompanied detailed accounts of behavior and distribution in some instances, which were innovations.

Darwin was working on the other major publishing enterprise that followed the *Beagle* voyage at the same time the *Zoology* project was proceeding. *The Geology of the Voyage of the Beagle,* although less spectacular in some ways, and less well illustrated than the *Zoology,* was scientifically more important. The three volumes initially appeared between 1842 and 1846. At many stages in the voyage, geological observations following his training in North Wales occupied more of Darwin's attention than other branches of natural history. Volume 1 of *Geology* was titled *The Structure and Distribution of Coral Reefs.* This includes some of his observations from Tahiti, Cocos, and Mauritius but also includes material from many other explorers and navigators on island groups. The book's importance lies in the fact that within it

Darwin in middle life, 1854. From an early edition of Darwin's works.

are to be found details of Darwin's theory of **corals and coral reefs** and atolls—the idea that fringing reefs, barrier reefs, and atolls are members of a single series; as a core volcanic island subsided (or as is now widely held) the sea level rose, one form was gradually converted into another. This idea seems to have occurred to Darwin during his crossing of the Pacific, late in 1835, and represents his first dalliance with the notion of **gradualism,** or the importance and effectiveness of long-continued gradual change. In this coral reef theory, too, is the idea of a dialogue or relationship between the physical environment and living things: as the coral grew, it changed the environment; as the environment changed, the conditions for coral growth changed. Both these latter aspects appeared much later in Darwin's theory of evolution by natural selection.

Geological Observations on Volcanic Islands followed and is in some respects a companion volume, with detailed observations on Cape Verde, St. Paul's, Ascension Island, St. Helena, Fernando Noronha, New Zealand, and the Azores as well as brief notes on Australia and the **Cape of Good Hope.** Interestingly, a somewhat analogous notion to the coral reef hypothesis seems to have gone through Darwin's mind in relation to volcanic rocks. He suggested that different rock types might differentiate out over time from a single magma or molten rock; as crystals of different minerals formed and sunk, so the chemical composition of what remained would change (gradualism again). The third volume was simply called *Geological Observations in South America.*

The woman he had been fond of in pre-*Beagle* days (**Fanny Owen**) married someone else during the first few months he was away, and a little over two years after his return (on January 29, 1839) he married his cousin **Emma Wedgwood** (1808–1896). The Darwins married their Wedgwood cousins three times in two generations, and at times Charles was haunted by the idea that this might have unfortunate effects; 3 of his 10 children died in infancy, although several of the others had long and distinguished lives. After a brief period of residence in London, Charles and Emma moved to **Down House,** Downe, in Kent, in September 1842, where, apart from fairly short visits to other parts of Britain, Charles spent the remainder of his days. Charles Darwin was comfortably off, particularly after the death of his father, and did not have to seek paid employment. He was able to devote his life, in the quiet of the Kent countryside, to science, while living the life of a country squire, employing several servants in his house and participating in the life of the village.

Settled into married and family life at Down House, and with the Herculean tasks represented by *Zoology* and *Geology* out of the way, Darwin embarked on a major study of a relatively obscure group of organisms—the **barnacles** or *Cirripeda*. This was the work that established his credentials as a painstaking scientist capable of extremely detailed observations. Work started in 1846 and continued for eight years; the volumes produced are Darwin's only contribution to formal taxonomy (the classification of plants and animals) and are still held in high esteem. The two studies, *Living Cirripeda* and *Fossil Cirripeda of Great Britain,* were based on careful study and dissection of hundreds of specimens sent to him from many parts of the world.

Evolution

Around the time of his marriage, Charles read **Thomas Malthus**'s (1766–1834) *Essay on Population,* with its emphasis on war, pestilence, and famine acting as checks to human population growth. This provided the mechanism for the evolutionary ideas with which he was experimenting (he tended, at this early time, to use the term "transmutability of species"). The environment "selected" certain "races" or strains of organisms that were best adapted to it, and those that were less well adapted tended to perish before they were able to reproduce. In that way, through many generations, change occurred. He wrote short drafts of his idea in the 1840s, but, although one can see the occasional evolutionary insight in some of his publications from those days, he did not publish his full theory. Possibly he felt he needed to accumulate overwhelming evidence, possibly he hesitated out of respect for his wife's religious susceptibilities—she was a devoutly religious woman. However, in the summer of 1858, he received a letter from **Alfred Russel Wallace** (1823–1913) enclosing the draft of an article that outlined theories similar to his own. An honorable man, he did not wish to be unfair to a colleague, but neither did he think it right that someone else should have priority in a matter upon which he had been working for over 20 years. His friends and colleagues—geologist **Charles Lyell** and botanist **Joseph Hooker**—took matters in hand and presented a cobbled-together version of material from both Wallace and Darwin to the **Linnean Society of London** on July 1, 1858. *On the Origin of Species,* in which the theory of **evolution through natural selection** was formally spelled out for the first time, followed a year later. While the Linnean Society presentation attracted relatively little attention, reception of *On the Origin* was much more lively. The book adduced a massive amount of evidence from, for example, the variations that occur in plants and animals under domestication, the geographical distribution of organisms, and fossil records. The difficulties of the theory were firmly faced.

The debate that followed publication has widely been seen as a challenge by science to the power and influence of the church, together with an affront to the belief that God made the world, all the plants and animals thereon, and humanity in six days, as described in the Old Testament. This is, in fact, a gross oversimplification. Charles Lyell, Darwin's geologist friend, never accepted all the implications of *On the Origin*. The zoologist **Richard Owen** was one of the most outspoken opponents of evolutionary views. On the other hand, many churchmen enthusiastically seized on the liberating nature of evolutionary ideas: no longer could they be expected to believe parts of the Old Testament that could not be literally true. The parson-naturalist **Charles Kingsley** (author of *The Water Babies*) became an enthusiastic supporter, and **Henry Baker Tristram** and Octavius Pickard-Cambridge were among the first naturalists to use Darwin's ideas in their work (on the birds of North Africa and spiders, respectively). Most liberal theologians now see no conflict between the acceptance of evolutionary ideas and religious belief.

Darwin had periods of illness during much of his life and led a somewhat quiet life at Down; he did not attend the Linnean Society meeting nor the "Great Debate" on his ideas at the **British Association for the Advancement of Science** meeting of 1860 at which **Thomas Huxley** sparred with **Samuel Wilberforce,** Bishop of Oxford. Although much criticized (and misquoted and misinterpreted), he took the criticism with a quiet grace, accepting that there were many who would never agree with him.

After *On the Origin*

On the Origin of Species says nothing directly about the origin of humans, although the implications are there, and at the very end of the book Darwin writes that, some time in the future, "light would be thrown on the origin of man and his history." Darwin took up this challenge more fully in *The Descent of Man,* published in 1871. Here he argued that humans had evolved from more lowly creatures, possibly something akin to modern primates, and that one of the important mechanisms of this evolution was "sexual selection"—the preference of members of one sex for certain characteristics in the other. This, he argued, tended to encourage the preferred characteristics, as they were passed from one generation to another. Individuals without these characteristics would be likely to have fewer offspring, and ultimately these characteristics would disappear. (In reality, sexual selection is a particular case of natural selection.) He wrote toward the end of *Descent*:

> The main conclusion arrived at in this work, namely that man is descended from some lowly organised form, will, I regret to think, be highly distasteful to many. . . . We must, however, acknowledge, as it seems to me, that man, with all his noble qualities, with sympathy which feels for the most debased, with benevolence which extends not only to other men but to the humblest living creature, with his god-like intellect which has penetrated into the movements and constitution of the solar system—with all these exalted powers—Man still bears in his bodily frame the indelible stamp of his lowly origin. (*Descent of Man*, chapter 21)

This thinking, of course, further aggravated some churchmen, who found the notion of a lowly origin for humankind incompatible with the doctrine of "man created in God's image," although it has acted as a springboard for much modern biology.

Darwin applied the gradualist notion to the development of coral reefs while aboard the *Beagle;* he later applied analogous concepts to the development of different types of igneous rocks from a single magma and, of course, to the development of life on Earth. He also applied similar ideas to the psychological development of children. And in his last book, *The Formation of Vegetable Mould through the Action of Worms* (1882), he emphasized vividly the important effects of long-continued but very small changes. The action of earthworms, by consuming soil and passing it through their bodies, resulted in the gradual burial and reburial of the surface, and the resultant "removal of all inequalities." In the last paragraph of this book, published very close to the time of his death, he returned to his first gradualist thought experiment, the development of coral reefs:

> It may be doubted whether there are many other animals which have played so important a part in the history of the world, as have these lowly organised creatures. Some other animals, however, still more lowly organised, namely corals have done far more conspicuous work in having reefs and islands in the great oceans; but these are almost confined to the tropical zones.

He published a stream of books and scientific papers, both before and after the publication of *On the Origin of Species,* on a wide range of scientific subjects. One of his entry points to evolution through natural selection was the notion of "artificial selection" in domestic animals and plants; humans selected the forms most suitable for their purpose and bred from them, gradually modifying their appearance. This work eventually led to *The Variation of Animals and Plants under Domestication* (1868). From very early in the *Beagle* voyage, the young Darwin showed his interest in the behavior of animals: the way in which an octopus changed its color, the aggressive behavior of a penguin in the Falklands as he approached it, the building of nests by birds and insects, and the tameness of animals on remote islands provide a few examples. This work led to important later studies on animal behavior and human psychology, such as his book *The Expression of Emotions in Man and Animals* (1872), which could also be regarded as an evolutionary work. The work aimed to show the essential unity of animals and humanity; for example, Darwin aimed to refute the idea that the facial muscles, so important in expression, were a special human feature and endowment.

Of the 1862 book *On the Various Contrivances by which British and Foreign Orchids Are Fertilised by Insects,* it was stated by Darwin's friend and American correspondent Asa Gray: "If the Orchid book had appeared before the *Origin,* the author would have been canonised rather than anathematised" by many churchmen. In many ways, the book is of the "natural theology" tradition. One reviewer, in a journal called *The Churchman,* argued that the volume was an indirect way of saying, "O Lord, how manifold are Thy works"; nevertheless, it does take an evolutionary stance, and Darwin himself remarked that he thought that the publication of this volume would "do good to the *Origin,* as it will show I have worked hard at details."

Darwin had, in fact, been interested in plants—particularly flowering plants—since his time with Henslow as a Cambridge undergraduate. Other important publications in this area included *On the Movements and Habits of Climbing Plants* (1865) and *Insectivorous Plants* (1875). The former, in its title and its emphasis on behavior was a companion to *Emotions;* both are evolutionary in character, because they emphasize the relationships between plants and other organisms (as does *Orchids*) and other aspects of the environment; *Insectivorous Plants,* for example, included a study of such plants' adaptations to "impoverished" conditions.

The Integrity of Darwin's Work

Although Darwin's published work covered a wide range of topics (and those mentioned above constitute a mere trifle from a long list), there is a certain unity about his work. Much of his work has—either clearly stated or implied—an evolutionary thrust. His research emphasizes change over time, adaptation to environment, and the oneness or wholeness of humanity and nature. Bearing in mind that he had rather poor health for much of the latter part of his life, he had (and loved) his large family, he entered fully into the life of his village, and he carried on a prolific correspondence with naturalists (and others) in many parts of the world, his output was formidable. One estimate is that, over the course of his life, he must have written over six million words.

One feature of the way Darwin worked was his constant revision. His notes from the *Beagle* period are heavy with annotations. For example, he constantly compared observations at one island of the 40 or so he visited with those from others. Sometimes he revisited a locality, and when he did this, the additional observations can be clearly identified. Sometimes he entirely rewrote his notes as his views changed and to take account of new information as it came to hand.

His published work was treated in the same way. Sometimes a later edition of a book contains additional material and modifications that render it a different work. For example, the fifth edition of *On the Origin of Species,* which appeared in 1869, was the first in which Herbert Spencer's phrase "the survival of the fittest" appeared, but it was not until the sixth edition, of 1872, that the word "evolution" appeared (although "evolved" was the last word of the text of all previous editions of this work, and "evolution" had appeared in *The Descent of Man* a year earlier).

Darwin died, after a period of illness, on April 19, 1882; a quiet funeral in the local parish church had been planned, but the scientific establishment took over, and, although he might be described as an agnostic, he was buried in Westminster Abbey after a service of considerable pomp on April 26.

It would be fair to say that Darwin's hypotheses changed the world; they were, of course, an incomplete expression of evolutionary ideas—genetics and molecular biology have carried them further than he could have envisaged. Sometimes they have been distorted (as in social Darwinism and Nazism, for example) in ways of which he would not have approved. **Karl Marx** claimed to have been influenced by Darwinian ideas and corresponded with him and sent him copies of his works. Some still disagree with Darwin's essential thrust, but few can deny his importance. His memory is maintained in place names in the Falkland Islands, South America, Australia, and New Zealand, and in the scientific names of many species of plants and animals.

Darwin in old age. From the monument in Westminster Abbey. Photo: Dean and Chapter of Westminster.

FURTHER READING

There have been numerous biographies of Charles Darwin; two of the most valuable and most recent are:

Browne, Janet. 1995. *Charles Darwin,* Vol. 1: *Voyaging;* Vol. 2 (2002), *The Power of Place.* London: Jonathon Cape.

Desmond, Adrian and James Moore. 1991. *Darwin.* London: Michael Joseph.

A guide to the published works of Charles Darwin is:

Freeman, R. B. 1977. *The Works of Charles Darwin: An Annotated Bibliographical Handlist.* Folkstone, England: Dawson.

Darwin, City of

Capital city of the Northern Territory, Australia, located at 12° 27' S and 130° 50' E.

After the conclusion of the voyage that carried Charles Darwin around the world, HMS *Beagle* went on another voyage of exploration, which included a passage around the northern coast of Australia. (This route had been suggested in the Admiralty's instructions to Captain **Robert FitzRoy** on the Darwin voyage, should this part of the world have to be traversed during the Southern Hemisphere winter, but it was not used.) The vessel was then under the command of John Clements Wickham; others of Charles Darwin's shipmates aboard included John Lort Stokes. The port was named after their former friend from the earlier voyage, in 1839.

Although Aboriginal people had inhabited the area for thousands of years, there was no European settlement until 1869. Shortly after this, the first poles of the overland telegraph were erected in Darwin, and this project, when completed, connected Australia to the rest of the world. The discovery of gold inland assisted the young colony's development.

In February 1942, Darwin was attacked by 242 Japanese aircraft (from the same fleet that attached Pearl Harbor, but more bombs were dropped on Darwin than on Pearl Harbor), killing some 250 persons, and causing major damage.

The city was largely destroyed by Cyclone Tracey on Christmas Day 1974; there were 50 deaths, and 70 percent of the buildings were destroyed. About 30,000 people were evacuated by air. The city was reconstructed using modern materials and design techniques and is now a modern port city, communications center, and seat of government for the Northern Territory. The population in 2004 was 110,000. It is the location of Charles Darwin University.

Darwin, Emma (née Wedgwood) (1808–1896)

Heiress of the Wedgwood pottery family; wife and inspirational supporter of Charles Robert Darwin for 43 years.

Darwins married Wedgwoods three times in two generations. Charles's father, Robert Darwin, had married Susannah Wedgwood (1765–1817); Josiah Wedgwood III had married Charles's sister Caroline (1800–1888), and Charles married Emma at the little church of St Peter's at Maer, in the county of Staffordshire on January 20, 1839. Moreover, the founder of the Wedgwood pottery dynasty, **Josiah I** had also married a distant cousin, Sally Wedgwood. There were other connections: Emma's uncle, John Wedgwood, had married her mother's sister (née Allen). Later in life, Charles expressed concern that this degree of cousinly inbreeding might have deleterious effects. Indeed, there is some slight evidence that one child of the marriage of Charles and Emma might have had Down's syndrome (Charles Waring) and died as a toddler of scarlet fever, one child (Mary) died a few weeks after birth, and another, **Annie,** also died young.

But this complex intertwining of inheritance had its advantages. Descended from a line of prosperous physicians (the Darwins), country gentry (the Allens, from west Wales), and brilliantly successful manufacturers (the Wedgwoods), the young couple would never want financially. It also meant a rare combination of talents and abilities. The Darwin and Wedgwood families had produced, and have continued to produce, persons of outstanding abilities for many generations.

Emma Wedgwood was born on May 2, 1808 at Maer Hall, then the Wedgwood family estate, in Staffordshire—a home that she loved and looked back upon with nostalgia all her days. She was the youngest of eight children—four girls and four boys. She and her sister Fanny, who was two years older, were considered as a unit by other members of the family, almost as one person—the "Dovelies." Yet these two were very different and were also referred to as "Miss Pepper and Salt": Fanny was freckled and very orderly—"Miss Memorandum"; Emma was lively, untidy but pretty—"Miss Slip-Slop." Emma was educated at home and seems to have had a lot of freedom. The children used to row a boat or go for walks around the estate's quarter-mile long lake. Emma learned to played the piano, and she enjoyed music throughout her life.

The Wedgwoods always attached great importance to education, and the views of **Josiah Wedgwood II** on the education of girls were in advance of many of his contemporaries. Besides having governesses and tutors at home, the Wedgwood girls and their mother were in 1818 taken on a feminine version of the Grand Tour of Europe, visiting Paris, Rome, Florence, and Geneva. Emma and Fanny had dancing lessons and entered into society. Emma became quite good at French. Then in 1822 they were sent to a school in Paddington Green (then a quiet rural location outside London), where, although her music was encouraged, Emma later claimed that she learned little. The two young girls became homesick and were brought home after a year. The fine library at Maer Hall probably provided sufficient stimulation.

Emma Wedgwood's degree of religious devotion fluctuated. The family had a strong Unitarian tradition, but Emma later became a regular worshipper at the village church (which was Church of England) at Downe and was thought of as rather devout, being very perturbed as some of Charles Darwin's ideas on evolution developed and he moved away from formal religion. But, apparently, Emma became less intense in her religious observance late in life. She was confirmed at the age of 16, perhaps partly for the sake of convention.

There was a great deal of social contact among the hoards of Darwin, Allen, and Wedgwood cousins. They put on plays together, and there seem to have been some fairly boisterous parties and dances and a good amount of flirtation. The young Charles Darwin frequently stayed over at Maer in the autumn for pheasant and partridge shooting. The estate provided a splendid environment for walking and riding, and "in the evening there was much agreeable conversation," he wrote. Yet there is little evidence of any special relationship or affection between the teenage Emma and Charles at this time. Charles admired the singing of Emma's sister Charlotte (there was music as well as conversation), and there is some evidence that Fanny Wedgwood had some interest in him. But Charles was not interested; he was passionately in love with another Fanny—**Fanny Owen,** the daughter of a neighboring country gentleman, who, a few weeks into the *Beagle*'s voyage, married someone else. However, at these times, and a little later, Sir James Mackintosh—barrister, member of Parliament, historian, and philosopher—used to visit Maer, and, noticing Charles Darwin, perceptively remarked: "There is something in that man that interests me."

And so the years tumbled by. In her early twenties, while Charles Darwin was traveling around the world, the attractive young Emma was engaged in a round of balls, charitable works, visits to nearby country houses and London, where her group visited the House of Commons, went to exhibitions, concerts, and lectures. Emma took an intelligent interest in the politics of the era—the era of the Great Reform Bill.

In August 1832, there occurred an event that had a profound affect on Emma: her childhood companion and sibling, dear, kind Fanny, died rather suddenly. There was cholera in the district but the family maintained that the cause was "some kind of inflammation" or biliousness. Perhaps this was to prevent panic from spreading through the village. Emma became more devout and more serious. At the same time, her mother's health was deteriorating, both physically and mentally, and Emma and her remaining sisters had to spend much time nursing her.

Charles returned from his voyage in the first week of October 1836, and, after visiting his home in Shrewsbury, within days was at Maer to thank his Uncle Jos (Josiah II) who had intervened with Charles's father, Robert, to encourage him to allow the young naturalist to go on the voyage. Emma was among the group who listened spellbound to tales of Patagonia and Tierra del Fuego, of mountains, forests, and islands. She appreciated that Charles, too, had changed. The immature beetle collector and sportsman had gone, and a mature, serious scientist had emerged. They each must have liked what they saw, for, although they did not meet much over the next few months—the scientist was sorting his specimens and discussing them with experts in London and Cambridge, as well as writing his reports—the friendship firmed. Emma also traveled: she revisited the continent and spent time with friends in Paris.

Darwin was certainly pondering marriage. He drew up a table, listing the advantages and disadvantages of the married state, but with no hint that he had anyone in particular in mind. Nevertheless, his conclusion was clear:

"Marry—marry—marry." But both parties were reticent. Finally, in November 1838, in the library at Maer Hall, he proposed. Emma accepted at once. They were married two months later—the wedding being described as being very like a marriage from one of Jane Austen's novels and conducted by another cousin, Allen Wedgwood. It was a quiet wedding, and almost immediately after, their carriage left for Birmingham so the happy couple could travel onward by the new railway line to London.

For a few years after their marriage, they lived in Gower Street, in London. They were extremely contented. Emma was pregnant within a few months but seems to have enjoyed keeping house. They employed servants, including a cook, but Emma seems to have done some of the cooking herself; her recipe book survives and tells a tale of sound, if somewhat plain, nourishing English fare. They entertained Charles's scientific friends: **John Henslow, Charles Lyell, Joseph Hooker, Thomas Huxley, Richard Owen,** and Charles Babbage (whose work on calculating machines paved the way for the modern computer). Emma found some of them rather dull.

Alas, the health of both of them deteriorated. Maybe it was the stress of city living coupled with London's pollution. And Emma was almost continually pregnant for the next 16 years. The precise nature of Charles's illness has been much discussed. As a very young man, he had had heart palpitations and severe migraines. It has been suggested that he might have picked up infections in South America. But it also has been surmised that his sickness was at least partially psychological; it does seem that occasionally he may, consciously or unconsciously, have exaggerated his symptoms to gain Emma's attention and sympathy, and possibly the sympathy of his doctor father. Nevertheless, his vomiting attacks, skin eruptions, and violent shivering seem to have been real enough. (See article on Ill Health and Diseases of Charles Darwin.)

The couple resolved to move out of London; with a growing family, they needed a larger house. Charles, in particular, sought a more peaceful life. Emma longed for a larger garden. They searched for a country house, not too far out of town, in the summer of 1842. Robert Darwin bought them Down House in the village of Downe in Kent, about 16 miles from London for £2,200, and they moved in in September 1842, Somewhat bleak and unprepossessing when they acquired it, over the years the home was improved and extended, the garden planted with flower beds and trees, and the house filled with love and children. It was to be a recreation of Maer Hall with cousins coming and going, and children and grandchildren returning again and again throughout the following decades.

Charles and Emma might have left the city, but their country home was busy with the noise of children: both parents delighted in playing with their offspring in a completely natural way.

In addition to the three that died young, Emma had seven other children. The eldest child, William, was born in 1839, within a year of their marriage, and the youngest, the sickly Charles Waring, was born in 1856, when Emma was approaching 50. The years must have been hard.

In Darwin's *Autobiography,* he summarized the years at Down:

> Few persons have lived a more retired life than we have done. Besides short visits to the houses of relations and occasionally to the seaside or elsewhere, we have gone nowhere. . . . During the first part of my residence we went a little into society and received a few friends here; but my health always suffered from the excitement, violent shivery and vomiting attacks being thus brought on. I have therefore been compelled for many years to give up all dinner parties.

Charles Darwin combined his researches in the study, the greenhouse, the garden, and the nearby countryside with the activities of a demonstrative and caring father—the antithesis of the stern Victorian patriarch. He and Emma had the normal worries of parenthood: the grief over the deaths of Annie, Mary, and Charles Waring and concerns over childhood illnesses and about the education and "advancement in life" of their offspring.

Charles never had to work for a living, but there is evidence that in some ways they were reasonably economical. They had several servants at Down, some of whom remained with them for years.

Emma maintained her enthusiasm for music through the decades at Down. She played for her own pleasure and to soothe Charles; he enjoyed her playing when he was feeling stressed or unwell. Darwin family tradition has it that she used to play lively tunes to which the children danced.

Charles discussed his work with Emma, and she supported him devotedly, although she was concerned about the religious implications of his evolutionary ideas. It seems that, on some occasions, they found it easier to express their feelings in writing. Toward the end 1844, he became concerned that, in the event of his early death, his ideas, of which he appreciated the importance, would be lost. He wrote out a summary of his views (see **Essay of 1844**), together with instructions to Emma for their publication, perhaps with the assistance of his friend Hooker. Much later, Emma also carefully checked the proofs of *On the Origin,* and it seems that the text was slightly adapted in a few places to acknowledge her sensibilities: for example, almost nothing is said about the origin of humans, a topic on which they disagreed strongly.

When *On the Origin of Species* was finally published in late November 1859, the first printing sold out immediately, and more copies were rushed from the presses. Emma rejoiced at the book's success, writing to their son William that his father would "never think small beer of himself again." The book's success in terms of its distribution (although Darwin never made any money from it) brought him into the limelight. His ideas were bitterly attacked in some quarters. Henslow, although he disagreed with parts, thought it a "stumble in the right direction." Sedgwick thought it was nonsense. But many younger scientific colleagues were impressed. Emma supported her husband throughout.

On the whole, the 1850s brought periods of better health to both Charles and Emma and they went out and about to a greater extent. They enjoyed a visit to the Great Exhibition in London in 1851. Visits to relations, the Lake District in northern England, and seaside resorts in Wales of the Isle of Wight (off the south coast of England) enlivened their days. Charles took to going to occasional scientific meetings in London.

But in the 1860s Charles Darwin was working on *The Descent of Man*, the work that sought to apply his evolutionary ideas to humanity, and the thought of the storm that would follow its publication made him ill. Emma read the manuscript and wrote to one of her daughters: "I think it will be very interesting but that I shall dislike it very much." She feared it would "put God further off." They were perhaps a little overconcerned, for reviews were quite civil. People were "talking about [the volume] without being shocked." Opinions had subtly changed in the decade since the publication of *On the Origin*.

Despite the worries and grief of earlier years, Emma and Charles had great joy from their children later in their lives. Several became very distinguished in their own fields. Leonard was a major in the Royal Engineers; **William** was a successful banker; and **Francis** (Frank) was a botanist—he was his father's assistant for many years, but later held academic posts at Cambridge, as well as edited his father's letters. **George** was a Cambridge mathematician, physicist, and astronomer and academically the most successful. **Horace** was less academic but founded the Cambridge Scientific Instrument Company. Emma and Charles visited Cambridge in the last years of Charles's life and enjoyed seeing their thriving children and grandchildren.

But by the very late 1870s, depression and ill health were again having their effect. A summer holiday at Patterdale in the Lake District in 1881 did something to restore Charles's spirits, but he realized that his work was done, and the idea depressed him. He was very ill in the cold of the succeeding winter. He had a serious heart condition and was in constant pain for long periods. One night, in April 1882, he woke in great distress, telling Emma that he could bear the pain better if she were awake. He wanted to die and sent his children an affectionate message. He died at about 4:00 P.M. on April 19, 1882. Emma remained remarkably calm in the days that followed. She and the rest of the family, and indeed Charles himself, had expected the funeral and burial to be in the village of Downe. But it was not to be. Powerful influences were at work, and, despite Charles's known agnostic views, in the presence of a vast congregation, the funeral and burial were held in Westminster Abbey. Emma did not attend, remaining alone at Down House.

She gathered up her life, spending some months in most years in Cambridge, but kept on Down House for the sake of the children and grandchildren in summer. She took to reading philosophy; as the family's matriarch she was a source of wise counsel for a large extended family. She died at Down on October 2, 1896, at the age of 88 years, and was quietly buried in Downe churchyard. (Incidentally, her death was 60 years to the day from when Charles had stepped ashore at Falmouth at the conclusion of the *Beagle*'s voyage.)

In Charles Darwin's autobiography, he addressed his children as follows:

> You all know your mother, and what a good mother she has been to all of you. She has been my greatest blessing and I can declare that in my whole life I have never heard her utter one word which I would have rather been unsaid. She has never failed in her kindest sympathy towards me, and has borne with the utmost patience my frequent complains of ill-health and discomfort. I do not believe she has ever missed an opportunity of doing a kind action to anyone near her. I marvel at my good fortune, that she, so infinitely my superior in every single moral quality, consented to be my wife. She has been my wise adviser and cheerful comforter throughout life, which without her would have been . . . a miserable one from ill-health. She has earned the love and admiration of every soul near her.

This says it all. It was Emma who kept him alive.

FURTHER READING

Healey, Edna. 2001. *Emma Darwin: The Inspirational Wife of a Genius.* London: Headline.

Darwin, Erasmus (junior) (Erasmus Alvey Darwin) (1804–1881)

Charles Darwin's elder brother; qualified as a medical doctor but was interested in literature rather than science, and mostly lived a life of leisure. Known as Eras or Uncle Ras by the family.

Erasmus Alvey Darwin was Charles Darwin's only brother. Like Charles, he attended **Shrewsbury** School and Christ's College Cambridge, completing his practical medical training in **Edinburgh,** just at the time that Charles was starting his. The two were close: as young lads they conducted chemistry experiments together in the garden shed at The Mount, in Shrewsbury.

But **Robert Darwin,** their father, thought as early as 1829 that Erasmus, apparently frail as a child, did not have the stamina to survive the strain "on body and mind" of a career as a successful medical doctor and provided an allowance for him to live in literary London. Erasmus seems to have been happy with this arrangement and passed much of his time attending fashionable dinner parties. His brother (later accompanied by his family) stayed with him in the city from time to time. While young, he seemed to have been something of a ladies' man, carrying on a (probably harmless) flirtation with Fanny Wedgwood (née Frances Mackintosh, who was married to Hensleigh Wedgwood). To distract the press, Erasmus was paired off with Emma Wedgwood. But they seem to have had little feeling for one another, and eventually Emma married Charles.

Later, Erasmus's name was linked to that of Harriet Martineau, the radical and feminist, and he spent much time driving with her in a carriage. On

April 1, 1838, when Charles was living nearby after his return from the *Beagle* voyage, he wrote to his sister Susan:

> and now for Miss Martineau, who has been as frisky lately as the Rhinoceros. Erasmus has been with her noon, morning and night: if her character was not as secure as a mountain in the polar regions she certainly would lose it. [Charles] Lyell called there the other day and there was a beautiful rose on the table, and she showed it to him and said "Erasmus Darwin gave me that." How fortunate it is, she is so very plain; otherwise I should be very frightened. (*Correspondence of Charles Darwin*, Vol. 2, 80 and Cambridge University Library, Darwin Archive)

"Very plain" was probably a euphemism. Robert Darwin was also concerned by the relationship: although Whiggish and liberal in outlook, he thought she was perhaps too radical for the Darwin family. But the radical Harriet Martineau and the dilettante Erasmus Darwin between them attracted "all the geniuses" in London around them, and the young Charles, working to establish himself among the scientific men, may have benefited from this society. Harriet seems to have been impressed by Charles, recalling him as "painstaking and effective." But the health of both parties (Harriet and Erasmus) deteriorated and they drifted apart.

Erasmus was on the fringes of the Abolitionist (antislavery) campaign, and dabbled in spiritualism and psychic research. He never married but doted on his many nephews and nieces, greatly enjoying playing with them. But he seems to have become addicted to opium, then widely used as a medicine, and his health deteriorated, his final years being rather unhappy.

Darwin, Erasmus (senior) (1731–1802)

Grandfather of Charles Darwin; physician, poet, and polymath.

A person of extraordinary energy and flexibility of mind, Erasmus Darwin was born at Elton in Nottinghamshire, the son of a lawyer and minor landowner. As a child, he was interested in science. He studied at **Cambridge** (St. John's College) and **Edinburgh** universities, and set up as a doctor first in Nottingham, and then in the cathedral town of Lichfield, where he became a prominent figure. His free-thinking opinions were instrumental in his being prevented by conservative pressures in the scientific establishment from his taking part in one of Captain James Cook's voyages. He kept a large botanical garden (and was an excellent botanist) and was also extremely interested in mechanical inventions, experimenting with electricity, telescopes, and devising a horizontal windmill. He saw links between his attempts at invention and his medical training, thinking of the body as an efficient machine. He knew Benjamin Franklin and worked with him on various projects; he was also associated with the Lunar Society—a pioneer scientific society in the

English Midlands. He was also extremely interested in philology and language and designed a "speaking machine." He married twice; after his second marriage, he moved to Derby. He also took a mistress—the governess of one of his children—by whom he had two daughters: the entire ménage seems to have lived happily together as a family.

It is, however, for his evolutionary ideas that Erasmus Darwin is particularly remembered. His book *Zoonomia or the Laws of Organic Life* was published in 1794, although he seems to have been working on it for several decades. The book contains much medical information, but also includes what has been called "the first complete view of evolution." Other works that hint at evolutionary ideas include *The Temple of Nature, or the Origin of Society* (published posthumously in 1802) and *The Botanic Garden* (1789, 1791). He was influenced by the French naturalist G.L.L. Comte De Buffon (1707–1788), who had speculated about the possibility of the transmutability of species.

In *Zoonomia,* he wrote of the adaptation of organisms to their environment and way of life:

> Some birds have acquired harder beaks to crack nuts, as the parrot. Others have acquired beaks adapted to break the harder seeds, as sparrows. Others for the softer seeds of flowers, or the buds of trees, as the finches. (Vol. 2, 235)

Erasmus Darwin wrote of the "family" of the whole of nature, stating that there was "a certain similitude" about the whole living world. In *The Temple of Nature* (1807 edition, 35), he wrote:

Portrait of Erasmus Darwin, senior. From an eighteenth-century print.

Organic life beneath the shoreless waves
Was born, and nursed in Ocean's pearly caves;
First forms minute, unseen by spheric glass,
Move on the mud, or pierce the watery mass;
These, as successive generations bloom,
New powers acquire and larger limbs assume;
Whence countless groups of vegetation spring,
And breathing realms of fin, and feet, and wing.

Thus the tall Oak, the giant of the wood,
Which bears Britannia's thunders on the flood;
The Whale, unmeasured monster of the main;
The lordly lion, monarch of the plain;
The eagle, soaring in the realms of air,
Whose eye, undazzled, drinks the solar glare;
Imperious man, who rules the bestial crowd,
Of language, reason, and reflection proud,
With brow erect, who scorns this earthy sod,
And styles himself the image of his God-
Arose from rudiments of form and sense,
An embryon point or microscopic ens!
(ens = entity or being)

Here are set out many aspects of the theory of evolution. The idea of competition in nature makes its appearance in the same work:

From Hunger's arm the shafts of Death are hurl'd
And one great Slaughter-house the warring world.

Although some of his ideas on how evolution might occur somewhat resemble those of Lamarck, Erasmus Darwin also described how competition and sexual selection might cause changes in species: "The [result of a] contest among males seems to be, that the strongest and most active animal should propogate the species which should thus be improved." Erasmus Darwin arrived at his conclusions through an integrative approach—combining his observations of domesticated animals and the study of animal behavior—and he utilized his vast knowledge of many different fields, such as paleontology, the study of the distribution of organisms, embryology, and comparative anatomy.

Many of the components of his grandson's theory of evolution through natural selection can by identified in Erasmus Darwin's writings. But despite the fact that his poetry was well received in literary circles, verse is not the best medium in which to propound scientific ideas if a writer intends to be taken seriously. Some of Erasmus's works were parodied and lampooned mercilessly. The time for evolution had not yet come. Charles Darwin knew of his grandfather's works (and certainly read some of them, possibly while at school).

Darwin, Francis (1848—1925)

Botanist and third son and seventh child of Charles and Emma Darwin.

Francis Darwin went to Trinity College, Cambridge, first studying mathematics (like his brother Charles), but then changing to natural sciences. He graduated in 1870. He then went to study for a medical degree in London, qualifying in 1875, although he never practiced medicine.

Francis Darwin married Amy Ruck in 1874; she died in 1876 four days after the birth of their son Bernard Darwin, who became an essayist and journalist. Francis then married Ellen Crofts and they had a daughter Frances, who married and became known as the poet Frances Cornford.

Francis Darwin worked with his father at **Down House** on experiments dealing with plant movement, especially phototropism (growth toward light) and they coauthored *The Power of Movement in Plants* (1880). He lectured in botany at Cambridge; it is said that when the chair of botany became vacant, although encouraged, he refused to apply, stating that a younger man needed the position more than he did. He was more interested in the arts and music than other members of the Darwin family of his day, and he experimented with psychical research and flirted with the eugenics movement.

Francis Darwin was elected a Fellow of the **Royal Society** on June 8, 1882, the same year his father died. He edited *The Autobiography of Charles Darwin* (1887) and his father's letters: *The Life and Letters of Charles Darwin* (1887) and *More Letters of Charles Darwin* (1905). He edited **Thomas Huxley**'s *On the Reception of the Origin of Species* (1887). His understanding of the history of science and of his father's role in it is epitomized by the following quotation:

> In science the credit goes to the man who convinces the world, not the man to whom the idea first occurs. (*Eugenics Review*, April 1914)

Darwin, George Howard (1845—1912)

Second son and fifth child of Charles Darwin; mathematician and physicist; Cambridge University professor.

At least one Darwin in every generation for five generations achieved the distinction of a Fellowship of the **Royal Society** (FRS), the highest scientific honor in Britain. The fourth in this illustrious line was George. George was passionately interested in natural history in childhood and as a teenager at Downe had a special interest in butterflies. During his years at Clapham Grammar School, he was taught by a brilliant mathematician.

Despite this background, he was described as a late developer and showed no great academic promise during his first couple of years as an undergraduate at Trinity College, Cambridge. But he was finally adjudged "second wrangler" (i.e., second on the list of those who gained first class honors in mathematics). It was some years after taking his degree that he realized that his life's work lay in the application of mathematics to scientific problems, and he studied the law, even qualifying as a barrister.

But like his father, George Darwin suffered from periodic ill heath, and it may be that he judged himself insufficiently strong to cope with life at the English bar. He withdrew to Cambridge (Trinity had given him a fellowship shortly after his degree had been awarded). He wrote papers on a variety of subjects—biological, philosophical, economic—although many of them had a statistical bent. Often he sent drafts to his father for comment. The flow of ideas was two-way, and Charles Darwin often sought the advice of his son when he thought him to be more knowledgeable than himself. George was also something of an artist (which Charles Darwin never was) and contributed illustrations to some of his father's books. He was also a skilled linguist and sometimes translated letters from French and German (and occasionally other languages) for his father. He assisted with the proofs of the second edition of *The Descent of Man* in 1873.

But George's main work was in geodesy (the precise measurement of the earth) and geophysics. He made important contributions to the study of the movements of the moon, the tides, and the escape of heat from the inner earth. He was appointed Plumian Professor of Astronomy at Cambridge in 1883. A host of other honors followed. He was president of the **British Association for the Advancement of Science** during its meeting in South Africa in 1905. He was knighted (allowed to use the title Sir, his wife becoming Lady Darwin) the same year, and was awarded the 1911 Copley Medal, the highest honor the **Royal Society** can bestow; in this he once again followed his father, who had received the award in 1864.

Professor Sir George Darwin's courtship, marriage, and family life have been charmingly described in two books by his daughters: *Period Piece* by **Gwen Raverat** and *A House by the River* by Margaret Keynes. He married an American, of Huguenot heritage, Maud du Puy, in July 1884. She reigned as matriarch over Newnham Grange—the house in Cambridge that was the home of the Darwin family from 1885 until she died in 1947—for 62 of her 86 years.

Darwin, Horace (1851—1928)

Distinguished engineer; youngest surviving son of Charles Darwin. He was interested in natural history as a child, is said to have had a charming nature but to have been a dreadful speller. He attended Trinity College, Cambridge, and made a career as a builder of scientific instruments. In 1885, he founded the Cambridge Scientific Instrument Company (eventually taken over by George Kent Group in 1968). He was the mayor of Cambridge from 1896–1897 and, as such, tried to bring together "town and gown"—traditionally great rivals. He was elected a Fellow of the **Royal Society** in 1903. Horace married Emma Farrer in January 1880, and they had three children, one of whom was Norah, who, later, as **Norah Barlow,** became a significant Darwin scholar, editing her grandfather's papers and diaries.

FURTHER READING

Cattermole, M.J.G. and A. F. Wolfe. 1987. *Horace Darwin's Shop: A History of the Cambridge Scientific Company 1878–1968.* Bristol, England: Adam Hilger.

Darwin, Robert Waring (1766–1848)

Medical doctor, businessman, father of Charles Robert Darwin.

Robert, the son of **Erasmus Darwin (senior)** obtained the degree of doctor of medicine at the University of Leyden in the Netherlands before he was 20 and completed his medical studies at Edinburgh in 1786. Late that year, he set up a medical practice in **Shrewsbury.** His father wrote to friends asking them to recommend Robert to their friends in the Shrewsbury area. Nevertheless, Robert himself deserves much of the credit for his success. He was sympathetic and observant, and it is said that he had more than fifty patients within six months. Robert Darwin was extremely successful throughout his 60 years of practice in Shrewsbury.

In 1796, when he was 29, Robert married Susannah Wedgwood, daughter of **Josiah Wedgwood I,** the master potter. Her dowry enabled him to purchase land at The Mount on high ground overlooking the River Severn and to build a substantial house, in which he lived until his death, 50 years later.

Robert Darwin became a dominating figure in the town of Shrewsbury; he was extremely successful in his medical practice, and it is asserted that he had the highest income of any provincial doctor. He was six feet two inches (1.88 meters) tall and extremely portly. He had to have stone steps constructed to help him mount his carriage and part of the dining table cut out to accommodate his girth. He gave up regularly weighing himself when he reached 24 stone (330 pounds or 152 kilograms). His well-built coachman was often sent ahead to test the floorboards for him before Darwin entered a new patient's house. Robert and his wife Susannah had two sons (Erasmus and Charles) and four daughters (Marianne, Susan, Caroline, and [Emily] Catherine). After his wife Susannah died in 1817, at age 52, Robert maintained close links with the family of her brother **Josiah Wedgwood II,** who lived at Maer, only a few miles from Shrewsbury, and who was an extremely important influence on the young Charles Darwin.

Despite his successful medical practice, his account books show that only about a third of his annual income came from medical fees: about £3,000 in a good year. He had an excellent head for business, and most of his income was from dividends from securities (he was, for example, a major shareholder in the Trent and Mersey Canal). He also had income from rents—as soon as he arrived in Shrewsbury he bought several houses. He received interest paid to him on mortgages raised on local property. In the days before the banks were efficiently organized to provides loans for business, particularly the expanding manufacturing industries, Dr. Darwin was a specialist in private money-broking, arranging loans to support business ventures, acting as a financial intermediary. He has been described as somewhat ruthless in some of his business dealings. Nevertheless, Charles described him as "the kindest man I ever met." Although there was some tension between Charles and his father—the elder Darwin was probably disappointed when his younger son decided to leave Edinburgh Medical School, unqualified. He initially thought the *Beagle* venture was a waste of time, but, once convinced of its value (when Charles gained the encouragement of Robert's brother-in-law Josiah Wedgwood II), he supported him and indeed funded him generously. It was because of the further financial support that Robert gave his son on his marriage and the inheritance provided on his death that Charles never had to seek paid employment, but was able to devote his life to science. He was also generous to his other children.

Darwin College, Cambridge

College founded in 1964, named after Charles Darwin.

Darwin College was the first college in Cambridge founded exclusively for graduate students. It was established on the initiative of three other **Cambridge University** colleges—St. John's, Gonville and Caius, and Trinity—with the active support of the university as a whole. The core of the college is Newnham Grange, a large house built in 1793 for a local corn merchant. This house was bought in 1883 by the second son of Charles, Sir **George Darwin** (1845–1912), Plumian Professor of Astronomy in Cambridge University; he also acquired the adjoining building, the Old Granary, in 1885. In due course, the Grange became the home of Sir **Charles Darwin** (1887–1962), a distinguished physicist and Sir George's son. On his death, with the active support of his widow, Lady Katherine, it was acquired for the college. The adjoining house, the Hermitage, a mid-nineteenth-century building, was acquired from St. John's College, and other properties have been purchased as they became available. New buildings, including a modern study center, have been added.

Thus, although the Charles Darwin of evolution fame never lived in the buildings that now form the college, there is a family link that reaches back to him. Darwin College commemorates a distinguished family, as well as Charles. Newnham Grange and the Old Granary were immortalized in *Period Piece: A Cambridge Childhood*, the book by Gwen Raverat, another grandchild of Charles Darwin.

The college prides itself on the international nature of its student body; in most years, over 50 countries are represented.

See also: Darwin, Charles Galton; Raverat, Gwen.

Darwinism and Literature

Although Darwin was a scientist and his influence on science was enormous, Charles Darwin's *Voyage of the Beagle, On the Origin of Species,* and *Descent of Man* can also be considered works of literature. He has an elegant style, even if some of his sentences are rather long for modern taste. Moreover, his works are constructed to tell a story, and he uses many of the literary devices of the novelist. He has a remarkable feel for rhetoric and uses this to make his points. Moreover, his message is conveyed largely in a series of metaphors, particular those associated with struggle and conflict. One need look no further than the full title of his main work to find an example of his use of metaphor: *On the Origin of Species, by Means of Natural Selection, or the Preservation of Favoured Races in the Struggle for Lif*e.

Darwin was profoundly influenced by what he read. While he was a teenager, in the summer of 1826, he read Gilbert White's timeless masterpiece *The Natural History of Selborne* and he came away from this book with a profound appreciation for wildlife.

While at Cambridge, Darwin was further inspired by literature in such works as **William Paley**'s *Natural Theology,* which he later said he found of great value; **John Herschel**'s *Preliminary Discourse on the Study of Natural Philosophy,* which taught him the basics of scientific methodology and the importance of sound, logical argument; and **Alexander von Humboldt**'s *Personal Narrative of a Voyage . . . A New Continent* on his South American travels. To some extent, *The Voyage of the Beagle* could be said to be modeled on this work.

During the *Beagle* voyage, Darwin often read Milton's *Paradise Lost.* Later, while living in London after the voyage, Darwin read some metaphysical books but did not like them. It was at this time in his life that he acquired a liking for the poetry of William Wordsworth and Samuel Taylor Coleridge.

In his later years, Darwin was fond of the novels of Jane Austen and Elizabeth Gaskell, the poems of Lord Byron, and the historical novels of Walter Scott. He did not enjoy novels with sad, depressing endings. His wife Emma sometimes would read novels to him twice a day while he reclined on a sofa in the drawing room at **Down House.**

Just as his research and his writing were influenced by what he read, so his work influenced other writers, including novelists and poets. It is claimed that one of the characters in Elizabeth Gaskell's *Wives and Daughters* (1866) is a fictionalized portrait of Darwin. But Darwin introduced a new world; existing paradigms were overthrown; religion and morality were reevaluated; science, instead of being mainly the realm of the specialist, and the dilettante, began to be common currency and its vocabulary more widely understood. Concepts such as the struggle for existence, favored races, selection (natural and sexual), evolution and change, extinction, chance, time, the influence of environment, and variation appear in novels, sometimes in ways much changed from how Darwin envisaged them.

An example can be found in George Eliot's *Middlemarch,* in which the author discussed the difficulty of coming to definite conclusions about the limitations and abilities of women:

> [I]f there were one level of feminine incompetence as strict as the ability to count three and no more, the social lot of women might be treated with scientific certitude. Meanwhile the indefiniteness remains, the limits of variation are really much wider than any one would imagine from the sameness of women's coiffure.

A single keyword may remind the reader of the whole debate. The importance of quantification is mentioned here, and science is associated with "certitude"; these allusions perhaps help focus the reader's attention on a particular way of thinking. But it is the word "variation" that is of greatest significance here. To what extent can similarities in form or appearance be used to show relationships between species? Organisms may resemble one another closely but belong to very different biological groups; superficial similarities may be, as Darwin put it in chapter 13 of *On the Origin,* "adaptive or analogical," the result of similar environmental, evolutionary pressures on organisms of different origins. The dugong, whales, and fishes superficially resemble one another because of their adaptation to the marine environment. The greyhound and the racehorse also have superficial resemblances because they have been bred for a similar purpose. Moreover, although it was the rigors of selection that contributed to the complexity and diversity of life, the raw material on which they worked was variation.

The word "variety" occurs three times in the first sentence of the first chapter of *On the Origin:*

> When we look to the individuals of the same variety or sub-variety of our older cultivated plants and animals, one of the first points that strikes us, is, that they generally differ much more from each other than do the individuals of any one species or variety in the state of nature.

Possibly this is George Eliot's source. Domestic life allows, it could be argued, little scope for variation; substantially less, perhaps, than that of which women are capable. A straightforward point about the restrictions of home life has been given a gloss by this glance toward a current (in the 1870s) topical point of discussion. Much variation exists, and it only needs the right environmental circumstances to display itself.

The works of **Thomas Hardy** provide another example of the use of Darwinian concepts, including that of sexual selection, by a Victorian English novelist.

Darwin himself was heavily indebted to **Charles Lyell**'s elegantly written *Principles of Geology* (first edition 1830–1832). This book was extremely popular and went through many editions. It espoused the doctrine of uniformitarianism—the notion that the present condition of the Earth is the result of long periods of gradual change, brought about by processes that can be observed today. **Gideon Algernon Mantell** (1790–1852) produced another popular geology text, *The Wonders of Geology* (1838), which also went into numerous editions and was heavily influenced by Lyell. Perhaps even closer to the central Darwinian theme was *Vestiges of Creation*, published anonymously in 1844 by **Robert Chambers.**

Hardy owned, and is known to have used, a copy of Mansell's book, and he borrowed heavily from it. Alfred, Lord Tennyson read *Vestiges* in 1844 and has been described as "anticipating" Darwin in some of his poetry. But Tennyson, influenced by the rather strange, almost mystical ideas in Chambers, saw evolution as an upward, spiritual journey. In his *In Memoriam*, written over 17 years from 1833 to 1850, in grief for the death of a friend, he wrote:

> I held it truth, with him who sings
> To one clear harp in divers tones,
> That men may rise on stepping-stones
> Of their dead selves to higher things. (*In Memoriam*, I, 1–4)

Later, we find again the idea of the refinement of the human soul. Suffering and grief are perhaps part of a process of the abandonment of animality:

> To shape and use. Arise and fly
> The reeling Faun, the sensual feast;
> Move upward, working out the beast,
> And let the ape and tiger die. (CVIII, 24–28)

Fragments of other generally Darwinian ideas appear. Here, Tennyson acknowledges extinction in nature using a geological metaphor:

> "So careful of the type?" but no.
> From scarped cliff and quarried stone
> She cries, "A thousand types are gone:
> I care for nothing, all shall go." (LVI, 1–4)

The notion of the survival of the fittest can be perceived where the poet, noting both the profligacy and severity of nature, observed:

> that of fifty seeds
> She often brings but one to bear. (LV, 10–11)

A mechanism for this selective process is not far away:

> Creation's final law—
> . . . Nature, red in tooth and claw. (LVI, 14–15)

Darwin gave the world a host of new ways of looking at itself. But he was integrating and refining notions that were already in the air and already having their influence. To this extent, he can be seen as a node—albeit a very important one—in a web of influences extending from before his day onward, throughout the Victorian period and long after.

FURTHER READING

Beer, Gillian. 1983. *Darwin's Plots: Evolutionary Narrative in Darwin, George Eliot, and Nineteenth Century Fiction*. London: Routledge and Kegan Paul.

Darwinism and Theology

Although many saw Darwin's theory of evolution, and the set of ideas associated with it, as contradictory to the precepts of conventional religion (particularly Christianity), the true position was much more complex.

Darwin cherished the following "compliment," sent to him anonymously in February 1875:

> The learned Darwin states that Moses taught confusion
> For Man, he boldly states, descends from Ape or Monkey.
> I, having read his book, come to this conclusion—
> Darwin (at least himself) descends from Ass or Donkey!

There were many among the conventional English, Anglican, establishment, and evangelical Christians in many countries (particularly in the United States), who concurred with the poet. But there were many who did not.

In the medieval period, and indeed until well into the sixteenth century, the notion that the Book of Genesis contained the literal truth concerning the origin of the universe, the Earth, and life was widespread. There was general agreement that the world had been created in six days and that this had happened not more than a few thousand years ago. James Ussher (1581–1656), Bishop of Meath and later Archbishop of Armagh (Ireland), wrote *Annales veteris et novis testamenti* (Annals of the Old and New Testaments) (1650–1654), stating that the date of creation was 4004 B.C.; the date and time of day were also specified. Bishop Ussher's chronology was widely accepted and was printed in some Bibles from 1701 onward, although it never was official Anglican doctrine. Other dates were supported by some scholars. Some early geologists saw their task as one of **reconciliation**—the reconciling the Book of Moses with the Book of the Rocks. John Burnet (1635–1715) was such a person: he attributed many features of the Earth's surface such as the mountains and valleys and the distribution of fossils to the flood described in Genesis, chapters 6–9.

But although the idea of a young Earth was given much credence, there were criticisms. **John Ray** (1627–1705), naturalist and theologian, was skeptical. He had personally seen shells atop high mountains—such as those of central Germany and in the Alps—but the idea that water had overwhelmed the highest of mountains all over the world at the same time stretched his credulity.

> Now that ever the Water should have covered the Earth to that height as to exceed the tops of the highest mountains, and for a considerable time abode

there, is hard to believe, nor can such Opinion be easily reconciled with the Scripture. If it be said that these Shells were brought in by the universal Deluge in the time of Noah, when the Mountains were covered, I answer that that Deluge proceeded from the Rain, which was more likely to carry Shells down to the Sea, than bring them up from it. (*Observations Topographical, Moral and Philosophical*, 1673, 125)

By the nineteenth century, although some such as **William Buckland,** professor of geology at Oxford, in the early part of his career, clung to the idea that the biblical flood was important in distributing superficial deposits, most geologists, particularly after the publication of **Charles Lyell**'s *Principles of Geology* (1831–1833), were convinced of the old Earth hypothesis—the idea that the world was much older than the likes of Bishop Ussher asserted and that it was possibly millions of years old. Sometimes interesting intellectual gymnastics were performed by those who accepted a longer Earth history but who still wished to reconcile. Some suggested that the six days of the creation described in Genesis were very long days—that they represented six extended periods of time rather than six modern 24-hour days. Others supported the idea that there was a long period between the initial creation and the six days specified in Genesis. Possibly William Galloway (1811–1903) was such a person: he accepted that a long period of sedimentary accumulation preceded the deluge. He was the popular, evangelical vicar of St. Mark's, Regent's Park, London, for nearly forty years (1849–1888), and it was said "His great aim in life was the defence of Scripture." He attempted, by mathematical and geological argument, to show that the flood had been caused by the Earth's equilibrium being altered and "a change of axis" of the Earth caused by the accumulation of sediments. His stream of pamphlets aimed at demonstrating scientifically that the Great Flood had occurred included: *Physical Facts and the Scriptural Record* (1872), *Science and Geology in Relation to the Universal Deluge* (1888), and *Testimony of Science to the Deluge* (undated, about 1895). The term "scriptural geologist" was sometimes applied to such persons, and Galloway seems to have been an extreme example.

Another English naturalist-parson who was reluctant to abandon the "Mosaic" approach was William Purchas, a clergyman in the diocese of Lichfield. He felt able to write the following after reading some Lyellian accounts of geology as late as 1889:

certain conclusions advanced . . . seem incapable of reconciliation with the Mosaic account of the Creation. . . . While it may be quite true that these conclusions may seem to be legitimate deductions now, or to be now demanded by the facts at present known to Geologists, it is equally true that in a science as young as Geology which is still youthful, new and important facts may any day be brought to light which may demand considerable modification of views now widely and very positively maintained, and that while we do not at present see how the testimony of Genesis & that of the rocks are to be harmonized, we may [be] best satisfied that a fuller understanding of the matter will shew there to be substantial accord. (Letter in Durham University Library)

The attitude was not unique. Those who wrote of the war between science and religion that coincided with and followed Darwin's enunciation of his theories were probably overstating the situation. By the 1850s, most scientists, although many were Christian, were not opposed to an old Earth hypothesis. Uncertainty about Darwin's theories, when they came forward in 1859, there may have been, but Ussher and the young Earth theory had by then largely been displaced.

In fact there was a wide variation in how Darwin's views were received. Certainly **Adam Sedgwick,** vice master of Trinity College, Cambridge, and Canon of Norwich Cathedral, when he was training the young Darwin in geological field techniques in North Wales in the summer of 1831 would not have attached a great deal of importance to James Ussher's computations. Devout Christian he may have been, but he was not an extreme literalist. Yet after reading *On the Origin of Species* for the first time in November 1859, he wrote a "kind yet slashing letter" to his former protégé, ending:

> I call (in the abstract) causation the will of God: & I can prove He acts for the good of all His creatures. He also acts by laws which we can study & comprehend. . . . We all admit development as a fact of history: but how came it about? . . . There is a moral or metaphysical part of nature as well as a physical. A man who denies this is deep in the mire of folly. (*Correspondence of Charles Darwin,* Vol 7, pages 396–397, and Cambridge University Library, Darwin Archive)

Sedgwick seems to broadly accept Darwin's idea of change over time— development—but argues more about mechanism. Sedgwick is clearly within **William Paley**'s natural theology tradition that sees the diversity, beauty, and complexity of the natural world as evidence of the creative power of God, and the adaptation of organisms to their environment as evidence that "He acts for the good of all His creatures."

The parson-ornithologist **Francis Orpen Morris** was an even more trenchant critic. He attacked Darwin's theories in pamphlets (such as *Difficulties with Darwinism* [1869] and *The Demands of Darwinism on Credulity* [1890]), sermons, and speeches for 50 years, seeing it as his life's work to discredit the "monstrous puerilities" expressed in Darwin's books. How could organisms change over time and yet inherit characters from their parents?

On the other side of the Atlantic, in 1873, Princeton theologian and evangelical Presbyterian Charles Hodge (1797–1878) mounted a multi-pronged assault on Darwin and Darwinism in *Systematic Theology*. He claimed that Darwin's ideas were atheistic:

> Mr. Darwin and his associates, . . . admit . . . only the creation of matter, but of living matter, in the form of one or a few primordial germs from which without

any purpose or design, by the slow operation of unintelligent natural causes, and accidental variations, during untold ages, all the orders, classes, genera, species, and varieties of plants and animals, from the lowest to the highest, man included, have been formed. Teleology, and therefore, mind, or God, is expressly banished from the world. (*Systematic Theology,* Vol. 2, 1873, 23)

Hodge appreciated Darwin's reputation as a naturalist, his "fairness and frankness," and the detailed observations displayed in his works. He outlined Darwin's theory of evolution through natural selection and makes four main comments. First, it is an assault on common sense to be informed that "the whale and the humming-bird, man and the mosquito" are derived from the same source. Second, the theory cannot be correct because it is based on an impossible assumption: that "matter does the work of mind." Hodge argues design in the Paleyan manner. His objection is that Darwin argues against the intervention of mind (a designer) anywhere in the process and that this is incredible. Third (an extension of the second point), "the system is thoroughly atheistic and therefore cannot possibly stand." Darwin asserts that God has had nothing to do with the universe since the creation of one or more living germ or germs, and, to Hodge, this is tantamount to atheism. Hodge's fourth remark is that the theory is a mere hypothesis and incapable of proof by its very nature. Some of the argument appears circular, but Hodge's works were (and to some extent still are) influential, especially in the United States.

But many naturalists saw no conflict between their Christian faith and Darwin's ideas. **Charles Kingsley,** Rector of Eversley, Hampshire, was an enthusiastic supporter almost from his first glance at *On the Origin.* On receiving the book, he wrote to Darwin "All I have seen awes me," and "I shall prize your book." After agreeing with Darwin's argument that species are impermanent, he concluded "that it is just as noble a conception of the Deity to believe" that original forms were created that could develop and change as to maintain that new forms had to be created to fill the gaps that "he himself had made."

There were many clergy in the Church of England and in other denominations who took a similar view (Roman Catholics excepted, until well into the twentieth century). Some found Darwin's ideas liberating; it was no longer necessary to believe the creation stories in Genesis as the complete literal truth, although they might have great value. By the nineteenth century, biblical scholars were pointing out discrepancies and differences within the scriptural texts. Parts of Genesis and other sections of the Old Testament were myths, or allegories, containing important truths and ideas perhaps, but which should not be regarded as accurate scientifically. In the United States, James McCosh (1811–1894), eleventh president of Princeton University, but originally from Scotland, was among those who saw evolution as the tool used by the deity for creation.

The Victorian era was the hey-day of the parson-naturalist. There were many English clergy trained in the natural theology tradition who saw the study of the living world as a logical extension of their work as priests. Those who studied lichens and liverworts, beetles and shield bugs, starfish and sponges believed that, by exploring the complexity and beauty of the living world, they were gaining an insight into the mind of the Creator. Many of them almost at once began to use Darwin's theories in this work. Examples include the Reverend Octavius Pickard Cambridge, a correspondent of Darwin's who wrote on the idea of sexual selection as it applied to spiders. Another enthusiast was **Henry Baker Tristram** (1822–1906), who perceived a gradual transition in form in a series of larks he collected from North Africa.

Darwin's theory changed the way humans saw themselves and their world. If one accepted that humans were descended from animals, it became clear that humans also *were* animals. The role of humanity in relation to the living world, God, and the universe had to be reconsidered. The natural world also took on a more somber color in the minds of many, as animals in the wild were understood to be in a constant state of competition with one another as they engaged in the "struggle for existence." The world was also seen in a less permanent fashion; since the Earth was apparently very different millions of years ago from the way it is now, the comfortable stability and certainty that many saw in the world about them was displaced. Nothing would be quite the same again, and theology had to adjust to the new ideas.

See also: Darwin's Death and Westminster Abbey Funeral; Religion in the Life of Charles Darwin.

FURTHER READING

Armstrong, P. H. 2000. *The English Parson-Naturalist: A Companionship between Science and Religion.* Leominster, England: Gracewing Publications.

Brooke, J. H. 1991. *Science and Religion: Some Historical Perspectives.* Cambridge, England: Cambridge University Press.

Gillispie, C. G. 1951. *Genesis and Geology.* Cambridge, Mass.: Harvard University Press (reissued with new foreword, 1997).

Roberts, M. R. 1998. "Genesis and Geology Unearthed." *The Churchman* 112 (3): 225–255.

Darwin's Death and Westminster Abbey Funeral

Charles Darwin died on April 19, 1882, and, despite his ambivalence toward conventional religion, was accorded a funeral with all the pomp that the British establishment could provide, in Westminster Abbey, wherein he is buried.

Since middle life, Charles Darwin had not enjoyed good health (although there had been occasional periods of improvement). It has been widely asserted that his illnesses were at least partly psychosomatic, the result perhaps of stress in appreciating what effect his revolutionary ideas might have on the world and of the criticism he had to withstand after the publication of *On the Origin of Species.*

Darwin had occasional heart palpitations since before the *Beagle* voyage, but, while visiting London in mid-December 1881, he had serious chest pains, staggering, stumbling, and grasping iron railings while walking along a street. The next day he seemed better and Dr. Clarke, his London physician, declared him well, and with rest he seemed to recover. Back at Down in early 1882, he worked hard on scientific papers, and occasionally walked around the Sandwalk (the sand-strewn path around a small area of woodland that Darwin had planted at Down). But he was weak.

A severe cough left him miserable in February 1882; he vomited frequently, and the chest pains returned. On March 7, he was walking slowly around the Sandwalk when he had another seizure; he was alone but managed to hobble back to the house, collapsing into Emma's arms. Dr. Clarke diagnosed angina and prescribed morphine for the pain, but Darwin became depressed and moved little for several days. But he rallied and briefly took part in family activities. Another doctor, Norman Moore, somewhat reassured the family by stating that Darwin just had a weak heart. But by early April, the attacks were becoming severe. The old Darwin, although he knew the end was not far off, retained the habits of a lifetime, carefully recording his symptoms—"much pain," "stomach excessively bad"—as though it was a final experiment. Doctors prescribed various medications. At a meal on April 15, he felt a violent stabbing pain in the head. He staggered into another room and fell onto the sofa, briefly losing consciousness. "Dropped down," he noted. It is recorded that he said to Emma, "It's almost worthwhile to be sick to be nursed by you." Although there were lucid moments, the next couple of days he was consumed with pain and nausea and experienced periods of unconsciousness. He died at about 4:00 P.M. on Wednesday, April 19, 1882, in Emma's arms, just a few weeks after his 73rd birthday. Not long before he passed, he was heard to utter "I am not at least afraid to die," but the oft-repeated myth that he "repented of his blasphemies" is completely untrue.

The family wished for Charles to be buried quietly in the churchyard at Downe, close to the graves of his brother Erasmus and two of his dead infant children; the village carpenter prepared a coffin. But John Lubbock, longtime neighbor, friend, and disciple intervened. Lubbock was a prosperous banker and an influential member of Parliament, and he induced 20 members of Parliament to petition George Bradley, Dean of Westminster, suggesting to him "that it would be acceptable to a very large number of our fellow countrymen . . . that our illustrious countryman, Dr Darwin, should be buried in Westminster Abbey." The press mounted a campaign, some journalists seeing such an event as a gesture of "reconciliation between Faith and Science." Thomas Huxley also put pressure on the Abbey clergy. Somewhat reluctantly, Emma and the family agreed: they thought he would have wished to accept the nation's "acknowledgment of what he had done."

Darwin's pallbearers at the funeral, which was held at noon on April 26, 1882, were **Joseph Hooker,** his great friend and colleague; his "bulldog," **Thomas Huxley; Alfred Russel Wallace,** co-originator of the notion of natural selection; and John Lubbock. Behind followed dignitaries of church and state. Darwin's eldest son William was chief mourner; the rest of the family, representatives of scientific bodies and universities, and people from the United States, Russia, and many European countries also accompanied the coffin. One commentator referred to "the greatest gathering of intellect . . . ever brought together."

As the procession made its way through the minster, a specially written anthem was sung: the words were from the book of Proverbs: "Happy is the man that findeth wisdom and getteth understanding." One picture from the service remembered by many is of eldest son William, feeling a draught on his bald head, placing his black gloves upon it.

Darwin, agnostic though he was, was buried in the Abbey in what has become known as Scientists Corner. He was laid beneath the monument to Sir Isaac Newton, quite close to his friend **Charles Lyell,** and next to his mentor Sir **John Herschel,** whose book on scientific method he had read five decades earlier, and whom he had met in Cape Town toward the end of the *Beagle*'s Voyage.

Although some voices were raised against the pomp associated with the funeral by those who felt that the great naturalist's ideas were an evil blasphemy, on the whole, the dignity attached to the proceedings was felt by the British nation (and the world) to have been appropriate.

See also: Ill Health and Diseases of Charles Darwin; Religion in the Life of Charles Darwin.

FURTHER READING

Desmond, Adrian and James Moore. 1991. *Darwin*. London: Michael Joseph. See especially chapters 41, 43, and 44.
Moore, James. 1994. *The Darwin Legend*. Grand Rapids, MI: Baker Books.

Darwin's Fungus

Cyttaria darwinii; a fungus that grows profusely and apparently parasitically on the *Nothofagus,* or **southern or antarctic beech** trees, in **Tierra del Fuego** and that was of immense interest to Darwin.

The species has been named after him. The names Indian bread and *pan de indios* are also used. In the indigenous languages of the island, it is called: *yoken ter* or *owachick.*

See also: Ecology.

Dawkins, Richard (-1941-)

British zoologist and controversial publicist for the evolutionary cause.

Richard Dawkins was born in Nairobi, Kenya, in 1941, and spent his early years in East Africa. His family returned to England in 1949, and he

Darwin's fungus, growing on southern beech trees, Tierra del Fuego. Photo: Patrick Armstrong.

studied at Oxford University, graduating in 1962. He remained at Oxford, studying for his doctorate under the Dutch-born ethologist (scientist who studies animal behavior) Niko (Nikolaas) Timbergen. From 1967 to 1969, he taught zoology at the University of California, Berkeley, returning to Oxford in 1970, ultimately becoming a fellow of New College.

Timbergen's influence on Dawkins was profound. Dawkins later recalled Timbergen's use of two phrases: "behaviour machinery" and "equipment for survival." When he wrote his first book, *The Selfish Gene,* in 1976, Dawkins combined them into the phrase "survival machine." Another important influence was Francis Crick's and James Watson's work in modern genetics and molecular biology. Organisms, in Dawkins's view, can be seen as machines, programmed by their genes. Genes were machines for ensuring their own replication above all else—immortal replicators. **Evolution through natural selection** was a concept that applied not only at the levels of the individual organism and the species and taxonomic group, but also at the level of the gene. He concludes this book with the words:

> The only kind of entity that has to exist in order for life to arise, anywhere in the universe, is the immortal replicator.

In his second book, *The Extended Phenotype* (1982), Dawkins pushed the outer limits of the replicator notion. The genes in an egg are referred to as an organism's *genotype,* and the expression of those genes—say, in an adult bird—are called the *phenotype.* The extended phenotype included its family, social group, tools, and the environments it created (in the case of a bird this might include its nesting behavior and the nest itself). These are part of the physical manifestation of the genes—the extended phenotype of the genetic code. The invisible code of the genes, therefore, influences substantial parts of the environment to the "selfish" advantage of those genes.

The title of *The Blind Watchmaker* (1986) is taken from the allusion to the watch found upon a heath, in *Natural Theology* by **William Paley.** (If someone found a watch in the open countryside, he or she would assume that it had had a maker, a designer. Design implies a designer, and the complexity and interrelations within nature imply the existence of a divine designer or creator.) *The Blind Watchmaker* emphasizes randomness in the evolutionary process: Dawkins uses the phrase "untamed chance." Much variation in nature is random, directionless, and it is the power of natural selection that works on the variation to produce life's diversity. In Dawkins's view, there is no need to invoke any creator.

> *Cumulative selection,* by slow and gradual degrees, . . . is the only explanation that has ever been proposed, for the existence of life's complex design. (*The Blind Watchmaker,* chapter 11)

Dawkins coined the term *meme* in 1976, basing the word on a shortening of the Greek *mimeme* (something imitated), making it sound a little like gene. The concept languished in relative obscurity until the late 1980s and 1990s, when it was enthusiastically adopted by a number of biologists and psychologists. Dawkins used the term to refer to any cultural entity (such as an aspect of fashion, a method of building, a song, an idea, or a religion) that might be considered capable of replicating itself. He hypothesized that many cultural entities could be considered replicators, generally replicating through exposure to humans, who have evolved as efficient (though not perfect) copiers of information and behavior. Memes do not always get copied perfectly, and might indeed become refined, combined with other ideas, or otherwise modified, resulting in the development of new memes, which may themselves prove more (or less) efficient replicators than their predecessors. Cultural evolution could thus be considered to have proceeded in a manner in some ways analogous to the theory of biological evolution based on genes. Memes advantageous to the survival of the individual or group (and the memes it held) would tend to survive, and be replicated; those deleterious would tend to be eliminated. Religion, according to Dawkins, might have survival value and therefore would tend to be perpetuated (whatever the fundamental truth, or otherwise, of its basic tenets).

In 2006, with the publication of *The God Delusion,* Richard Dawkins carried his ideas of a mechanistic universe to their logical conclusion, setting forth his controversial ideas for a militant atheism. Dawkins had, in fact, throughout his career, consistently argued that the concept of God has no role in science. He has campaigned against the teaching of religion in schools, colleges, and universities, and indeed for the elimination of faith-based institutions of education and learning. Some of his most eminent scientific colleagues have been among those who have disagreed absolutely with some of Dawkins's more extreme views.

Professor Richard Dawkins has been much honored (by the **Royal Society,** the Royal Society of Literature, and several universities) for his important reinterpretation of Darwinian ideas and for his outstanding contribution to the public understanding of science, but he is a controversial figure who has generated much heated argument and emotion.

See also: Origin of Life.

Descent of Man

Charles Darwin's second important evolutionary text, published in 1871, in which his ideas were applied to humanity.

In *On the Origin of Species,* published in 1859, Darwin avoided discussing the evolution of humans, although the implications of what he had said for humanity were clear to many. He realized the sensitive nature of this matter, and he waited for over a decade before publishing the work that made this its main theme. As in *On the Origin,* he provided an enormous array of facts arranged to support his strong arguments.

The full title of the work is *The Descent of Man; and Selection in Relation to Sex.* This emphasizes that the book is divided into two parts—in a sense, two rather separate books, which, in the first edition, appeared as two discrete volumes. In subsequent editions they were combined.

In the introduction, Darwin announces:

> The sole object of this work is to consider, firstly, whether man, like every other species, is descended from some pre-existing form; secondly, the manner of his development; and thirdly, the value of the differences between the so-called races of man.

The book is also of great significance because the word "evolution" appears on page 2 (i.e., in the introduction) of the first volume of the first edition. This is the first time the word appears in any of Charles Darwin's works: this anticipates its use in the sixth edition of *On the Origin.*

Chapter 1 rehearses the evidence for the descent of modern man from some lower form. It describes the homologous (similar in form) structures, notes similarities in habits and behavior, and comments on similarities in the diseases that affect humans and other animals, particularly the great apes and monkeys. He also notes the striking similarities in the range of parasites that infect them. The similarity of the embryonic forms of humans and other mammals is noted, along with the presence of rudimentary organs: it is argued, for example, that the thin layer of hairs on the body of most humans is a relic of the thick coat of hair or fur on the bodies of other mammals.

Chapter 2, Manner of Development, applies the concepts set out in *On the Origin* to humans—examples of variation, competition, and "the struggle for existence" are given. Chapters 3 and 4 compare the mental powers of humans and the lower animals, and chapter 5 speculates on the possibility of "the advancement of intellectual powers through natural selection." The final two chapters of Part 1 discuss the various races of humanity and their formation, differentiation, and affinities—in other words, Darwin seeks to apply evolutionary ideas to the various members of the human family.

The second part of the book is devoted to sexual selection. Darwin realized that the principle of natural selection was responsible for the differences between the sexes in animals. Usually (but far from universally) it is the male that is more flamboyant in coloration or has the more elaborate secondary sexual characteristics. Male stag beetles have massive claws or mandibles, peacocks have their striking tails, stags (male deer) may have enormous antlers, male butterflies are frequently much more brightly colored than the females. Male humans have beards and hairy chests. Darwin expresses the notion that these adornments convey a selective advantage: a female was more likely to mate with the male that had the more spectacular adornment, the antlers that led to victory in conflict, or a more striking courtship display. Sexual selection thus provided a special case of natural selection.

The reception of *Descent* was perhaps only marginally less controversial than *On the Origin*. To some extent, he had been preceded by **Thomas Huxley**'s 1862 *Man's Place in Nature*. Nevertheless, in the preface to the second edition, Darwin mentions the "fiery ordeal through which this book has passed." The clamor following *On the Origin* had died down, and the notion of transmutability of species had been accepted by many, but the specific assertion that humans were descended from apelike ancestors still transgressed some Victorian mores.

The book appeared in the United States within months of its release by John Murray in Britain, and had been translated into Dutch, French, German, Italian, Swedish, and Russian within a little over a year—and into several other languages during Darwin's life time. There have been literally hundreds of editions and printings since, in about thirty languages.

DNA

Deoxyribonucleic acid is a complex chemical that contains the genetic instructions for the development of almost all forms of life.

The concept of inheritance was vital to Charles Darwin's theory of **evolution through natural selection.** All life forms vary, and these variations are inherited from one generation to another. The selection of organisms with certain favorable characteristics and their perpetuation in future generations depend on the mechanism of inheritance, about which Darwin understood little. The rediscovery of **Gregor Mendel**'s work early in the twentieth century provided some genetic basis for Darwin's ideas, and the publication of the DNA code in the 1950s explained much of the mechanism of inheritance.

DNA is a polynucleotide; its molecule is a long polymer (a compound formed by the combination of many simpler compounds) of nucleotides, which encodes the sequence of amino acids in proteins using the genetic code.

DNA is thus responsible for the genetic propagation of most inherited characteristics (in humans, for example, these range from eye color and height to resistance to disease). The genetic information encoded by an organism's DNA is often referred to as its genome.

Three groups of scientists in the 1950s were attempting to determine the structure of DNA. The first group to commence was at King's College, London University, under Maurice Wilkins, who later was joined by Rosalind Franklin. Another, much better known, group at the Cavendish Laboratory, Cambridge, was led by Englishman Francis Crick (1916–2004) and American James Watson (born 1928). Yet another group, at the California Institute of Technology in the United States was led by Linus Pauling (1901–1994), who in 1948 discovered that the molecules of many proteins included helical (spiral) shapes. All these individuals and institutions made important contributions to the unraveling of the structure of DNA, although there has been a good deal of controversy (some of it ill tempered) concerning their relative importance.

Crick and Watson built physical models using metal rods and balls, in which they incorporated the known chemical structures of the nucleotides as well as the known position of the linkages between them. At King's College, New Zealander Maurice Wilkins (1916–2004) and Rosalind Franklin (1920–1958) examined X-ray diffraction patterns of DNA. Of the three groups, only the London group was able to produce good quality diffraction patterns and thus produce sufficient quantitative data concerning DNA's structure.

The double helix (twofold spiral) structure allows DNA to replicate itself during cell division. In most organisms, the most DNA is packed onto chromosomes—rodlike structures in the cell nucleus that divide on cell division, carrying the DNA with them. During reproduction, the DNA is transmitted to offspring.

DNA is thought to have originated some 3.5 to 4.6 billion years ago. The replication of the DNA at each cell divi-

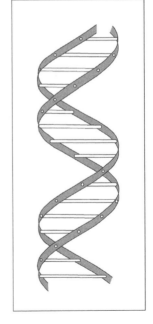

Diagram showing the "double helix" structure of the DNA molecule.

145

sion and reproduction allows the genetic signature (where DNA survives) to be tracked throughout geological time. Similarity in the DNA of two organisms therefore provides powerful evidence they have a similar evolutionary origin. Moreover, the replication of DNA is sometimes less than absolutely perfect: there are occasional "errors" as the DNA is copied; one estimate is that there is 1 to 2 percent change in DNA per million years, but this rate probably varies considerably. (Work near Marlborough Sound, New Zealand, examined the DNA of related fish in two rivers, which, on the basis of geological evidence, were thought to have separated some 100,000 years ago. The differences in the fish DNA suggested a considerably greater rate of change.) In late 2006, it was announced that the DNA from the skull of a 45,000–year-old Neanderthal man from Zagreb in Croatia had been compared to modern human DNA, suggesting that Neanderthal and modern humans diverged about 315,000 years ago. The oldest DNA so far recovered was from plant material 400,000 years old. It is thought highly unlikely that DNA from dinosaur bones hundreds of millions of years old could be recovered, as was hypothesized in the movie *Jurassic Park* and several other movies and TV programs with a similar theme. Nevertheless, the understanding of DNA has provided substantial evidence that Charles Darwin's theory was substantially correct and provides insights to how the evolutionary process proceeds.

FURTHER READING

Crick, Francis. 1990. *What Mad Pursuit: A Personal View of Scientific Discovery.* New York: Perseus Books.

Watson, James D. 1998. *The Double Helix: A Personal Account of the Discovery of the Structure of DNA.* New York: Scribner.

Watson, James D. and F. H. Crick. 1953. "Molecular Structure of Nucleic Acids; A Structure for Deoxyribose Nucleic Acid." *Nature* 171(4356): 737–738.

Domestic Animals

The study of domestic animals was one of Charles Darwin's entry points into his evolutionary ideas and formed the basis of one of his important books.

Several times during the course of the voyage of the *Beagle,* Charles Darwin made careful observations of the different types of domestic animals and plants he encountered, speculating on how changes might have occurred over time, how characteristics might have been inherited, and methods of reproduction. He had, for example, several opportunities of seeing how, when a domestic animal was turned out on a remote island, it sometimes, as he put it, had "retrograded" into an "original form." He noted in March 1834 the vast, aggressive wild bulls on East Falkland that looked "like ancient sculptures," and also observed the behavior of feral horses on the same island. On a tiny islet in the Chonos Archipelago in December of the same year, he observed "there were many wild goats," probably "turned out a century since." "Their colour was pretty uniform," he continued in his diary, "being a dark reddish brown. Many had a white mark on the forehead & a few had one on the lower jaw. All appeared to have a singular outline of forehead." Here was a small, isolated island population that had inherited the characteristics of the founder population. Not far distant, on the island of Chiloé, he noted in detail the vegetative propagation of apples by an unusual method.

In later life, he was something of a landowner, made the acquaintance of farmers, and made a special study of the variation and inheritance of characteristics in populations of the many breeds of the domestic pigeons that he kept at Down House.

The first chapter of *On the Origin of Species* is titled Variation under Domestication and commences as follows:

> When we look to the individuals of the same variety or sub-variety of our older cultivated plants and animals, one of the first points that strikes us, is, that they generally differ much more from each other, than do individuals of any one species or variety in a state of nature.

The artificial selection of particular traits by farmer, stock-breeder, and gardener from the natural variation of plants and animals, he argued, was responsible for the great diversity of breeds domesticated or cultivated by humans. The last words in chapter 1 of *On the Origin* were:

> I am convinced that the accumulative action of Selection, whether applied methodically and more quickly, or unconsciously and more slowly, but more efficiently is by far the predominant Power.

Darwin went on to Variation under Nature in chapter 2, and then Struggle for Existence and Natural Selection. His consideration of the variability of domestic plants and animals is thus the important first element in his argument set out in the book as a whole.

Charles Darwin expanded his ideas in this field in *Variation of Plants and Animals under Domestication,* published in 1868. In this work, his intention was to:

> give under the head of each species only the facts I have been able to collect or observe, showing the amount and nature of the changes which animals and plants have gone undergone whilst under man's dominion, or which bear on the general principles of variation. (chapter 1)

This book was, in fact, the only part of his "Big Species Book" that was published in his life time. (For some years before receiving Wallace's letter—the bolt from the blue—Darwin had been at work on an enormous manuscript on natural selection and evolution [eventually published as *Charles Darwin's Natural Selection* by Cambridge University Press in

1975]. *On the Origin of Species* was merely an "abstract" of this massive work, published in what was an emergency situation.)

In *Variation of Plants and Animals,* he considered cats, dogs, pigs, horses, asses, cattle, sheep, goats, rabbits, chickens, ducks, geese, peacock, turkeys, guinea fowl, goldfish, and hive bees—although his most detailed case study was of pigeons, firmly based on his own research and observations. Cereals and vegetables are also considered. The purpose of the book (which went into several editions) is to show how normal variation is acted on by deliberate selection by humans, and the "accidental" selection pressures of the field and farmyard to produce the diversity of breeds and strains that exist today. Thus it served to drive home one of the main points on which he had based the argument in *On the Origin of Species.*

Down House

The Darwin family home from September 14, 1842, when Charles and his family moved from London, until the death of Emma in 1896. It is now preserved as The Charles Darwin Memorial. The house is situated in the village of Downe in Kent, about 15 miles (24 kilometers) from central London.

Early records show that a Kentish farmer acquired the land on which the present house stands in 1681, and he probably built a house. However, the central portion of the house, as it now exists, was built in 1778. When Charles and Emma moved in, it was said to be dull and unattractive: "a square brick building of three storeys with shabby whitewash." The surroundings were open and bleak.

Rear garden at Down House, after extensions. From: *Letters of Charles Darwin,* 1887.

Soon after the family moved in, they had the adjoining lane lowered and a high flint wall constructed, so that the property was not overlooked; bay windows were built on the garden side of the house, extending up the entire three stories; further building work took place in 1843. A drawing room was added in 1858, and a verandah was constructed on the garden side of this in 1874. A new study constructed on the front of the house in 1877. Today the house gives the impression of a largish, but by no means grand, country house, for the most part whitewashed, rather gaunt in appearance from the front, but attractive and sheltered by trees and shrubberies when viewed from the garden.

After Emma Darwin's death, it was rented for a while. The house had a variety of uses, including a school and a private residence, before coming into the possession of the Royal College of Surgeons in 1952. It is now under the care of English Heritage and is open to the public. The old study in which Darwin wrote most of his books and the drawing room, where he and Emma entertained the likes of **Joseph Hooker** and **Charles Lyell,** are set out very much as they were in the life time of the great naturalist, and they are furnished with many items of furniture and pictures associated with Charles and his family.

To the back of the house is the large garden, which still resembles the garden that Charles Darwin knew, and in which his many children and grandchildren played. One of his daughters, Henrietta (later Mrs. Lichfield) recalled:

> Many gardens are more beautiful but few could have a greater charm, and nowhere do I know one where it was so pleasant to sit out. The flower-beds were under the drawing room windows, and were filled with hardy herbaceous plants, intermixed with bedded-out plants and annuals. It was often untidy but had a particularly gay and varied effect. On the lawn were two yew-trees where the children had their swing. Beyond the row of lime-trees was the orchard, and a long walk bordered with flowering shrubs let through the kitchen garden to the "Sand-Walk." This consisted of a strip of wood planted by my father with varied trees, many being wild cherries and birches, and on one side bordered with hollies. At one end was an old pit, out of which the sand was dug the sand which gave [the path which surrounded the strip of woodland] its name. The walk on one side was always sheltered from the sun and wind, the other sunny, with an outlook over the quiet valley on to the woods beyond, but windy when it blew from the north and east. Here we children played, and here my father took his pacings for forty or more years. (H. Litchfied. 1915. *Emma Darwin: A Century of Family Letters, 1792–1896*)

Many of the trees are gone, but close to the house is a mulberry said to have been planted in 1609. It was described in **Gwen Raverat**'s (Darwin's granddaughter) account of Down House in the late 1880s and 1890s:

> A great old mulberry tree grew right up against the windows. The shadows of the leaves used to shift about on the white floor, and you could hear the plop of the ripe mulberries as they fell to the ground, and the blackbirds sang there in the early mornings. (Gwen Raverat, 1952, *Period Piece,* chapter 8)

While Charles Darwin lived at Down House, he took the part of the village squire, taking an active part in the affairs and institutions of the village. It was also from here that he wrote the greater part of his scientific work; a stream of articles and papers in scientific journals; and his geological studies of *Coral Islands* (1842), *Volcanic Islands* (1844), and the *Geology of South America*. He then devoted over seven years to the detailed study of barnacles (1847–1854). *On the Origin of Species* was published in 1859, following his receipt of a letter from **Alfred Russel Wallace** that contained the draft of

Darwin's study at Down House, 1882. From: *Letters of Charles Darwin*, 1887.

an almost identical theory in 1858. Some of the discussions (with the likes of Charles Lyell and Joseph Hooker) on Charles's publication of his own theory took place in the drawing room at Down House. In 1862 appeared *The Ferilisation of Orchids,* some of the researches for which were done in a greenhouse on the grounds of Down House. Variation of *Animals and Plants under Domestication* appeared in 1868 and included work on pigeons done by Darwin at Down. Darwin's last book, *The Formation of Vegetable Mould through the Action of Worms* (1881), has a special association with Down House; it contains numerous detailed observations made in the Down garden, some made very soon after he moved in. Not far from the house is the "worm stone," a device put there to measure the rate at which the activities of earthworms buried a large circular stone.

Charles Darwin died at Down House on April 19, 1882; it was at first suggested that he should be buried in the Downe village churchyard. But the powers of the nation's scientific establishment intervened, and he was interred in Westminster Abbey. Emma continued to reside at Down House until 1896, although she spent part of the year in Cambridge, where two of her sons and several of her grandchildren lived.

Down House, although close to London, is still surrounded by countryside. It is open to the public and still casts a spell on visitors. In the house and garden, one can feel closer to the great Victorian naturalist than anywhere else.

E

Earthworms

Earthworms belong to a large phylum (major biological group), the Annelida, or the segmented worms. They belong to the class Oligochaeta, which means "few bristles" and refers to the few (usually four) bristles, or *setae,* on each segment of the worm's body. This is in contrast with the many setae of marine annelids in the class Polychaeta ("many bristles").

About 3,000 species of earthworms are known, and they vary in length from a fraction of an inch to nearly 10 feet (a few millimeters to about three meters). There are some freshwater forms, but most earthworms live in the soil, particularly in damp, well-vegetated regions. They were of immense interest and importance to Charles Darwin.

The final paragraph of Darwin's final book, published a few months before his death, reads as follows:

> It may be doubted whether there are many other animals which have played so important a part in the history of the world, as have these lowly organised creatures. Some other animals, however, still more lowly organised, namely corals have done far more conspicuous work in having reefs and islands in the great oceans; but these are almost confined to the tropical zones. (*Vegetable Mould and Earthworms,* chapter 7)

Moreover, among the first scientific papers that Darwin presented to the **Geological Society of London** in 1837, just months after his return from the *Beagle* voyage, were one on coral reefs and one on earthworms and "the formation of mould." Studies of coral organisms and earthworms thus occupied Darwin's mind both at the beginning of his scientific career and at the end, 45 years later. On both occasions, and in relation to both groups of creatures, emphasis was on the immense changes that can be wrought by the long-continued action of very slow processes. Bearing in mind how the theme of gradual change runs though the entire body of Darwin's work, this is of great significance and importance.

Further, this last work, the full title of which was *The Formation of Vegetable Mould through the Action of Worms with Observations on Their Habits*, encapsulates much of what Darwin attempted during his career. It combines the natural history or biological approach—the study of organisms—with the geological approach—the study of the processes that shape the surface of the planet. As the title implies, Darwin considers in detail the behavior of the earthworms (from the *Beagle* days onward, Darwin was ahead of his day in considering the behavior of animals as well as their morphology or form). He uses the experimental approach to investigate earthworms' sensitivity to light, sound, vibration, and other stimuli and also employs quantitative methods. He performed a series of experiments with leaves of different species of trees and triangles of paper to test the worms' ability to recognize and manipulate them into the entrances to their burrows. He presented the results of these tests in a series of statistical tables; again, in doing this, he was somewhat ahead of his time.

But perhaps Darwin's most important contribution in this book is his appreciation of the rate of burial of objects at the surface of the ground through the regular delivery by worms of castings (pellets of soil excreted by worms, the organic matter within the soil having been digested and absorbed) to the surface. As the result of his observations and experiments near his home, he calculated:

> If we assume that they work for only half the year—though this is too low an estimate—then the worms in this field would eject during the year 8.387 pounds per square yard; 18.12 tons per acre, assuming the whole surface to be equally productive in castings. (*Vegetable Mould,* chapter 3)

Darwin backs up such statements by references to how the remains of ancient Roman villas and medieval abbeys have been buried by earthworms' activities. In his garden at Down House, he attached measuring instruments to a large stone to compute the rate of burial accurately. He also emphasizes the role of worms in creating "mould" (the name he gives to the dark, upper layer of the soil) through their burrowing and pulling leaves and other organic material into the soil.

In a chapter of the book titled "The Action of Worms in the Denudation of the Land," Darwin speculates that the burrowing of worms allows air, water, and humic acids to penetrate the soil and affect the parent rock beneath. He goes on: "Not only do worms aid indirectly in the chemical disintegration of rocks, but there is good reason to believe that they likewise act in a direct and mechanical manner on the smaller particles." By comminuting the soil particles that pass through their bodies, the worms reduce them to a fine powder, which is more likely to be washed or blown away.

Thus:

> Worms have played a more important part in the history of the world than most persons would at first suppose. In almost all humid countries they are extraordinarily numerous. . . . In many parts of England a weight of more than ten tons [10,016 kilograms] of dry earth annually passes through their bodies and is brought to the surface on each acre of land. (*Vegetable Mould,* chapter 7)

Elsewhere in the same concluding chapter, he reminds readers that worms have a number of ways of perceiving their environment; are capable of complex behavior in burrowing, lining their burrows with leaves, and, in some species, producing towerlike castings. "They act in nearly the manner as would a man, who had to close a cylindrical tube with different kinds of leaves, petioles, triangles of paper, &c., for they commonly seize such objects by their pointed ends."

In this final chapter, then, of his final book, Darwin sees a continuity between these lowly earthworms and humanity; he emphasizes the importance of gradual change in producing spectacular effects; and he stresses the intimate relationships between organisms and their environment, both physical and biological. These are the three themes that run through Darwin's life and work.

FURTHER READING

Darwin, C. 1881. *The Formation of Vegetable Mould through the Action of Worms.* London: John Murray.

Ecology

The science that deals with relationships among organisms and between organisms and their environment.

The term *oekologie* is said to have been coined in 1866 by the German biologist and firm Darwin supporter Ernst Haeckel (1834–1919), although it seems that Henry David Thoreau (1817–1862), the American philosopher, naturalist, and essayist had already invented it as early as 1855. The word is derived from the Greek *oikos* (home or household) and *logos* (word, study). Ecology is thus the study of the household, or the economy of nature.

The word appeared in the French language for the first time around 1874. Indeed, one of the first enterprises within the discipline of ecology started with a comprehensive study of the Mont Ventoux area in France.

However, long before the subject became established as a discipline in its own right, there were many naturalists who emphasized the relationship between plants and animals and their environment. **John Ray** (1627–1705) frequently wrote of plants in relation to their habitats. Ray, in turn, profoundly influenced **William Paley** (1743–1805), who wrote extensively on the adaptation of organisms to their environment and way of life in *Natural Theology,* a book that Darwin read at Cambridge University. **Alexander von Humboldt** (1769–1859)—the reading of whose book on travels in South America inspired Charles Darwin to undertake the *Beagle* voyage, emphasizes the zonation of plants on mountains in South America. Another influence on Charles Darwin's ecological point of view was his grandfather, **Erasmus Darwin (senior)** (1731–1802), who touched on similar ideas in the poetic *The Botanic Garden* and *Zoonomia.*

Whatever the influences, from an early point in his voyage, Darwin was seeing plants and animals in relation to their surroundings and seeing them as components of whole communities. On the tiny islet of **St. Paul's Rocks,** he noted the limited number of species or organisms and speculated on the links between them. He described, too, how only a few species colonized low islets just emerging from the sea. He detailed the relationship between hermit crabs and the shells of mollusks they colonized.

> The large claw or pincers of some of them [hermit crabs] are most beautifully adapted when drawn back, to form an operculum to the shell, which is as perfect as the proper one which the living molluscous animal formerly possessed. I was assured, & as far as my observations went it was confirmed, that there are certain kinds of these hermits which always use certain kinds of old shells. (*Diary,* April 2, 1836)

There was, in fact, often a tripartite ecological relationship among the hermit crabs, the shells, and the **sea anemones** that lived atop the shells.

One finds in Darwin's writings phrases such as "exquisite adaptation" and "perfectly adapted."

A key notion of modern ecology is that organisms are influenced by abiotic factors (those that are nonliving, such as climate and the salinity of water) and biotic factors (those of other living things). Darwin was alert to this distinction and, for example, noted that the assemblage of coral forms that lived on the wave-swept outer reef of a coral island was different from the corals that inhabited calmer inshore waters, and different again from those of the tranquil lagoon. In the lagoon environment were fish, he noted, that grazed off the living coral, grinding the stony coral material, and excreting "a calcarious sandy mud."

Darwin also understood the existence of whole complexes or communities of plants and animals. The coral reefs he studied on the Cocos Islands and Tahiti—which consisted of the many species of corals, the fish that lived on or among them, the holothuriae (sea cucumbers), and the "numerous burrow-

ing shells, and the nereidous worms that perforate every block of dead coral"—
were all related to one another and were components of a whole community.
Similarly, the eucalyptus of the **Australian** forests that had vertically arranged
leaves with a waxy layer to protect them in the fierce sun, the marsupial mammals, the dry climate, fire, and the Aborigines were all interdependent.

One of the most important developments in twentieth-century ecology
was the development of the *ecosystem* concept by British botanist Sir Arthur
Tansley in 1935. An ecosystem can be defined as a segment of nature, with
all its included organisms, in their environment. An ecosystem thus includes not only the plants, animals, and micro-organisms in a community,
but also the soil, water, and atmosphere, and also the relationships among
all these components. It is the ecosystem—English oakwood, tundra, Canadian boreal forest, Wisconsin lake, Arizona desert, coral island—that is
now the preferred unit of study in ecology.

Although the term ecosystem was not coined until a century after Darwin's voyage, some of his descriptions of environments—tropical forests,
coral reefs, Australian bush, and **kelp and kelp beds**—showed that he understood the concept.

An even wider point that runs through much of Darwin's work is the
idea of a dialogue between living things and their environment. For example, he sees the development of coral islands in terms of a struggle or contest between land and sea. The apparently weak coral organisms grow slowly,
resulting in the building of reefs and atolls despite the power of the waves
and the activities of the creatures that consume the coral structures and
grind them down to particles of sand and mud on the lagoon floor. Natural
selection was another example of the same phenomenon: pressures of the
environment work on the natural variability of living things. The theory of
evolution through natural selection is in fact a very ecological idea. Moreover, because the organisms in ecosystems are strongly linked to one another and the evolution of all the organisms in a community is occurring
simultaneously, it should be noted that ecosystems—whole environments—
are constantly evolving. This comes through in the final elegant paragraph
of *On the Origin of Species*. Darwin perhaps saw in his mind's eye a hedge-
bank in the countryside of Kent, close to where he lived at Downe.

It is interesting to contemplate an entangled bank, clothed with many plants of
many kinds, with birds singing on the bushes, with various insects flitting
about, and with worms crawling through the damp earth, and to reflect that
these elaborately constructed forms, so different from each other, and dependent on each other in so complex a manner, have all been produced by laws
acting around us. These laws, taken in the largest sense, being Growth with
Reproduction; inheritance which is almost implied by reproduction; Variability
from the indirect and direct action of the external conditions of life, and from
use and disuse; a Ratio of Increase so high as to lead to a Struggle for Life, and
as a consequence to Natural Selection, entailing Divergence of Character and

the Extinction of less-improved forms. Thus, from the war of nature, from famine and death, the most exalted object which we are capable of conceiving, namely, the production of the higher animals, directly follows. There is grandeur in this view of life, with its several powers, having been originally breathed into a few forms or into one; and that, whilst this planet has gone cycling on according to the fixed law of gravity, from so simple a beginning endless forms most beautiful and most wonderful have been, and are being, evolved.

Edinburgh

Scottish capital and intellectual and industrial center on the southern shore of the Firth of Forth in eastern Scotland. The location of Charles Darwin's unsuccessful medical training.

Medical training at Edinburgh Medical School was a tradition in the Darwin family. Charles Darwin's grandfather, **Erasmus Darwin,** had undertaken medical training there, as had his father Robert and his brother, also named Erasmus.

The city made a profound effect on the young Charles Darwin, who was sent there by his father in October 1826, at the age of 16. The contrasts it represented were summarized by the two nicknames of the city: "Auld Reekie" on account of the pall of smoke that hung about parts of it and "The Athens of the North" on account of some of its fine classical style buildings. The city is located on and around a group of hills: Castle Rock (348 feet, 106 meters) lies at the center, Arthur's Seat (824 feet, 251 meters) is to the southeast, and Carlton Hill (350 feet, 106 meters) is to the east. The castle dominates the city: its rich mix of architectural styles reflects its complex history and role as a fortress and seat of kings. The tiny St. Margaret's Chapel, Edinburgh's oldest building, dates from 1093. Crown Square, the principal courtyard, was developed in the fifteenth century, and the Great Hall, with its impressive hammerbeam roof, was built by James IV. The Half Moon Battery was created in the late sixteenth century. Edinburgh Castle looms over Princes Street, to the north of which is the classical New Town, largely dating from the eighteenth century, and to the south is the Old Town, dominated by tall tenement buildings, narrow alleys, and dark courtyards. The architecture of the city is austere, and the place has a somber, northern character.

In October 1826, the two Darwin lads rented accommodation on the fourth floor of one of these tall buildings, close to the university. They explored, and were impressed by, the ancient city, with its many fine buildings. On Sundays, they sampled a variety of churches; they occasionally went to the theater. Edinburgh had a reputation for being a cosmopolitan center of learning in a way that Cambridge and Oxford had not. The ancient English universities were Church of England (Anglican) foundations that were not open to dissenters (nonconformists), Catholics, or Jews. North of the border, the situation was different: Scotland was Presbyterian, not Anglican. There were strong links with continental universities, particularly those of Holland and France; students might take a year at Paris or Leiden and return with the latest European ideas.

Edinburgh had the reputation of being the leading medical school in Britain and had much better facilities than English universities. In Charles's year, there were 900 medical students. Yet the school was in decline. He attended lectures in chemistry and geology and medicine; most were uniformly dull. Moreover, the sight of blood disgusted him, and the sight of operations being conducted—in those days without the benefit of anesthesia—was an unbelievable horror. Within 18 months, he knew that medicine was not for him, and he left without a degree.

Nevertheless there were benefits to his time in Edinburgh. He collected marine life along the Firth of Forth and explored the hills, perhaps taking an interest in the varied rock types for the first time. He joined the Plinian Society and both listened to and gave papers on scientific topics. He was befriended by Dr. Robert Edmond Grant, an Edinburgh-born doctor of liberal views who had forsaken the practice of medicine for the study of marine organisms. He was a freethinker and disagreed fundamentally with the doctrines of natural theology. He was a devotee of French revolutionary radical ideas, including the evolutionary notions of **Jean-Baptiste Lamarck.** Although their acquaintance was relatively brief, it was important to the young Darwin. And the smattering of human anatomy Darwin learned served him well. He was always interested in humans, and some of his descriptions of physiognomy of native peoples encountered on the *Beagle* probably owe something to his time in Edinburgh.

Eight Stones

Reputed group of islets in the Atlantic Ocean.

Early in January 1832, a few days into the *Beagle*'s voyage, Darwin wrote his diary: "We looked for the eight stones and passed over the spot where they are laid down on the charts. Perhaps their origin might have been Volcanic and they have since disappeared." Captain Robert FitzRoy's account confirms that they searched hard for the islets, without success. If they ever existed, they no longer do. Volcanic islands sometimes collapse, but regardless of whether this is the explanation for the disappearing Eight Stones, the fact that Darwin considered it is interesting. It implies that at a very early point in the voyage he was already appreciating that he lived in a dynamic, changing world.

Essay of 1844

Darwin's full summary of his evolutionary ideas, written in the summer of 1844.

In the early summer of 1842, Charles Darwin wrote a brief and very rough summary of his ideas on the transmutability of species, probably mainly to clarify his own thoughts: this manuscript has become known as the **Sketch of 1842.** Exactly two years later, he prepared a much fuller treatment, to which the title Essay of 1844 has become attached. This is a much longer document—it runs to 230 pages—and the style is more polished. Some passages are virtually identical with the *Sketch*—for example, the original concluding sentence beginning "There is a grandeur in this view of life." Many of the same themes are taken up, but much greater detail is given, and the notion of the transmutability of species is set out in full. He provides detailed instances of the bearing on his theories of embryology, geographical distributions, affinities between organisms, the flora of remote islands, and "the improbability of finding fossil forms intermediate between existing species." He goes into some detail on the "principles of selection applicable to instincts."

The manuscript is a clear blueprint for his later work. An extract from it appeared in the July 1858 Darwin-Wallace **Linnean Society of London** presentation. Yet some argue that there are subtle differences in emphasis. It has been stated that the Essay is somewhat more Lamarckian than *On the Origin of Species* and that "sports" (the modern term would be mutations) are more prominent in the earlier documents than in *On the Origin* (although there is some variation between the 1859 and later editions).

Darwin clearly attached great importance to the Essay. On July 5, 1844, he wrote a long letter to his wife that begins:

> My Dear Emma,
>
> I have just finished my sketch of my species theory. If, as I believe that my theory is true & it is accepted even by one competent judge, it will be a considerable step in science.
>
> I therefore write this, in case of my sudden death, as my most solemn & last request, which I am sure you will consider the same as if legally entered in my will, that you will devote £400 to its publication, and further will yourself, or through Hensleigh [Wedgwood, Emma's brother], take trouble in promoting it.

He suggests how this was to be accomplished. As well as some competent person receiving the modest honorarium, it was proposed that he receive all Darwin's natural history books that contained relevant material, scored or annotated by Darwin. Possible editors included Charles Lyell, Joseph Hooker, and John Henslow. The notes on possible editorship were amended later. If all else failed, the Essay was to be published as it was.

Two copies of the full manuscript—the original and a fair copy—are held in the Darwin Archive of the Cambridge University Library. The personal memorandum to Emma is in the library of the Natural History Museum in London.

FURTHER READING

de Beer, Gavin, ed. 1958. *Evolution by Natural Selection*. Cambridge, England: Cambridge University Press. This contains the text of the Essay in full at pp. 91–254 and the letter at pp. 35–37.

Evolution, Convergent

The process whereby organisms that are not related come to resemble one another.

Sometimes plants or animals living in widely separated ecosystems and belonging to different biological groups come to resemble one another or assume other characteristics in common. This may be because a similarity in the environments imposes similar selection pressures. Examples include the evolution of winged flight in birds, bats, insects, the extinct pterosaurs, and perhaps flying fish. The lenses of eyes have evolved separately in different groups of animals. Structures that are the result of convergent evolution are sometimes referred to as analogous structures or homoplasies.

The fur of several different groups of mammals has developed into spines for protection, and thus echidnas (monotremes), hedgehogs (insectivores), and porcupines (rodents) look superficially similar. Euphorbias

Mangroves, northwest Australia. The mangrove form has evolved in many different plant groups. Photo: Patrick Armstrong.

161

and cacti have both developed adaptations to survive in dry conditions, and the two plant groups appear similar. The selection pressures imposed by the conditions of gently shelving, muddy tropical shores has led to convergent evolution in many different plant groups to produce mangroves. The mangrove form has evolved in about twenty different plant families.

Evolution, History of the Concept

Originally a general term implying any change over time.

In the eighteenth century, when the term evolution was applied to living beings, it referred to what is now known as embryological development, the development of an embryo or fetus. For Charles Bonnet (1720–1793) and Albrech von Haller (1708–1777), it implied the gradual unrolling of preexisting components.

In a modern sense, the term was first used in 1832 by geologist **Charles Lyell** (1797–1876) when he was discussing the ideas of **Jean-Baptiste Lamarck** (1744–1829), who did not himself used the word. Charles Darwin used the term sparingly: he preferred the terms "mutability of species" or "descent with modification."

Philosopher and psychologist **Herbert Spencer** (1820–1903) was the great popularizer and promoter of the term. Initially he used it to include all forms of progressive or directional development, but later distinguished between embryological development and the "transformation of forms." At the end of the nineteenth century, the word evolution usually implied *progressive* change, or change in the direction of increased sophistication and structural complexity, although Darwin insisted that change did not necessarily mean change in the direction of increased complexity. In the twentieth century, the idea that evolution was necessarily associated with progress weakened. Indeed, the term may be used for a change associated with a *reduction* in the level of complexity. The term is now used for specific examples of change (phylogeny) or for change in general.

The ancient Greek philosophers were the earliest to formulate an evolutionary concept of origins. These philosophers were, however, not scientists or experimentalists; rather they speculated on the origin of the universe in a manner consistent with their religious and philosophical beliefs. Although some of the earliest Greek philosophers considered their gods to be creators, this began to change with the influence of Thales of Miletus (fl 585 B.C.), who founded the Milesian school of philosophy. One of the basic assumptions of this school was that the origin of everything could be explained in terms of its material composition. The origin of things was explained, therefore, by a process of self-assembly from some fundamental material element. Thales believed that water was that basic element from which everything else evolved. Others in this school maintained that air or fire were the fundamental elements from which other entities, including living organisms, were derived.

Heraclitus of Ephesus (535–475 B.C.) advanced the idea of limitless change. He eliminated any necessity for a creator by postulating a constantly changing world with neither beginning nor end.

Empedocles (c. 492–432 B.C.) went further, proposing that everything in the universe evolved from four basic elements—water, air, fire, and earth. He theorized that all parts of living organisms were formed independently and were brought together in random combinations. Combinations that were not well suited to life perished, while the better-suited combinations survived. There are similarities between the ideas of Empedocles and the Darwinian notion of the survival of the fittest—and even in more modern strands of evolutionary thought.

The thinking of Epicurus (341–270 B.C.) also has similarities with modern evolutionary thinkers and cosmologists. He thought that everything in the universe evolved by random combinations of moving elementary particles called atoms! Epicurus was the founder of a philosophical system known as *Epicureanism,* which taught that the universe was eternal and that nothing could influence it from without.

More striking analogies with Darwinian thought can be seen in the Epicurean philosopher Lucretius's *De Rerum Natura* (*On the Nature of Things*) written in the first century B.C. Lucretius came close to Darwin's theory of natural selection when he speculated on the former existence of monstrous creatures that had disappeared through their being unsuited to their changing environment.

Western thought lost sight of these speculations for over a millennium, and the notion of the mutability of life did not reemerge until about the eighteenth century. With the development of modern science and a greater emphasis on an experimental approach and detailed observation, clear ideas emerged on what constituted a species. Species were generally regarded as having been stable and fixed since creation. The date of creation was calculated in 1664 by Archbishop Usher on the basis of information he gleaned from the Bible to have been on October 26, 4004 B.C. (although many other dates were discussed). The assumed young age of the Earth provided relatively little time for change either in the Earth's form or in living things.

The French mathematician-astronomer Pierre de Maupertuis (1698–1759) is often credited with being among the first to develop a coherent theory of evolution. His theory included a process of random change plus natural selection. In his book *Essaie de Cosmologie (Essay on Cosmology)* he argued that chance had produced a vast number of individuals but only a small proportion of these were organized in such a way that the organism's organs could satisfy their needs. A much greater number showed neither adaptation nor order. These ill-adapted forms have all perished. Thus, the living forms seen are only a small proportion of the large number that a blind destiny produced. Benoît de Maillet (1656–1738), **Carl (Carolus) Linnaeus** (1707–1778), and G.L.L. Buffon (1707–1788) were others who suggested that new forms have come into existence during the Earth's history, although these thinkers could not account for the great range of biological diversity or suggest a coherent mechanism.

The first hypothesis that came anywhere near accomplishing this was that of **Jean-Baptiste Lamarck,** who in 1800 advanced the notion that the simplest life forms had formed spontaneously as the result of the interplay of "heat, light, electricity and moisture" and that all others had been successively produced. In his *Philosophie Zoologique (Zoological Philosophy)* in 1809, he maintained that change had been the result of two factors:

- the power of life—the inherent tendency within animal life toward increasing complexity
- the inheritance of acquired characteristics. Animals, he believed, responded to changes in the environment by developing new habits, which in turn led to changes in their structure. These changes could be passed to their offspring, although it might take many generations for the change to be noticeable.

Opponents of Lamarckism argued that the fossil evidence did not reveal the gradual changes between forms that Lamarck's theory required. At the time, the Earth was thought of as being relatively young, and it was considered that there had been insufficient time for the changes to be accomplished.

Etienne Geoffrey St. Hilaire (1772–1844) emphasized that there was a common plan for animals, because not only were there similarities in the basic structure of vertebrates and invertebrates, but indeed between the two groups. He thought that interference at some stage in the early development of the organism—the embryo or fetus—might lead to advancement or holding back—that new species might arise as "monsters."

The idea of development through time was advanced in England in a book titled *Vestiges of the Natural History of Creation* (*Vestiges*), published anonymously in 1844. Long after his death, it was revealed that the author was **Robert Chambers** (1802–1871), a prolific publisher and author from Edinburgh. He, too, emphasized that changes might be occasioned by some dislocation or change in the development of the earlier stages of life of individuals: "All . . . changes may be produced by a mere modification of the embryotic progress." Moreover, although he perceived a hierarchy of complexity—seeing, for example, the egg-laying mammals (platypus, echidna) as more primitive than the **marsupials** (kangaroos, wallabies) and these lower on the scale than the placental mammals—he postulated a branching arrangement.

It has been already intimated, as a general fact, that there is an obvious gradation amongst the families of both the vegetable and animal kingdoms, from the simple lichen and animalcule respectively up to the highest order of dicotyledonous trees and the mammalia. Confining our attention, in the meantime, to the animal kingdom—it does not appear that this gradation passes along one line, on which every form of animal life can be, as it were, strung; there may be branching or double lines at some places. . . . But still it is incontestable that there are general appearances of a scale beginning with the simple and advancing to the complicated. (Robert Chambers, 1844, *Vestiges of the Natural History of Creation.* Soho, England: John Churchill, 191)

Chambers included a treelike diagram to show the divergence of fish, reptiles, and birds from common ancestors. He was vague on the precise mechanisms. He saw development extending from the origin of the Earth from swirling masses of gas, through the geological eras, each with its own assemblage of organisms, this development ultimately including the improvement of humanity.

Darwin remarked that *Vestiges* was important in preparing many people to accept his own theory of evolution. It attracted vitriolic criticism and was, to a modern view, flawed in a number of ways—but it did prepare the ground in a firmer way than did the verses of **Erasmus Darwin (senior)** (Charles's grandfather, 1731–1801), despite the strongly evolutionary flavor of some of these.

The theory of evolution through natural selection was independently developed by Darwin and **Alfred Russel Wallace** (1817–1911). Although vague ideas about the possible mutability of species may have drifted through Charles Darwin's mind while he was aboard the *Beagle,* he did not fully adopt the evolutionary point of view until about March 1837, some months after his return from the sea, while he was sorting his specimens and discussing them with other naturalists in Cambridge and London. However, the mechanism was not entirely clear to him until he read Malthus's *Essay on Population* (probably the 1832 edition) in about September–October 1838.

Darwin spent the next 20 years gathering further evidence to support his ideas by reading, by correspondence, and through observation. He sketched out a brief statement of his views in 1842, elaborating it to the **Essay of 1844** and was, meanwhile, working on his study of **barnacles.** In early June 1858, he received a letter from Alfred Russell Wallace, enclosing a manuscript entitled "On the Tendency of Varieties to Depart Indefinitely from the Original Type." The final words of Wallace's paper were:

We believe we have now shown that there is a tendency in nature to the continued progression of certain classes of varieties further and further from the original type—a progression to which there appears no reason to assign any definite limits. . . . This progression, by minute steps, in various directions, but always checked and balanced by the necessary conditions . . . may . . . be followed out so as to agree with all the phenomena presented by organised beings, their extinction and succession in past ages, and all their extraordinary modifications of form, instinct and habits they exhibit. (*Journal of the Linnean Society (Zoology)* 3 (1859): 45–62)

Darwin was extremely concerned. He wrote to Charles Lyell: "if Wallace had my MS sketch written out in 1842 he could not have made a better short abstract." Many of the phrases used by Wallace echoed terms used by Darwin. Darwin, honorably said that he would forward it to a journal. But, Darwin continued, "my originality . . . will be smashed." Charles Lyell and Darwin's other close scientific friend, **Joseph Hooker,** acted promptly. In just over a fortnight, they had obtained from Darwin a brief summary of his ideas, the text of a letter he had written to **Asa Gray** in the United States dated September 6, 1857, and Wallace's manuscript and made a joint presentation to the **Linnean Society of London** on July 1. The cobbled-together paper was published the following August. Justice had been done to both parties, although neither Wallace nor Darwin was present. Wallace was in the Dutch East Indies; Darwin remained at Down House because he had other matters on his mind: His baby son (Charles Waring) had died of scarlet fever on June 28 after a final few hours that were "miserable beyond expression"; his daughter Henrietta had diphtheria; and his sister Marianne had just died.

For many years, Charles Darwin had been collecting material for and writing what he called his Big Species book. It was still far from finished in July 1858, and it would have taken years to complete it. He therefore commenced writing an abstract or condensed version of this while on holiday on the Isle of Wight (on the south coast of England) in late July 1858. He must have worked at a relentless pace considering the burden of the bereavements and anxieties of a few weeks before. He wrote that he completed 44 pages in one evening. The manuscript of *On the Origin of Species by Means of Natural Selection, or the Preservation of Favoured Races in the Struggle for Life* was, remarkably, completed by March the following year. It was published in November 1859.

Whereas the evolutionary writings of Erasmus Darwin, Lamarck, Chambers, and the rest had been speculative and, on the whole, not enthusiastically received, Darwin's *On the Origin of Species* was the volume that made evolutionary ideas scientifically respectable. By providing far more evidence than the earlier theorists had and by suggesting natural selection as a mechanism, coupled with the notion of adaptation to environment with its echoes of William Paley, Darwin broke new ground. He backed his theories with evidence from many fields of science: the variation in domestic animals and plants, the geographical distribution of organisms, comparative anatomy, embryology, animal behavior, and paleontology. He did not avoid difficulties, and he gained the support of distinguished scientists such as Thomas Huxley and Joseph Hooker. In the United States, Asa Gray at Harvard University was a firm supporter.

Darwin never asserted that natural selection was the only process involved in evolution, and in the later editions of *On the Origin,* he modified his approach slightly, even tilting slightly toward Lamarckism (it should be remembered that the mechanisms of heredity were not fully understood). In

Descent of Man (1871), he speculates on sexual selection—the idea that the selection of one sex by another might provide a mechanism for evolution.

The latter years of the nineteenth century saw the widespread acceptance of evolution and of wide-scale attempts to accumulate evidence for it—particularly from paleontology. For example, the discovery in the 1860s of specimens of ***Archaeopteryx*** from late Jurassic rocks in Germany provided evidence for a link between reptiles and birds. Later, a small horselike fossil was discovered in North America, to which the name *Eohippus* was given (it is now called *Hyracotherium*). A sequence of horse fossils from *Eohippus* to the modern horse (*Equus*) was described and given wide publicity by Thomas Huxley, among others. Museums, including the American Museum of Natural History and the British Natural History Museum in London assembled popular exhibits showing the evolution of the horse. Other examples of gradations through a sequence of fossils such as the Ammonites were documented. Nevertheless, the incompleteness of the fossil record and the relative rarity of transitional forms remained a problem.

Late in the nineteenth century, Fritz Muller (1822–1897) and Ernst Haeckel (1834–1919), the person who coined the term **ecology,** developed the notion of the **recapitulation** of an organism's evolutionary history during its life history. A mammal, therefore, was seen to develop from a single-celled organism (the fertilized egg) through a fishlike ancestor (the young embryo) to the modern form during the gestation period.

But despite the contributions of the embryologists and paleontologists, by the end of the nineteenth century, the exact nature of the mechanisms of heredity and of variation were still not understood. There was even a resurgence of Lamarckian ideas. It was only after about 1900 that **Gregor Mendel**'s (1822–1884) work in the monastery garden at Brno in what is now the Slovak Republic became well known and theory of particulate inheritance (the idea that individual characteristics were passed to succeeding generations as separate units and in accordance with ascertainable rules and ratios) could be blended with Darwinian evolution through natural selection. The complete reconciliation of Mendelian genetics with Darwin's natural selection was an interdisciplinary enterprise. Field naturalists and ecologists familiar with the adaptation of organisms and the details of geographical variations and speciation emphasized the idea of a species as a population (perhaps showing considerable variation) rather than an ideal type. Experimental biologists such as Wilhelm Johannsen (1857–1927) showed the distinction between the phenotype (the appearance of the organism, which might change with time) and the genotype (which was fixed for life). They also showed that mutations (striking, random, genetic changes) could be inherited in a Mendelian manner. Population geneticists put forward mathematical models suggesting how factors such as mutation rate, selection, recombination, immigration, and emigration might affect the frequencies of particular genes in a population. The analysis of genes in natural populations was pioneered in Russia (former Soviet Union) by Sergei Chetverikov (1880–1959) and further developed in the United States by his student Theodosius Dobzhansky (1900–1975). The synthesis of Mendelism and evolution through natural selection could be said to be largely achieved through the publication of *Evolution: The Modern Synthesis* by Julian Huxley (1887–1975, Thomas Huxley's grandson) in 1942.

In 1953, collaboration between English physicist Francis Crick (1916–2004) and American biologist James Dewey Watson (1928–) led to the proposal of the double-helical structure for **DNA** and an explanation of the replication scheme that was responsible for the one-way movement of information from gene to organism and its flow from generation to generation.

Nevertheless, the problems of gaps in the evolutionary sequence and the incompleteness of the fossil record to some extent remained. Ernst Mayr (1904–2005) attempted to solve this difficulty through the concept of the peripheral isolate—a small section of the population, separated for a period, possibly a long period, from its parent population, perhaps by climatic change (e.g., the separation of the continuous band of the tropical rain forest into a number of separate "islands" of forest during the cooler, dryer weather of the quaternary [the Ice Age]). The idea of the peripheral isolate needs to be considered alongside the theory of punctuated equilibrium that was suggested by Neil Eldredge and **Stephen Jay Gould** (1941–2002) in the 1970s. They suggested that in isolated populations, because of factors such as relatively small population numbers and limited range of variation, speciation (the evolution of new species) would be relatively rapid. This, they argued, might explain why the fossil record shows relative stability of a species form for long periods and the rapidity with which a new species appears. In other words, they argue that long periods of stability or equilibrium alternate with intervals of much more rapid change.

Eldredge and Gould were among those who argued that the concept of natural selection might occur at various levels—at the level of the individual, the population, the species, or some larger unit such as the family, class, or phylum. Oxford zoologist **Richard Dawkins** (1942–) in a series of popular books including *The Selfish Gene* (1976), *The Blind Watchmaker* (1986), and *Climbing Mount Improbable* (1996) has suggested that selection occurs most significantly at the level of the gene. He divided the world between replicators—structures that can be copied, such as DNA molecules—and vehicles—the devices that enable the copying to occur, the organisms. Dawkins further suggests that there are certain ideas or beliefs (for example, religious ideas) that confer a selection advantage in human populations: he calls these *memes*. He argues that people holding certain religious or ethical ideas will tend to pass them on to those close to them, including their offspring, and that, if holding these beliefs confers some advantage, they and the ideas will tend to prosper and expand. Some of Dawkins's suggestions have been controversial. Evolutionary ideas compete with one another in a Darwinian way, and will continue to evolve.

FURTHER READING

Darwin, Charles R. 1859. *On the Origin of Species.* London: John Murray. Many subsequent editions.

Dawkins, Richard. 1976. *The Selfish Gene.* Oxford, England: Oxford University Press (revised 1989).

Dawkins, Richard. 1986. *The Blind Watchmaker.* London: Longmans (revised 1991).

Gould, Stephen J. and Neil Eldredge. 1977. "Punctuated Equilibria: The Tempo and Mode of Evolution Reconsidered." *Paleobiology* 3:115–151.

Huxley, Julian. 1942. *Evolution: The Modern Synthesis.* London: George Allen and Unwin.

Evolution, Saltatory

The evolution of new species or major biological groups through a major jump, perhaps through the large-scale repatterning of chromosomes rather than as the result of gradual change. It might be considered an extreme form of **punctuated equilibrium.** It is probably rare.

See also: Evolution through Natural Selection; Gould, Stephen Jay.

Evolutionary Ideas after On the Origin

Although most scientists came to accept the essential truth of Darwin's ideas within two decades of the publication of his book in 1859, there have been subtle changes of emphasis.

Darwin's friend **Thomas Huxley** became a vigorous supporter of the theory of evolution and specifically used his knowledge of the anatomy of apes to argue for human evolution in his 1863 *Evidence as to Man's Place in Nature.* Darwin took up this challenge in *Descent of Man,* published in 1871. His earlier **On the Origin of Species** was somewhat ambivalent on the evolution of humans and says little about it.

The evolutionary theme runs through much of Darwin's later work: for example, his *The Expression of Emotion in Man and Animals,* published in 1872, has a profoundly evolutionary taint. Even the title implies a similarity in the emotions and behavior of animals and humans and a unity between them.

Darwin never assumed that natural selection was the only mechanism of evolution, although *On the Origin* clearly implies that it is the dominant one. Nevertheless, the idea is briefly alluded to:

> Sexual Selection . . . depends not on a struggle for existence, but on a struggle between the males for the possession of the females; the result is not death of the unsuccessful competitor, but few or no offspring. Sexual selection is therefore less rigorous than natural selection. (*On the Origin,* first edition, chapter 4)

In *Descent of Man,* the subtitle of which was *Selection in Relation to Sex,* the idea is developed at greater length. It has even been suggested that there are traces of Lamarckian theory—the idea that characteristics are acquired during the life time of an individual organism—can be detected in some of the later editions of the *On the Origin*.

With the exception of traditionalists such as comparative anatomist **Richard Owen** (who was at one time friendly with Darwin and wrote the *Fossil Mammalia* volume of *The Zoology of the Beagle*) and Louis Agassiz, many late Victorian scientists embraced the theory of evolution and the grand sweep it represented. However, many had difficulties with Darwin's proposed mechanism for evolution. Some scientists actively opposed the suggestion that it was natural selection that was the primary driver of evolution. Many were unhappy about the idea of the importance of chance and of random variation in Darwin's schema. **John F. W. Herschel** is alleged to have described *On the Origin* as "the law of higgledy-piggledy" and in 1861 wrote that:

> An intelligence, guided by a purpose, must be continually in action to bias the direction of the steps of change—to regulate their amount—to limit their divergence—and to continue them in a definite course. (John F. W. Herschel, *Physical Geography*, 1861, 12)

The notion of undirected evolution in the face of what could be interpreted as a steady progress from primitive forms of life to modern, civilized humanity seemed unsatisfactory. There must surely be something purposeful or directional in the steady march from the primeval slime to the English country gentleman. On the European continent, Ernst Haeckel's *History of Creation* (1876) and *Evolution of Man* (1879) represented expressions of the directionality of evolution. Evolution was represented as a tree with humanity atop it. The early exponents of Mendelian genetics tended to see **Gregor Mendel**'s ideas as an alternative to Darwin's evolutionary framework. Some historians of science see an eclipse of Darwinism in the late nineteenth and early twentieth centuries. Another problem that Darwin acknowledges and that preoccupied late Victorian and some early twentieth-century scientists was the absence of **transitional forms** both in the fossil record and among living plants and animals—hence the idea that evolution had proceeded by a series of "saltations" or sudden jumps rather than through gradual adaptation. This idea has some similarities with the notion of **punctuated equilibrium** espoused by **Stephen Jay Gould** in the late twentieth century. An attack from a different direction came from physicists. William Thomson (later Lord Kelvin) argued that the Earth was gradually cooling and could not have existed in its present state for long enough to provide the time for the very slow process of evolution through natural selection to have taken its slow course (it is now known that radioactivity provides a source of energy to maintain the heat of the inner Earth for immense periods of time). Physical scientists also criticized Darwin's methodology, which was quite different from the established experimental approach: there was no experimental evidence that natural selection could produce new species, and the theory did not make testable predictions.

Thus, while the notion of a broad sweep of evolution persisted, variations circulated—some involving divine intervention, some Lamarckian in character, and some emphasizing saltatory change.

In the 1930s, however, a number of biologists, geneticists, and statisticians (particularly R. A. Fisher) developed the *modern synthesis of evolution*, which merged Darwinian selection theory with more sophisticated statistical understandings of Mendelian genetics. The understanding of the role of chromosomes in the cell made clear how the inheritance of characteristics and the variations on which natural selection depended could occur. Further evidence for evolution came from biogeography—the study of the geographical distributions of plants and animals. A critical point came with the 1942 publication of *Evolution: The Modern Synthesis* by Julian Huxley (grandson of Darwin's friend Thomas Huxley). Later still, further reinforcement came from the understanding of the molecular structure of **DNA** and of the nature of mutations.

See also: Hooker, Joseph Dalton.

FURTHER READING

Bowler, P. J. 1990. *Charles Darwin: The Man and His Influence*. Cambridge, England: Cambridge University Press.
Huxley, Julian. 1942. *Evolution: The Modern Synthesis*. London: George Allen and Unwin.

Evolution of the Horse

In the 1870s, Othniel Charles Marsh (1831–1899) published descriptions of some recently discovered horse fossils from North America. At that time, few **transitional forms** were known apart from *Archaeopteryx*. The sequence of horse fossils that Marsh described (and that **Thomas Huxley** widely publicized) was presented as an example of evolution taking place in a single lineage. It was apparently possible to trace the history of horses from the fossil species *Eohippus* (now called *Hyracotherium*) through a series of clear intermediates, which were eventually transformed into their very different-looking descendent, the modern horse (*Equus*).

Later, the American Museum of Natural History in New York City assembled an exhibit of these fossil horses, designed to show this gradual evolution from *Eohippus* (literally "dawn horse") to modern *Equus*. Such exhibits directed attention to the horse family not only as evidence for evolution, but to a model of gradual, straight-line evolution, with *Equus* being the end point or goal of the evolutionary sequence. This version of the horse family history was included in many biology textbooks.

Hyracotherium was a small forest creature of the early Eocene epoch, about 55 million years ago. This animal was 10 to 20 inches (30 to 50 centimeters) tall at the shoulder and had a somewhat doglike appearance, with an arched back, stumpy neck, short snout, short legs, and long tail. It was an herbivore, browsing on fruit and foliage. Its legs were flexible and rotatable, with all major bones present and unfused. The skeleton had the typical mammalian structure, and there were four toes on each front foot and three on the hind feet. Traces of the first (in front) and second (rear) toes were present. It had a relatively small brain with particularly small frontal lobes. It had the typical dentition of a browsing mammal with low-crowned teeth with three incisors, a single canine, four distinct premolars, and three grinding molars in each side of each jaw.

In the early middle Eocene epoch (approximately 50 million years ago), there was a transition from *Hyracotherium* to a close relative, *Orohippus.* However, the vestiges of the first and second toes had disappeared. There was also a significant change in the teeth. The last premolar had become more like a molar, giving *Orohippus* one more grinding tooth. Also, the crests on the teeth were more pronounced, suggesting that *Orohippus* was eating tougher plant material.

Mesohippus appeared in the late Eocene epoch (approximately 40 million years ago) as the climate of North America was becoming dryer, the grasslands were expanding, and the forests were shrinking. This creature was a little larger than *Epihippus,* its back was less arched, the legs and neck a little longer. *Mesohippus* had three toes on its hind and front feet, and the fourth front toe had been reduced to a vestigial fragment. Its cerebral hemispheres were notably larger and its brain more distinctly equine. Also, its last three premolars resembled molars, so that the animal had six similar grinding teeth, with one premolar in front. Like *Epihippus, Mesohippus* had sharp and well-formed tooth crests for chewing tougher vegetation.

In the Miocene epoch (about 18 million years ago), horses became specialized more to eating grasses. Teeth became better adapted for chewing stringy, fibrous stems. The crests on the teeth enlarged and came together in a series of distinctive ridgelike structures for grinding. Moreover, there was a gradual increase in the crown, the teeth developed the capacity to grow out of the gum continuously as the tops were worn down, and they became harder.

Horses also became specialized runners: there was an increase in body size, leg length, and length of the head. The bones of the legs began to fuse, and the leg bones and muscle system became adapted for efficient forward-and-back strides. Most significantly, the horses began to permanently stand on tiptoe (another adaptation for speed). *Merychippus* was about 40 inches (1.1 meters) high.

A one-toed horse called *Dinohippus* arose about 12 million years ago. Its precise ancestor is uncertain. The early species in this genus are *D. spectans, D. interpolatus,* and *D. leidyanus.* They look remarkably like modern horses in their foot structure, dentition, and form of the skull. The teeth were somewhat straighter than those of *Merychippus.* A later species, *D. mexicanus,* had even straighter teeth and a skull structure even more like modern forms. *Dinohippus* was the most common horse in North America in the late Pliocene epoch and may have given rise to *Equus*.

Equus appears on the scene about four million years ago; this is the genus that includes all modern equines. The first *Equus* species were about 52 inches (1.33 meters) tall—the size of a small pony—with a classic horselike body: a rigid spine, long neck, long legs, fused leg bones with no rotation, a long nose, flexible muzzle, and deep jaw. The brain was somewhat larger than in earlier forms. The genus *Equus* was (and is) one-toed, with side ligaments that prevent twisting of the hoof, and has high-crowned, straight grazing teeth with strong crests lined with hard cement. It should be noted that six species of *Equus* survived into modern times: three species of African zebra, the true horse (*E. caballus*), the donkey (*E. asinus*), and the kiang (*E. hemionus*) of the deserts of Asia. Ironically, the horse became extinct in North America, the locale of much of its important evolution, shortly after the end of the Ice Age, about 7,000 years ago, only to be reintroduced by the Spaniards in the late fifteenth and sixteenth centuries.

Certain trends can be identified in the sequence that can be attributed to adaptation to an open plains rather than a forest environment: larger size; limbs adapted for speed rather than a life creeping through the undergrowth; teeth adapted to eating tough, silica-rich grasses rather than soft, leafy foliage. However, there are complexities. In the Miocene epoch (about 24 million years ago), there appeared a short-lived group of small horses such as *Archeohippus*. And in different lineages, the various changes proceeded at different rates. There appears to be a trend from multi-toed to single-toed forms, because the three-toed horse became extinct relatively recently. If just one or two three-toed horse species had survived, the generalization would be less valid. As new fossils have been discovered, it has became clear that the old straight-line model of horse evolution is unsatisfactory. In some cases, a lineage can be traced through several species, but sometimes species split from one another. At certain times, there seems to have been a burst, with many new forms developing within a comparatively short time. There are also dead ends—isolated branches that led nowhere, the species making them up becoming extinct and leaving no progeny. A branching model is perhaps more appropriate in the case of the horses, as it is in the case of many other fossil groups (including humans). Another complexity is that members of the genus *Equus* still seem to retain the genes for making side toes. Usually these express themselves as the vestigial splint bones of the second and fourth toes around the large central third toe. But sometimes a modern horse appears with small but fully formed side toes. Genes may lie latent within a population and might reassert themselves should conditions change.

FURTHER READING

Gould, Steven Jay. 1983. *Hen's Teeth and Horses' Toes*. New York: W. W. Norton & Co.

Gould, Steven Jay. 1992. "The Case of the Creeping Fox Terrier Clone." *Bully for Brontosaurus: Reflections in Natural History*. New York: W. W. Norton & Co., 155–167.

MacFadden, Bruce J. 1988. "Horses, the Fossil Record, and Evolution: A Current Perspective." *Evolutionary Biology* 22: 131–158.

MacFadden, Bruce J. 1992. *Fossil Horses: Systematics, Paleobiology and Evolution of the Family Equidae.* Cambridge, England: Cambridge University Press.

Simpson, George Gaylord. 1951. *Horses.* Oxford, England: Oxford University Press. (A 1971 reprint is much outdated but a classic reference.)

Evolution through Natural Selection

Charles Darwin's principle theory, set out with great clarity in his book ***On the Origin of Species,*** published in November 1859.

The basic theory is based on a limited number of generalizations and the inferences that can be drawn from them.

- Species of plants and animals are frequently very fertile. Far more offspring are produced than can survive to adulthood.
- Populations remain approximately constant over the long term, albeit with modest fluctuations.
- Food and other resources are finite, and they are relatively constant most of the time.
- From the above three observations, it may be inferred that, in an environment, there will be a struggle for survival among individuals or competition between them.

Adaptation to environment: The baobab (*Adansonia gregorii*) in northern Australia has an immensely swollen trunk to store water through a long tropical dry season. Photo: Patrick Armstrong.

Adaptation to environment: the European snipe (*Gallinago gallinago*) showing concealing coloration (camouflage). Photo: the late Edward Armstrong.

- In sexually reproducing species, generally no two individuals are identical. Variation is almost universal.
- Much of this variation is heritable; it is passed on from one generation to the next.
- Therefore, in a world of stable populations where each individual struggles to survive, the individuals with the best, fittest, or most favorable characteristics will be more likely to survive, and these traits will be passed to their offspring.
- These advantageous characteristics are then inherited by following generations, becoming dominant among the population through time. This is natural selection.
- Plants and animals, therefore, through time, become adapted to their environment.

See also: Evolution, History of the Concept.

Expression of Emotions

Short title of book published in 1872 comparing human and animal behavior; the culmination of Charles Darwin's many decades of work on animal behavior and psychology.

From his earliest days aboard HMS *Beagle,* Darwin displayed a high degree of interest in the behavior of animals. In the **Cape Verde Islands,** he noted the movements, behavior, and change in color of the octopus. In South America, he observed the habits and songs of birds. He noted also the extraordinary tameness of birds on remote islands and the behavior of feral cattle on the **Falkland Islands** and of goats on islands off South America. He experimented on the irritability and powers of perception of organisms as varied as **sea anemones** and **planaria** (flatworms). He collected the elaborate nests of some insects. Later he made extensive observations of the behavior of primates and other animals at London Zoo.

The full title of the work was *The Expression of Emotions in Man and Animals,* and the book represented the third stage in Darwin's long campaign to demonstrate that humans have evolved from other species of animals. Many human emotions and mental abilities can be seen in animal ancestors. Darwin gives many striking examples based on his detailed observations over many years. He attempts to establish a conceptual framework for the study of human and animal emotions and, in doing so, provided an important part of the basis of modern psychology and ethology (the study of animal behavior).

I will begin by giving the three Principles, which appear to me to account for most of the expressions and gestures involuntarily used by man and the lower animals, under the influence of various emotions and sensations. I arrived, however, at these three Principles only at the close of my observations. . . .

I. *The principle of serviceable associated Habits.*—Certain complex actions are of direct or indirect service under certain states of the mind, in order to relieve or gratify certain sensations, desires, &c.; and whenever the same state of mind is induced, however feebly, there is a tendency through the force of habit and association for the same movements to be performed, though they may not then be of the least use. Some actions ordinarily associated through habit with certain states of the mind may be partially repressed through the will, and in such cases the muscles which are least under the separate control of the will are the most liable still to act, causing movements which we recognize as expressive. In certain other cases the checking of one habitual movement requires other slight movements; and these are likewise expressive.

II. *The principle of Antithesis.*—Certain states of the mind lead to certain habitual actions, which are of service, as under our first principle. Now when a directly opposite state of mind is induced, there is a strong and involuntary tendency to the performance of movements of a directly opposite nature, though these are of no use; and such movements are in some cases highly expressive.

III. The principle of actions due to the constitution of the Nervous System, independently from the first of the Will, and independently to a certain extent of Habit.—When the sensorium is strongly excited, nerve-force is generated in excess, and is transmitted in certain definite directions, depending on the connection of the nerve-cells, and partly on habit: or the supply of nerve-force may, as it appears, be interrupted. Effects are around broad themes and his effective laying of the foundations of a new subject were formidable achievements. When one appreciates that his work on psychology and behavior was proceeding alongside his efforts in biology (both zoology and botany) and geology, one can hardly fail to be impressed by Darwin's genius.

See also: Child Development; Evolution through Natural Selection; Instinct; *On the Origin of Species.*

thus produced which we recognize as expressive. This third princi}
may, for the sake of brevity, be called that of the direct action of t
nervous system.

These principles might be expressed differently today, but the in
tance of these great themes remains. Darwin elaborates on these ide
the first three chapters of the book.

Chapter 4 is on the "Means of Expression in Animals." He discusse
the vocal expressions of sound, concentrating on birds and mammal
goes on to consider nonvocal sounds, such the rattling of the quill:
porcupine, the thumping of the ground by rabbits, and the sounds
birds produce with their feathers. He goes on to list many examples of
sound communication and expression of emotions, such as the erecti
the dermal appendages, hairs, and feathers under the emotions of ango
terror and the drawing back of the ears by some mammals as a prepa:
for fighting and as an expression of anger, together with the erection
ears and the raising the head as a sign of attention or concentration. (
ter 5 gives some examples of special expressions of dogs, cats, rumi
horses, and monkeys. For example, Darwin illustrates the posture of
when terrified, arching its back, perhaps attempting to make it seem a:
as possible. Appropriate comparisons with human responses are mad

Most of the remaining chapters discuss and provide detail on s}
human emotions such as suffering, anxiety, grief, despair, joy, dev
hatred, anger, contempt, disgust, guilt, pride, surprise, and fear.

The final chapter emphasizes the evolutionary significance of em
and behavior. The importance of inheritance in behavior is empha
many animals display behavior that could not possibly have been l
from copying others. The similarity and differences in how emotio
displayed is discussed in some detail. The penultimate paragraph
book reads:

> We have seen that the study of the theory of expression confirms to a cer
> limited extent the conclusion that man is derived from some lower an
> form, and supports the belief of the specific or sub-specific unity of the se
> races; but as far as my judgment serves, such confirmation was hardly nee
> (*Expression of Emotions*, chapter 14)

Some might argue that Darwin pushes his argument too far. In st
the essential unity of animal life and the common origins of huma
animals he becomes too anthropomorphic, attributing to animals di:
human emotions and values—for example, when he describes the
that a dog has for its puppies or the manner in which a dog licks a c
which it is "friends." From a modern perspective, this may be fai
ment, but Darwin was working in his own time with the vocabular
able to him. His organization of a tremendous wealth of observe

F

Falkland Islands

A group of islands in the southwest Atlantic Ocean, about 280 miles (450 kilometers) northeast of the island of **Tierra del Fuego** and about 370 miles (600 kilometers) east of **Patagonia** in Argentina. Visited twice by Darwin.

The islands lie between the latitudes of 51° and 52° 30' S and between 57° 30' and 61° 30' W longitude. The two main islands—West Falkland and East Falkland—have areas of about 1,300 and 2,000 square miles, respectively (approximately 3,500 and 5,000 square kilometers) and are separated by the long, narrow expanse of Falkland Sound. There are many hundreds of smaller islands. The climate is described as subantarctic; although there is not a great deal of snow, the islands are exceedingly bleak and windswept, and the terrestrial vegetation is mostly scrubby, open moorland. The seas surrounding the islands abound with rich beds of giant seaweeds—**kelp beds.** Geologically, the rocks are related to those of South Africa, from which the Falklands miniplate broke off at the time of fragmentation of the former Southern Hemisphere land mass of Gondwana, over 100 million years ago. The principal settlement today is the little town of Stanley (East Falkland). The present population of the archipelago, including British military personnel, is a little more than 2,000.

HMS *Beagle* visited the Falklands twice—March 1 to April 6, 1833, and March 9 to April 7, 1834—during which periods the ship remained close

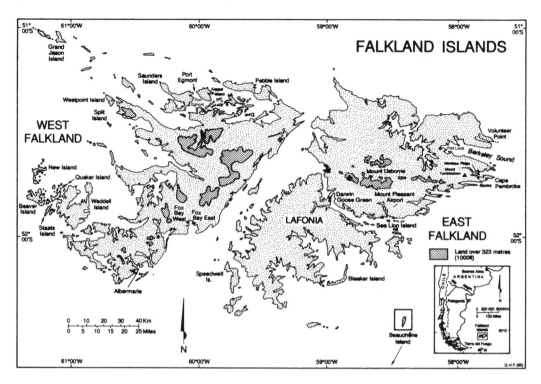

Map of the Falkland Islands. Map drawn at Geography Department, University of Western Australia.

to the tiny settlement of Port Louis. It is thought that the visits (which alternated with visits to Tierra del Fuego) were of considerable importance to Charles Darwin's intellectual development.

During his two visits, Darwin explored a good deal of East Falkland (he probably did not land on West Falkland, although others from the expedition did, and they provided him with information). He beachcombed along the shores of Berkeley Sound, collecting a wide variety of forms of marine life, explored well to the north and to the south of Port Louis, and traveled overland with a group of gauchos to a point close to the present settlements of Goose Green and Darwin. His experiences on East Falkland, where he spent more time than at many of his ports of call and covered dozens of pages with his notes, were pivotal. He had with him Lyell's *Principles of Geology,* which espoused a gradualist or uniformitarian view of the world's development rather than a catastrophist interpretation, which emphasized sudden dramatic change and was then widely accepted. On East Falkland, Darwin was between these two extremes: he observed the processes of gradual erosion and deposition, but also (in the privacy of his own notes) speculated that the stone runs might have been created by earthquakes shaking rock masses from the nearby mountains. (Stone runs are a characteristic element in the Falklands landscape; they are glacierlike masses of angular boulders, up to a mile in length and several hundred yards in width.

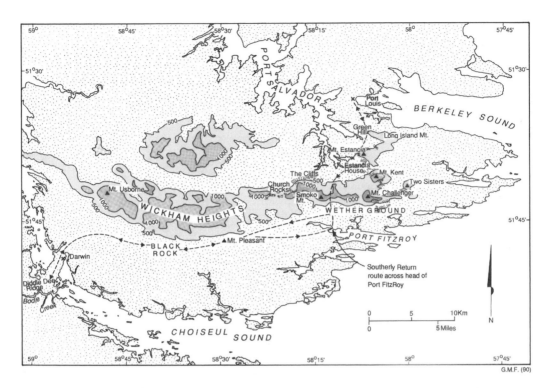

Map showing Darwin's overland journey, East Falkland, 1834. Map drawn at Geography Department, University of Western Australia.

Open moorland, East Falkland. Photo: Patrick Armstrong.

They are now thought to have been created by frost action when the climate was colder.)

He noted that the foxes (or **warrahs**) from East and West Falkland were different, long before he made a comparable observation on the birds of the Galapagos Islands. He did not describe the kelp beds of Berkeley Sound as ecosystems, but described the tight network of relationships of the organisms within them in a remarkably integrated way.

The folded strata of the islands confirmed in his mind that he lived in a dynamic, changing world. He compared the barren moorlands of East Falkland with the richness of the warm shallow seas of the Paleozoic, evidence of which he found in fossiliferous strata near Port Louis, understanding, therefore, that the climate and environment must have changed. He also contrasted the species-poor terrestrial environment with the kelp beds that were full of marine life of many kinds. He described the behavior of birds, such as penguins and caracaras (a bird of prey) at a time when morphology and appearance were considered by naturalists to be more important, opening the way for his later psychological studies (e.g., *The Expression of Emotions in Animals and Man*); he was particularly struck by the tameness in organisms. He noted that some invertebrate forms he found in the sound produced tens of thousands of eggs and yet were not numerous—just a step away from the ideas of competition and natural selection expressed in *On the Origin of Species*. He observed the appearance

Stone runs, East Falkland. Photo: Patrick Armstrong.

and behavior of the feral cattle and horses: one of his entry points to evolutionary ideas, much later, was through the study of **domestic animals** (*Animals and Plants under Domestication*). He wondered about the mechanisms of dispersal of plants and animals to the islands, noticing that some of the forms found on the Falklands were similar to those of Tierra del Fuego, at the southern tip of South America—which led him to speculate about **long-distance dispersal.** He wondered, for example, whether "furious gales" or migrating birds might be partly responsible for the transport of plants from South America. These ruminations are important, because long-distance dispersal can be seen as the handmaiden of evolution. If all life has evolved from a common origin or is derived from a very few simple forms, then it follows that living beings on remote islands (or their possibly remote ancestors) must have made the journey thither.

There were other events of a more personal nature that influenced Darwin's impressions of the Falklands. During the 1833 visit, one of his shipmates, E. H. Hellyer, the captain's clerk, drowned, tangled in kelp while attempting to recover a bird specimen, and was buried on "a lonely headland." The shores of Berkeley Sound were strewn with the wreckage of ships: the French whaling ship *La Magellan* had come to grief a few months before, and the crew was living in improvised tents made from sails. Captain **Robert FitzRoy** had to make arrangements for their repatriation. On the second (1834) visit, it was discovered that several murders had been

Stone runs, East Falkland (detail). Photo: Patrick Armstrong.

committed in the tiny settlement of Port Louis, and the ringleaders were brought aboard the *Beagle* in irons. The body of a Lieutenant Clive was found (he had been lost from another visiting British ship some months before) and was buried close to the grave of the crew's lamented shipmate. The weather was sometimes awful. It is not surprising that Darwin had no great affection for the place, despite its profound scientific interest.

The islands had originally been colonized by the French in the late eighteenth century (hence the French character of place names such as Port Louis), but they ceded sovereignty to Spain, the Argentineans remaining when the countries of South America achieved independence. However, by the early 1830s, the Buenos Aires government had virtually abandoned the islands, and there was no real authority. The British takeover, initially somewhat half-hearted, has been a source of irritation to relations between Britain and Argentina ever since. Darwin wrote, with great prescience: "These islands have long been a bone of contention between nations." How right he was; the strains continued for over a century and a half. Argentina, convinced of the validity of her long-standing claim, invaded the islands in 1982, and this led to several months of war between the two countries before British authority was reasserted. By the early twenty-first

Fossils from the same site near Port Louis as Darwin collected. Photo: Geography Department, University of Western Australia.

Port Louis as it was in 1988. Photo: Patrick Armstrong.

century, relations had improved somewhat, and a certain degree of cooperation over matters such as fisheries management had been established, but the sovereignty issue remains alive.

It would not be true to say that Darwin's Falklands experiences were all-important any more than his Galapagos experiences were of overwhelming significance. But the Falklands sojourn, along with his visits to so many other islands, provided important and unique opportunities for him.

See also: Catastrophism; Uniformitarianism.

Port Louis as it was in the 1830s. From: *Narrative of the Surveying Voyages*, 1839.

FURTHER READING

Armstrong, Patrick. 1992. *Darwin's Desolate Islands, a Naturalist in the Falklands, 1833 and 1834.* Chippenham, England: Picton Publishing.

Fernando Noronha

Small island in the south Atlantic; now an exclusive tourist destination.

In late February 1832, Darwin spent a few hours on the island of Fernando Noronha (Ilha Fernando de Noronha), 350 miles (about 600 kilometers) southwest of **St. Paul's Rocks,** at 3° 50"S and some 270 miles northeast of the pointed shoulder of Brazil, which still has sovereignty over the small, 10 square mile (26 square kilometers) isle. Darwin was always one for comparisons and noted the complete contrast with St. Paul's: "The whole island is one forest . . . so thickly intertwined that it requires great exertion to crawl along. The scenery was very beautiful . . . large magnolias and laurels and trees covered with delicate flowers," he remarked. He found a termites' nest and noted the volcanic structure of the island. He climbed to the top of a pinnacle, which from its geological nature he surmised had been injected as fluid magma. But, he commented, substantial denudation must have occurred to reveal this steep hill formed of material that had originally been injected inside a volcano. He was beginning to appreciate that he lived in a changing world.

Fertilisation of Orchids

Book, the full title of which was *On the Various Contrivancies by which British and Foreign Orchids Are Fertilised by Insects, and on the Good Effects of Intercrossing,* published by Charles Darwin in 1862. It had an important evolutionary thrust and was well received.

See article on Botany.

Fieldwork and Collecting Methods of Charles Darwin

Darwin does not say a great deal in his writings about his methods, and to some extent they have to be deduced from chance remarks in notebooks and letters. He was instructed in biological fieldwork and collecting by Professor **John Henslow** and in geological field methods by Professor **Adam Sedgwick**. Concerning the latter, Darwin's *Autobiography* contains an account of their excursion into **North Wales** in the summer of 1831. Darwin had had instruction in the use of a direct transect across country, the inspection of rock exposures, and the collection of rock specimens. He had a geological hammer (for knocking off fragments of rock as specimens), a clinometer for the measurement of angles of dip of strata, an aneroid barometer for estimating heights, and a compass. With the instruction he had received from Henslow and Sedgwick, he was able to combine fragments of geological information collected in the field to produce a simple geological map. He also had the knack of seeing in three dimensions and produced, while on the *Beagle* voyage, some very good geological cross-section diagrams. He collected many hundreds of rock specimens—some from almost every port and island he visited. Because of his excellent powers of observation and ability to see how strata and rock masses related to one another, he was frequently able to make good assessments (for example, in the **Cape Verde Islands, Tasmania,** and in the **Falkland Islands**) of the relative ages of rocks and the manner of their origins.

Darwin had been a collector of natural history objects since the age of eight. He collected marine specimens from rock pools along the shore while in **Edinburgh** and **beetles** while at Cambridge. In his biological fieldwork on the *Beagle,* although his concentration was on collecting rather than on showing the relationships between organisms (the detailed study of **ecology** lay far in the future), he shows some insightful ecological glimpses. He collected many thousands of specimens: insects, shells, reptiles, birds mammals, fish, and a few amphibians. The birds and mammals were skinned, but some invertebrates, fish, and reptiles were preserved in spirits. He collected insects, including aquatic creatures, using a sweep nets. Marine plankton were collected by dragging a homemade net behind the ship. Just south of the Tropic of Cancer in the Atlantic Ocean, he:

> proved today the utility of a contrivance which will afford me many hours of amusement & work, it is a bag four feet [1.2 meters] deep, made of bunting, & attached to a semicircular bow: this by lines is kept upright and dragged behind the vessel. This evening it brought up a mass of small animals & tomorrow I look forward to a greater harvest. (*Diary,* January 10, 1832)

Darwin also seems to have had angling equipment (see article on **fishes**). He had a telescope, a microscope, and dissecting instruments. He used "fly nippers" for insects and had several guns for shooting birds and larger mammals (although on **St. Paul's Rocks,** he set about seabirds with his geological hammer, and in Chile a fox was dispatched in the same way). He had some sort of small traps for small mammals such as mice; he refers at one point to a trap baited with cheese. Carrion, dead wood, dung, and decaying fungi were inspected for insects, and some tiny creatures were extracted from mosses and lichens growing on trees (see article on **beetles**) and from spiders' webs. Some beetles, as in his youth, were extracted from beneath the bark of trees. Some of the insects were pinned, and some specimens were kept in small pillboxes.

It is important to note that this was not mere accumulation; Darwin kept detailed notes on where and when he collected specimens (in his **Geological** and **Zoological Diaries**). He also was careful to note the habits or behavior of the creatures he observed and collected, and indeed their ecology. Here is his account from the Birds volume of *The Zoology of the Voyage of the Beagle* (but based on his notes) of one of the most spectacular: the gray or brown petrel (*Procellaria cinera*):

> It generally frequents the retired inland sounds in very large flocks; although occasionally two or three may be seen out at sea. I do not think I ever saw so many birds of any other sort together, as I once saw of these petrels, behind [i.e., to the east of] the island of Chiloe. Hundreds of thousands flew in an irregular line, for several hours in one direction. When part of the flock settled on the water, the surface was blackened; and a cackling noise proceeded from them, as of human beings talking in the distance. At this time, the water was covered by clouds of small crustacea. The inhabitants of Chiloe told me that this petrel was very irregular in its movements; sometimes they appeared in vast numbers, and on the next day there was not one to be seen. . . . Their flight was direct and vigorous and they seldom glided with extended wings in graceful curves, like most other members of this family. They are very wary, and seldom approach within gun-shot of a boat or ship: a disposition strikingly different from that of most of the other species. (*The Zoology of the Voyage of the Beagle,* Vol. 3, 137–138)

He went on to state that inside the stomach of one he (or probably his servant **Syms Covington**) shot were "seven prawn-like crabs" and in another "the beak of a small cuttlefish." The account is interesting for the amount of information it contains on the behavior of the species—flight, social behavior, voice, and wariness are all recorded. Darwin compares the behavior with that of other species. The account is also ecological because the food and habitat are noted. Not only was he an excellent observer, distinguishing carefully his own observations from those of others, but he observed in a different way from many naturalists of his day, who were mainly concerned with only the appearance of an organism. Elsewhere he discussed the forms of the nests of birds and insects, the songs and calls of birds, and their aggressive and courtship behavior. The study of **animal behavior** was then in its infancy, and Darwin was a pioneer. His studies culminated in *The Expression of Emotions in Man and Animals*, published in 1872. For a note on the extent to which Darwin used ecological ideas in his field studies, see the article on **kelp and kelp beds.**

Perhaps because of his long association with botanist John Henslow, the plant collections from the *Beagle* period are also quite extensive. His notes on them, however, are much less systematic. He makes occasional references to plants in his diary and notes, for example, the grass trees of King George's Sound, the Eucalyptus forests of New South Wales, some distinctively formed apple trees on the island of Chiloé, and sometimes comments on the relationships among plant life, soil, the effects of burning, and other factors. But there is seldom the wealth of detail given in some of his observations on animals. However, there are exceptions. He seems to have a particular interest in what we would now call the plant biodiversity of some islands. In view of his later ideas on evolution and long-distance dispersal, this is of considerable interest. He noted that the number of species that made up the thick forests on Tahiti was much less than those that inhabited the forests of South America. On the Cocos (Keeling) Islands in the Indian Ocean he thought (somewhat mistakenly) that there were only five or six kinds of trees and about a dozen other native plant species. He made what he thought was a full collection, which Henslow later described in detail. He seems to have had some method of drying specimens aboard the *Beagle*.

Darwin was careful about labeling his specimens. Usually a label on the specimen linked it to full particulars in some notebook or list. Syms Covington assisted with some of this work, both on the voyage and in the months following it. Packages of specimens were sent back to Henslow in Cambridge, who unpacked and sorted them and reported on their condition in letters. In a letter dated January 1833, Henslow describes the insects Darwin sent as "most excellent" and many of the other materials as "capital," although one or two of the birds had lost their labels, and a few specimens had become moldy. Advice was given on the best way of packing, and the types of specimens that would be most valuable.

After the voyage, the specimens were often given to experts in the various fields to study and write up, although some he retained himself at least temporarily. Henslow took the plants, **George Waterhouse** some of the insects, **John Gould** the birds, and **Leonard Jenyns** the fishes. The specimens are thus widely scattered. The plants are mostly in the University Herbarium in Cambridge, and the rock specimens in the nearby Mineralogy and Petrology Museum. The fishes (preserved in spirit) are in the Natural History Museum in London, along with some of the other vertebrates. Some of the insects are in Dublin, others in Oxford. Small numbers of plants are located in the Gray Herbarium at Harvard, the Missouri Botanic Garden, and in Florence, Italy. Sometimes the notes relating to specimens are held in a different location from the specimens themselves. Much of Darwin's material was described and published within a few years of his return, by himself and by Waterhouse, Jenyns, Henslow, Gould, and others. But some was not published until well over a century later; there are probably still many *Beagle* specimens lurking in collections around the world that have never been properly identified and described.

The study of humanity was perhaps less developed than that of botany, geology, and zoology, and Darwin, although he was intensely interested in his fellow humans, sometimes did not have a firm conceptual framework upon which to place his descriptions. Sometimes the Edinburgh medical student who didn't quite make it can be heard in the descriptions. He was perhaps relying on his Edinburgh training when he described the "emaciated body & strange drowsy expression" of an opium addict in Mauritius or when he described the way in which the tattoos on a Maori man followed the muscle contours of his body. Sometimes he was driven back to animal comparisons; here he describes the New Zealand Maori custom of rubbing noses:

> The women on our first approach began uttering something in a most dolorous and plaintive voice, they then squatted down & held up their faces; my companions standing over them placed the bridges of their own noses at right angles to theirs, & commenced pressing; this lasted rather longer than a cordial shake of the hand would with us; as we vary the force of the grasp of the hand in shaking, so do they in pressing. During the process they utter comfortable little grunts, very much in the same manner as two pigs do when rubbing against each other. (*Diary*, December 23, 1835)

Hardly complimentary, but vivid enough.

Sometimes the comparisons went the other way. Darwin could frequently be accused of anthropomorphism (imparting human qualities or abilities to animals). He describes birds (and other creatures) as "crafty," "bold," "brave," or "inquisitive." But then he did not have the terminology or concepts to do much else.

However, the comparative method illustrated above was one the keys to Charles Darwin's success. At an early moment in his career, he wrote: "The habit of comparison leads to generalization." In the field, in his cabin in the *Beagle* writing up his notes, and later in the study at **Down House,** Darwin was constantly comparing one thing with another. By comparing the various coral islands he saw on his travels, he arrived at the coral atoll theory; by comparing the volcanic islands of **St. Helena, and Ascension Island, Cape Verde,** the **Azores,** and the **Galapagos Islands** (and the rocks of which they are composed), he put forward a similar model for the development of volcanic islands. He arranged the human communities he encountered the—Fuegians, Aborigines, **Maoris,** and Tahitians—along a sort of ladder of civilization. And, of course, the development his theory of evolution depended in no small way on his comparisons of organisms with one another.

Darwin was a first-rate observer, diligent collector, and a very conscientious recorder. He had had brief, but effective, training from Sedgwick and Henslow, who continued to support him on his voyage. He was well equipped for fieldwork and for preserving and storing specimens, within the limits of what was available in his day. His enthusiasm for the different branches of natural history varied throughout the voyage. His thirst for information and his frequent use of the comparative method when processing it were the secrets of his success.

FURTHER READING

Porter, D. M. 1985. "The Beagle Collector and His Collections." In *The Darwinian Heritage*, ed. D. Kohn. Princeton, NJ: Princeton University Press, 973–1019.

Fishes

Vertebrate class of organisms; Darwin was very interested in fishes, although the group was not of fundamental importance in the development of his ideas.

As a boy and young man, Darwin enjoyed angling; a letter written by his elder brother Erasmus when Charles was 19 says: "As to the tackle you are quite welcome to have it all except the line whose beauties you don't appreciate properly." Three years later, he was having instruction in angling from a Mr. Slaney, member of Parliament for **Shrewsbury,** who described Darwin as "a very flourishing pupil." He sometimes went trout fishing with his elder brother in Wales and also fished at Maer (the property of his uncle, Josiah Wedgwood). He was certainly familiar with Izaak Walton's (1593–1683) *Compleat Angler* (1653) and kept a field list of fishes. Possibly his skill at angling and in handling fish assisted him on the *Beagle,* for he amassed quite a substantial collection of fishes while on the 1831–1836 voyage. Sometimes he bought interesting specimens caught by the other sailors. Here is an extract from his journal relating to an incident during the brief stay at St. Stephen's Bay, in the Galapagos:

> The Bay swarmed with animals; Fish, Shark & Turtles were popping their heads up in all parts. Fishing lines were soon put overboard & great numbers of fine fish 2 & even 3 feet long were caught. This sport makes all hands very merry; loud laughter & the heavy flapping of fish are heard on every side. (*Diary,* September 17, 1835)

Most of his fish specimens of the *Beagle* period are in the Natural History Museum in London; his original notes on them—*Fish in Spirits of Wine*—are in the Darwin Archive in the Cambridge University Library. These specimens and notes were used by Leonard Jenyns in his 1842 production of *The Zoology of the Voyage of the Beagle, Part IV, Fish,* which describes about 135 species collected by Darwin on the voyage.

As in almost all matters, Darwin's observations are excellent. Here is an account of a burrfish or porcupine fish for Darwin's *Zoological Notes,* made while at Bahia, Brazil:

> March 10th [1832] a Diodon [modern generic name *Cuclichthys*] was caught swimming unexpanded near the shore. Length about an inch: above blackish brown, beneath spotted with yellow, On head four soft projections: the upper ones longer like the feelers of a snail. Eyes with pupils dark blue: iris mottled

with black. The dorsal, caudal and anal fins are so close together that they act as one. These, as well as the Pectorals which are placed just before the branchial apertures, are in continuous state of tremulous motion even when the animal remains still. The animal propels its body by using these posterior fins in the same manner as a boat is sculled, that is by moving them rapidly from side to side, with an oblique surface exposed to the water. The pectoral fins have great play, which is necessary to enable the animal to swim with its back downward.

When handled a considerable quantity of fine "Carmine red" fibrous secretion was emitted from the abdomen and stained paper. . . . The fish has several means of defence: it can bite & squirt water some distance from its Mouth, making at the same time a curious noise with its jaw. After being taken out of the water for a short time, & placed in again, it absorbed by the mouth (perhaps likewise by the branchial apertures) a considerable quantity of water and air, sufficient to distend it to a perfect globe [i.e., swallowing both air and water] & then forcing it into the body, its return being prevented by a muscular contraction which is externally visible & by the dilation of the animal producing suction. . . . When the body is distended the papillae with which it is covered become stiff [and pointed] . . . The animal being so much buoyed up, the branchial openings are out of water, but a stream flowed out of them which was constantly replenished by the mouth.

After having remained on the surface in this state for a short time, the air & water would be expelled from the branchial aperture & the mouth. (*Zoological Notes*, Cambridge University Library, Darwin Archive)

Darwin not only shows his powers of detailed observation—the colors, shape, and dimensions of the creature are carefully documented—but he also describes the behavior of the organism in fascinating detail. From his days on the *Beagle* onward, he attached great important to the behavior of animals, before its study was recognized as being of much significance, and he wrote at length on this topic throughout his subsequent career. Moreover, his writings on fishes, as with many other organisms, are remarkably integrative; he frequently shows the relationships among ethology (behavior), ecology (habitat and food relationships, for example), and morphology (form). Here is Darwin describing the parrot fishes in the Cocos (Keeling) Islands in the Indian Ocean:

[T]here are here two species of fish, of the genus Sparus [actually *Scarus*], which exclusively feed on coral. Both are coloured of a splendid bluish-green, one living invariably in the lagoon, and the other amongst the outer breakers. Mr Liesk [a British resident on the atoll] assured us that he had repeatedly seen whole shoals grazing with their strong bony jaws on the tops of the coral branches. I opened the intestines of several, and found them distended with yellow calcareous matter. This fish, together with the lithophagous [rock-consuming] shells and nereidous animals [bristle worms] which perforate every block of dead coral, must be very efficient agents in producing the finest kind of mud. (*Diary*, April 6, 1836)

The appearance of the fishes is here linked to its habits and food supply and is described with details of their habitat. (Note also the careful separation of his own observations from those of another and his experimental approach in the dissection of one fish.)

Fishes provided important examples for the development of Darwin's evolutionary ideas. A single example must suffice. In 1856, Darwin wrote to his long-time American pen-friend, **James Dwight Dana** concerning a paper he had read in an American scientific journal on the creatures that lived in Mammoth Cave in Kentucky. Were the blind or nearly blind insects, crustaceans, and fish found in the dark cave system generally found only in the Americas? He found that some of them were, and they were different from the creatures found in caves in Europe, despite the similarity in their habitats (see **convergent evolution**). In a letter to A. Murray a few years later, he wrote:

> With respect to cave animals, reflect on the cave-Rat, the fish Amblyopis & Astacus in America—the Proteus in caves of Europe, & you will admit that on [the] creation doctrine, there has been surprising diversity for such habitations. (Letter to A. Murray, May 5, 1860, in *Correspondence,* Vol. 8, 190–191)

The cave ecosystems of Europe and North America had been isolated from one another, and so the faunas had evolved quite separately. Darwin firmly believed that the distinctiveness of the cave biotas of different regions firmly supported his ideas.

In his "Big Species Book" (the large manuscript of which *On the Origin of Species* was a summary, not published until 1975), he stated:

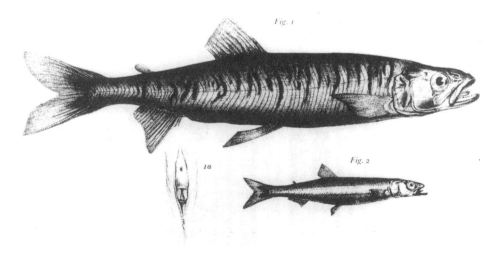

A plate from *The Zoology of the Voyage of the Beagle,* Part IV, Fishes, 1842. The upper fish, Aplochiton zebra, was caught in the Falkland Islands; the lower specimen is of a related species from Tierra del Fuego.

[I]n the caves of Kentucky there are, also, blind insects, crustaceans, fish & a Rat. The various stages of abortion of the eyes of these Kentucky animals is very curious; some have no trace of an eye, some a rudiment, & the Crustacean has the footstalk for the eye without the organ,—it has the stand for the telescope without the instrument. Now as the existence of useless eyes could hardly be injurious, I should attribute their blindness to simple disuse. . . . Although . . . many of the cave animals of Europe & No. America, though exposed to closely similar conditions . . . are except for their blindness very little allied. According to my views, these animals were not created in their respective caves, but American animals must have got into the Kentucky caves, & European animals into those of Styria [part of Austria] slowly penetrating, century after century into the profounder abysses, & gradually have become blind by disuse; they would also, become modified in any other way, through selection fitting them for their new & dark homes. (R. C. Stauffer, ed., 1975, *Charles Darwin's Natural Section,* Cambridge, England: Cambridge University Press, 295–296; written in about 1856)

Many generations of life in the dark of caves, Darwin argued, had resulted in the atrophying of the eyes, as they evolved adaptations to life in their distinctive environment. In fact, the maintenance of functioning eyes in a habitat where they provide no selective advantage, is "injurious" because it requires energy that might with greater advantage be used elsewhere. So it is not a case of "simple disuse" that caused the eyes of generations of cave-dwelling fish to atrophy, but their competitive advantage. The loss of the functionality of the eyes actually increased their owners' fitness or competitiveness. The progressive degeneration of the eyes in cave-dwelling fish has been studied and ceases when it begins to interfere with other closely related, but still useful, organs. Darwin, although incorrect in detail, was more correct than he thought in terms of the broader picture.

Daniel Pauly, a Canadian fish biologist who has made a special study of Darwin's work on fishes, has calculated that 0.7 percent of Darwin's written output (about 45,000 out of some six million, published and unpublished, words) was on this biological group, concluding that fish were not of enormous importance to him. Nevertheless, he points out that *On the Origin* contains a number references to fish, including sexual selection in fishes, relict forms, flying fish, the development of swimming bladders, the metamorphosis of flat fish, the significance of barriers such as the Isthmus of Panama in the evolution of fishes, and how seeds in the guts of fish might be distributed by fish-eating birds (an interesting ecological link). Not all of these occur in all of the six editions published in Charles Darwin's lifetime, and he changed some of his ideas, sometimes quite substantially, between one edition and another. *Variation of Animals and Plants under Domestication* (1871, 1877) contains a section on the origin and variation in form of the goldfish. Clearly, even if they were not all-important, fish were of considerable interest and significance to the great naturalist.

See also: Evolution through Natural Selection.

FURTHER READING

Pauly, Daniel. 2002. *Darwin's Fishes: An Encyclopedia of Ichthyology, Ecology and Evolution.* Cambridge, England: Cambridge University Press.
Pauly, Daniel. 2003. "Charles Darwin, Ichthyology and the Species Concept." *Fish and Fisheries* 3: 146–150.

FitzRoy, Robert (1805–1865)

Brilliant hydrographer, naval commander, meteorologist, and later a colonial governor; captain of HMS *Beagle* during its famous voyage of 1831–1836.

Robert FitzRoy was born on July 5, 1805 (the year of the Battle of Trafalgar) at Ampton Hall, near Euston in Suffolk, in eastern England. He was the second son of the second son of the Third Duke of Grafton. Robert's father, after service as an army officer, became a country squire, represented a Suffolk constituency in Parliament, and was described as a "farming, gardening and fox-hunting country gentleman." The family was well connected politically, and the family tree abounded with army and naval officers, some of great distinction and gallantry.

When Robert was four years old, the family moved to Wakefield Lodge in Northamptonshire, in the middle of England, but before he was 13, the young Robert FitzRoy was enrolled at the Royal Naval College at Portsmouth. The normal course at the college lasted from two and a half to three years, but he completed it in one year and eight months. The coursework (physics, astronomy, navigation, naval history, geography, naval architecture, and French) was intense. Robert passed with full marks and a gold medal. He saw service as volunteer, midshipman, lieutenant, and flag lieutenant on the *Owen Glendower, Hind, Thetis,* and *Ganges* in his teens and early 20s. These ships had tasks as varied as discouraging smuggling around the Cornish coast and ferrying ambassadors to their posts. His service in British waters, the Mediterranean, and South America trained him well; his ships were involved in the occasional skirmish but in no spectacular action. An officer, Lieutenant (later Admiral) **Bartholomew Sulivan,** who served with FitzRoy described him as "one of the best practical seamen in the service" and one "with a fondness for every type of observation useful in navigating a ship."

Early in 1828, the *Adventure* (captained by **Philip Parker King**) and the *Beagle* (under the command of Pringle Stokes) were undertaking a hydrographic survey of the wild confusion of islands, inlets, and promontories of **Tierra del Fuego.** Faced with severe weather and serious privations, the strain on Stokes became unbearable, and he shot himself in the head; he died in great pain a few days later. Although there was another officer who could have been considered to have a greater claim on the position, Admiral Sir Robert Otway, then in charge of the South American Station, gave Robert FitzRoy, at the young age of 23, command of the 10-gun surveying brig, HMS *Beagle.* The confidence was not misplaced.

Many months of further survey followed, and FitzRoy completed the tasks assigned to him with flair. However, at one stage a whaleboat was taken by a group of Fuegian natives, and FitzRoy took several Fuegians hostage, hoping to exchange them for the boat. The tactic was unsuccessful. The names Fuegia Basket (a young girl), Boat Memory, and **Jemmy Button** were given to the members of the group. A young man to whom the name York Minster had been given was also picked up from the island to which the name of the ecclesiastical building had been given by Captain James Cook (1728–1779) several decades earlier. FitzRoy resolved to take the group to Britain, to have them educated (and "christianised"), and returned. This he did, returning in October 1830, and the group was placed in the hands of the Reverend William Wilson at Walthamstow, near London. They became quite notorious and were presented to King William IV and Queen Adelaide, but history relates little of what the parties thought of each other. While the British naval authorities (the Admiralty) were not enthusiastic about FitzRoy's scheme, they agreed not to interfere with his plans and indeed provided medical care for the Fuegians at a naval hospital. At one stage it looked as though the Admiralty might default on the agreement to allow FitzRoy to return the Fuegians on a naval vessel, so he started to make plans to charter a vessel at his own expense. However, perhaps partly because of his connections, the authorities agreed that the survey could continue.

Just after Christmas 1831, therefore, HMS *Beagle* set off again for the South Atlantic, intent on completing the hydrographic survey of the southern tip of South America and returning the Fuegians (except for Boat Memory, who had died of smallpox) to their homeland, in the company of a missionary. The west coast of South America was then to be surveyed, and "a chain of meridians" around the world was to be established. An accurate method of establishing longitude had only recently been developed, and the precise position of many points was still uncertain. Charles Darwin was chosen by FitzRoy to act as a companion and to assist with natural history observations on this second *Beagle* voyage. There is every reason to believe that the discussions and the sometimes vigorous arguments that Darwin and FitzRoy had while sharing the cramped quarters aboard ship were a significant influence on the young naturalist. (FitzRoy had something of a temper and could sometimes be autocratic and difficult. His shipmates on occasion evaluated his mood by asking: "How much hot coffee had been served to the Captain?") Despite occasionally strained relations between the two, on the whole Darwin and FitzRoy interacted well, sometimes visiting geological and other sites together (e.g., Bald Head, southwestern Australia, and some of the islands of the Cocos group). FitzRoy allowed the ship's boats to be used to set Darwin down at a location from which he wished to collect specimens or make observations. The history of science would have been very different were it not for the manner in which these two were thrown together for nearly five years.

After visiting Bahia (now Salvador) in **Brazil,** FitzRoy spent several weeks surveying the Abrolhos Islands and around **Tierra del Fuego** in late 1832 and early 1833; during this period, the Fuegians were returned, but the attempt to establish a mission station was unsuccessful. The missionary (Richard Matthews) was attacked, and his was property taken, so FitzRoy had to remove him, taking him eventually to New Zealand. The *Beagle* then sailed for Port Louis, Berkeley Sound, East Falkland, to repair the ship after serious storms experienced off the southern tip of South America and to replenish stocks of beef and water, but FitzRoy also completed detailed hydrographic charts of the **Falkland Islands.**

The captain frequently had diplomatic, administrative, or other official duties to perform in the ports visited, and, at a number of locations, Robert FitzRoy had to sort out petty squabbles or act in some other official capacity. The visits of the *Beagle* to Berkeley Sound in the Falkland Islands were typical. On the first visit, FitzRoy found a group of French seamen living in tents made from sails; the French whaling ship *La Magellan* had been "totally wrecked." FitzRoy wrote: "After due enquiry, I promised to carry as many as I could to Monte Video, and to interest myself in procuring passage for the rest." He went on: "[T]here was no constituted authority on the islands," the Argentineans having recently apparently abandoned them. The settlement had allegedly been ruined in 1831 by some of the crew from USS *Lexington;* the few gauchos living there used to "gamble, quarrel and fight with long knives." The crews of French, British, and American whalers armed with clubs and rifles provided no lack of elements of discord. "And it was with a heavy heart and gloomy forebodings that I looked forward to the months . . . without the presence of a man-o-war, or the semblance of any regular authority." FitzRoy's forebodings were well grounded; in the year that elapsed between the two *Beagle* visits there were enacted, as Darwin put it, "complicated scenes of cold-blooded murder, robbery, plunder, suffering and infamous conduct." Several murders were committed, and some of the desperados responsible were taken on board the *Beagle* in irons (April 1834).

The *Beagle* also picked up and carried to safety a group of seamen from an American whaling vessel who had jumped ship on the west coast of South America and had been "living rough" for over a year. In New Zealand, he had to deal with the mutinous crew of another whaling ship, and, in Tahiti, FitzRoy had to negotiate with Queen Pomare in an attempt to obtain compensation for the loss of a British ship that had been seized. Captain FitzRoy seems to have dealt with all of these irritations (among others) with diplomacy, completed the hydrographic surveys with great efficiency, and collected much information on the islands and ports that were visited. At every port of call, navigational and astronomical instruments were set up, and magnetic and positional observations were made. Admiral Beaufort, in charge of hydrographic work at the admiralty, wrote to him several times in 1832 and 1833 complimenting him on the high standard of his work.

The voyage of the *Beagle* continued from South America, via the **Galapagos Islands** and **Tahiti,** to the **Bay of Islands, New Zealand,** and on to Port Jackson (Sydney) in **New South Wales.** From there the ship sailed to Hobart Town in **Tasmania** and King George's Sound, close to the southwest corner of Australia. The Indian Ocean was traversed with brief sojourns at the **Cocos (Keeling) Islands** and **Mauritius.** A short stay at the **Cape of Good Hope** was followed by visits to **St. Helena and Ascension Island.** Bahia was touched at for the second time (completing the chain of meridians) before the *Beagle* made brief calls at the **Cape Verde Islands** and the **Azores.** Falmouth, in Cornwall, in the southwest corner of England was gained on the stormy night of October 2, 1836. FitzRoy spent the next three years completing the charts from the data he had gathered, compiling reports for the Admiralty, and writing his *Narrative of the Surveying Voyages of the Beagle.* He gave evidence to a House of Lords committee. He had a brief period in Parliament, followed by a couple of years (1843–1845) as governor of **New Zealand.** Partly because of his autocratic manner, his tenure in this position was not a success. Back in Britain, he was posted to HMS *Arrogant,* the first screw-driven ship of the Royal Navy. In 1850, partly because of ill health, he resigned from the full-time service of the Navy. Always interested in meteorology (he invented a type of barometer), he was appointed the first head of the newly established Meteorological Office. He was promoted to rear-admiral and developed a system of synoptic charts, weather forecasts, and storm warnings. He was a great success in some of these activities, but he had his own priorities, which were not always those of his political masters. He tended to make enemies; sometimes (as with weather forecasts today) his forecasts were wrong, and he was bitterly criticized, which he took hard. A traditionalist in many matters and an evangelical, estrangement with Darwin followed the publication of *On the Origin of Species* in 1859 and the Great Debate at the **British Association for the Advancement of Science** meeting in Oxford in 1860 (which he attended). Periods of ill health and depression became longer and more intense and eventually destroyed him: on April 30, 1865, he took his own life, cutting his throat with a razor. There is a bitter irony in this because it was the suicide of one of his naval colleagues that gave him the command of the *Beagle.* One of his naval forbears had also committed suicide.

In some ways a caricature of a naval officer of his day, Robert FitzRoy had defects in his character, but he was a brilliant man. It is for his hydrographic charts and his contribution to meteorology that he is remembered. In the British Hydrographic Office in Taunton, in the west of England are a number of exceptionally fine manuscript charts countersigned by FitzRoy. Indeed, his name appeared on some published marine charts still in use at the end of the twentieth century. The precise extent of his influence on Darwin can never be known, but it was considerable. His name is commemorated in place names in the Falkland Islands, South America, and Australia, as well as in a meteorological sea area in the Atlantic Ocean.

FURTHER READING

Mellersh, H.E.L. 1968. *FitzRoy of the Beagle*. London: Rupert Hart-Davis.
Nichols, Peter. 2003. *Evolution's Captain*. New York: HarperCollins.

Forms of Flowers

The widely used short title of Charles Darwin's book *The Different Forms of Flowers on Plants of the Same Species*. The work was one of the author's most important botanical works and was of considerable evolutionary significance because it illustrated how certain variations in flower structure were adaptations to ensure cross-pollination and the production of high numbers of progeny.

In 1862 Darwin had published in the *Journal of the Linnean Society* an article with the striking title "On the Two Forms or Dimorphic Condition of the Species of Primula, and on Their Remarkable Sexual Relations." This paper was but one step along the road of Darwin's interest in the role of sex in evolutionary theory. Although he did not understand the precise nature of inheritance, he did appreciate that sexual reproduction, enabling the mingling of both parents' characteristics, promoted variation on which natural selection operated. Moreover, sexual selection—an idea developed in *Descent of Man*—provided a mechanism for the encouragement of certain traits in a population at the expense of others. In plants, the fertilization of one gamete rather than another was a more passive affair than in the higher animals, but nevertheless the forms of flowers sometimes provided a strategy whereby certain fertilizations were encouraged and others were rendered less likely or impossible, with beneficial effects on the progeny. Cross-fertilization was encouraged because of the advantages in terms of variation that it promoted.

Forms of Flowers commenced with a detailed case study of the variation in the flowers in the genus *Primula* that formed the basis of Darwin's earlier paper. He considers the cowslip (*Primula veris*), primrose (*P. vulgaris*), and oxslip (*P. elatior*)—all of which are quite common in the English countryside. He applies the similar method of inquiry to the variable blackberry or bramble (genus *Rubus*), the flax (genus *Linum*), and numerous other species.

Forms of Flowers was published in 1877 by John Murray—the firm that published many of Darwin's books. It is dedicated "as a small tribute of respect and affection" to his American botanist friend, **Asa Gray**. The book attracted much less interest than some of his others. Only two printings of 1,250 each appeared in his life time; another thousand copies were produced with a preface by his son **Francis Darwin** in 1884. The book has been reprinted and translated much less than some of Darwin's other works.

Fossils

The remains or traces of past life. The branch of science that studies fossils is known as *paleontology*. Darwin had been interested in fossils and their significance since his student days, and he collected many fossils on the *Beagle* voyage. Later he emphasized them as being an important, but not perhaps all-important, source of evidence for evolution.

A fossil may be the whole or any part of an animal or plant. It is often chemically changed, or it may be an impression (a mold or a cast) of the shape of an organism. Fossils also include the remains of the effects of organisms, including tracks (such as dinosaur tracks or worm trails), excrement, or burrows (trace fossils). Fossils assist in dating and correlating sedimentary strata: a *zone fossil* is one that only occurs in a restricted layer or in particular series of layers or strata. Derived fossils are those that formed in one stratum, were later eroded out, and redeposited elsewhere, enclosed in a much later stratum. On the whole, the fossil evidence shows that, throughout geological time, there has been a progression from simple to more complex forms of life.

Apart from some uninspiring lectures attended while Darwin was an unsuccessful medical student at Edinburgh, he learned most of the geology he was ever taught in the summer of 1831, after taking his degree from Cambridge. He did some undirected fieldwork around his Shrewsbury home—including the exploration of a limestone quarry at Llanymynech, about 14 miles (22.5 kilometers) northwest of **Shrewsbury** that he probably visited in late July. His fortnight's tour through **North Wales,** a couple of weeks later, under the supervision of **Adam Sedgwick** was much more directed. However, the notes of neither of these excursions say a great deal about fossil collecting, although he found *Madrepores* (corals but it is possible that Darwin mistook Bryozoans for corals) near Cwm Idwal in North Wales.

As the result of knowledge gained at **Edinburgh,** from Sedgwick and **John Henslow** at Cambridge, and through his own study, by the time the *Beagle* voyage was a few months old, Darwin was a competent finder of fossils. He was able to offer a rough identification, although he was never a specialist paleontologist, always relying on others for exact identifications.

A few examples of the fossils that Darwin encountered on the voyage and their possible significance to him will be mentioned.

In South America he collected a number of fossil mammals (some he found himself, some he bought); these included **Megatherium,** a giant slothlike form, from Bahia Blanca and from Uruguay. He also found the remains of what later turned out to be the remains of an extinct form of llama. These, written up in the Fossil Mammalia volume of the **Zoology of the Voyage of the Beagle** by **Richard Owen,** proved to be important. They demonstrated to Darwin that extinct forms of animals were to be found in the same general area of the world as the living forms. From this fact, it was a simple step to suggest that there might be an evolutionary link between them—but this came much later, after his return to England.

At the small settlement of Port Louis in the **Falkland Islands,** after being somewhat bored by his long stay in a bleak location, he recorded:

> The whole aspect of the Falklands Islands was however changed to my eyes from that walk; for I found a rock abounding with shells; & they of the most interesting geological aera. (*Diary,* March 10–17, 1833)

In his geological notes, he goes into much greater detail:

> I was therefore the more surprised to find near the settlement within the slate, beds of sandstone which abounded with impressions and casts of shells. The sandstone is fine grained and soft: it is often slaty, in which case it generally contains scales of mica. . . . The included organic remains are found in seams or beds between the sandstone strata. In some cases the casts form the whole mass, in others they are embedded in sandstone, and very often in a matrix of hard blue compact rock. The shells belong to Terebratula and its subgenera; there are also species of Entrochitus and vestiges of some other remains the nature of which I could not ascertain. (*Geological Notes,* Cambridge University Library, Darwin Archive)

Darwin speculated about the exact age of the fossils (they are now thought to be from the Devonian period, about 350–400 million years ago) and wondered how they compared with fossils of similar age from other parts of the world. (He later handed over these fossils to two Geological Society colleagues, John Morris and Daniel Sharpe, who wrote an account of them in a paper in the *Proceedings of the Geological Society* in 1846.)

The layer indeed contains dozens of fossils of brachiopods, crinoids, and trilobites. Darwin's phrase "abounding with shells" is entirely appropriate. He noted the bleak and infertile landscape that surrounded him: the island was everywhere "[t]he same entire absence of trees & the same universal covering of brown wiry grass." It was monotonous, and there were few insects or land invertebrates. He was struck by the great contrast of this cold, bleak environment of the Falkland Islands with the prolific seas, which perhaps experienced a much warmer climate that might have existed in the geological past when the sandstones "abounding with shells" were deposited.

> Do not the Entrochitus & other organic remains indicate a climate previously warmer? Where the latitude of the place is 51 degrees in the southern hemisphere is considered even a remote possibility on such a point becomes interesting. (*Geological Notes,* Cambridge University Library, Darwin Archive)

This experience no doubt emphasized in his mind that he lived in a dynamic, changing world. Things had not always been as they are now.

In Tasmania, too, he collected important fossils that he eventually passed on to specialists for identification, but that impressed him at the time. He understood that fossils were not mere curiosities but were to be considered in the context of the rock that contained them. Here he notes the older formation in the Hobart area:

[There are] Clay-Slates, white Cherty or Flinty rocks . . . & Limestones. . . . Perhaps the most abundant varieties might be named whitish flinty Slates. These rocks abound with impressions of Organic remains—the most abundant are those of the smaller stony Corals . . . there are likewise the casts of numerous Terebratula [a genus of brachiopod, a type of shelled creature abundant in ancient seas]. (*Geological Notes,* Cambridge University Library, Darwin Archive)

Darwin also noted the presence of coral fossils in coralline rock on islands such as Cocos and Mauritius, giving him insights into the history of the islands as he developed his coral atoll theory. He found shells in the sedimentary rocks of Tierra del Fuego and other areas of southern South America, which helped him to establish their approximate age and the broad structure of the continent for his book on *The Geology of South America.* Although his paleontological studies sometimes lagged behind his work in other areas in the *Beagle* days, they were important and gave him a number of important insights.

Although the study of fossils was not a major route through which Darwin reached his evolutionary views, it was significant, and he devoted two chapters of **On the Origin of Species** to this field. Chapter 9 was titled "On the Imperfection of the Geological Record," and chapter 10 was titled "On the Geological Succession of Organic Beings."

In the first of these, Darwin asks:

Why then is not every geological formation and every stratum full of . . . intermediate links? Geology assuredly does not reveal any such finely graduated organic chain; and this perhaps, is the most obvious and gravest objection which can be urged against my theory. The explanation lies, as I believe in the extreme imperfection of the geological record.

He goes on to comment not only on the extreme length of geological time, but on its complexity. Periods of erosion and deposition, uplift and subsidence have alternated; species may have migrated from one area to another.

In order to get a perfect gradation between two forms in the upper and lower parts of the same formation, the deposit must have gone on accumulating for a very long period, in order to have given sufficient time for the very slow process of variation; hence the species undergoing modification will have had to live on the same area throughout this whole time.

Nevertheless, Darwin argues the evidence of paleontology is often persuasive:

> If we look . . . [at] distinct but consecutive stages of the same great formation, we find that the embedded fossils, though universally ranked as specifically different, yet are for more closely allied to each other than are species in widely separated formations.

In any event, exactly what constitutes a species and a variety is often a matter for debate among paleontologists. Further, he argued, at that time, little was known of the geology of countries other than those of Europe and the United States. Darwin hoped that as other areas of the world were studied, further information would be revealed on the transition of one form to another in the fossil record. To a limited extent, he has been vindicated, although perhaps not as convincingly as he would have wished.

In chapter 10, Darwin argues that different species are likely to have evolved at different rates—some species and biological groups much more rapidly than others. He gives the oft-quoted example of *Lingula,* which is found in Silurian rocks and yet is also found almost indistinguishable from this ancient form in modern seas. On the other hand, the trilobites and ammonites seem to have evolved more rapidly and are now entirely extinct. Some shells found in rocks of the lower Tertiary are almost identical to forms still living, yet they may be "in the midst of a multitude of extinct forms."

> I believe in no fixed law of development, causing all the inhabitants of a country to change abruptly, or simultaneously, or to an equal degree. The process of modification must be extremely slow. The variability of each species is independent of all others.

A species, or a biological group as a whole, once extinct, never reappears—a fact that would be difficult to explain if one believed in a separate creation for each geological formation, as some did, but entirely explicable if each species evolved once, had a finite life span, and then disappeared, perhaps though competition with other, more successful evolving species or groups.

The fossils in formations of the same age in widely separated parts of the world resembled one another. Although fossils the same age as the European Chalk formation (with which Darwin would have been familiar, living in Kent, south of London) are not identical to the rocks of North and South America and at the Cape of Good Hope, there is a strong measure of similarity—"forms of life change simultaneously throughout the world," as he put it.

Darwin summarizes chapters 9 and 10 of *On the Origin:*

> If then the geological record be as imperfect as I believe it to be, . . . the main objections to the theory of natural selection are greatly diminished or disap-

pear. On the other hand, all the chief laws of palaeontology plainly proclaim, as it seems to me, that species have been produced by ordinary generation: old forms having been supplanted by new and improved forms of life, produced by the laws of variation still acting around us, and preserved by Natural Selection.

In short, Charles Darwin felt, and he has substantially been found correct, that the paleontological record supported his evolutionary ideas. There are those, however, for whom the rarity of intermediary forms and the suddenness with which some fossil groups "burst on the scene" remain difficulties.

See also: Evolution through Natural Selection; Lyell, Charles.

Fox, William Darwin (1805—1880)

Clergyman, naturalist, and cousin of Charles Darwin.

William Fox was the son of Samuel Fox (1765–1851) and Anne Darwin, the sister of Erasmus Darwin (senior). Like Charles Darwin, Fox studied for the Church of England priesthood at Cambridge University. They were also both enthusiastic naturalists and keen collectors of beetles. At Cambridge, Fox and Darwin became friends, and Fox instructed his younger cousin on entomology and was probably partly responsible for developing Darwin's enthusiasm. Fox graduated from Cambridge a year or two before Darwin and later became rector of Delamere in Cheshire (1838–1873). He then retired to Sandon on the Isle of Wight and is buried there. The two cousins corresponded on family matters and natural history throughout their lives.

Fox married twice and had 16 children. His first wife was Harriet Fletcher (1799–1842), daughter of Sir Richard Fletcher, whom he married in 1834. His second wife was Ellen Sophia (1820–1887), daughter of Basil George Woodd of Hillfield, Hampstead, whom he married in 1846.

Frankland, George (1800—1838)

Surveyor General of **Tasmania** (Van Diemen's Land); Darwin's guide on the island in 1836. (Some sources give the date of his birth as 1797.)

George Frankland was Surveyor General of Tasmania for 10 years (1828–1838) during the formative stages of the development of the island. He explored parts of the island, including the forests of the Huon Valley (1829) and the Lake St. Clair area in the mountainous center of the island (1835). He befriended Charles Darwin when he visited Hobart in February 1836, and they went on several days' fieldwork together, Darwin visiting him in his home.

Frankland's name is commemorated in several place names in Tasmania.

G

Galapagos Finches

A group of rather inconspicuous birds found on the **Galapagos Islands** in the Pacific Ocean; they interested Darwin on his visit in September to October 1835, and have been the subject of much subsequent evolutionary research.

In the later editions of *The Voyage of the Beagle* appears the following sentence:

> Seeing this gradation and diversity of structure in one small, intimately related group of birds one might fancy that from an original paucity of birds in this archipelago, one species has been taken and modified for different ends. (*Voyage of the Beagle*, chapter 17)

Here is Charles Darwin quietly asserting his belief in evolution. It is not surprising, therefore, that this interesting group of birds has become known as Darwin's finches. The name was first coined in 1836, and was popularized by the publication of the first modern ecological and evolutionary study of that title by David Lack in 1947. Darwin does little more than mention them in his diary, and, after a brief description in *The Voyage* and the publication of the Birds volume of *The Zoology of the Voyage*, edited by **John Gould,** Darwin does not mention them much in his writings.

Darwin's finches are similar to each other in size, coloration, and habits. Their main difference is in the size and shape of their beak, although beak shapes can be highly variable, and the beak of one individual can extend into the size range of another species. Fourteen species of birds are currently recognized as Darwin's finches—13 in the Galapagos and 1 on Cocos Island, an isolated isle hundreds of kilometers to the northeast—not to be confused with the Cocos (Keeling) Islands in the Indian Ocean.

There is some disagreement, however, as to how the 14 species are grouped. Traditionally, the finches have been divided into four genera: the ground finches (*Geospiza*), the tree finches (*Camarhynchus*), the warbler finch (*Certhidea*), and the isolated Cocos finch (*Pinaroloxias*). As a group, the tree finches are more heterogeneous than the ground finches, and it is current practice to subdivide the tree finches into three categories: *Camarhynchus* (the true tree finches), *Platyspiza* (the vegetarian finch), and *Cactospiza* (containing the woodpecker and mangrove finches). On the other hand, some experts argue that splitting the finches into six discrete genera emphasizes their differences, and they suggest grouping all of them into the single genus *Geospiza* to stress their similarities. But whether you split them into six genera or lump them into one (avian taxonomists have traditionally been divided into the "splitters" and "lumpers"), there is general agreement on the existence of 14 species.

Different combinations of species are found on different islands of the archipelago: some are found on only one or two islands, and some are found on almost all of the larger isles.

In the isolated environment of a remote archipelago, there is a low species diversity—relatively few land birds have been able to reach the Galapagos—and so there is less competition than there is in a mainland environment. The finches have thus evolved to fill different ecological niches: some are insect feeders, some feed on seeds. One uses a cactus spine to extract insects from crevices. The Galapagos finches thus provide an example of adaptive radiation.

The problems that exist in the identification of the different finches are rooted in precisely what makes them so interesting and important to an understanding of the evolutionary process. If two species share a common ancestor, then as one traces them back in time, they should become more and more similar in appearance. At the point at which they separated, the two species should become ambiguous. Some of Darwin's finches still seem to be in the process of separating. There is some evidence that a fertility barrier between individuals of different species has not yet completely formed, and there is evidence of some hybridization between species (which, of course, makes identification difficult).

There are populations of the large cactus finch (*Genospiza conirostris*) on Genovesa (Tower Island) and Española (Hood Island), but their beaks differ. On Genovesa, the large ground finch coexists with the large cactus finch (*Genospiza magnirostris*). During the rainy season, when there is sufficient food to go round, the two species can feed in each other's ecological niches with negligible competition occurring between them. However, during the dry season, when food is much more scarce, the two species are compelled to specialize in their food sources. Assuming that the two originally evolved on separate islands, their present association in overlapping ranges has tended to make them diverge. Despite the fact that some of the finches show a broad variation in beak type, the diversity of the large ground and large cactus finches on Genovesa is small. Any large cactus finch whose beak overlapped in size with the beaks of the large ground finch will be less able to successfully compete with other members of that species. On Española, however, the large ground finch either never arrived, or it became extinct, and this island now only has the large cactus finch. But without the competition, the beak of the large cactus finch can exhibit more variability, and, indeed, its beak is intermediate in size between the two forms of the finches that occur on Genovesa. On Española, this species can apparently feed equally well in both niches all year round.

Island environments, because of their relatively low biodiversity, sometimes allow ecological and evolutionary processes to be seen more clearly than amid the biological and ecological complexity of continental locations. The Galapagos are of particular interest not only because they seem to have played a role in the development of Darwin's ideas (more in looking back after his visit rather than during his actual sojourn on the islands), but they have been found to be important locales for the study of evolution as it appears to be proceeding today.

FURTHER READING

Lack, David. 1947. *Darwin's Finches.* Cambridge, England: Cambridge University Press.
Weiner, J. 1994. *The Beak of the Finch: A Story of Evolution in Our Time.* London: Jonathon Cape.

Galapagos Islands

Archipelago of volcanic origin in the tropical Pacific Ocean.

This group of islands, which is part of Ecuador, has an area of about 1,885 square miles (4,880 square kilometers) and a population of about 12,000. It is one of the world's most written about groups of islands. It is often asserted that it was on the Galapagos Islands that Darwin had his flash of inspiration regarding the nature of evolution. He recalled in his **Autobiography:**

> During the voyage of the *Beagle* I had been deeply impressed . . . by the South American character of most of the productions of the Galapagos archipelago, and more especially by the manner in which they differ slightly on each island of the group.

But a careful scrutiny of the notes that the young naturalist made while he was aboard the *Beagle* indicates that there was no such flash of enlightenment while he was in the archipelago in September and October 1835. When he wrote of the Galapagos in his autobiography (an account intended only for his family) over four decades later, he seems to have given the wrong impression. Although some of the observations he made in the Galapagos were important, while on the islands he was sometimes uncertain as to the exact geographical affinities of some of the creatures he found. There is evidence that vague ideas on the mutability of species drifted through his mind during the voyage, but it was not until about March 1837, some months after he returned to England, that he was converted to an evolutionary outlook.

Darwin spent about 19 days on land while in the archipelago. He landed on only four islands: Albemarle (now called Isabela), Charles (Floreana), Chatham (San Cristobel), and James (Santiago). Throughout the remainder of the weeks that the *Beagle* was among the Galapagos Islands, he was on board the ship while she was engaged in hydrographic survey or voyaging between islands. His impressions of the islands were often negative. He wrote in his diary: "The black rocks heated by the rays of the vertical sun, like a stove, give to the air a close and sultry feeling." He described the vegetation using phrases such as "small leafless brushwood," "ugly little flowers," "stunted trees," "little signs of life," "the plants smell unpleasantly." He compared the landscape to that of the "infernal regions." There were "most disgusting, clumsy lizards" that were referred to as "imps of darkness." For a while he seems to be thinking of the Galapagos archipelago as some sort of stark, hot hell on Earth. The tortoises hissed at him. Once he compared the chimneylike forms of volcanic features to the "iron furnaces near Wolverhampton" in the industrial areas of the English Midlands and described the bare volcanic rock as being "rough and horrid." When he and a couple of companions found some water in small depressions on the northern part of Albemarle Island, it was "not good"; the country was "arid & sterile." A couple of days later, he wrote of the same island that he thought it would be difficult to find "in the intertropical latitudes a piece of land 75 miles long, so entirely useless to man or the larger animals." Despite all this, he continued to make thoughtful observations; for example, he describes the suite of volcanic forms and his exploration of them very lucidly:

To the South of the Cove [Targus Cove] I found a most beautiful Crater, elliptic in form, less than a mile in its longer axis & about 500 feet deep. Its bottom was occupied by a lake, out of which a tiny Crater formed an Island . . . The . . . lake looked blue & clear. I hurried down the cindery side, choked with dust, to my disgust on tasting the water found it Salt as brine. This crater & some other neighbouring ones have only poured mud or Sandstone containing fragments of Volcanic rocks; but from the mountain behind, great bare streams have flowed, sometimes from the summit, or from small Craters on the side, expanding in their descent, have at base formed plains of Lava.

Despite the heat, thirst, and dust, his observations of animals remained astute. He carefully compared the terrestrial lizards he found in the mountains with the marine forms he had encountered by the shore; he thought, from their structure, that they were "closely allied" to the "imps of darkness." He noted that this species lived in burrows, into which it hurried when frightened; the creatures had a ridge and spines along the back, and were orange-yellow with the hinder part of the back brick red; they weighed 10 to 15 pounds (4.5 to 6.8 kilograms) and were 2 to 4 feet (0.6 to 1.2 meters) in length. They were considered good eating, and, Darwin commented, "this day forty were collected."

Besides reptiles, he collected birds, plants, and insects (grasshoppers, beetles, flies) in dozens. However, he made mistakes; he only realized the significance of the fact that the giant tortoises (of which he wrote much) differed in the shape of their shells from island to island very late in the day. And he seems to have intermingled the bird specimens from different islands, so that when he was working on his specimens after the voyage, he had to appeal to others who had collected specimens on the islands—Captain FitzRoy, his servant Syms Covington, and the ship's surgeon, Benjamin Bynoe—because in some cases their material was better labeled.

Darwin, in the frantic months after the voyage, was particularly interested in the **Galapagos finches**—the *Geospizinae,* now often called Darwin's finches—and also the mockingbirds from the islands. He noted that there seemed to be something of a gradation in the form of the different species of finch and that they differed from island to island. In the first edition (1839) of the *Journal of Researches* (later editions were titled *The Voyage of the Beagle*) he wrote,

> [I]n the thirteen species of ground-finches, a nearly perfect gradation may be traced, from a beak extraordinarily thick, to one so fine, that it may be compared to that of a warbler. I very much suspect, that certain members of the series are confined to different islands; therefore if the collection had been made on *one* island, it would not have presented so perfect a gradation. It is clear, that if several islands have each their peculiar species of the same genera, when these are placed together, they will have a wide range of character.

But at that time Darwin did not follow up the matter: "There is not space in this work, to enter on this curious subject." In later editions, he is more open. In the 1845 edition, adjacent to woodcut sketches of some of the finches with their varied beaks, he notes that there had originally been few species on the groups of islands and that "one species had been modified for different ends."

Darwin was clearly by then using evolutionary ideas privately, but had not yet gone public with them. There are other hints of the way in which he was thinking a couple of pages earlier.

The natural history of these islands is eminently curious, and well deserves attention. Most of the organic productions are aboriginal creations, found nowhere else [i.e., endemic]; there is even a difference between the inhabitants of the different islands. . . . The archipelago is a little world within itself, or rather a satellite attached to America, whence it has derived a few stray colonists.

After noting the substantial distance from the nearest land and the relative geological recency of the volcanic islands, he mused:

Hence, both in space and in time, we seem brought somewhat near to that great fact—that mystery of mysteries—the first appearance of new beings on this earth.

He seems to be postulating, a little obliquely, that initially barren islands were colonized by long-distance movement, perhaps from the Americas, and subsequently became adapted to the island environment.

In the months and years following the voyage, Darwin did a good deal of thinking about the Galapagos and its suite of endemic beings. The archipelago may have been significant in kick-starting some of his evolutionary thoughts, but their significance was in the fact that, by the end of the voyage, he had many other island groups with which to compare them. He was perhaps conscious of the limitations in his collecting and labeling because he does not specifically mention the Galapagos finches in *On the Origin of Species.*

Although he collected many specimens there and he found much of interest, he made mistakes and he did not particularly like the Galapagos. The archipelago seems to have been of some significance in the development of his ideas, but only after the voyage, following his comparison of them with other environments, especially other islands.

FURTHER READING

Sulloway, F. J. 1985. "Darwin and the Galapagos." *Biological Journal of the Linnean Society* 21: 29–59.

Geological Society of London

A scientific society that has as its primary objective "investigating the mineral structure of the Earth." Darwin was an enthusiastic member.

The Geological Society is the oldest national geological society in the world and, with 9,000 members, the largest in Europe. It has an important role in publishing research and organizing conferences. Since 1874, the Society has been based at Burlington House, Piccadilly, London.

The Society was founded in 1807, partly from the basis of a previous club known as the Arkesian Society. Among the more prominent founders were William Babbington, Sir Humphry Davy, and George Bellas Greenough. It received a Royal Charter from King George IV in 1825.

To begin with, and for some decades, the Society had the character of a rather exclusive dining club. Members dined together the first Friday of every month from June until November. Dinner was served at precisely 5:00 P.M., followed by the business of the evening—the reading of papers and discussion—at 7.00 P.M. Initially it was seen as something of a rival to the Royal Society, some members of which felt that the existence of the young interloper was unnecessary.

Charles Lyell was an early member. Here, from his diary, is a recollection of a meeting he attended in 1831, while he was still a young man (although he had published the first volume of *Principles of Geology* the previous year). It illustrates the flavor of the Society in its earlier decades:

> Dined at the Geological Society Club . . . a pleasant club—Stokes, Greenough, Buckland, Lord Cole . . . and a few more. Murchison was pheasant-shooting in the country but cut in for the meeting. A short paper on Springs, and another by Mr Hutton on the Whin Sill of Yorkshire, drew up Buckland, Greenough, Murchison and De La Beche, and they seemed disposed to go on for ever, Buckland speaking five times, but not once too often. I was glad to sit quiet. (H. H. Woodward, 1907, *History of the Geological Society of London,* Geological Society of London, 97)

Charles Darwin undertook important geological research during the period 1831 to 1836, while he was aboard the *Beagle,* and realized that he would need to become a member. **Adam Sedgwick** had, in fact, offered to propose him for membership before he departed on the voyage, but nothing came of this offer. Charles, therefore, wrote to his mentor **John Henslow** from the island of St. Helena in July 1836, and he was proposed for membership in early November of the same year.

The Geological Society was supremely important to Darwin at several critical times of his career. Even before he was a member, Adam Sedgwick read extracts from some of his letters to Henslow to a meeting (November 18, 1835), and thus the two of them eased the young geologist's entry into the London scientific community. After his return and election to membership, he read a number of papers to the Society in quick succession (they were subsequently published by the society). Perhaps the most important was his coral atoll theory paper titled "On Certain Areas of Elevation and Subsidence in the Pacific and Indian Oceans as Deduced from the Study of Coral Formations," which he presented on May 31, 1837. It demonstrated that the fringing reefs, barrier reefs, and atolls were members of a single series formed by subsidence; this was Darwin's first use of the effects of gradual change in a publication. Moreover, the paper also contains the suggestion:

> That some degree of light might thus be thrown on the question, whether certain groups of living beings, peculiar to small spots are the remnants of a former large population, or a new on springing into existence.

This is Darwin's first published reference to evolution. It does not seem to have caused much comment at the time. Other papers at about this time were on the elevation of the coast of South America, volcanoes, and the unfortunate account of the Parallel Roads of **Glen Roy** (this sought to establish that these scars in the hillsides of Scotland were the result of sea level change; they were eventually shown to have been cut by glacial lakes in the Ice Age, and Darwin admitted that the paper was a "great failure"). An important piece on erratic boulders in South America appeared in 1842.

Darwin presented specimens to the society. He had been advised within months of his return from the *Beagle* that he should not waste his time running societies. Nevertheless, he was at a very early stage elected to the Council of the Geological Society and by early 1838 was appointed its secretary—"although," he wrote to Henslow, "it is an office I do not relish." He continued with this job despite protests and having to miss meetings because of illness until February 1841; nevertheless, he remained on the Council for many years. In 1859—the year of the publication of *On the Origin*—he was awarded the Wollaston Medal, the highest award of the Society.

Geological Time Scale

The method of delineating time used by geologists and other scientists to describe the timing and relationships between events that have occurred during the Earth's history. Darwin's geological and evolutionary work cannot be understood without reference to a geological scale of this sort.

Two approaches to geological time are encountered:

Relative time—whereby subdivisions of the Earth's geological history are arranged in a specific order based on relative age relationships (usually their vertical or stratigraphic position or their position in relation to other rocks above or below them in the geological column). The subdivisions are named, and most of the names can be recognized throughout the world, usually on the basis of the fossils the rocks contain.

Absolute time—numerical ages in millions of years (Ma). These are nowadays usually obtained via radiometric dating methods (based on the rate at which radioactive elements [or isotopes] decay into other elements; see below). Absolute time measurements can be used to calibrate, or place numerical values on, the relative time scale.

Some early attempts at establishing the history of the earth were based on the scrutiny of biblical sources, particularly the book of Genesis. Theophilus of Antioch, in A.D. 180, gave the date of the creation at 5515 B.C. Better known is the estimate of Archbishop James Ussher, who, in the 1650s, suggested that the date of creation was 4004 B.C. There were estimates from the eighteenth century that the world was about 74,000 years old.

The basic principles of geological time scales as they are understood today were established by Nicholas Steno (1638–1686), a Danish philosopher who argued that strata or layers of rock are deposited in succession and that each layer or stratum represents a slice of time. He formulated the law of superposition, which states that, in a section of horizontally bedded rocks, any given stratum is likely to be older than those above it but younger than those below it. While Steno's principles were simple, applying them to the real world proved complex. (Rocks often have been tilted, eroded, distorted or even overturned, so application of the rule is not always easy.)

Despite what is often asserted, by about 1825, most educated people in the West, Christian or not, realized that the earth was millions, possibly many millions, of years old, and by a decade or two later, the broad outline of the geological time scale and the names of many of the units had been established. Nevertheless, for some time, providing precise numerical dates for the various units remained almost impossible.

In 1862, three years after the publication of *On the Origin of Species*, Lord Kelvin (William Thomson, 1824–1907) made the first numerical calculation of Earth's age based on real scientific data. He knew that Earth's temperature increased one degree Fahrenheit for each 50 feet (12 meters) into the Earth. He suggested that the Earth began as molten rock at about 7,000° F (3,800° C). He calculated how long it would have taken to cool

Horizontally bedded sandstones, northwestern Australia. The law of superposition states that "in a set of undisturbed strata, the oldest will be at the bottom." Photo: Geography Department, University of Western Australia.

Steeply folded rocks, East Falkland. Sedimentary rocks may be almost vertical, or even overturned. This makes assessing its age difficult. Photo: Patrick Armstrong.

to produce that surface temperature gradient. He thus computed that it would have taken about 100 million years to reach the observed value. Thus, he estimated that the Earth was about 100 million years old.

To the disappointment of some biologists and geologists, Kelvin's calculations for the age of the Earth did not seem sufficient time for evolution to occur. Moreover, by 1899, he had revised this figure down to 20 to 40 million years. A few biologists and geologists, however, suggested figures of up to 100 times greater.

The discrepancy was not resolved until the early twentieth century, when Ernest Rutherford (1871–1937) found that radioactivity provides the Earth with an internal heating source that works in opposition to the process of cooling through the loss of heat from the surface. Current estimates suggest that the planet is at least 4,600 million years old.

Radioactivity also provided a method for the accurate dating of individual rocks: the rate at which radioactive isotopes (forms of chemical elements) decay—for example, uranium into lead, potassium into argon, carbon-14 into carbon-12—can allow an estimate to be made of the time that has elapsed since a rock has formed. There are many difficulties with this method of geological dating: one problem is that fragments of older rocks may be incorporated into younger rocks (for example, recent lavas from Hawaii have given anomalously old dates, probably because some of

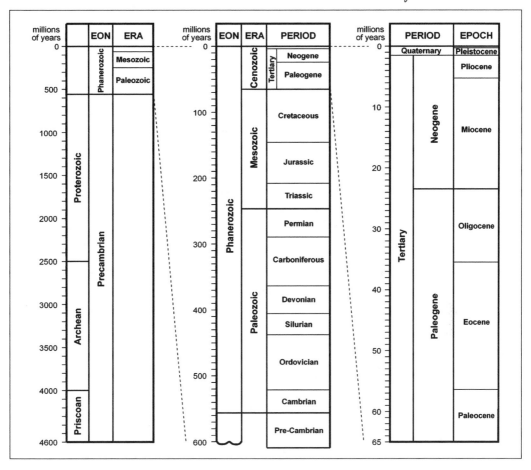

The divisions of geological time. It should be noted that there is some difference of opinion among geologists on the exact timing of the divisions. In North America the Carboniferous is sometimes divided into the Mississippian and Pennsylvanian.

the magma has come from deep within the Earth). The table gives some idea of the absolute ages of some of the geological periods as they are now understood.

Arthur Holmes provided as early attempt to integrate relative and absolute geological time in *The Age of the Earth* in the 1930s; there have been numerous revisions since, but the amount of change with each revision has become smaller. The date of the boundary between the base of the Tertiary and the upper Cretaceous periods has remained at about 65 million years for some time.

FURTHER READING

Blatt, H., W.B.N. Berry, and S. Brande. 1991. *Principles of Stratigraphic Analysis*. Boston: Blackwell Scientific Publications.

Grotzinger, J. P., S. A. Bowring, B. Z. Saylor, and A. J. Kaufman. 1995. "Biostratigraphic and Geochronologic Constraints on Early Animal Evolution." *Science* 270 (October 27): 598–604.

Harland, W. B., R. L. Armstrong, A. V. Cox, L. E. Craig, A. G. Smith, and D. G. Smith. 1990. *A Geologic Time Scale.* Cambridge, England: Cambridge University Press.

Holmes, Arthur. 1937. *The Age of the Earth* (new edition, revised). London: Nelson.

Roberts, Michael. 2007. "Genesis Chapter 1 and Geological Time from Hugo Grotius and Martin Mersenne to William Conybeare and Thomas Chalmers (1620–1825)." In *Myth and Geology, Geological Society of London, Special Publications* 273, eds. L. Piccardi and W. B. Masse, 39–49.

Geology of the Voyage of the Beagle

A series of three books, written in the years following his voyage, that describe Darwin's geological observations and the conclusions he deduced from them.

Very early in the voyage, at St. Jago in the **Cape Verde Islands,** in January 1832, Charles Darwin thought that he might be able to write a book about geology. He recalled the flash of inspiration decades later:

> It then first dawned on me that I might perhaps write a book on the geology of the various countries visited, and this made me thrill with delight. That was a memorable hour to me. (*Autobiography,* 81)

In fact, he wrote three books, or at least three volumes in one series. He commenced writing the first, and probably the most important, of these, *Coral Reefs,* in October 1838. He seems to have enjoyed writing it, but the process was not without its difficulties. He wrote to **Leonard Jenyns (John Henslow**'s brother-in-law) on July 13, 1839:

> I am hard at work, preparing the first volume of my geology—it is very pleasant easy work putting together the frame of a geological theory, but it is just as tough a job collecting & comparing the hard unbending facts—I have been for the last six weeks employed over one map to illustrate my views on coral formations. (*Correspondence,* Vol. 2, 207; original in Bath Reference Library)

Darwin ran into other problems in getting the book published. Darwin had been able to negotiate a grant of £1,000 to assist with the costs of producing the *Zoology of the Voyage of the Beagle,* and he had hoped that there might be some of this left over to help defray the costs of the *Geology of the Voyage.* It was not to be: he wrote to his wife Emma on May 9, 1842, just before publication, to say: "the government money has gone much quicker than I thought & expenses of the coral volume are greater, being as far as we can judge 130£ to 140£." He thought he would have to put a couple of hundred pounds into the project and was worried about Emma's attitude to this. He grumbled that he spent three years and seven months on the project.

Nevertheless, the finished book was worth the effort. It is a well-written and well-crafted book and, on the whole, it was well received. It starts with a case study of a coral atoll—the **Cocos (Keeling) Islands** in the Indian Ocean that he visited in April 1836. He then discusses atolls more generally and proceeds to a discussion of barrier reefs and fringing reefs. Chapter 4 deals with the distribution of coral and the conditions (in terms of temperature and sea depth) in which they can form. Chapter 5 outlines his theory of the formation of the different classes of coral reefs, suggesting that one form gradually developed into another as the result of gradual submergence. This is important because it represents Darwin's use of uniformitarian or gradualist principles in a major theory. The final chapter integrates his theory with his observations and notes on distribution, suggesting that there are great areas of the oceans that have submerged and other areas of emergence. There are a number of maps and diagrams (the engraving of which was perhaps the cause of the expense).

Volume 2, *Geological Observations on Volcanic Islands,* gave him less trouble; he started on the project in October 1842, and he wrote to his publishers that he had almost finished in October 1843 (although he did not actually deliver the manuscript until January 1844). He adopted a rather different approach to the structure than the one he used for the coral reefs volume. He describes each archipelago and island, starting with St. Jago. **Fernando Noronha,** Terceira in the **Azores, Tahiti,** and **Mauritius** are briefly mentioned, but **St. Helena and Ascension Island** and the **Galapagos Islands** warranted a chapter each. Chapter 6 is, like the final chapter of the coral reefs volume, an integrative one. He discusses the distribution of the islands, noting particularly their alignment and their possible age. Interestingly, he suggests a process based on the settling out of crystals within magma, so that a lava of one composition might "evolve" into that of another over time. The theme of elevation recurs, and, as with *Coral Reefs*, the work is strongly comparative. Because volume 3 of the series was to deal with South America, and not wishing to leave anything out, the final chapter cobbles together his observations from **Australia** (**Tasmania, New South Wales,** and King George's Sound), **New Zealand,** and the **Cape of Good Hope;** he admits that this material does not fit well with the main theme of the book.

Geological Observations on South America was commenced on October 29, 1845, and the last proof was corrected 11 months later on October 1, 1846. He drew together his observations from that vast area and again suggested that many aspects of the geology (and geomorphology) or the region could be explained by elevation. He also showed the relationship between **igneous rocks** and **metamorphic rocks.** Although by now a firm disciple of **Charles Lyell**'s approach, called **uniformitarianism** or **gradualism**—stressing the changes that had taken place over very long periods of time—Darwin nevertheless, in his emphasis on sea-level change and other topics, on occasion takes a firmly independent line. Always an integrator, he frequently compared (and combined) his ideas with those of others. For example, he discusses the views of the French geologist and paleontologist Alcide d'Orbigny, repeatedly differing from them. He explains d'Orbigny's view that the rocks of the pampas formation were laid down suddenly as the result of a single catastrophic event or *débâcle*. Darwin, on the other hand, using his own observations and those of others, opines that the rocks had been laid down successively over a considerable time under brackish or estuarine conditions. D'Orbigny sees the preservation of fossils in the position of life as evidence of very rapid uplift; Darwin took the opposite view. Gradualist views triumphed over catastrophism.

It was 10 years almost to the day between Darwin's coming ashore from the *Beagle* and the completion of the final volume of *Geology of the Voyage* (although he had been involved in much else, such as the **Zoology of the Voyage of the Beagle** and early work on his species theory later set out in *On the Origin of Species* at the same time). Taken together, the three books are a plea for the uniformitarian approach, the importance of changes in level, and the comparative method. The breadth of knowledge, the originality of the theoretical constructs, and an integrative way of working that the series displayed played a large part in establishing the scientific reputation of Charles Darwin at an early stage in his career.

The three books were reissued as a single volume in 1851. A second, slightly revised edition of *Coral Reefs* appeared in 1871. There have been many subsequent reprints of all three memoirs, some of which have contained an authoritative introduction by Professor J. W. Judd. There have been translations of at least one of the three volumes into French, German, Italian, Japanese, Russian, and Spanish.

Glaciation

The formation of glaciers and the processes and landforms associated with them.

Glaciers are masses of snow and ice that are sufficiently large to become deformed under their own weight and to flow downhill. It is now understood that there have been periods on Earth when the climate has become colder and glaciers became larger and more extensive in their distribution. Ice caps are dome-shaped glaciers from which the ice flows radially; the term ice sheet is used when the area covered is more than 50,000 square kilometers (about 13,000 square miles). During the most recent Ice Age, between about 2 million and 10,000 years ago, there were several periods when ice sheets covered much of Europe and North America, and in upland areas, such as the Alps, Scandinavia, and the Rockies, valley glaciers extended well below their present levels. Evidence of glaciation includes that of erratic boulders (far-traveled rock masses) and moraines (ridges of material deposited by ice). In upland areas, glaciers cut out U-shaped valleys.

Until well into the nineteenth century, the layer of drift deposits that covered much of northern Europe (deposits now referred to as boulder clay or glacial till) were ascribed to the flood described in the book of Genesis. (And their existence used to demonstrate the truth of the Old Testament and, by implication therefore, the literal truth of the whole Bible.) Darwin's approximate contemporary, the eccentric Oxford geologist **William Buckland** (1784–1856), was originally of this view and propounded it extensively. However, in 1840, Louis Agassiz (1807–1873), a Swiss naturalist, professor at the University of Neuchâtel and later at Harvard University, published *Études sur les glaciers* (*Studies of Glaciers*), which documented the behavior of Alpine glaciers and showed that glaciers and ice sheets had been much more extensive. (He had outlined of his ideas to the Swiss Natural History Society in 1837.)

Interestingly, when the young Charles Darwin traveled through **North Wales** with **Adam Sedgwick** in the early summer of 1831, they did not notice the evidence of glaciation that was all around them. As late as 1838, Darwin attributed the Parallel Roads of **Glen Roy** in Scotland to sea-level change rather than to the existence of ice margin lakes dammed by ice masses now thought to explain them; he later acknowledged his error.

This oversight is all the more surprising because Darwin had had considerable first-hand experience of glaciers in the Cordilleras of South America and in **Tierra del Fuego.** January 1833 found him with a group of shipmates in the Beagle Channel:

In many places, magnificent glaciers extended from the mountains to the water's edge. I cannot imagine anything more beautiful than the beryl blue of these glaciers, especially when contrasted with snow. The occurrence of glaciers reaching the water's edge & in summer, in Lat. 56° is a most curious phenomenon: the same thing does not occur in Norway under Lat 70°. From the number of small ice-bergs the channel resembled in miniature the Arctic Ocean. One of these glaciers placed us for a minute in most imminent peril. . . . a large mass fell roaring into the water. Our boats were on the beach; we saw the great wave rushing onwards, & instantly it was evident how great was the chance of their being dashed to pieces. (*Diary,* January 29, 1833)

Darwin was one of those who saved the day, rushing to hold the boats. He modestly says nothing about this in his journal, but Captain **Robert FitzRoy** was impressed, and he named the nearby Mt. Darwin after him. Darwin ended his account, however: "If they [the boats] had been washed away, how dangerous would our lot have been, surrounded on all sides by savages & deprived of all provisions."

In a short piece on the sighting of a rock in an iceberg by antarctic explorer Enderby in the *Journal of the Royal Geographical Society* in 1839, Darwin wrote: "Every fact on the transportation of fragments of rock by ice is of importance, as throwing light on the problem of 'erratic boulders,' which has so long perplexed geologists." It seems as though he was appreciating the importance of ice in modifying the Earth's surface before Agassiz's work had been published in Britain.

By the 1840s, in his revision of the *Voyage of the Beagle* for its later editions, Darwin had entirely absorbed the Ice Age theory.

> Few geologists now doubt that those erratic boulders which lie near lofty mountains, have been pushed forward by glaciers themselves. . . . The connexion between the transportal of boulders and the presence of ice in some form, is strikingly shown by their geographical distribution over the earth. (*Voyage of the Beagle*, chapter 11)

In fact, as early as 1841, he presented a paper to the **Geological Society of London** titled "On the Distribution of the Erratic Boulders on the Contemporaneous Unstratified Deposits of South America." He maintains that boulders might be transported by sea ice as well as by glaciers on land.

Later, Charles Darwin used the Ice Age theory extensively in his evolutionary writings:

> We have evidence of almost every conceivable kind, organic and inorganic, that within a very recent geological period, central Europe and North America suffered under an Arctic climate. The ruins of a house burnt by fire do not tell their tale more plainly, than do the mountains of Scotland and Wales, with their scored flanks, polished surfaces, and perched boulders, of the icy streams with which their valleys were lately filled. So greatly has the climate of Europe changed, that in Northern Italy, gigantic moraines, left by old glaciers, are now clothed by the vines and maize. Throughout a large part of the United States, erratic boulders, and rocks scored by drifted icebergs and coast-ice, plainly reveal a former cold period. (*On the Origin of Species*, 1st edition, chapter 11, Geographical Distribution)

He went on to show how climatic change has altered the distribution of plants, isolating populations and commingling others, and that this might well have had evolutionary consequences.

Gladstone, William Ewart (1809–1898)

British statesman, prime minister, reformer and pamphleteer, author, and scholar. His contribution to the evolutionary debates of the 1880s was not, however, one of his greatest triumphs.

The Right Honourable William Ewart Gladstone was a British Liberal politician holding the office of prime minister four times (1868–1874, 1880–1885, 1886, and 1892–1894). He was known for his populist speeches and was, for many years, the main political rival of Benjamin Disraeli. Gladstone was famously at odds with Queen **Victoria** for much of his career. She once complained: "He always addresses me as if I were a public meeting." Gladstone was known as the Grand Old Man or the People's William. He dominated the political life of Britain for the latter part of the nineteenth century.

Born in Liverpool in 1809 (the year of Charles Darwin's birth), William Ewart Gladstone was the fourth son of the merchant Sir John Gladstones and his second wife, Anne MacKenzie Robertson. (The final *s* was later dropped from the family surname.) John was a member of Parliament (1818–1827).

Although William Gladstone was born and brought up in Liverpool, and always retained a touch of a north country accent; he was of Scottish descent on both of sides of his family. William was educated at Eton College and in 1828 entered Christ Church, Oxford, where he took classics and mathematics, obtaining a double first. While an undergraduate, Gladstone was president of the Oxford Union, the student debating society, where he developed a reputation as a fine orator—a reputation that followed him into the House of Commons. At university, Gladstone was a Tory and firmly denounced the Whig proposals for parliamentary reform in a long-remembered debate at the Oxford Union.

He first considered a vocation as an Anglican priest (i.e., a Church of England clergyman); he was dissuaded from this by his father, although he was a devout Anglican all his life. He was first elected to Parliament in 1832 as conservative member of Parliament for Newark, partly as the result of the support of the Duke of Newcastle (with the son of whom he had been at university). Initially he was a somewhat reactionary High Tory. His first speech on June 3, 1833, established his reputation as a parliamentary performer. He held minor office in the short government of Sir Robert Peel, 1834–1835, as a junior minister at the treasury, and later as undersecretary for the colonies.

In 1839, he married Catherine Glynne, the daughter of Sir Steven Glynne of Hawarden Castle, North Wales, not far from the English city of Chester. Catherine was a woman of charm, wit, and discretion and bore William eight children (several of whom went on to make their own contribution to British public life). The marriage lasted for 49 years, until his death; it provided Gladstone with a secure and loving home life and great happiness, as well as providing a link (which he found exceedingly useful) with the British governing and aristocratic class.

He was re-elected in 1841, and in succeeding governments served as president of the Board of Trade, colonial secretary, chancellor of the exchequer, and prime minister. He held some of these offices several times (he was four times prime minister) and sometimes held more than one office simultaneously. He variously represented Oxford University, Newark, South Lancashire, Greenwich, and Midlothian. He eventually left the Conservatives, joining the Liberals in 1859. Gladstonian Liberalism, as it came to be known, was a major reforming influence; it was characterized in the 1860s and 1870s by a number of policies intended to improve individual liberty and loosen political and economic restraints. First was the reduction of public expenditure, on the basis that the economy and society were best helped by allowing people to spend as they saw fit. Gladstone advocated a foreign policy aimed at promoting peace and improving understanding, on the basis that this would help reduce expenditure and taxation as well as help trade. Finally, there was the reform of government institutions that prevented people from acting freely to improve themselves—particularly in the army, the civil service, and in local government—to cut restrictions on individual advancement. For example, he abolished the sale of commissions in the army. During this period, the franchise (the right to vote) was gradually extended. And as the result of successive reform acts, Parliament modernized: "rotten boroughs" (constituencies controlled by a small number of votes) became a thing of the past, and the distribution of parliamentary seats more closely reflected the distribution of population. He advocated free trade. His great aim of pacifying Ireland and bringing Home Rule to that unhappy island was not achieved, and he paid a heavy political price for it. One mistake he regretted was making a speech that appeared to favor the South in the American Civil War, when Britain's official stand was that of neutrality.

Gladstone was not solely responsible for all the improvements of his day, but his imprint on British politics profoundly influenced the tone and temper of life in Britain during the Victorian period—a period of progress and innovation and of the advancement of the common man at the expense of the inherited privilege of the landed gentry and aristocracy (despite his own background).

Gladstone was a prolific reader throughout his life—he is said to have read 20,000 books—and was a considerable classical scholar and theologian. He certainly read some of Charles Darwin's works and was interested in them, but his strong support of traditional Anglicanism made it difficult for him to accept the evolutionary point of view in its entirety. In November 1885, Gladstone wrote an article in a periodical called *Nineteenth Century* titled "Dawn of Creation and of Worship." In this Gladstone revealed himself as a "reconciler" (see **reconciliation**), one who attempts to reconcile the book of Genesis with modern scientific thought. He saw the point of departure as a "formless mass, created by God, out of which the earth was shaped and constituted a thing of individual existence" (Gen. 1–2). Later, light and dark, water and land came into existence, then plants that water creatures, then land creatures and finally man. Gladstone, like other reconcilers, seems to have envisaged a Genesis day as being far longer than a literal day. He asserts that modern paleontology provides support for these views.

> Now this same . . . order is understood to have been so affirmed in our time by natural science, that it may be taken as a demonstrated conclusion and established fact.

Darwin's great supporter **Thomas Huxley,** although he was not named in Gladstone's article, took this as an attack on Darwin and answered the next month with "The Interpreters of Genesis and the Interpreters of Nature," a piece that has become known as a classic of polemical literature. Outwardly polite, Huxley's sarcasm is vicious:

> If Mr. Gladstone's latest information on these matters is derived from famous discourse prefixed to the "Ossemens Fossiles" [one of **Georges Cuvier**'s works, published in 1812], I can understand the position he has taken up; if he has ever opened a respectable modern manual of palæontology, or geology, I cannot. For the facts which demolish his whole argument are of the commonest notoriety.

Gladstone exercised his right of reply soon after, in the January 1886 issue of *Nineteenth Century.* In fact, the two may not have been so far apart as Huxley's polemic suggested. In an essay full of allusions to biblical scholarship and the Greek and Latin classics, Gladstone declaimed:

> Nor can I comprehend the rapidity with which persons of authority have come to treat the Darwinian hypothesis as having reached the final stage of demonstration. To the eye of a looker-on their pace and method seem rather too much like a steeplechase. But this may very well be due to their want of appropriate knowledge and habits of thought. For myself, in my loose and uninformed way of looking at Evolution, I feel only too much biased in its favour, by what I conceive to be its relation to the great argument of design.

In asserting that Darwin's views were anything but "in their final stage of demonstration" and that there were indeed links between the doctrine of evolution and that of "the great argument of design," Gladstone was simply stating facts. Evolutionary notions have developed considerably since the nineteenth century; and William Paley's argument of design, expressed in *Natural Theology,* a work that greatly impressed Darwin, have their echo in the twenty-first-century notion of intelligent design. Many today have no difficulty with the idea that "evolution is the creator's tool."

The debate continued for some months, and others entered the fray. Huxley felt he had "polished off" the Grand Old Man, reporting in letters to his friends in the succeeding months that he had "dissected him" as "an anatomico-psychological exercise." It was not quite so simple as that.

What is, however, perhaps even more important than his personal ideas on evolution is that Gladstone's reforms, his enthusiasm for technology and education, and his encouragement of liberal ideas (even when he did not altogether agree with them) contributed to an environment in which Darwin's doctrines could flourish. In 1876, while visiting members of his party in the area, William Gladstone visited Darwin at his home at Down

House, talked of political matters, and tried to be friendly. Darwin felt much honored by the visit, for, despite differences that may have existed, the Darwins were always on the Whig or Liberal side of politics and approved of many of Gladstone's efforts on behalf of education and the common people.

Gladstone was a Liberal and an advocate of peace to the last. As late as 1896 he spoke in Liverpool, denouncing the massacres of the Armenians by the Ottoman Turks. He died of cancer in 1889 at age 88 at Hawarden Castle, in North Wales, originally his wife's family home and his own for much of his life. The nation mourned. He, like Darwin, was buried in Westminster Abbey.

FURTHER READING

Bebbington, D. W. 1993. *William Ewart Gladstone: Faith and Politics in Victorian Britain.* Grand Rapids, MI: Eerdmans.
Jenkins, Roy. 1995. *Gladstone.* London: Macmillan.
Matthew, H.C.G. 1998. *Gladstone, 1809–1898.* Oxford, England: Clarendon Press.

Glen Roy

Valley in Scotland; site of Charles Darwin's "great failure."

Glen Roy, near the Great Glen in the Scottish Highlands, displays a number of glacial features (land forms created during the Ice Age), but the most famous is its set of striking parallel "roads." These roads are the remnant shorelines of a glacial lake (ice-dammed lake) that existed in the glen during the last phase of the Ice Age. There are three levels of parallel roads in the glen, each corresponding to a different former lake level. These features are unique for their excellent preservation and for the fact that they are partly cut into the bedrock.

Approximately 11,000 to 10,000 years ago, there was a cold period—locally referred to as the Loch Lomond Stadial—at which time glaciers readvanced through parts of Scotland. At Glen Roy, the glaciers advancing from the south and west dammed a glacial lake in the valley, and the lake existed long enough to form shorelines high on the valley sides. The three levels of parallel roads are: 855, 1066, and 1168 feet (260, 325, and 350 meters respectively) above the present sea level.

Charles Darwin studied the geology of this area in late June 1838. But his interpretation was quite different. He had been preoccupied during the latter stages of the *Beagle* voyage—especially while he was developing the coral atoll theory—with the idea of changes in sea level. He thought that major areas of the Earth's crust had subsided and others had risen. He had found what he thought were raised shorelines high above the present sea level on the west coast of South America. He looked for bold, universal theories, attempting to find the *vera causa* or true cause of phenomena rather than erecting an ad hoc theory that would serve on a single occasion. His interpretation of the roads was that Glen Roy had once been an arm of the sea, and that they were "raised beaches" cut when the sea level was much higher. He gave a paper expressing these ideas to the **Royal Society** in February 1839. It was titled "Observations on the Parallel Roads of Glen Roy, and of Other parts of Lochaber in Scotland, with an Attempt To Prove that They Are of Marine Origin" and was later published in the *Philosophical Transactions* of the society. Darwin made comparisons with sites he had observed during his voyage in an attempt to universalize his ideas of sea level rise and fall. Although the paper includes a mass of detailed observation and is carefully argued, Louis Agassiz was at the same time developing his ice age theory that much of the Northern Hemisphere had been covered by ice—ice that had blocked Glen Roy, causing the lake to form and cutting the roads in the hillside. This was an idea that had been hinted at some years before Darwin's visit to the Highlands. Eventually Darwin conceded: he acknowledged that his Glen Roy paper had been a "gigantic blunder" or a "great failure." Even the greatest minds are sometimes in error.

See also: Glaciation.

Gould, John (1804–1881)

English ornithologist who worked on the bird specimens that Darwin collected on the *Beagle* voyage; he was best known, however, as a prolific producer of lavishly illustrated natural history books, which now command enormous prices among collectors.

John Gould, the son of a gardener, was born on September 14, 1804, at Lyme Regis, Dorset. Gould learned taxidermy at Windsor Castle, where his father was foreman of gardeners. In 1827, he was appointed animal preserver to the Zoological Society of London. The arrival in 1830 of a collection of bird skins from the Himalayas enabled him to produce the first of many splendid folio volumes, *A Century of Birds from the Himalaya Mountains* (1831–1832). Gould's sketches were transferred to lithographer's stone by his wife Elizabeth (née Coxon), whose great artistic talents enhanced many of John Gould's works until her death in 1841, perhaps partly as the result of overwork. The five-volume *Birds of Europe* (1832–1837) and *Monograph of the Ramphastidae* (Toucans) (1834) were so successful that the Goulds were able to spend two years (1838–1840) in Australia, where they amassed a large collection of birds and mammals. These collections resulted in Gould's most famous work, *The Birds of Australia,* in seven volumes (1840–1848, with supplements appearing in 1851–1869) and *Mammals of Australia,* in three volumes (1845–1863). In total he produced over 40 volumes, containing over 3,000 colored plates.

John Gould's books on birds were famous for their illustrations. "Chlorospiza melamoderna" from his *Zoology of the Voyage of the Beagle*, Part 3, Birds, 1841. The modern scientific name for this Falkland Islands species is *Melamoderna melamoderna*, the black-throated finch.

Gould was a first-rate field observer as well as being an excellent museum taxonomist. While in Australia, he described in great detail the manner in which the beaks of the honey-eaters (family *Meliphagidae*) were adapted for seeking nectar from the blossoms of Australian plants.

His many scientific papers, mostly devoted to descriptions of new species, established his scientific reputation, and it was for this reason that Darwin contacted him for help with his bird specimens and for assistance with the *Birds* volume (part 3) of ***Zoology of the Voyage of the Beagle*** (1843). He and his wife left for the Australian bird-collecting expedition before the work was completed; nevertheless, the advice John Gould gave Darwin, particularly on the bird specimens he had collected from the Galapagos, was extremely important. In early 1837, John Gould carefully examined the bird specimens from that group of islands and pronounced that the specimens Darwin had collected there, and in his mind assigned to different biological groups on account of their wide variety of beak forms, were in fact closely related; they were "a series of ground finches, which are . . . peculiar"; they constituted "an entirely new group containing 12 species." In fact, the final total was slightly more than this. Darwin, like us all, made mistakes, and one of his more consequential errors was his failure to label some of the Galapagos specimens with the name of the island from which they came; he had to seek information from some of his shipmates who had taken specimens. However, Gould had much more to say. Darwin had labeled a set of mockingbirds by island: these Gould told him were distinct species. And they were related to, but not identical with, South American forms. These fragments became extremely important to Darwin as he began to develop his theories. The birds of the Galapagos Islands (which he thought [correctly] were young, geologically) had arrived from the mainland and changed after arrival; in some cases, each island had its own distinctive assemblage of creatures. A little later, they discussed the South American rhea specimens; one was a new species, which Gould designated *Rhea darwinii*. This too is interesting, because Darwin's first speculative evolutionary notes appear in his notebooks from this time: "Why were there no intermediates between the big and little species [of rhea] at the Rio Negro";

was the change from one form to another progressive or had it been "produced at one blow?" Clearly much more thinking and working was required, but the young Darwin was on his way—and John Gould, unwittingly, perhaps—had helped him there.

Gould was elected a fellow of the **Royal Society** in 1843.

He was an active conservationist. Spending the period (1837–1840) in Australia, he wrote:

> Short-sighted indeed are the Anglo-Australians, or they would have long ere this made laws for the preservation of their highly singular indigenous animals; and . . . wishing to introduce to Australia the productions of other climes, whose forms are not adapted to that country.

He was extremely prescient in this; he foresaw the extermination of the Tasmanian wolf or thylacine; it would, he thought, "speedily diminish" and become "like the wolf in England and Scotland, be recorded as an animal of the past." It is appropriate, therefore, that the Gould League, established in Australia in 1909, commemorates his life and work by encouraging an interest in natural history and conservation among young people.

He died in London on February 3, 1881. His final wish was that his epitaph should be "here lies John Gould, bird man."

FURTHER READING

Lambourne, Maureen. 1987. *John Gould: Bird Man*. Milton Keynes, England: Osberton Productions.

Gould, Stephen Jay (1941–2002)

American evolutionist, paleontologist, and historian and popularizer of science.

Stephen Jay Gould was born and raised in New York City, in a nonpracticing Jewish household. When he was five years old, his father took him to the Hall of Dinosaurs in the American Museum of Natural History. It was there that he first saw a specimen of *Tyrannosaurus rex:* "I was awestruck," he later recalled. It was at that moment he decided to become a paleontologist. He graduated from Antioch College and received his doctorate from Columbia University in 1967. For the remainder of his career, he was based at Harvard University. In 1973, he became professor of geology and curator of invertebrate paleontology at the university's Museum of Comparative Zoology; nine years later, he received the title Alexander Aggaziz Professor of Zoology. A good deal of Gould's scientific research was on land snails.

Gould was a passionate believer in the theory of evolution and wrote a series of popular books on the subject, including *The Panda's Thumb* (1980), *The Mismeasure of Man* (1981, revised 1996), *Wonderful Life*

(1989), and *Bully for Brontosaurus* (1991). Some of these consisted primarily of articles he wrote for the magazine *Natural History*.

One of the problems that has beset evolutionary theory is that intermediates between species and between the major biological groups are rare. In the fossil record, organisms tend to remain the same for an appreciable period and then disappear. Indeed, the concept of zone fossils in geology—the use of a particular fossil to identify a particular stratum—depends on this. In 1979, Gould and Miles Eldredge suggested the idea of **punctuated equilibrium.** They argued that there were periods of rapid evolution that were perhaps the result of mutations interspersed with comparatively long periods of stability. Alongside the notion of punctuated equilibrium goes the idea of peripheral isolation. The relatively sudden changes envisaged by Gould might occur in a very small area, and thus direct evidence for the change might seldom be found (e.g., in the fossil record). Gould did not totally disown the possibility of slow, natural selection–induced evolution—he remained a great admirer of Darwin's ideas—but he thought that this was not the only mechanism. He emphasized that competition and selection could occur at a variety of levels—population, species, and higher taxonomic groups.

Another innovation in evolutionary theory was the borrowing of the architectural term *spandrel* for evolutionary biology. Architecturally, a spandrel is the space between two arches or between an arch and a rectangular enclosure: such a structure may be elaborately decorated, but such decoration was not its original purpose. In evolutionary biology, a spandrel is a characteristic that evolved as a side effect of a true adaptation. It is a structure that arose as a necessary consequence of other features rather than through natural selection. Not every feature of every organism has arisen by adaptation; sometimes a structure developed to fulfill one function may take on another.

Gould emphasized the chanciness of evolution; there was a randomness about which species or major biological groups survived. In *Wonderful Life* (based largely on the research of others), he considered the bizarre fossil fauna of the Cambrian Burgess Shale of British Columbia. Gould maintained that as many as half the organisms preserved there belonged to unknown phyla (i.e., they belonged to groups that were totally different from the forms in younger rocks). There had been some form of mass extinction; some organisms had survived, some had not, and pure chance had influenced this. If some other combination of forms has survived the catastrophe, he argued, the whole nature of the subsequent development of life on earth might have been very different. (There were those who disagreed, stating that there was considerable continuity between the Burgess Shale's fossils and later forms.) Gould, however, carried the randomness of the evolutionary process much further: "Humans," he argued, are not the "result of predictable evolutionary progress, but . . . a fortuitous cosmic afterthought, a tiny little twig on the enormously arborescent bush of life, which if replanted from seed, would almost surely not grow this twig again."

Gould appeared to enjoy controversy. He emphasized the importance of the whole organism (and the species, population, and biological group) and its fitness (or otherwise) for its environment rather than a part of the individual, let alone the gene. In this he was strongly in opposition to **Richard Dawkins,** of Oxford, who argues that evolution, above all else, can be envisaged as competition between genes. John Maynard Smith, another critic of Gould's emphasis on sudden mutations, felt that he had underemphasized adaptation yet approved of how he had reinvigorated evolutionary paleontology. Another source of conflict between Dawkins and Gould was Dawkins's extreme antipathy to religion. Although of Jewish background, Gould described himself as an agnostic; yet he stated more than once that acceptance of evolution was entirely compatible with Christian (or other religious) belief. He maintained that religion and science were "nonoverlapping magisteria." Each had their role and place, and neither should attempt to usurp the position of the other. He was particularly critical of scientific creationism, which attempted to adduce scientific evidence to prove the literal truth of the creation stories of the book of Genesis. Gould also sought to strengthen links between science and the social sciences and humanities.

Gould died in May 2002, after a battle with cancer that he documented in the scientific press. There were fulsome obituaries; even those who opposed some of his views admired his single-mindedness in the promotion of, and protection of, science in general and evolutionary ideas in particular.

Gradualism

The notion that any phenomenon is affected by long-continued, gradual change. The idea may be applied in geology, geomorphology (the study of land forms), biology, paleontology, psychology, and astronomy.

See also: Uniformitarianism.

Gray, Asa (1810—1888)

American botanist; supporter and publicist of Darwinian ideas in the United States.

A farmer's son, Asa Gray was born in Paris, Oneida County, New York. Like a number of his scientific contemporaries, he commenced his career with medical training (**Thomas Huxley** and **Joseph Hooker** were medically qualified, and **Charles Darwin** undertook two years of study at Edinburgh Medical School). After schooling at Clinton Grammar School, he studied medicine at Fairfield Academy, graduating with the degree of MD in 1831. He became interested in science as a discipline, and in the relationship between science and religion, while working with John Hadley. However, he soon abandoned the practice of medicine and took a series of part-time teaching and library appointments. Already having amassed a substantial collection of plants, he began working closely with John Torrey of New York, then the leading botanist in the United States. Gray's first paper on botany appeared in 1834, and thereafter a stream of papers and textbooks on botany followed. These included *Elements of Botany* (1836), *Botanical Text-book for Colleges* (1839), *How Plants Grow* (1858), and *Field, Forest and Garden Botany* (1869). Of greater scientific importance, however, was his *Manual of the Botany of the Northern United States,* which first appeared in 1847 but went through many editions.

Gray was selected to be a member of the U.S. Exploring Expedition, 1838–1842, but partly because of delays in its getting under way and partly because he had been offered a university chair, he withdrew from the expedition. (See article on **James Dwight Dana.**) He later, however, assisted with the scientific study of the specimens collected. He also studied, evaluated, and classified material from a number of expeditions to the American West, which was in the 1840s and 1850s being explored and opened up. His *Synoptical Flora of North America,* a project planned and executed with John Torrey, was the product of many years of work and appeared in 1878. In 1842, he accepted the Fischer professorship of natural history at Harvard University and was responsible for developing a curriculum of systematic botany and establishing a botanic garden and an outstanding herbarium. In 1874, he was appointed to the board of regents of the Smithsonian Institution in Washington, DC, succeeding Louis Agassiz. He also held the position of president of the American Academy of Arts and Sciences from 1863 to 1873. He was elected a foreign member of the **Royal Society** of London in 1873.

Despite adhering to the Presbyterian tradition and having a strongly evangelical outlook, Gray was very much an empirical scientist, applying the utmost rigor in his work and eschewing the transcendentalism of some New England thinkers. For much of his career, Asa Gray was interested in the distribution of plants, and in the 1850s compared the plants of the United States with those of Japan, applying rigorous statis-

Asa Gray, Darwin's American correspondent and publicist.

tical methods where possible. It was this interest in distribution that cemented his relationship with Charles Darwin, and they corresponded frequently; nearly 40 letters between them are known from the years 1851–1859. They had met at Kew early in 1851; at that time, Jane Gray referred to Darwin as a "lively, agreeable person." In an important letter in 1857, Darwin admitted Asa Grey into the small group of confidants with whom he had discussed his evolutionary views. There was obviously a real warmth between them, for Darwin refers to Gray's "extraordinary kindness" in his providing information and assistance and his "warmest feelings of respect." In an enclosure with this letter, he sets out his views in some detail:

> I cannot doubt that during millions of generations individuals of a species will be born with some slight variation profitable in some part of its economy; such will have a better chance of surviving, propogating, this variation, which again will be slowly increased by the accumulative action of Natural selection; and the variety thus formed will either coexist with, or more commonly will exterminate its parent form. (Charles Darwin to Asa Gray, September 5, 1857; *Correspondence of Charles Darwin,* Vol. 6, 448, Harvard University, Gray Herbarium)

Parts of this letter were included in the joint Darwin-Wallace presentation, cobbled together by **Joseph Hooker** and **Charles Lyell,** to the **Linnean Society of London** in 1858. As Gray began to adopt Darwin's ideas on transmutability, he expressed the notion that the floras of the United States and Japan were not entirely separate creations, but were the descendants of a common flora that had been pushed south by **glaciation.** This brought Gray into direct conflict with Louis Agassiz, who was a proponent of the stability of species.

Gray was known for his fair, balanced, and often very literary reviews of scientific texts. His review of *On the Origin of Species,* which was published a few months after his work on the relationship between Japanese and American floras was published, has been described as by far the most competent to appear in the United States. Although he had misgivings about certain aspects of Darwin's theory—he worried particularly about the chanciness of natural selection mechanisms—he made it his business to see that the book would be received fairly. He saw *On the Origin* as a continuation of Paleyan thinking on natural theology; in his view, natural selection did not exclude design, and he stressed that acceptance of the theory of evolution did not necessarily imply atheism. The term "Darwin's retriever" has been used for Gray, in that he retrieved evolutionary thought for Christians. Those, like Agassiz, who saw the racial implications of evolution, did not welcome an approach that suggested that "the Negro and the Hottentot" were blood relations of modern Europeans and white Americans.

Gray wrote important works that publicized Darwin's ideas in North America; these included *A Free Examination of Darwin's Treatise on the Origin of Species* (1861), *Essays and Reviews Pertaining to Darwinism* (1876), and *Natural Science and Religion* (1880). This is not to say he was uncritical: he admitted that the lack of any clear understanding of the mechanisms of variation and inheritance posed difficulties.

Sometimes Gray continued his work on the reconciliation of evolutionary ideas and theism in cooperation with a Congregationalist pastor from Andover, Maine, George Frederick Wright. They both saw the "exquisite adaptation" manifest in the natural world, brought about by evolution, as evidence *for* design in nature rather than *against* it. The fact that Wright was something of a geologist assisted in the propagation of these views. After Gray's death, Wright continued with his geological research (he wrote *The Ice Age in North America* (1889) and *Man and the Glacial Period* (1896)) and his attempts to harmonize religion and science.

H

Hardy, Thomas (1840—1928)

Considered perhaps the greatest of the Victorian English novelists; also a distinguished poet. Although he lived into the post–World War I era, his life overlapped with that of Charles Darwin by over 40 years, and they read each other's works.

Some literary scholars maintain that the structure, and to some extent the detail, of Hardy's, novels—set in Wessex, the county of Dorset, and the adjacent landscapes of the West of England—were profoundly influenced by his interpretation of Darwin's writings, particularly *On the Origin of Species* (1859) and *Descent of Man* (1871). Influences of other broadly Darwinian authors—**Charles Lyell, Thomas Huxley, Herbert Spencer,** and **Gideon Algernon Mantell** for example—can also be detected, and indeed were acknowledged by Hardy.

Thomas Hardy was born in the village of Upper Brockhampton, Dorset, the son of a master mason and building contractor. He was educated in the nearby country town of Dorchester, and at the age of 16 was apprenticed to a firm of architects that specialized in the restoration of churches—skills that were in demand in the mid-Victorian period. At the age of 22, he moved to London, working with the architectural firm of Arthur Blomfield. He attended evening classes in French, went to the opera and to the plays of Shakespeare. He read works by Charles Darwin, social evolutionist **Herbert Spencer** (1820–1903), and empirical philosopher John Stuart

Mill (1806–1873), whose positivist thinking affected him. He started to write poetry about rural life but found little market for his work.

In 1867, he returned to Dorset and, for a while, to architectural work. He had a brief engagement to a 16-year-old relative, Typhena Sparks. The relationship did not last, and he married Emma Lavinia Gifford, who, although the marriage had its ups and downs, encouraged him to think of writing as his true vocation. Not achieving success with his poetry, he was advised by the novelist George Meredith (1828–1909) to attempt a novel. *Far from the Madding Crowd* appeared in 1874. Hardy then became a full-time novelist and published a series of works set among the fields, hedgerows, farms, and villages of Wessex, just before the main burst of the industrial revolution. He had a feel for the landscape:

> Here, in the valley, the world seems to be constructed upon a smaller and more delicate scale . . . the prospect is a broad rich mass of grass and trees, mantling minor hills and dales within the major. Such is the Vale of Blackmoor. (*Tess of the d'Urbervilles*, chapter 2)

Interestingly, passages describing cultural landscapes, broadly similar in temper and economy, can be found in *The Voyage of the Beagle*.

Hardy's works were tragedies and, for the most part, deeply pessimistic in tone; they emphasize the helplessness of individuals at the hands of fate and the manner in which individuals, often influenced by profound passions, are sometimes the instruments of their own destruction. *The Return of the Native* appeared in 1878 and the *Mayor of Casterbridge* in 1886. Casterbridge was the thinly disguised town of Dorchester. Although popular today as a lyrical pastoralist, Hardy was heavily criticized at the time. One reviewer of *Tess of the d'Urbervilles* stated that the novel, "except for a few hours spent with cows, has not a gleam of sunshine." It was *Tess* (1891) and *Jude the Obscure* (1896) that particularly challenged contemporary Victorian conventions of religious and sexual conduct and that received particularly astringent criticism, touching as they did on seduction, illegitimacy, adultery, desertion, and murder. One editor wrote that he disliked *Tess* because the allegedly emotive word "succulent" was used several times for the fertile Frome Valley. There are a number of such instances in which the landscape stands as an allegory for human sexuality, and such references contributed to the difficulty in getting the novel published. When *Tess* appeared, however, it, along with Hardy's other novels, were very successful, and he became a quite wealthy man.

Hardy continued to hold a generally Christian outlook throughout his early life, indeed until shortly after his reading of *On the Origin,* but evolutionary ideas soon influenced him and he later renounced theism, adopting a mechanical, determinist approach to nature's seeming brutality. It was a short step to imposing this paradigm on the human condition. *Tess* and

Jude were castigated by some as atheist novels, and Hardy's marriage suffered as the result of the public outrage.

Here is a single example of Hardy's early flirtation with evolutionary ideas, from the early novel, published in 1873, *A Pair of Blue Eyes* (chapter 22). Henry Knight has fallen down a steep cliff and is perched precariously on a small, unstable knob of rock; not surprisingly, his thoughts turn to death:

> [O]pposite Knight's eyes was an imbedded fossil, standing forth in low relief from the rock. It was a creature with eyes. The eyes, dead and turned to stone, were even now regarding him. It was one of the early crustaceans called Trilobites. Separated by millions of years in their lives, Knight and this underling seemed to have met in their death. It was the single instance within reach of his vision of anything that had ever been alive and had had a body to save, as he himself had now.
>
> The creature represented but a low type of animal existence, for never in their vernal years had the plains indicated by those numberless slaty layers been traversed by an intelligence worthy of the name. Zoophytes, mollusca, shell-fish, were the highest developments of those ancient dates. The immense lapses of time each formation represented had known nothing of the dignity of man. . . . He was to be with the small in his death. . . .
>
> Time closed up like a fan before him. He saw himself at one extremity of the years, face to face with the beginning and all the intermediate centuries simultaneously. Fierce men, clothed in the hides of beasts, and carrying, for defence and attack, huge clubs and pointed spears, rose from the rock. . . . They lived in hollows, woods, and mud huts—perhaps in caves of the neighbouring rocks. Behind them stood an earlier band. No man was there. Huge elephantine forms, the mastodon, the hippopotamus, the tapir, antelopes of monstrous size, the megatherium, and the myledon—all, for the moment, in juxtaposition. Further back, and overlapped by these, were perched huge-billed birds and swinish creatures as large as horses. Still more shadowy were the sinister crocodilian outlines—alligators and other uncouth shapes, culminating in the colossal lizard, the iguanodon. Folded behind were dragon forms and clouds of flying reptiles: still underneath were fishy beings of lower development; and so on, till the lifetime scenes of the fossil confronting him were a present and modern condition of things.

Hardy uses the trilobite (no longer considered a crustacean) as a peg on which to hang Knight's thoughts on life, death, and time, but there is a strong evolutionary thrust in the piece. Hardy shows that he knows about Darwin's views on the evolution of life, although it seems that some of the material in the above extract is derived from Gideon Algernon Mantell's *The Wonders of Geology, or a Familiar Exposition of Geological Phenomena*, first published in 1838, two decades before *On the Origin*. Mantell's semi-popular work distils the thoughts of Darwin's geologist friend Charles Lyell.

It is, however, *Tess of the d'Urbervilles* that has been described as showing the strongest Darwinian influence. Charles Darwin's notion of natural selection or Herbert Spencer's term "survival of the fittest" is based on the combined effects of chance variations and the pressures of the environment, including competition. It was this process that led to evolutionary change. John Holloway identifies the seven phases of the novel (as Hardy called them) with the Darwinian themes of organism, environment, struggle, adaptation, fertility, survival, and resistance. An individual is seen as passing through the same cycle as a species: origin, establishment, extinction. Hardy himself grouped *Tess, Jude, Casterbridge,* and *Madding Crowd* (and several others) as his "novels of character and environment," suggesting that he saw the environment, and indeed the landscape, as important influences on the course of human life.

Darwin's *On the Origin of Species* does not, apart from a vague reference in the final paragraph, make much mention of human evolution. He reserved this for *Descent of Man,* published over 12 years later. Although he saw natural selection as the primary process in evolution, in this later work he emphasized sexual selection. One might select a mate with certain characteristics and therefore, through genetic inheritance, influence the form of the progeny of the union—and ultimately the course of evolution of the species. In "Thomas Hardy's Comedies and Tragedies of Fickleness," in *Flirt's Tragedy,* R. A Kaye maintains that Hardy's plots explore Darwin's notion of sexual selection. Powerful, dominating female characters operate an "elaborate male beauty contest." The heroines find themselves in entanglements where they have to deal with two or more lovers. In *Under the Greenwood Tree* (1872), a young schoolteacher, Fancy Day, succumbs to Dick Dewy, but Dick eventually realizes that Fancy has a roving eye. In *A Pair of Blue Eyes* (1873), Elfride Swancourt, engaged to be married to the debonair Stephen Fitzmaurice Smith, abandons him for another (geologist and writer Henry Knight) in the face of family disapproval, but her happiness is destroyed when her fiancé discovers her previous relationship. In *Madding Crowd,* Bathsheba Everdene embodies an archetypical flirt. In *Jude,* Sue Bridehead combines coquetry with poor judgment. Many times, according to this interpretation, Hardy distorts sexual selection, prolonging and distorting the moment of choice. The flirtatious female can "interrupt evolutionary progress," as various types of catastrophe proceed from the determinist logic of sexual selection. It has to be said, however, that such a Darwinist view of the novels has not been universally accepted.

The criticism of *Tess of the d'Urbervilles* and *Jude the Obscure* disturbed Hardy, and he resolved to write no more novels, devoting much of the rest of his life to poetry. His enormous blank-verse panorama of the Napoleonic Wars, *The Dynasts,* was written between 1903 and 1908 (the theme of struggle persisting). The last book published during his life time was *Human Shows, Far Phantasies, Songs and Trifles* (1925), but *Winter Words in Various Moods and Metres* was published posthumously (1928).

His first wife Emma died in 1912, and two years later he married his secretary, Florence Dugdale, a woman forty years younger than he. From 1920 to 1927, Thomas Hardy worked on his autobiography, which was published in two volumes in 1928 and 1930.

Although reviled by certain establishment figures in Hardy's earlier decades, the tide turned. In 1909, he followed his friend George Meredith into the presidency of the Society of Authors. King George V conferred on him the Order of Merit, and in 1912 he was awarded the Gold Medal of the Royal Society of Literature. He is said to have refused a knighthood, but, after he died in Dorchester on December 11, 1928, he was buried, despite his atheistic outlook, in Poets' Corner of Westminster Abbey, just a few feet from where Charles Darwin, who held similar, although not identical, religious views, is buried.

See also: Darwinism and Literature.

FURTHER READING

Holloway, John. 1960. *The Chartered Mirror: Literary and Critical Essays.* London: Routledge and Kegan Paul.

Kaye, Richard A. 2002. *The Flirt's Tragedy: Desire without End in Victorian and Edwardian Fiction.* Charlottesville: University of Virginia Press.

Henslow, John Stevens (1796–1861)

Parson-naturalist, botanist, Cambridge University professor, and Darwin's mentor.

He authored over 130 publications—including several books on topics as varied as botany, zoology, archaeology, geology, agriculture, and theology—was an educational pioneer, a political pamphleteer, and held the Cambridge chairs of mineralogy and botany. Henslow will, however, be remembered primarily as Darwin's teacher and the person influential in gaining for him his position on the *Beagle*.

In many ways Henslow was a typical example of that supremely important figure in British science, the Victorian clergyman-naturalist. He came from a reasonably well-to-do, upper-middle-class family. His grandfather, Sir John Henslow(e), was a distinguished naval architect and, for many years, chief surveyor to the Royal Navy. His father (John Prentis Henslow) was a solicitor but later went into business with his uncle as a wine merchant in Rochester; and later still married the daughter of a rich brewer, Thomas Stevens. John Prentis's father-in-law took him into partnership, and the couple set up house in Rochester in Kent, and John Stevens was born February 5, 1796, the eldest of 11 children, 3 of whom died in infancy. Both his parents collected natural history specimens, and their bright young son followed their example. There is a tale of young John dragging home a fungus "almost as big as himself." Boarding school on the outskirts of London followed; here his interest in natural history was further encouraged. He attended St. John's College, Cambridge, a large and wealthy college. He studied mathematics and philosophy but also attended lectures in chemistry, geology, and mineralogy. He graduated with first-class honors in mathematics in 1818, having won several university prizes along the way. He remained in Cambridge after graduating, helping professors with their researches and in preparing demonstrations for students. He undertook several geological expeditions to different parts of the British Isles—the Isle of Wight (off southern England) and the Isle of Man (in the Irish Sea) in 1819 and the Isle of Anglesey (off the north coast of Wales) in 1820 and 1821. Work done on these journeys formed the basis of his first few scientific papers. He was elected to the chair of mineralogy in May 1822 (at what would now be considered the extremely young age of 26) and commenced lecturing in early 1823.

He married Harriet Jenyns, the daughter of a country clergyman from a landowning family in December 1823 (in the eighteenth and nineteenth centuries, English clerical and landowning families were closely connected with each other by kinship and marriage).

John Stevens Henslow was ordained deacon in April 1824 and priest in November of the same year, immediately prior to his taking the position of perpetual curate (effectively the same as vicar) of Little St. Mary's Church, Cambridge. The following year, he added to his list of appointments (and presumably his income) by taking the chair of botany. The holding of more than one church and university appointment at the same time was not then considered unusual. In March 1827, he gave up the mineralogy chair to concentrate on the botany appointment.

It was around this time that Henslow commenced holding his Friday evening soirées for those who were interested in science. These became a Cambridge institution, and some distinguished visitors attended, including the American artist and ornithologist John James Audubon in March 1828.

Henslow had the reputation of being an excellent teacher, giving well-prepared lectures illustrated by diagrams of his own drawing. Perhaps even more important was his agreeable, affable manner: he was at home with the most distinguished scholar and the youngest student (or school child) and answered queries, no matter how naïve, with courtesy and care,

John Stevens Henslow, Darwin's mentor and life-long friend. National Portrait Gallery, London.

as though whatever observation was brought to him was a matter of interest and importance.

In 1829, Charles Darwin attended some of Henslow's soirées and some of his lectures, and their lifelong friendship was established. They went for botanical walks in the Cambridgeshire countryside, and Darwin became known as "the man who walks with Henslow." The tuition that Charles Darwin obtained in these various formal and informal ways was formative in the young naturalist's development. Darwin stated that his meeting with Henslow was the one event "which influenced my career more than any other." In the spring and early summer of 1831, Henslow encouraged Darwin to take an interest in geology, and a few weeks later suggested his name as a possible companion for Captain **Robert Fitz-Roy** on the *Beagle* voyage. Henslow also directed Darwin's reading constructively, suggesting, for example, that he take Lyell's *Principles of Geology* on the voyage, although he cautioned his young student that, "on no account" should he accept everything in it. Also, in the frenetic period of planning for departure, Henslow gave detailed advice on preparing and preserving specimens.

While Darwin was voyaging, the two kept in contact by letter. Crates of specimens were sent to Henslow for preliminary inspection, sorting, and safekeeping—the first box was received in 1833—and extracts from Darwin's letters were printed and circulated. Thus, when Darwin returned from the sea, the scientific community in London and Cambridge already knew a

Parish church at Hitcham, Suffolk. Photo: Patrick Armstrong.

good deal about him and was ready to receive him to its heart. Henslow looked through many of the specimens Darwin had collected on the voyage, writing papers on the flora of the Galapagos and the Cocos Islands on the basis of Darwin's collected material.

In 1839, Henslow gave up his Cambridge house and many of his Cambridge commitments and moved to the parish of All Saints, Hitcham, a small village in Suffolk, about 35 miles (56 kilometers) from Cambridge. He retained his university professorship but concentrated his lecturing into a few weeks a year. He was thus a rector of a small rural parish for the remainder of his days. He entered fully into village life, financially supporting, encouraging, and teaching in the village school. He became interested in agriculture and used his knowledge of botany and geology for the benefit of the local farmers. He supported the museum in the nearby town of Ipswich. He also encouraged a medical club, a children's clothing club, a ploughing match society, and a cricket club. Every year he arranged an agricultural show for the village of Hitcham that included a marquee museum at which specimens of all kinds were exhibited, including some sent by Darwin. The link through correspondence continued, to the benefit of both parties, although Henslow, a liberal churchman in some of his views, never entirely accepted the conclusions expressed in *On the Origin of Species*.

Henslow's final illness commenced in mid-March 1861, when he caught a severe cold on a visit to friends in southern England. He returned to Suffolk on March 23, obviously very ill with chest pains and having difficulty breathing. Doctors diagnosed bronchitis and congestion of the lungs, but little could be done for him in a world without antibiotics. He lingered for several weeks, with several of his former colleagues and family members around him. He was described in those days as being "calm, resigned and quite happy . . . full of peace and love."

He died on May 16, 1861, at the age of 65. His funeral was on May 22; he was buried close to his wife, who predeceased him by some years, near the church tower in the Hitcham churchyard.

Darwin continued to be influenced by his friend and teacher long after Henslow had died. Darwin had constructed a heated greenhouse at his home at Down House in 1863, and some of his best botanical experimental work followed. His correspondence—for example, with Joseph Hooker—shows that he was frequently using Henslow's writings, especially his *Principles of Descriptive and Physiological Botany* (1835).

Charles Darwin's assessment of his mentor, given in the autobiography he wrote for his family late in life (1873) was as follows:

> His strongest taste was to draw conclusions from long-continued minute observations. His judgement was excellent and his whole mind well balanced, but I do not suppose that anyone would say that he possessed much original genius.

246

To which Henslow biographers S. M. Walters and E. A. Stow add:

[F]or the progress of science as for the welfare of mankind, a flair for teaching which releases genius may be as important as the genius itself. Without Henslows there are no Darwins. (*Darwin's Mentor*, 2001, Cambridge University Press, 261)

FURTHER READING

Russell-Gebbet, Jean. 1977. *Henslow of Hitcham*. Lavenham, England: Terrence Dalton.
Walters, S. M. and E. A. Stow. 2001. *Darwin's Mentor: John Stevens Henslow, 1796–1861*. Cambridge, England: Cambridge University Press.

Herschel, John F. W. (1792–1871)

Astronomer, mathematician, meteorologist, biologist, chemist, and philosopher of science. Important source of inspiration to the young Charles Darwin.

John Herschel was a member of a family dynasty of scientists particularly noted for their contributions to astronomy. John Herschel's father William, of German origin, was the discoverer of the planet Uranus and maker of some of the best telescopes of his day.

While a student of mathematics at Cambridge, John was instrumental in introducing some of the latest continental ideas on mathematics and physics to Britain. He also wrote on chemistry and was a pioneer of photography. He wrote an influential book on the philosophy of science titled *A Preliminary Discourse on the Study of Natural Philosophy* (1830), which emphasized the need for repeated observation, comparison, and logical reasoning. Charles Darwin read this while at Cambridge, and was much inspired by it; his annotated copy still exists. Indeed it contributed to the young Darwin's resolve to make a contribution to science and influenced his manner of collecting and utilizing information.

One of Herschel's most important astronomical works was his 1847 catalogue of Southern Hemisphere stars. In this he was continuing his father's work in cataloging the northern stars. Sir John Herschel lived and worked at the **Cape of Good Hope** for about four years (1834–1838), cataloging 70,000 southern stars and many thousands of nebulae and double stars. It was while he was in residence at the Cape that Charles Darwin met him, along with a group of several other distinguished scientists then living in Cape Town. The discussions that this group had must have been a great encouragement to Darwin after his lonely four and a half years aboard HMS *Beagle*. Darwin and Sir John Herschel dined together, possibly several times, during the period June 8–15, 1836. Darwin described this as "the most memorable event which, for a long period, I have had the good fortune to enjoy." Although there is no strong evidence, the possibility exists that they discussed the notions of the mutability of species that were, during the voyage, hovering, vague and unformed, at the back of Darwin's mind.

Hooker, Joseph Dalton (1817—1911)

Botanist, biogeographer, close friend, and collaborator with Charles Darwin.

The younger son of Sir William Jackson Hooker and his wife Maria, Joseph Hooker was born in the small town of Halesworth, Suffolk, in eastern England, on June 30, 1817. His family moved to Glasgow in Scotland when he was very young, and he attended Glasgow High School and later Glasgow University, where his father was Regius Professor of Botany. Like a number of other significant biologists and naturalists of his age, Hooker undertook medical training and graduated with an MD in 1839.

Hooker attended his father's botany lectures at the university from the age of seven and developed an interest in plant distributions. He also had an early interest in travel and exploration; in later life, he recalled sitting on his grandfather's knee looking at the pictures in Captain Cook's *Voyages.* He was particularly struck by one of Cook's sailors killing penguins on Kerguelen's Land (Isles Kerguelen), and he remembered thinking that "I should be the happiest boy alive if ever I would see that wonderful arched rock, and knock penguins on the head."

He did not have very long to wait. He secured the position of assistant surgeon on HMS *Erebus,* which, together with the *Terror,* explored the Southern Ocean, including the outer fringes of Antarctica, reaching as far south as 78° 17' S under the leadership of Sir James Clark Ross, between 1839 and 1843. Captain Ross had stated that he wanted "such a person as Mr Darwin" on the voyage.

Before Joseph Hooker set sail, Charles Lyell of Kinnordy, Scotland (the father of **Charles Lyell,** the geologist), gave Hooker the proofs of Charles Darwin's *Voyage of the Beagle.* Hooker read Darwin's account of his voyage with enthusiasm, wondering whether he would have the abilities needed in a naturalist who aspired to follow in Darwin's footsteps. But Hooker's role with Ross was somewhat different from Darwin's with Captain FitzRoy. Hooker was no self-funded "gentleman's companion"; the position of assistant surgeon was a relatively lowly one, and Hooker was subject to naval regulations and had a multitude of tasks to perform. Nevertheless, he was able to collect specimens and undertake valuable scientific work when the expedition visited the **Falkland Islands,** Kerguelen, **New Zealand,** and **Tasmanica.**

When the expedition returned to England in 1843, Hooker worked hard to establish his scientific reputation and searched, unsuccessfully, for a paid appointment in the field of botany. His father had been appointed first director of the Royal Botanic Gardens at Kew in 1841, following its coming under official government control. Although this was not a well-paid position, it was a prestigious and influential one. William Hooker was able to secure an Admiralty grant of £1,000 for his son in the same way that Darwin had secured funding for some of the scientific publications that followed the voyage of the *Beagle*. This grant was intended to cover the cost of the *Botany of the Antarctic Voyage*. Moreover, Joseph received his assistant surgeon's pay for some of the time he worked on this project. The work eventually appeared in the form of six large volumes: two each for the *Flora Antarctica* (1844–1847), the *Flora Novae-Zelandiae* (1851–1853), and the *Flora Tasmanica* (1853–1859). These were important milestones in the development of Southern Hemisphere botany.

During the period 1847 to 1849, Hooker obtained another government grant for a visit to the central and eastern Himalayas. The Admiralty gave him free passage to India. Hooker visited Calcutta and Darjeeling, where he consulted with Brian Houghton Hodgson, an expert on Nepalese culture and Buddhism as well as an enthusiastic naturalist. It was planned that the two of them would make the journey into the Himalayas together. However, in 1848, Hodgson became too ill to accompany him, and Archibald Campbell, a British civil servant, went instead. Hooker was sometimes an obstinate and difficult man (Darwin at one stage described him as "impulsive" and "peppery"), and the expedition managed to annoy the rajar and the chief minister of the tiny mountain state of Sikim in a number of ways. They deliberately ignored some instructions, including the request that they not cross into Tibet, and at one stage Hooker and Campbell were imprisoned. Intervention by the British government soon secured their release, but the incident reflected little credit on any of the parties involved. Following his release, Hooker spent 1850 traveling with Thomas Thomson in Bengal, returning to Britain in 1851. They wrote the first volume of a projected *Flora Indica* (1855); however, the project was never completed because of a lack of funding. Hooker eventually produced the *Flora of British India* (1872–1897). The introductory essay on the geographical relationships of the flora of the Indian subcontinent was one of Joseph Hooker's most important publications on biogeography. Altogether, Hooker collected about 7,000 species in India and Nepal, and their classification and naming continued for much of the remainder of his career. His book *Himalayan Journals* (1854) was dedicated to Darwin.

Shortly after his return from India, in August 1851, Hooker married Frances Harriet, eldest daughter of the Reverend **John Stevens Henslow,** the Cambridge professor of botany who had been Darwin's mentor and who had been influential in securing Darwin's position aboard HMS *Beagle*—thus further consolidating the close network of family and marriage relationships that existed in English science at the time. (See article on **intellectual aristocracy.**) They had four sons and two surviving daughters. Hooker, like Charles Darwin, was very close to his children and enjoyed playing with them. One specially loved daughter, Minnie (Maria Elizabeth), died in September 1863 when she was just six years old—an experience that he shared with Darwin, as

Annie Darwin had died about 12 years earlier. His grief was long-lasting and immense. He wrote to Charles Darwin on the day of Minnie's death:

> Dear dear friend,
> My darling 2nd girl died here an hour ago, & I think of you more in my grief than any other friend.

Meanwhile Joseph's father, William Hooker, had been successful in developing the Botanic Gardens at Kew. By the early 1850s, they extended over 300 acres (120 hectares), had 20 greenhouses, and contained 4,500 growing plants. The herbarium held 150,000 specimens. In 1855, the government agreed that the expansion now warranted the appointment of an assistant director, and Joseph was appointed to assist his father.

In 1865, William Hooker, Joseph's father, died, and Joseph succeeded him as director of Kew. He was by this time a botanist with a worldwide reputation, but nevertheless nepotism played a part in his advancement. He might not have secured the position without his father's constant assistance and support. For example, William Hooker offered to leave his large personal herbarium to the nation on the condition that his son was appointed to succeed him.

Joseph Hooker remained director of Kew until his retirement in 1885. These years were marked by the continuation and expansion of Kew's imperial role. In 1859–1860, William Hooker and Kew had provided essential assistance in effecting the transfer of cinchona trees (from the bark of which quinine was made) from South America to India. This enabled this important crop to be grown in a British dominion that had plenty of cheap labor. Because malaria was a severe problem in many of Britain's tropical colonies, the availability of a cheap, reliable source of this drug had important economic implications. His father's success with the cinchona transplantation was repeated under Joseph Hooker's directorship when, in the 1870s, rubber trees (*Hevea brasilensis*) were removed (without permission from the government of Brazil) to be grown in British colonies in Asia.

Hooker undertook a massive amount of taxonomic work to name and classify plants, but throughout his life he was interested in the distribution of plants. He placed great emphasis on the former existence of land bridges. Disjunct distributions (when a species or biological group occurs in two or more widely separated regions) were sometimes explained by former dry land connections that have subsequently disappeared through a rise in sea level. Although the rise in sea level that has occurred over the past 10,000 years as the result of melting ice caps that once covered large areas of the northern hemisphere has caused the drowning of some land connections, Hooker invoked the land bridge mechanism in circumstances where other processes, such as plate tectonics (the lateral movement of the Earth's crustal plates) or long-distance dispersal, are now thought more attractive.

Darwin, although he acknowledged that there had been changes in sea level, was never very attracted to the land bridge theory. Nevertheless, the two men shared massive amounts of information about plant (and, to some extent, animal) distributions. For this reason, as well as their close personal friendship, Joseph Hooker was, from a relatively early stage, within the small circle of those who were privy to Darwin's developing ideas. Hooker had offered to describe some of the *Beagle* plant specimens. Darwin replied to Hooker early in 1844:

> I have been now ever since my return engaged in a very presumptuous work & which I know no one individual who would not say a very foolish one. I was so struck with [the] distribution of Galapagos organisms . . . & with the American fossil mammifers . . . that I determined to collect blindly every sort of fact, which could bear in any way on what are species. . . . At last gleams of light have come, & I am almost convinced that species are not (it is like confessing to murder) immutable . . . I think I have found out (here's presumption!) the simple way in which species become exquisitely adapted to various ends. (*Correspondence of Charles Darwin*, Vol. 3, January 1844, 214, and Darwin Archive, Cambridge University Library)

Hooker replied that: "There may in my opinion have been . . . a gradual change. I should be delighted to know how you think this change may have taken place." From then on, the association between the two naturalists almost amounted to collaboration. Darwin showed Hooker his 1844 *Essay,* in which the essential concept of natural selection was outlined: Hooker approved. They met several times in London and at Downe in 1844, and there were times when they wrote to one another almost daily, exchanging information—particularly on plant and animal distributions and especially those of the Southern Hemisphere because both had visited Australia, New Zealand, Tierra del Fuego, and the mainland of South America. Both had visited a number of remote islands. It is not surprising, therefore, that there are traces of evolutionary thinking in some of Hooker's southern *Flora* books. For example, in the *Flora Tasmanica,* after discussing the varied and local flora of southwestern Australia, he speculated that the development of this "under the theory of creation by variation have might have occupied a great length of time"—a statement that closely resembles "evolution through natural selection." Hooker also drew attention to the strikingly individual biotas of remote islands and was among the first to describe the similarity between the "Beech [*Nothofagus*] districts of the southern lands," preparing the way for modern ideas such the doctrine of plate tectonics.

During Joseph Hooker's period as director of the Botanic Gardens at Kew, he managed to court controversy in a number of ways. He was a firm defender of the scientific and utilitarian (i.e., economic) purpose of Kew and had little patience with those who wished to use it only as a venue for recreation. For a long period, only serious botanists and artists were allowed admittance to the gardens in the morning; the general public had to wait until the afternoon. There was friction with the government in 1872, when it was proposed that the Kew Herbarium be transferred to the Natural History Museum (as a cost-cutting measure). This would have shattered the scientific mission of the gardens as Hooker envisaged it and would have reduced Kew to little more than a park for "romping," as Hooker dismissively put it. He fought this with strong support from the scientific community, including Darwin and Charles Lyell. They won.

Yet despite Hooker's outspoken opposition to anything he regarded as detracting from Kew's scientific importance, he was strongly in favor of widening public participation in science. In 1866, he addressed the **British Association for the Advancement of Science** (BAAS)—whose meetings the public were encouraged to attend—and delivered a lecture on "insular floras." He renounced the land bridge theory—the notion of the foundering of "imaginary continents"—and adopted Darwin's theory that attempted to explain many plant distributions by **long-distance dispersal** or migration. Hooker made a major contribution to the work of the BAAS, presiding over the of zoology and botany section in 1874 and over the geography section in 1881. Hooker was elected president of the **Royal Society** in 1873, initiating a number of reforms the purpose of which was to broaden public participation. He also traveled widely, visiting the Middle East in 1860, North Africa in 1871, and the Rocky Mountains in 1877.

Joseph Hooker is often seen, in the history of science, as an appendix to the Darwinian story. In fact, despite his strong support for the theory of evolution through natural selection and his close personal friendship with Darwin's good friend **Thomas Huxley,** he attempted to remain on good terms with non-Darwinians. This was perhaps because of the need to avoid alienating his extensive network of correspondents and collectors all over the world, on which the success of Kew no small way depended.

Hooker's contribution to science was enormous. He established the study of plant distributions as a discipline in its own right, he worked on the taxonomy of many groups of plants, and he opened up the botany of the Indian subcontinent. He studied the floras of both remote islands and great continents, and he wrote about the arctic, the antarctic, and the tropics. He wrote and edited floras that were still in use over 50 years after his death. For these achievements, he was much honored in his own life time. He received honorary degrees from many universities, including Oxford and Cambridge. He was created a Companion in 1869, he was knighted in 1877, and he received the Order of Merit in 1907. The Royal Society gave him the Copley medal in 1887 and the Darwin medal in 1892. He was honored by numerous foreign scientific societies.

Hooker died in his sleep on December 10, 1911, after a short illness. He was buried, in accordance with his wishes, alongside his father in the St. Anne's churchyard on Kew Green. His widow (his second wife Hyacinth; Frances had died in 1874) was offered the option of having him buried alongside Darwin in Westminster Abbey. It is as well that she refused, for despite the significance of his link with Darwin, such an interment would perhaps have perpetuated the notion of Joseph Hooker as a secondary, subordinate figure. It was botany, Kew Gardens, and family that were important to him above all, and that determined his resting place.

FURTHER READING

Allan, M. 1967. *The Hookers of Kew, 1785–1911*. London: Michael Joseph.

Human Evolution

Charles Darwin said relatively little on human evolution until quite late in his career. Many (but not all) of his speculations on the subject, it turns out, were well founded.

The appreciation that there are strong similarities between humans and the great apes is an old one. Although *On the Origin of Species* did not comment on the matter of human evolution apart from a somewhat vague reference in the final paragraphs, the implications of Darwin's theory were clear to many of his readers. **Thomas Huxley** commented on many of the similarities (and also some of the differences) between humans and apes in his *Man's Place in Nature,* published in 1863. By the time Darwin published *Descent of Man* in 1871, the possibility of the evolution of humans from apelike ancestors was well aired, although far from universally accepted. Darwin prefaced his 1871 work with the words:

> During many years I collected notes on the origin or descent of man, without any intention of publishing on the subject, but rather with the determination not to publish, as I thought that I should thus only add to the prejudices against my views. It seemed to me sufficient to indicate, in the first edition of my Origin of Species, that by this work "light would be thrown on the origin of man and his history."

Even some of his supporters, such as **Charles Lyell** and **Alfred Russel Wallace,** boggled, initially at least, at the notion that such a blunt instrument as natural selection could have produced humans, with their enormous mental capacity. Lyell's important work *The Geological Evidence of Antiquity of Man* appeared in 1863, and, although it is in general supportive of Darwin's views, there seems to be a slight hesitation.

Darwin picked up the discussion in 1871. On the apparent absence (at that time) of prehuman fossils, he wrote:

> With respect to the absence of fossil remains, serving to connect man with his ape-like progenitors, no one will lay much stress on this fact who reads Sir C. Lyell's discussion, where he shows that in all vertebrate classes the discovery of fossil remains has been a very slow and fortuitous process. Nor should it be forgotten that those regions which are the most likely to afford remains

connecting man with some extinct ape-like creature, have not as yet been searched by geologists.

Darwin's 1871 work, was thus based primarily on observations on living humans (including some of the groups he had met on the voyage of the *Beagle*), comparative anatomy, patterns of behavior, and embryology. Many, but not all, of Darwin's deductions have been confirmed from modern research on fossil forms.

In the later nineteenth century, many speculated that humans' closest living relatives were chimpanzees and gorillas; since both of these (and many other species of primates) were found in Africa, it was suggested that a common ancestor to both humans and the apes might have at one time have existed in that continent and that fossils of human ancestors might one day be found in Africa. Darwin, no doubt recalling his research on both living and fossil forms in South America (and the similarities between them), put it as follows.

> In each great region of the world the living mammals are closely related to the extinct species of the same region. It is therefore probable that Africa was formerly inhabited by extinct apes closely allied to the gorilla and chimpanzee; and as these two species are now man's nearest allies, it is somewhat more probable that our early progenitors lived on the African continent than elsewhere.

And so it has subsequently been proved to be the case. In 1924, Raymond Dart described a young australopithecine, found in a cave at Taung, in the Transvaal, South Africa. Dart gave it the name *Australopithecus africanus*. The fossil material consisted of a skull and an internal cast of a small brain (410 cubic centimeters); the brain, however, was more like that of a modern human than that of an ape. There were short canine teeth, and Dart thought, on the basis of certain features of the skull, that the creature was bipedal (i.e., it stood upright, moving on two legs), and he suggested that it was a transitional form between apes and humans. It was, however, another 20 years, following the discovery of other material, before his claims were taken with any degree of seriousness.

Darwin appreciated the importance of bipedality:

> Man alone has become a biped: and we can, I think, partly see how he has come to assume his correct attitude, which forms one of his most conspicuous characters. Man could not have attained his dominant position in the world without the use of his hands which are so admirably adapted to act in obedience to his will.

Hands could not, he argued, have assumed the tasks of manipulating tools and weapons while still supporting the weight of his body or while specially adapted to tree-climbing. Subsequent evidence from Africa suggests that bipedalism preceded the expansion of the brain by some two million years.

DNA evidence further suggests that, between four and eight million years ago, first the gorilla and then the chimpanzee (genus *Pan*) diverged from the lineage leading to humans. There is, however, no fossil record for the African great apes, probably because bones are unlikely to be preserved as fossils in tropical rain forest environments. Hominines (the group that includes humans and the australopithecines) seem, therefore, to have been one of the mammal groups (with antelopes, hyenas, elephants, and horses) that became adapted to open grasslands as soon as this vegetation type appeared around eight million years ago. Fossils of these are more common, having been found in several parts of Africa.

The australopithecines as a group—some five or six, possibly more, species have been identified—lived about two to four million years ago and are now generally thought to be ancestors of the genus *Homo,* the genus which includes modern humans, *Homo sapiens* (*sapiens* is Latin for wise or intelligent). There is some uncertainty as to whether *A. africanus* truly is a direct ancestor to modern humans; it might have been more like a cousin, occupying an evolutionary cul-de-sac branching off the main stem. The australopithecines were originally described as being either gracile or robust. The robust form of *Australopithecus* was later reclassified as *Paranthropus,* but there is continuing dispute about the exact relationships between the forms.

Similar arguments have enveloped the classification of the various forms of *Homo* that have been identified—from Africa and from elsewhere. *Homo habilis,* of which many specimens have been found in many parts of Africa, lived between about 2.5 and 1.5 million years ago. He was usually a little over a meter in height and weighed 30 to 55 kilograms. He had a brain capacity larger than the australopithecines at about 600 cubic centimeters but much smaller than that of modern humans.

Homo erectus has been found in many parts of Africa and in Asia (Indonesia, China, and the Caucasus). The form lived from about two million to 500,000 years ago. The early phase, *H. ergaster,* is considered to be a separate species, or it is seen as a subspecies of *erectus, Homo erectus ergaster.*

In the Pleistocene epoch, one to one and a half million years ago, in Africa, Asia, and Europe, *H. habilis* evolved larger brains (900 to 1,100 cubic centimeters) and made more elaborate stone tools; these and other differences have encouraged some scientists to classify them as a new species. In addition, *Homo erectus* may well have been the first human ancestor to walk truly upright. This was made possible by the evolution of firmly locking knees and a different location of the foramen magnum (the opening in the skull where the spinal chord enters). They may have used fire, and they were probably about the same height and weight as modern humans.

Homo neanderthalensis lived from about 350,000 to as recently as 30,000 years ago. Neanderthal bones were found in Europe in 1864: he seems to have had a height, weight, and brain capacity similar to that of *Homo sapiens,* although he was probably more heavily built. Darwin knew of the discovery, but says little about it in his writings. Also sometimes classified as *Homo sapiens neanderthalensis* (i.e., as a subspecies of modern humans), there is continuing debate over whether the Neanderthal man was a separate species or a subspecies of *H. sapiens.* While the debate remains unresolved, the currently most accepted view, based on DNA from Neanderthal bone, indicates that little or no gene flow occurred between *H. neanderthalensis* and *H. sapiens* (i.e., they did not interbreed), and therefore they constitute distinct species. Although they lived in Europe until well within the time scale of modern humans, they were almost certainly not ancestral to them. The two separate species may have lived alongside one another. Here is another instance of a form that represented an evolutionary blind alley.

Homo sapiens has lived from about 200,000 years ago to the present. Between 400,000 years ago and the second interglacial period (the time between two major ice advances in the Ice Age) in the middle Pleistocene, about 250,000 years ago, the trend in enlargement of the brain (and the cranium, the part of the skull that contained it) and the development of stone tool making provides evidence for a transition from *H. erectus* to *Homo sapiens. H. erectus,* as mentioned above, migrated out of Africa. But a further speciation of *H. sapiens* from *H. erectus* occurred in that continent. (There is little evidence that this speciation occurred elsewhere.) Then a dispersal of *H. sapiens,* within and without Africa, eventually replaced the earlier dispersed *H. erectus* though competition.

Humans throughout the world are genetically homogeneous, meaning that the DNA of any two individual *Homo sapiens* is more alike than is usual for most species, probably the result of the species' relatively recent evolution. Distinctive characteristics have developed, however, primarily as the result of small groups of people moving into new environments. Such small populations are often highly inbred, allowing the relatively rapid transmission of traits favorable to the new circumstances. These traits are a very small component of the total *Homo sapiens* genetic structure or genome and include such outward characteristics as skin color, limb length, and nose shape, in addition to internal characteristics such as lung capacity, which provides the ability to breathe efficiently in high altitudes.

Brief mention must be included of *Homo floresiensis,* a form of human described in 2004 from cave sites on the island of Flores in Indonesia that has captured the public imagination internationally. This creature, it has been suggested, lived about 100,000 to 12,000 years ago. It has been nicknamed the hobbit (after the imaginary creatures described in the novels of J.R.R. Tolkien) because of its small size. This may have been a product of insular, or island, dwarfism. (It is not unusual for populations of animals on islands to have a smaller size than analogous populations on mainland environments: this enables a larger number of organisms containing greater genetic variety to be compacted into the same biomass or weight of living material—a substantial evolutionary advantage.) *H. flore-siensis* is interesting both because of its small size and its young age. It may comprise an example of a recent species of the genus *Homo* that exhibits derived (i.e., not original) characteristics not shared with other modern humans. *H. floresiensis* shared a common ancestor with modern humans but split (relatively recently) from the main modern human lineage to follow its own distinct evolutionary path, partly in adaptation to its distinctive island environment. The most important find was a fossil believed to be a woman of about 30 years of age. This specimen has been dated to about 18,000 years. Her brain size was a very small 380 cubic centimeters (even small for a chimpanzee). She was just over three feet (about one meter) in height.

There is an ongoing debate about the status of *H. floresiensis.* Is it indeed a separate species? Some scientists believe that *H. floresiensis* was a modern *H. sapiens* suffering from pathological dwarfism and that the small stature was the result of disease. The modern humans who live on Flores, the island where the fossil was found, are generally small. This fact, some argue, together with pathological dwarfism, could indeed result in a hobbitlike creature. Another issue in the debate is that *H. floresiensis* material was found with tools hitherto known only to be associated with *H. sapiens.*

A number of other forms of *Homo* (and other hominids) have been described. Some of these may be local variants or subspecies of more widespread types. The study of human evolution is rapidly advancing, and the above discussion must be considered a brief and tentative snapshot of current thinking.

Charles Darwin's attempt to bring humanity within the scope of his theory of evolution was well grounded. Although the path of evolution is not absolutely clear—the above interpretations are just some of many—it can be stated with some certainty that the evolutionary paths that led to modern humans and the great apes separated a few million years ago. DNA studies have shown that the genome of the gorilla, the chimpanzee (and the orangutan in Asia), and modern *Homo sapiens* are very similar. The mainspring of human evolution was in Africa, and, although significant gaps and inconsistencies exist, it appears that hominid fossils can be arranged in order of increasing cranial capacity over time.

Humboldt, Alexander von (1769—1859)

German traveler, explorer, naturalist, geographer, and polymath. His *Personal Narrative of Travels to the Equinoctial Regions of the New Continent during the years 1799–1804* was an inspiration to Charles Darwin, who described him as "the greatest scientific traveller who ever lived."

Humboldt was born in Berlin, Germany (Prussia). His army officer father died when he was nine years old, and so he and his elder brother Wilhelm were brought up by their rather distant, cold, and unaffectionate mother. Tutors provided their early education, which emphasized languages and mathematics.

Alexander later studied at the Freiberg Academy of Mines under the famous geologist Abraham G. Werner. Humboldt also met George Forester, Captain James Cook's scientific illustrator from his second voyage, and they traveled around Europe. In 1792, at the age of 22, he obtained a position as a government inspector of mines in Franconia, Prussia. When he was 27, Humboldt's mother died, leaving him a substantial fortune, and so, the following year, he left government service and began to plan travels with Aime Bonpland, a French botanist and medical doctor. The pair traveled to Madrid and obtained special permission from King Charles II to explore South America (then mostly under Spanish colonial administration).

They studied the flora, fauna, and topography of the continent. In 1800, Humboldt mapped over 1,700 miles of the Orinoco River. He and Bonpland discovered and mapped the Casiquiare Canal, the only natural canal in the world that connects two major river systems (the Orinoco and the Negro River, a tributary of the Amazon). This was followed by a trip into the Andes, which included a climb of Mt. Chimborazo (in modern Ecuador), then believed to be the highest mountain in the world. They were not able reach the summit because of a steep cliff, but they did climb to over 18,000 feet (5,500 meters). While on the west coast of South America, Humboldt discovered and measured the Peruvian Current (often now known as the Humboldt Current). He also made some of the first accurate drawings of Inca ruins in South America (he visited the remains at Canar, Peru). In 1803, they explored Mexico, where Humboldt was offered, but refused, a position in the Mexican cabinet. The scientist Carlos Montufar (who later became a revolutionary in Ecuador) accompanied them on part of their travels.

The pair was persuaded to visit Washington, DC, by an American diplomat. They stayed in Washington for three weeks, and von Humboldt had many meetings with Thomas Jefferson; they became firm friends.

Humboldt sailed for Paris in 1804 and wrote *Personal Narrative of a Voyage to the Equinoctial Regions of a New Continent, 1799–1804,* outlining his field studies in the Americas. During his expeditions in the Americas and Europe, he had recorded and reported on magnetic declination. He also described in detail the altitudinal zonation of climate and vegetation and undertook pioneering studies on geology and geomorphology (e.g., the development of rounded domes through the weathering of granitic rocks). Humboldt and Bonpland collected plant, animal, and mineral specimens; studied electricity (including discovering and reporting an animal that produced electricity, *Electrophorus electricus,* the electric eel); observed astronomical phenomena; and made many other scientific observations.

Humboldt remained in France for about 23 years, meeting there with many other writers, scientists, and scholars. Ultimately, Alexander von Humboldt's fortunes were exhausted by his travels and by the costs of publishing his reports. In 1827, he returned to Berlin, where he obtained a steady income by becoming the King of Prussia's advisor. From 1827 to 1828, Humboldt gave extremely popular public lectures in Berlin. Humboldt was later invited to Russia by the tsar and, after exploring that nation, visiting the Ural Mountains and Siberia, and describing permafrost (permanently frozen ground in the northern tundra region), he recommended that Russia establish weather observatories across the country. The stations were established in 1835 and Humboldt was able to use the data to develop the concept of continentality—the idea that the interiors of continents have more extreme climates due to a lack of moderating influence from the ocean. He also developed the first isotherm map (isotherms are lines joining all places of equal average temperatures). He was the first person to recognize the need to preserve the cinchona plant (its bark contains quinine, which is used to cure malaria, and it was severely overexploited at the time) and to reveal the importance of guano (the dried droppings from fish-eating birds) as an excellent fertilizer.

As Humboldt aged, he decided to compile a compendium of everything known about the Earth. He called his work *Kosmos,* and in it he attempted to convey the idea of the unity of science. The first volume was published in 1845, when he was 76 years old. It was well written and well received. This volume, a general overview of the universe, sold out in two months and was translated into many languages. Other volumes focused on such topics as the human effort to describe the Earth, astronomy, and Earth and human interaction. Humboldt died in 1859, and the final volume was published in 1862 based on his notes for the work. He is buried at Tegel in Germany.

Baron Alexander von Humboldt, as he ultimately became known, was once described as the "last universal scholar in the field of the natural sciences." "When Humboldt died, no individual scholar could hope any longer to master the world's knowledge about the earth" (Geoffrey J. Martin and Preston E. James, *All Possible Worlds: A History of Geographical Ideas,* 2005).

In his own country, Alexander von Humboldt is commemorated in the Humboldt University in Berlin. In the United States, there are at least eight townships with Humboldtian names, along with counties, rivers, mountains, marshes, and state parks. On the moon, the *Mare Humboldtianum* (Humboldt's Sea) was named after him.

Humboldt's influence on Darwin was profound. *A Personal Narrative* inspired a young Charles Darwin while he was an undergraduate at Cambridge. While aboard the *Beagle,* Darwin was constantly reading Humboldt and seeing the world through Humboldt's eyes. He corresponded with him after his return, cited him in his books, and met him at least once.

During his last few months at Cambridge, Darwin spent many hours reading Humboldt's accounts of his journey (in translation) and copying out long sections. He later said that this was one of the books that imparted to him "a burning zeal to add even the most humble contribution to the noble structure of natural science."

Darwin was particularly interested at that time in the Isle of Tenerife, which Humboldt describes in some detail. Darwin resolved to arrange an expedition to go there, although this was "knocked on the head by the voyage of the *Beagle*." But that summer spent reading the *Narrative* enthused Darwin for tropical environments, encouraged him to learn some geology, and pick up sufficient Spanish to be useful in South America. Alas, Darwin was prevented by quarantine restrictions from actually landing on Tenerife during the voyage.

Not only was Humboldt responsible for firing the young English naturalist's enthusiasm prior to the voyage, but he was (via his *Personal Narrative*) present with him aboard the *Beagle,* pointing out things worthy of notice and sometimes providing a framework for describing them. In addition to having a copy of Humboldt's *Personal Narrative,* Darwin also had several other Humboldtian writings with him on the voyage.

The structure of Darwin's book (*The Voyage of the Beagle*) has similarities to Humboldt's *Personal Narrative*. Both take the form of a diary, with the entries rearranged and with scientific digressions. Moreover, one of the charms of Darwin's descriptive style in his diary—the version of it that was revised for publication—*The Voyage of the Beagle*—is the manner in which he describes landscapes. He often dwells for several lines on the light, clouds, colors of the sky, atmospheric haze, or the blurring of colors on a distant hillside. One day, early in his visit to Rio de Janeiro, Darwin recorded:

> I was particularly struck with a remark of Humboldt's, who often alludes to "the thin vapour which, without changing the transparency of the air, renders its tints more harmonious, and softens its effects." . . . This is an appearance I have never noticed in the temperate zones. The atmosphere, seen through a short space of half or three-quarters of a mile, was perfectly lucid, but at a greater distance all colours blended together into a most beautiful haze, of a pale French gray, mingled with a little blue. (*Voyage of the Beagle,* chapter 2)

And elsewhere in Brazil, after describing the scene at Bahia, with the convents and porticos and the ships in the bay:

> But these beauties are nothing compared to the vegetation; I believe from what I have seen Humboldt's descriptions are & for ever will be unparalleled: but even he with his dark skies & the rare union of poetry and science which he so strongly displays when writing on tropical scenery, with all this falls short of the truth. The mind is a chaos of delight . . . I am fit only to read Humboldt; he like another sun illumines everything I behold. (*Diary,* February 28, 1832)

Humboldt describes in great detail the form of volcanic craters; Darwin seems almost to use these descriptions as a template when he described the volcanic districts of New Zealand, the Galapagos, and the Azores. Humboldt also described the almost spherical rock masses and the granite domes of South America; Darwin answers in his geological notes on King George's Sound in southwest Australia:

> [O]n entering the Sound in the vessel, I saw that peculiar form of bare, smooth, conical hills appearing to be composed of great folding layers, which is found in Brazile & in the Mountains of Venezuela, I at once suspected that the observation of Humboldt of the frequency of this form in the hills of gneiss-granite, would be verified in this part of Australia. (*Geological Notes*, Cambridge University Library, Darwin Archive)

Humboldt was not only setting a research agenda by drawing Darwin's attention to phenomena of interest, he was influencing his writing style and even the broad structure of his written texts.

The relationship to Humboldt continued after Darwin's return from the sea. Darwin sent him a copy of *The Voyage of the Beagle*. An earlier letter (now lost) had advised him of its imminent arrival and said something of Darwin's debt to Humboldt. Humboldt wrote back (September 18, 1839) a letter sprinkled with similar laudatory phrases: "your work is remarkable . . . you have enlarged and corrected my views." In this long letter Humboldt discusses many interests that touch on the voyage: the distribution of tropical vegetation, climatic change, temperature of the inner Earth as measured in mines, glaciation, and ocean currents. The exchange continued; a letter from Darwin dated November 1, 1838, gives Humboldt information on the temperature of the sea at locations in the Pacific as well as containing further compliments. A few years later, they met for breakfast in London. Darwin was "a little disappointed by the great man," although he was "very amiable and talked much." Darwin cited *Humboldt's Personal Narrative* in many of his works: *Volcanic Islands, The Geology of South America, Descent of Man,* and *The Expression of Emotions in Man and Animals* and on topics as varied as volcanoes, lavas, granites, saline encrustations, the expressions of monkeys and mules, the speech of parrots, and South American tribes. Moreover, Humboldt is extensively quoted in the Transmutation Notebooks in which Darwin jotted down ideas as he developed his theories of evolution. With the exception of his close friends **Charles Lyell, Joseph Hooker,** and **Thomas Huxley,** it is difficult to name a person who had a greater influence on Darwin than Alexander von Humboldt.

Huxley, Thomas (1825–1895)

Physician, physiologist, anatomist, anthropologist, educator, and friend and supporter of Darwin—sometimes called "Darwin's bulldog."

Thomas Henry Huxley was born in Ealing, London. His only formal education was two years at the local school where his father taught mathematics. However, the young Huxley read widely in history and philosophy, science and languages. He obtained a medical apprenticeship (then an alternative to university study for entry into the medical profession) and obtained a scholarship to study at Charing Cross Hospital in London. He did well, gaining a gold medal for his work in physiology and anatomy, and publishing his first scientific paper at the age of 20.

There are a number of similarities in the lives of Charles Darwin and Thomas Huxley, although Huxley came from a much poorer family. Darwin, too, had had medical training; he had endured two unsuccessful years at Edinburgh Medical School, after serving what amounted to a few months apprenticeship to his doctor father Robert. After his training at Charing Cross, Huxley obtained a position as assistant surgeon on HMS *Rattlesnake*. But while Darwin had a relatively privileged position on HMS *Beagle,* sharing quarters with Captain **Robert FitzRoy,** the position of assistant surgeon was not a prestigious one. Huxley later described the accommodation as "degradingly offensive" and crawling with cockroaches. However, like the *Beagle,* the *Rattlesnake* was engaged on a voyage of hydrographic survey (1846–1850). Like the *Beagle,* the *Rattlesnake* visited Australia, calling at Sydney. But Darwin did not find a girl he liked there, whereas Huxley immediately fell in love with Henrietta Heathorn in Sydney, and eventually married her. Both Darwin and Huxley spent a good deal of time on board ship collecting and studying marine invertebrates. Huxley, like Darwin, but perhaps even more systematically, had posted the results of some of his researches back to England, and so found the ground already prepared for him in the scientific establishment when he returned to London. Huxley's paper "On the Anatomy and the Affinities of the Family of Medusae" was published in the *Philosophical Transactions of the Royal Society* in 1849. He was elected a fellow of the **Royal Society** at the age of 25 (Darwin was several years older before he attained this honor)

They both shared the friendship of **Joseph Hooker** and **Charles Lyell.** But while Darwin never had to work for a living, Huxley did not have the benefit of family financial support. His naval salary continued while he wrote up the results of his researches during the voyage, and he wrote articles on popular science. In 1854, he acquired a lectureship at the School of Mines (appointments in science at that time were few and far between); he also worked for the Geological Survey. Honors came thick and fast: he was elected to the council of the Royal Society and received the Royal Medal in 1851. He gave the Croonian Lecture in 1858. He was appointed Hunterian Professor of comparative anatomy at the Royal College of Surgeons (1863–1869) and Fullerton Professor of physiology at the Royal Institution (1863–1867). He was president of the Royal Society from 1883 to 1885.

Huxley was initially an opponent of evolutionary ideas, taking particular exception to the directionality or teleological nature (i.e., the idea that evolution was a progress or movement toward a goal) of the evolutionary models of **Jean-Baptiste Lamarck** and **Robert Chambers;** indeed Huxley's review of Chambers's book *Vestiges* was vitriolic. However, when he first read *On the Origin of Species,* he remarked "How stupid of me not to have thought of that!"

His remarkably prescient letter to Darwin (dated November 23, 1859) on his first reading of the book is worth quoting at some length:

> My dear Darwin
>
> I finished your book yesterday. . . . Since I read Von Bär's Essays [on recapitulation] nine years ago no work on Natural History Science I have met with has made so great an impression upon me & I do most heartily thank you for the great store of new views you have given me.
>
> Nothing . . . can be better than the tone of the book—it impresses those who know nothing about the subject. As for your doctrines, I am prepared to go to the Stake if requisite in support. . . .
>
> I trust you will not allow yourself to be in any way disgusted or annoyed by the considerable abuse & misrepresentation which unless I greatly mistake is in store for you. Depend on it you have earned the lasting gratitude of all thoughtful men. And as to the curs which will bark & yelp, you must recollect that some of your friends . . . are endowed with an amount of combativeness . . . which may stand you in good stead. (*Correspondence*, Vol. 7, 390–391, and Cambridge University Library, Darwin Archive)

Huxley was not accepting of every aspect of the theory. It the same letter he said to Darwin, for example, that "You have loaded yourself with an unnecessary difficulty in adopting 'Natura non facit saltum' [nature does not make leaps] so unreservedly. I believe she does make *small* jumps." In this he was anticipating the ideas of **Stephen Jay Gould** and Miles Eldredge—on **punctuated equilibrium** and **saltatory evolution**—over 100 years later.

Despite his reservations, Thomas Huxley became one of Darwin's most staunch defenders—hence the nickname Darwin's bulldog. Perhaps Huxley is best known for his role in championing the evolutionary point of view in the Great Debate at the Oxford meeting of the **British Association for the Advancement of Science** in June 1860, held under the chairmanship of the Reverend Professor **John Stevens Henslow.** Huxley's opponent in the debate was **Samuel Wilberforce,** Bishop of Oxford. During the debate (which Darwin did not attend), Wilberforce—who, although he had some knowledge of science, had been coached by **Richard Owen**—ridiculed the concept of evolution. Accounts of the debate vary, but the Bishop is said to have asked Huxley whether he would prefer to be descended from an ape on his grandfather's or grandmother's side. In a letter written by Huxley, he stated that his reply was:

> If . . . the question is put to me would I rather have a miserable ape for a grandfather or a man highly endowed by nature and possessed of great means of influence & yet who employs these faculties for the mere purpose of introducing ridicule into a grave scientific discussion—I unhesitating affirm my

preference for the ape. (T. H. Huxley to Frederic Daniel Dyster about September 1860, *Correspondence,* Vol. 8, 271–272)

Joseph Hooker and other Darwin friends and supporters proclaimed Huxley the winner of the debate; some less partisan people in the audience, estimated at 700 to 1,000, asserted that it was more evenly balanced.

Perhaps Huxley's most notable book was *Evidence on Man's Place in Nature,* published in 1863—five years after *On the Origin,* in which Darwin had said nothing on human evolution, stating only at the end of the book that eventually "light will be thrown on the origin of Man." Huxley's *Evidence* attempted to review what was known of primate and human paleontology and behavior. This was the first book to deal systematically with the topic of human evolution.

Again this caused a confrontation with Richard Owen. Owen claimed that the human brain contained parts that were not present in the brains of apes, and thus humans could not possibly be descended from apes. Huxley showed that the brains of apes and humans were fundamentally very similar.

Although Huxley described himself (as did Darwin in later life) as an agnostic, he was on remarkably good terms with a number of clergy, such as **Charles Kingsley.**

The Huxleys are among the most notable of English intellectual families. Thomas's son Leonard (1860–1930) was a biographer, poet, and essayist. Leonard had three sons, all very distinguished. Sir Julian followed his grandfather into zoology and edited an important book that aimed to bring Darwin's ideas up to date for the mid-twentieth century (*Evolution: The Modern Synthesis,* 1942); Sir Andrew (1917–) was a physiologist who studied nerve transmission and was awarded the Nobel Prize for Physiology or Medicine; Aldous was a novelist and essayist whose best-known book was the dystopian work *Brave New World.* And among many other notable Huxleys, Julian's son Francis was a well-known anthropologist, and a more distant relative, Leonard George Golden Huxley (1902–1988), who spent much of his life in Australia, was a physicist.

See also: Intellectual Aristocracy.

FURTHER READING

Desmond, Adrian. 1997. *Huxley: From Devil's Disciple to Evolution's High Priest.* Reading, MA: Addison-Wesley.

Hydrography

The mapping or charting and the scientific study of the seas and adjacent land.

See also: Royal Navy in the Nineteenth Century.

I

Igneous Rocks

Rocks formed when molten material—magma—solidifies either within the Earth's crust or at the surface. In the latter case, the rocks are referred to as volcanic, and the resultant land forms are volcanoes.

The term igneous comes from the Latin *ignis,* fire, referring to their origin from heated material. Plutonic rocks are those such as granite that cooled slowly, deep within the Earth, and have large crystals. Volcanic rocks cooled at a much faster rate and have small crystals (like basalt). The term *hypabyssal* is used for rocks that formed at an intermediate depth. Sometimes the term extrusive is used for volcanic rocks and intrusive for hypabyssal and plutonic.

Igneous rocks were of considerable interest to Charles Darwin at various times in his career. He made their acquaintance when on the tour through North Wales in the summer of 1831 with **Adam Sedgwick** and must have at least taken a passing interest in the basalt while walking over Arthur's Seat when he was a medical student in Edinburgh. But it was at St. Jago in the **Cape Verde Islands** that excitement gripped him: "The first examining of Volcanic rocks, must to a Geologist be a memorable epoch," he wrote in his diary.

Darwin's eye for detail when examining volcanic rocks is excellent. Here he is on James Island in the Galapagos:

[O]ne side of Fresh-water Bay . . . is bounded by a promontory, which forms the last wreck of a large crater. On the beach of this promontory, a quadrant-shaped segment of a small subordinate point of eruption stands exposed. It consists of nine separate little streams of lava piled upon each other; and an irregular pinnacle, about fifteen feet in height, of reddish brown vesicular basalt, abounding with large crystals of glassy albite and fused augite. . . .

In the lava . . . of this little crater, I found several fragments, which, from their angular form, and their granular structure, their freedom from air-cells, their brittle and burnt condition, closely resembled those fragments of primary rocks which are occasionally ejected . . . from volcanoes. These fragments consist of glassy albite, much mackled, with very imperfect cleavage, mingled with semi-rounded grains, having tarnished glassy surfaces of a steel-blue mineral. . . . (C Darwin, 1844, *The Geology of the Voyage of HMS Beagle, Part 2, Geological Observations on the Volcanic Islands*. London: Smith, Elder & Co., 109–111)

Darwin was always an integrator: he was interested in volcanic rocks and their relationship to the land forms that comprised them. For example, he ascended to the summit of Saddle Mountain, the highest hill on Charles Island (in the Galapagos), which modern maps show to be about 2,700 feet (825 meters) in height, finding there "the remains of an old crater" covered with "coarse grass & Shrubs." He also counted 39 volcanic conical hills on the comparatively small island, in the summit of each of which "was a more or less circular depression." From the thickness and fertility of the soil, the relatively smooth outline, and the covering of vegetation, he deduced that it had been long since the lava streams that covered the lower part of the island had flowed from these craters. Darwin combines information from the land forms, rocks, soils, and the vegetation to reconstruct the history of the island. While on St. Helena, he observed that some layers of lava were eroded and were covered with a layer "one inch in thickness of a reddish earthy matter." He speculated that considerable intervals of time had elapsed between the different volcanic events.

Darwin applied similar techniques—evaluating and comparing the gross form of the volcanic cones and craters and the detailed mineralogy of the rocks in the volcanic islands of the **Galapagos Islands, St. Helena and Ascension Island, Mauritius, Tahiti,** the **Azores, New Zealand,** and St. Jago in the **Cape Verde Islands.** He noted the way different types of lava overlay one another, the way some craters and cones were eroded or "broken down," sometimes bare of soil and vegetation, and sometimes richly clothed. He was thus able to build chronologies and geological histories. He noted that the later lavas of a sequence were often of different mineralogy (and therefore chemical composition) from the younger ones. On many of the volcanic islands he visited, he commented that the lower or older lavas were of trachyte, the younger of basaltic rocks. He therefore suggested that that, as crystals settled out of a magma (molten rock), its composition changed—an early use of a concept that was essentially evolutionary.

In parts of South America, during his few days at the **Cape of Good Hope** in Africa, and in parts of **Australia,** Darwin was in the realm of much more ancient crystalline rocks such as granite (a plutonic rock) and dolerite (a hypabyssal rock for which Darwin used the term "greenstone"). At King George's Sound in March 1836, he described the landscape as an uninviting flat land with rounded granite domes protruding from it:

> The country, viewed from an eminence, appears a woody plain, with here and there rounded and partly bare hills of granite protruding. (*Voyage of the Beagle,* chapter 21)

Darwin started his geological observations and speculations before the *Beagle* came to anchor in the sound, noticing the similarity of the landscape to that described by **Alexander von Humboldt** in his accounts of granite landscapes in South America—and perhaps recalling his own observations in Brazil and elsewhere in South America. He predicted that he would encounter granitic rocks in this part of Australia. His prediction was absolutely correct: the rounded and conical domes that surround King George's Sound are indeed of granite. He studied the rock carefully, noting that it was "a handsome stone composed of very large crystals of feldspar, little quartz, black mica, which latter infrequently replaced by hornblende." A couple of months later, he described similar landforms—granite masses weathered to rounded—sometimes almost spherical—domes near Paarl at the **Cape of Good Hope** in South Africa.

Although Darwin heard of active volcanoes and hot springs in **New Zealand,** he did not visit them. The only place where he came into contact with anything that could be described as active thermal activity was at the Furnas do Enxofre—the fumaroles or steam vents in the center of the Isle of Terceira in the **Azores** where he saw the steam seeping out of the ground at the bottom of a deep ravine (as it still does) and smelled the sulfurous, chemically charged gases that attacked the rocks surrounding the vents.

In Chile, Darwin experienced an earthquake (and witnessed the effects of the resulting tsunami), and he asked about the occurrence of earthquakes at many of the localities he visited. He was struck by the coincidence of the areas of volcanic (and other igneous) rocks, recent volcanism and geothermal activity, earthquake occurrence, and other evidence of earth movement. He noted the alignment of islands and volcanoes in, for example, the Pacific Ocean and in the Azores, and he hypothesized that there were areas of the world where major uplift was occurring and also areas of subsidence. This work neatly linked his studies of coral reefs and atolls and sea level change with his work on volcanic islands. He was always on the lookout for a *vera causa* or bold theory—an integrative theory that would explain more than one phenomenon. He first set out his notions in a paper given to the **Geological Society of London** in 1838 (published in 1840) titled "On the Connexion of Certain Volcanic Phenomena in South America; And on the

Formation of Mountain Chains and Volcanos of the Same Power by Which Continents Are Elevated." In his book on *Volcanic Islands* (part 2 of ***Geology of the Voyage of the Beagle***), he developed these ideas further, illustrating his ideas with detailed case studies of a number of islands and island groups.

See also: Metamorphic Rocks, Sedimentary Rocks.

Ill Health and Diseases of Charles Darwin

Charles Darwin was dogged by ill heath, manifest in a variety of symptoms, throughout much of his later life. The nature of his indisposition has given rise to much speculation about whether it had an organic origin or was psychosomatic.

In boyhood and early manhood, Darwin had a vigorous, active, and outdoor life. Although not favoring organized sports, he went for walks along the River Severn, fished, rode, shot partridges, went beachcombing along the shore while in Edinburgh, and, during the Cambridge years, explored the fields and fens of East Anglia and the hills of Wales with **John Henslow** and **Adam Sedgwick.** He enjoyed feminine company but also association with his fellow (then all male) undergraduates. There is every indication that he had all the attributes of a normal, healthy, young man. He drank wine, although seldom to excess. His father **Robert Darwin** was a doctor, as was his brother **Erasmus;** in his late teenage years he (unsuccessfully) studied at **Edinburgh** Medical School. It can be assumed that from such sources he received advice on the importance of good exercise and a sound diet.

During the years of the **HMS** *Beagle* voyage, some of his exploits and travels required enormous stamina, including travel by small boat along rivers and up narrow inlets, on horseback or on foot across deserts, and through forests. Darwin ascended the Andes, climbed to high points in **Tierra del Fuego,** and trekked across the peat bogs and stone runs of East Falkland with a party of gauchos. These activities would have discouraged and debilitated many.

Nevertheless, there are references to indisposition in his diary from the *Beagle* (December 1831 to October 1836). He experienced palpitations before the *Beagle* set sail but said nothing, for fear he should be discouraged from departing. He often endured the incredible misery of seasickness, sometimes accompanied by giddiness, for days on end. On the third day of the voyage, crossing the notorious Bay of Biscay, he noted:

> I have felt a good deal of nausea several times a day . . . the misery is excessive. . . . I found the only relief to be in a horizontal position. (*Diary,* December 29, 1831)

As so it continued, intermittently, throughout much of the voyage. It has been suggested (but mostly dismissed by medical opinion) that the continued retching caused some permanent injury to the stomach that manifested itself in later life.

On October 2, 1832, while riding in Argentina between Buenos Ayres and Santa Fe, he suffered from heat stroke.

> Unwell & feverish, from having exerted myself too much in the sun . . . I was much exhausted & was very glad to procure an unfurnished room. (*Diary*)

He was unwell in bed for the next two days, and on the 5th, although he was on the move again, he describes himself as "not quite well." Again it is suggested that this might have done him some permanent harm, but there is little evidence for this, for he recovered quickly.

More lasting were the effects of what seems to have been a case of food poisoning in Chile in September 1834. While visiting some gold mines, he "drank some Chichi, a very weak, sour new made wine." (*Chicha* is a sweet wine with a high alcohol content that is still made in some parts of Chile.) This, he thought, was the cause of his disordered stomach, his terrible weakness, and the loss of appetite that laid him low for several weeks. He was in bed for a month and was very ill indeed. The *Beagle*'s surgeon, Benjamin Bynoe, visited him (Darwin was staying in a house in Valparaiso) and prescribed rest and "a good deal of calmomel" (mercury chloride— formula Hg_2Cl_2—a dense white or yellowish-white, odorless solid which was, in the 1830s to 1860s, widely given as a diuretic or purgative; its use for this purpose has long since been abandoned because of its toxic nature).

More serious causes of Darwin's illnesses may have been insect bites he received, possibly on two or three occasions by *Triatoma infestans* (Heteroptera). The best documented occasion occurred just south of Mendoza, in western Argentina, at the foothills of the Andes:

> At night I experienced an attack, & it deserves no less a name, of the Benchuca, the great black bug of the Pampas. It is most disgusting to feel soft wingless insects, about an inch long, crawling over one's body; before sucking; they are quite thin, but afterwards round & bloated with blood, & in this state they are easily squashed. They are also found in the Northern part of Chili & in Peru: one which I caught at Iquiqui was very empty; being placed on a Table & though surrounded by people, if a finger was presented, its sucker was withdrawn, & the bold insect began to drawn blood. It was curious to watch the change in their size of the insect's body in less than ten minutes. There was no pain felt. This one meal kept the insect fat for four months; in a fortnight, however, it was ready, if allowed, to suck more blood. (*Diary*, March 25–26, 1835; obviously written up much later)

Eventually, after keeping the bug for four and a half months, Darwin killed it to keep as a specimen, but this has disappeared. This insect is the vector of a protozoan parasite (*Trypanosoma cruzi*), which enters the human body though broken skin. The bugs often defecate during their blood meal, and it is from the feces that the organism of infection may enter the body, causing American trypanosomiasis or Chagas' disease. It is often asserted that much of the ill health that Darwin experienced in his later life was due to this infection. However, although Darwin was at severe risk of catching this disease, the evidence that he actually did is not overwhelming. Two of the symptoms are swelling of the eyelids and swollen lymph nodes, and Darwin does not mention anything of the sort. And although the disease can remain without visible symptoms for many months or years, victims often present with severe cardiac problems and often do not survive to Darwin's age. Important exceptions occur, however. One suggestion is that Darwin was infected, but the disease did not fully develop in him. The matter cannot be regarded as completely resolved.

Other suggestions have been made that Darwin's illnesses were due to such things as chemicals added to red wine to enhance its color or the use of arsenic for skin outbreaks on his lips and fingers when he was collecting insects while at Cambridge. Again, evidence is thin.

Darwin suffered more or less chronic ill health from the ages of 30 to 60. There seems to have been some improvement in the final decade of his life, which seems to argue against an organic origin (such as Chagas' disease) for his ill health. From his own and other accounts, symptoms during this period included flatulence, stomach acidity, shivering, fainting, blurred vision, dots before the eyes, ringing in the ears, overexcitement at the prospect of meeting groups of people, and skin eruptions or eczema. He often felt tired; sometimes, he complained, he was only able to work for a few hours a day.

A good deal recent thinking suggests that much of Darwin's ill health was largely psychogenic. Da Costa's syndrome, hyperventilation syndrome, and anxiety disorder have frequently been mentioned. Both physiological and psychological factors are involved.

The immediate cause of symptoms may be an increase in the level of anxiety or fear associated with an increase in breathing, without any increase in activity or energy use. When an organism experiences fear or anxiety, increased oxygen intake often is called for, because it prepares for "fight or flight." In the absence of this activity and energy consumption, the increased and unstable breathing leads to a lowering and fluctuation in the level of carbon dioxide in the blood. Persistent overbreathing may cause the carbon dioxide level to remain at a level slightly above that at which symptoms are produced. Any situation, even if quite trivial (animated conversation, meeting with a group of people, or being left alone might be sufficient), can lower the level still further and produce symptoms. These symptoms may cause further worry and arousal; the patient may believe that he or she has some defect of the heart or stomach and that he or she may become very ill or die; this may lead to a panic attack, and a vicious circle of positive feedback may be produced.

The intensity of Darwin's symptoms varied. He seems to have had health problems in the weeks before departing on the *Beagle;* in September 1837 (shortly after his conversion to an evolutionary outlook) and when he was working hard on writing up the material from the voyage; at the end of 1839 before the birth of his first child; in 1848 to 1849 at the time of his father's final illness and death; and in 1863 to 1864, three years or so after the publication of *On the Origin of Species,* as opposition grew.

Some thus have argued it was during periods of overwork and in periods of great stress or anxiety that Darwin's illnesses became worse. The attacks that he suffered took their toll. The situation was perhaps aggravated by the fact that, just as Charles was convinced he was an invalid, his wife **Emma Darwin** seemed to be more than happy to nurse him—another case of positive feedback. The more Emma pandered to his worries, the more convinced Charles was that he was an invalid. **Gwen Raverat** in *Period Piece* maintained that there was something of a Darwin family tradition of hypochondria. Another suggestion is that, because of the loss of his mother at the age of seven and the sometimes rather strained relationship he had with his father, Charles was somewhat predisposed to psychological problems and possibly depression.

All sorts of treatments were prescribed by a small army of medical advisers: a bland diet was suggested, but also plenty of wine; abstention from snuff (popular in the nineteenth century); being wrapped in brass and zinc wires moistened with vinegar; hydroelectric chains; and various patent medicines. He went from time to time to the then-fashionable hydropathic spas such as those of Dr. James Gully in Malvern and Dr. Edward Lane at Moor Park. Sometimes he was wrapped in cold wet sheets or given cold baths, and he was of the opinion that some of this helped him, but perhaps these tortures just took his mind off other worries.

In the final year of his life, his health deteriorated again, and Darwin seems to have had a premonition that the end was near. He almost collapsed while in London before Christmas 1881, and again a few months later while walking around the Sandwalk at Down House. He suffered chest pains (probably angina), a weak pulse, nausea, and extreme weakness. He was treated with quinine and amyl nitrate (an antispasmodic); he was in great pain, coughing up blood, and cried out that he wanted to die. He passed away at 4:00 P.M. on April 19, 1882, with many members of his family nearby.

Darwin's medical history remains an enigma. The various theories raise as many questions as they answer. Probably both organic and psychological factors were involved, linked to each other in complex ways. Much about Darwin, including his ideas, depends on the interplay of many factors; his medical history is no exception.

See also: Darwin's Death and Westminster Abbey Funeral.

FURTHER READING

Adler, S. 1959. "Darwin's Illness." *Nature* 184 (October 10): 1102–1103.

Bowlby, J. 1990. *Charles Darwin: A New Biography.* London: Hutchinson.

Colp, R., Jr. 1977. *To Be an Invalid: The Illness of Charles Darwin.* Chicago: University of Chicago Press.

Insectivorous Plants

Important book on experimental botany published by Charles Darwin in 1875. It could be considered part of Darwin's series of evolutionary works because it stresses the adaptation of plants to poor soils.

Darwin, ever the field naturalist, introduced this work as follows:

> During the summer of 1860, I was surprised by finding how large a number of insects were caught by the leaves of the common sun-dew (*Drosera rotundifolia*) on a heath in Sussex. I had heard that insects were thus caught, but knew nothing further on the subject. I gathered by chance a dozen plants, bearing fifty-six fully expanded leaves, and on thirty-one of these dead insects or remnants of them adhered; and, no doubt, many more would have been caught afterwards by these same leaves, and still more by those as yet not expanded. On one plant all six leaves had caught their prey; and on several plants very many leaves had caught more than a single insect. On one large leaf I found the remains of thirteen distinct insects. Flies (Diptera) are captured much oftener than other insects. (*Insectivorous Plants*, 1875, chapter 1)

By the early 1870s, Darwin contacted a number of his old friends and colleagues hoping to gain their assistance with a series of experiments on insectivorous plants; these included **Joseph Hooker** and his assistant (and eventual successor) William Thistelton-Dyer at Kew and **Asa Gray** at Harvard.

Some of these colleagues assisted with experimental work. Inquiries to the journal *Nature* brought sacks of letters to be dealt with by his son **Francis Darwin,** who acted as his assistant. Plants also arrived from many countries and were grown in Darwin's greenhouse at Down House. He was particularly interested in plants of the genus sundew (*Drosera*), butterwort (*Pinguicula*), and the aquatic bladderwort (*Utricularia*). He conducted many experiments. The following passage shows the care with which he carried out his experiments (in this case on sundew) and recorded his results:

> The central glands of a leaf were irritated with a small stiff camel-hair brush, and in 70 m. [minutes] several of the outer tentacles were inflected; in 5 hrs. [hours] all the sub-marginal tentacles were inflected; next morning after an interval of about 22 hrs. they were fully re-expanded. In all the following cases the period is reckoned from the time of first irritation.

Another leaf treated in the same manner had a few tentacles inflected in 20 m.; in 4 hrs. all the submarginal and some of the extreme marginal tentacles, as well as the edge of the leaf itself, were inflected; in 17 hrs. they had recovered their proper, expanded position. I then put a dead fly in the centre of the last-mentioned leaf, and next morning it was closely clasped; five days afterwards the leaf re-expanded, and the tentacles, with their glands surrounded by secretion, were ready to act again. (*Insectivorous Plants,* 1875, chapter 1)

Darwin and his colleagues conducted about 450 experiments on insectivorous plants. He fed the plants with fragments of boiled egg, beef, and pieces of plant material and treated them with various chemicals varying from ammonia and phosphates to tea. One of the objects of the study was to find out the extent to which plants resembled animals in being capable of digestive processes (they did) and possessing a nervous system (they did not).

The comparison with animals comes out in the following passage:

The absorption of animal matter from captured insects explains how Drosera can flourish in extremely poor peaty soil, in some cases where nothing but sphagnum moss grows, and mosses depend altogether on the atmosphere for their nourishment. Although the leaves at a hasty glance do not appear green, owing to the purple colour of the tentacles, yet the upper and lower surfaces of the blade, the pedicels of the central tentacles, and the petioles contain chlorophyll, so that, no doubt, the plant obtains and assimilates carbonic acid from the air. Nevertheless, considering the nature of the soil where it grows, the supply of nitrogen would be extremely limited, or quite deficient, unless the plant had the power of obtaining this important element from captured insects. We can thus understand how it is that the roots are so poorly developed. These usually consist of only two or three slightly divided branches, from half to one inch in length, furnished with absorbent hairs. It appears, therefore, that the roots serve only to imbibe water; though, no doubt, they would absorb nutritious matter if present in the soil; for as we shall hereafter see, they absorb a weak solution of carbonate of ammonia. A plant of Drosera, with the edges of its leaves curled inwards, so as to form a temporary stomach, with the glands of the closely inflected tentacles pouring forth their acid secretion, which dissolves animal matter, afterwards to be absorbed, may be said to feed like an animal. But, differently from an animal, it drinks by means of its roots; and it must drink largely, so as to retain many drops of viscid fluid round the glands, sometimes as many as 260, exposed during the whole day to a glaring sun. (*Insectivorous Plants,* 1875, chapter 1)

Darwin is at his best here; the passage shows careful observation and shrewd deduction as well as integrative abilities. It clearly emphasizes the plants' adaptation to environment (soil and climate, insects), but also relates the plant's form to its environment and physiology. Darwin is pushing home the evolutionary message of adaptation to environment stressed 15 years before in *On the Origin.*

The demand for Darwin as an author was shown when, in early July 1875, the first printing of *Insectivorous Plants* sold out quickly, and a 1,000 copy reprint sold out within a fortnight. A U.S. edition appeared a few months later, and a second edition, revised by Francis Darwin appeared in 1888. French, German, Italian, and Russian translations appeared in Darwin's life time.

Instinct

A stereotyped pattern of behavior that is similar in all individuals of the same species and is triggered by particular stimuli. It is usually assumed that instinct is partly or perhaps mainly inherited.

Some discussion of the instinctive behavior of animals can be found in the writings of Ancient Greek philosophers (such as Anaximander), those of the medieval period, and of the European Enlightenment. For example, René Descartes (1596–1650) is often regarded as the founder of modern dualism because of his emphasis on the distinction between body and mind and is the originator of a materialistic or mechanical interpretation of nature. **Jean-Baptiste Lamarck** wrote of instinct as inherited habit and, like his fellow-evolutionist, Darwin, after him, believed that adaptive changes might appear first in behavior.

Probably one of the sources that influenced Charles Darwin most in his thinking on this subject is **William Kirby** and William Spence's four-volume *Introduction to Entomology* (Kirby was a Suffolk country clergy-man, Spence a northern England industrialist). The book first appeared in 1815 and quickly went into several editions; the fifth edition appeared in 1828. Darwin and his cousin William Darwin Fox were enthusiastic insect collectors while undergraduates at Cambridge and probably had access to the book there. There was certainly a copy on board the *Beagle*—it was a composite made up of different volumes from different editions. There is evidence from his notes that Darwin used this work frequently both during the voyage and after. A heavily annotated copy, presumably the one taken aboard the *Beagle,* remains in the Darwin Archive at Cambridge University. Like its predecessor, Gilbert White's *Natural History of Selborne,* this work is written as a series of letters, and the lengthy (over 60 pages) Letter 27, in volume 2, is on "Instinct of Insects." Moreover, other letters on hibernation and societies also refer to instinct extensively.

Interestingly, both Kirby and Darwin are extremely wary of attempting a definition of instinct. The following excerpt, from the beginning of chapter 7 of the 1859 edition of *On the Origin of Species* is as close as Darwin gets to defining instinct:

An action, which we ourselves should require experience to enable us to perform, when performed by an animal, more especially by a young one, without any experience, and when performed by many individuals in the same way, without their knowing for what purpose it is performed, is usually said to be instinctive.

While he admitted the possibility that a habit may sometimes be inherited, he continued that it would be a serious error to suppose that the "greater number of instincts have been acquired by habit one generation and then transmitted to succeeding generations."

Darwin assumes that instincts are as important as structure or form to the welfare of the species. (Very seldom is an instinct in one species of value to another.) Darwin envisages trifling yet profitable variations in behavior gradually accumulating through natural selection into complex patterns of behavior.

Analogous to his arguments based on the effects that artificial selection has had on the physical form of animals that have experienced domestication and centuries of association with humans, he argues that instincts have, to some extent, been shaped by artificial selection over generations in the farmyard. Tameness has developed in chickens. Farm dogs rarely attack domestic animals because it has been bred out of them; those that do habitually attack are likely to be destroyed so that nonattackers predominate in the population. Tumbler pigeons display a behavior pattern that is unnatural in wild populations but that has been enhanced by selective breeding.

Complex patterns of instinctive behavior—such the building of complex nests by birds and the construction of perfect hexagonal wax cells for the storage of honey by bees (an example discussed at considerable length by Kirby)—could be built up though natural selection working to accentuate minor changes in behavior over generations. Possibly the hexagonal pattern of the modern beehive developed from an earlier form of spherical cells, he argued, giving examples of intermediate forms.

Another example that Darwin discusses in some detail in *On the Origin* is the instinctive behavior of the European cuckoo (*Cuculus canorus*). The female of this species visits the nests of smaller birds, apparently selecting nests that contain eggs that generally match hers in color, and replaces an egg of the host with one of her own. She typically lays four or five eggs at two-day intervals, each in a different nest (meadow pipits, *Anthus pratensis,* reed warblers, *Acrocephalous scirpaceus,* and hedge sparrow or dunnock, *Prunella modularis* or are often used). The young cuckoo, usually being larger than its nest mates, removes them from the nest and becomes the sole recipient of its foster parents' care; the young cuckoo has a depression in its back to assist in this procedure. Interestingly, some New World cuckoos have very light and flimsy nests, and there has been some discussion concerning the extent that they may be parasitic. There are records of normally nonparasitic bird species occasionally laying in the nests of other birds.

A young European cuckoo (*Cuculus canorus*) instinctively removes the competing eggs or nestlings from its host's nest. Here an egg is being removed from a hedge-sparrow or dunnock's (*Prunella modularis*) nest. Photo: the late Edward Armstrong.

Darwin wrote:

> Now let us suppose that the ancient progenitor of the European cuckoo . . . occasionally . . . laid an egg in another bird's nest. If the old bird profited from this occasional habit, or if the young were made more vigorous by advantage having been taken of the mistaken maternal instinct of another bird, than by their own mother's care, . . . then the old birds or the fostered young would gain an advantage. . . . [T]he young thus reared would be apt to lay their eggs in other birds' nests, and thus be successful in rearing their young. By a continued process of this nature, I believe that the strange instinct of our cuckoo could be, and has been generated. (*On the Origin,* chapter 7)

Also of interest is that the European cuckoos' eggs laid in dunnock nests do not resemble the sky-blue eggs of the host, suggesting that the colonization of the dunnock may be a recent development and that the species has not yet acquired the ability to distinguish cuckoo eggs from its own. Other species tend to remove eggs that are markedly different from their own. Thus, some sort of possible evolutionary sequence can be established.

Darwin bolstered his argument by pointing out that species that are closely related—even if they live in widely separated parts of the world—often have very similar instincts. Thrushes in North America line their nests with mud as do European thrushes. The male wrens (*Troglodytes*) of North America build multiple cock's nests as do the closely related European species.

Darwin collected a massive amount of material on instinct. **Animal behavior** had been of interest to him since his days on the *Beagle* and possibly before, and some of what he collected was unpublished in his life time. He wrote of migration patterns of birds, fish, and mammals; feigning death by some creatures; and the tameness (i.e., the absence of the instinct of flight from humans) of wild birds on remote islands.

Darwin concludes his chapter on Instinct in *On the Origin*:

> [I]t is far more satisfactory to look at such instincts as the young cuckoo ejecting its foster-brothers,—ants making slaves,—the larvae of ichneumonidae [ichneumon flies] feeding within the live bodies of caterpillars,—not as specially endowed or created instincts, but as small consequences of one general law, leading to the advancement of all organic beings, namely, multiply, vary, let the strongest live and the weakest die.

FURTHER READING

Romanes, George John. 1883. *Mental Evolution in Animals: With a Posthumous Essay on Instinct by Charles Darwin*. London: Kegan Paul, Trench & Co., 355–384.

Intellectual Aristocracy

It has been asserted that there is only one English intellectual family. During the latter part of the eighteenth century, throughout the nineteenth, and well into the twentieth, the leading academic families of England were so closely interconnected by kinship and marriage that it was almost impossible to separate them. Comparisons might be made with English aristocratic and landowning families (the two networks intermesh to a limited extent), or the tight network of relationships within European royal families.

Charles Darwin married his Wedgwood cousin. So too did his sister Caroline, as did his father Robert Waring (FRS). His grandfather, Josiah Wedgwood I (FRS), founder of the pottery dynasty, had married another Wedgwood. This was just one set of twigs from a tree that penetrated British intellectual life for generations. As well as Robert Waring Darwin, the son of Erasmus (FRS), Josiah II (Josiah I's son) had as brothers-in-law Sir James Mackintosh, barrister, philosopher, and public servant who described the young Charles as "interesting" and J. C. Sismondi, the Geneva economist. His brother Thomas Wedgwood was a pioneer photographer. The next generation, as well as Charles Darwin (FRS), contains Hensleigh Wedgwood, the Cambridge etymologist, and Henry Allen Wedgwood, barrister and author. The children of Charles Darwin included Sir George Darwin (FRS), mathematical physicist and astronomer, Sir Francis Darwin

(FRS), botanist and editor of his father's correspondence, and Leonard Darwin, army officer and president of the Royal Geographical Society. The third knight (and FRS), Sir Horace Darwin, was a scientific instrument maker.

The next generation of Darwins contains another distinguished physicist, Sir Charles Galton Darwin (FRS), master of Christ's College, Cambridge, and director of the National Physical Laboratory. His sister Gwen (later Raverat) became an artist of international repute as well as chronicler of the Darwin family. Sir Charles's marriage provides a link between Oxford and Cambridge: he married a daughter (Kathleen) of F. W. Pember, the warden of All Souls College, Oxford. Another of the offspring of Sir George Darwin was Margaret, who married Sir Geoffrey Keynes (surgeon and bibliographer), linking the Darwins to another great English intellectual family.

One of Horace Darwin's daughters, Norah, married Alan, the son of Sir Thomas Barlow, president of the Royal College of Physicians and personal physician to Queen Victoria and two subsequent sovereigns; Sir Alan became a senior civil servant. Norah was a distinguished scholar in her own right, editing her grandfather's diaries and notebooks.

Sir Francis Darwin's son Bernard was originally a barrister but gave up the law for journalism and authorship. He was a correspondent of the London *Times*. Bernard's son Robin became principal of the Royal College of Art in London. Sir Francis's daughter by his second wife was called Frances; she was a poet and married Professor Francis Cornford, fellow of Trinity College, Cambridge.

The following are also cousins of Darwins. Dr. Ralph Vaughan-Williams, one of England's greatest musicians (his maternal grandparents were a Wedgwood and a Darwin), the novelist Arthur Wedgwood, Sir Ralph Wedgwood, railway director, and his daughter Dame Veronica, the historian and literary editor of the journal *Time and Tide*. The first Lord Wedgwood married the daughter of a judge, Lord Bowen; his son was a distinguished artist, and one of his daughters, Camilla Wedgwood, was an anthropologist.

Doubling back to the Keynes family, Margaret, one of the granddaughters of Charles Darwin, who married Sir Geoffrey Keynes, the surgeon, had as a brother-in-law John Maynard Keynes, later Lord Keynes, a civil servant and the founder of modern economics. John Maynard was the product of an already distinguished Cambridge academic family; his father was John Neville Keynes, economist and logician. Sir Geoffrey's son was Richard Keynes (FRS), professor of physiology at Cambridge and also historian of ideas, for he edited the writings of and wrote on both Charles Darwin and John Maynard Keynes. So too did Randal Keynes in the next generation.

Among Charles Darwin's friends and associates, there was a tight network of intermarriages among members of the Hooker, Henslow, Jenyns, and Huxley families. (Reference is made to some of these links in the articles on the individuals concerned.)

The above few notes have touched on the complex web of relationships that makes up the intellectual elite of Britain over the last two centuries. The net could be extended to include the Trevelyans, Arnolds, Macaulays, Butlers, Venns, Conybears, and Dickens families. It is not altogether surprising that this network exists. Until the Second World War, Oxford University and Cambridge University dominated England's intellectual life (London and Durham entering on the scene after the 1830s). Like-minded academics associated (as they still do) for social as well as academic purposes—often there is no distinction. And it is entirely natural that young people should look for partners among the offspring of their parents' friends. There is also the tendency to at least look favorably on persons known to one when seeking to fill an appointment. All of these processes tend to perpetuate the network. But the system was open: it has always been possible for poor, working-class children of outstanding ability to gain university scholarships. And, from time to time, English academics have gone outside the network for partners. Both George Darwin in the nineteenth century and C. H. Trevelyan (son of G. M. Trevelyan) married Americans; marriages to Swiss and French persons also have occurred. These brought in, as the cynics might put it, new blood and perhaps new ideas and new money.

The list above contains many fellows of the **Royal Society,** an honor awarded to scientists of the highest distinction. Also sprinkled in the network are a good number of knighthoods (Sir), peerages (Lord), and baronetcies (hereditary knighthoods), traditionally given by the sovereign to persons who have made great contributions. This is a web of relationships that includes the highest elites. Its existence has both promoted intellectual and scholarly excellence but is, to some extent, also the product of it.

Further Reading

Annan, N. G. 1955. "The Intellectual Aristocracy." In *Studies in Social History: A Tribute to G M Trevelyan,* ed. J. H. Plumb. London: Longmans.

Cannon, W. F. 1964. "Scientists and Broad Churchmen: An Early Victorian Intellectual Network." *Journal of British Studies* 4 (1): 65–88.

Islands

Areas of land surrounded by water. During the *Beagle*'s voyage, Darwin set foot on about 40 islands, varying in size from tiny fragments of rock to the continent of Australia. Dozens of others he inspected from a distance. They were extremely important to his intellectual development.

"The zoology of archipelagoes will be well worth examination," wrote Darwin, in his *Beagle* notes early in his career. Indeed, the study of plants and animals on islands, particularly remote islands, has contributed substantially to evolutionary theory and provides some of the clearest evidence for evolution.

An island has a certain intrinsic appeal. Some islands (including many that Darwin visited) are extremely beautiful. An island is (usually) smaller than a continent or ocean and simpler in its geology and biology, so relationships can be more clearly discerned. They are also numerous and vary in their size, shape, degree of isolation, the extent to which they have been affected by humans, and their ecology. They, therefore, can be compared to each other and provide a whole series of natural experiments in which biological and other hypotheses can be tested. Moreover, the phenomenon of insularity is an almost universal one: rock pools on a seashore, caves, lakes, remote mountain tops, fragments of woodland in a landscape that has been cleared, and parklands in a large city all have islandlike properties. Scientific ideas, from the age of Charles Darwin (and before) generated from the study of islands have found applicability elsewhere.

Continental islands are usually underlain by rocks such as granite, slate, and sandstone typical of the continental masses. (**Australia,** of course, is a continent as well as an island.) Other, smaller continental islands may have been separated by a rise in sea level, by earth movement, or a combination of both from the larger continental masses of which they were once a part. Among the islands that Darwin visited, the **Falkland Islands, Tierra del Fuego, Chiloé,** the islets of the Chonos archipelago off the Chilean coast, **New Zealand,** and **Tasmania** all have, at least in part, continental-type rocks beneath them, even if they show varying degrees of isolation.

Oceanic islands have never had a connection with, or formed a part of, a major continent. They have, quite literally, arisen out of the ocean as the result volcanic activity (as in the cases of **St. Helena and Ascension Island,** Terceira in the **Azores,** and **Fernando Noronha**); through coral growth (Cocos); or as the result of a combination of volcanic activity and the growth of corals (**Tahiti, Mauritius**).

Scientists today recognize that, despite potentially striking differences, islands have in common the following characteristics:

1. Usually relatively small size. (There are obvious exceptions.)
2. Isolation; an island is defined as a fragment of land surrounded by water, and so any island is isolated from other terrestrial environments, if only by a narrow channel.
3. Relatively low species diversity. Isolation—in some cases, extreme isolation—may mean that fewer species of plants and animals have been able to establish themselves than on mainland environments (assuming the hypothesis of independent creation is rejected).
4. Very clear boundaries.
5. A degree of endemism. Isolation means that at least some of an island's biota may be unique. The flow of genetic material between the island ecosystem and an outside source of variability may be impossible, or almost so.

6. Small populations: the relatively small physical size of many islands means that they have a small population (that can be relatively easily counted, in the case of larger organisms).
7. Relatively simple networks of ecological relationships; the low species diversity, the small size, and small populations of plants and animals on islands, along with their distinctive boundaries often means that islands are relatively easy to study. It is thus often argued that it is easier to figure out what is going on a tiny islet than on a great continent.
8. Comparability. Although each island represents a unique combination of physical factors and biological species, the fact that there are so many islands means that comparisons can be made. And, as Darwin knew well and wrote of in his diary during the final days of his voyage, "the habit of comparison leads to generalization."

For these reasons, islands have had great attractions for modern scientists, and there has been a great deal of investment in the study of their geology, biology, and ecology.

Darwin, when he first boarded HMS *Beagle,* understood only a small part of this. However, he had a brilliant, creative mind. He had been trained in certain critical skills, and he had the incredible good fortune to visit a wide range of these natural island laboratories.

In some cases, it is possible to trace the development of an idea or group of ideas through the course of the voyage. An example is provided by Darwin's coral atoll theory. Simply stated, this is the notion that fringing coral reefs, barrier reefs, and atolls are members of a series and that the main vehicle driving the transformation is a rise in sea level or a subsiding land level. (**Charles Lyell,** in *Principles of Geology* expressed the view that circular coral atolls were the result of the growth of coral around the lip of a volcanic crater; Darwin, at a fairly early stage rejected this notion.)

Coral growth had interested Darwin since he had seen a few tiny coral-like forms along the Scottish coast while he was a medical student in Edinburgh. How much bigger and more spectacular were the corals growing in the sea at his feet as he sat on the shore of Quail Island, at St. Jago in the **Cape Verde Islands,** a few weeks into the voyage! Moreover, the limestones on the shore behind him told a story of uplift. This site seems to have been that of his scientific awakening, the point where he began to appreciate in a vivid way that he lived in a dynamic, changing world. A few weeks later, he scrambled ashore the islets of the Abrolhos, apparently composed almost entirely of coral, and noticed the huge brain corals in the sea nearby. Although Darwin did not land again on a true coral island for several years, there is evidence that some of the associated ideas ran through his mind while he was in the Falklands, on Chiloé, and around the coast of South America as he searched for evidence of change in the relative levels of land and sea.

His letters and notebooks show that his interest in a theory of coral islands was reawakened shortly before he left the west coast of South America. Glimpses of distant atolls, perhaps from the mast of the *Beagle,* followed as the ship crossed the Pacific Ocean. From a high point in Tahiti, he was able view the Isle of Eimeo (Moorea), seeing a coral barrier reef in all its glory. During the same visit, from an outrigger canoe and with a jumping pole, he was able to examine the detailed form of coral reefs. He appreciated that different parts of the reef were associated with different species of corals and that corals only thrived in shallow, disturbed water. Captain **Robert Fitz-Roy**'s hydrographic surveys showed that, offshore from Tahiti, the seabed fell away steeply; clearly, the coral formations were the necklaces around caps of isolated submarine mountains. Between Tahiti and New Zealand, the first full draft of the coral atoll theory was prepared. The **Cocos (Keeling) Islands,** visited after he left Australia, provided a case study. It was the first true atoll upon which he had set foot, and, although he probably overestimated the rate of change in level, the study of the archipelago provided striking confirmation of his theory. Soundings offshore showed that the bed sloped away steeply, and a glimpse of the tiny atoll of North Keeling, a few hours to the north of the main archipelago, provided another example.

There were clear links between the development of the coral atoll theory and his study of volcanic islands. While atolls had developed through gradual change as the result of subsidence, time and again, Darwin stated that he thought that some volcanic islands were rising; he thought that rises in one part of the ocean floor were compensated for by subsidence elsewhere. Certainly he thought he had seen evidence of rise at St. Jago, where limestones containing the remains of marine organisms that were still around were raised above sea level. On Mauritius, surrounded by coral reefs but with a volcanic island core, he found coral material raised above the level of the beach.

Explorations along the coasts of Australia, especially Tasmania (areas that were visited after St. Jago, the **Galapagos Islands,** and Tahiti but before Cocos and Mauritius), further convinced him that at these localities, also, changes in sea level were also occurring. (Not all of his suggestions were well grounded; he does not seem to have understood that the long, narrow inlets of Sydney Harbour, the Derwent Estuary in Tasmania, and the almost circular King George's Sound in southwest Australia were formed by a rise in sea level relative to the land, inundating the preexisting valleys. He incorrectly thought that, along vast stretches of the coast of southern Australia, the sea had formerly stood higher and that there had been emergence rather than submergence.)

Islands were significant to Darwin's biological research, too. He noted that both coral islands and volcanic islands had a low biodiversity—they supported very few species of plants and animals. Of Tahiti he commented:

> It must not . . . be supposed that these woods at all equalled the forests of Brazil. In an island, the vast number of productions which characterise a continent cannot be expected to occur. (*Diary,* November, 17 1835)

Similarly, on the Cocos Islands, although there was a thick, tangled, jungle-like vegetation, the young Darwin was not deceived; the number of species was low:

> Besides the Cocoa nut which is so numerous as to first appear the only tree, there are five or six other kinds. One called the Cabbage tree, grows in great bulk in proportion to its height & has an irregular figure; . . . Besides these trees the number of native plants is exceedingly limited: I suppose it does not exceed a dozen. (*Diary,* April 2, 1836)

He went on:

> There are no true land birds, a snipe & land-rail are the only waders, the rest are all birds of the sea. Insects are very few in number: I must except some spiders & a small ant, which swarms in countless numbers at every spot and place.

The snipe was probably in fact a turnstone, *Arenaria interpres.* The land-rail, later identified as *Rallus philippensis andrewii,* is an endemic subspecies now confined to North Keeling. A fragment of paper kept with Darwin's zoological notes lists the 12 specimens: flies, ants, a couple of moths, and a beetle. In his published version, *Voyage of the Beagle* he amends the total to 13 species. He records a single species of lizard. In his writings on the land, plants, and animals of the archipelago, words such as "few," "only," "scanty," and "paucity" occur. He made similar observations concerning the low numbers of species present on other remote islets. On Cocos, he referred to the remote atoll as a "refuge for the destitute," a phrase that implies not only a long and difficult journey for ocean-carried seeds and fruits, wind-blown insects, or other floating or rafted organisms, but the rarity of events such as the arrival of such a colonizing "diseminule" (the fragment of living material—seed, fruit, spore, wind-blown insect—that is disseminated) on the remote atoll.

He could not always be sure, but Darwin sometimes appreciated that animals might be endemic (i.e. unique, found nowhere else) locally restricted to an island or island group. He certainly thought this was the case with some of the birds he encountered in the Galapagos, and indeed many months before he visited that archipelago, he hinted in his notes that the forms of Falklands fox, or **warrah,** on the islands East Falkland and West Falkland might be distinct varieties.

Darwin, while aboard the *Beagle,* thought that coral atolls and, to some extent, volcanic islands provided examples of changing environments; coming under the influence of Lyell, he appreciated that the Earth was undergoing gradual change. He appreciated that islands were impoverished in terms of the numbers of plants and animal species, and he had some idea that the biotas (floras plus faunas) of remote islands were distinctive.

Possibly partly as the result of his island experiences, and partly through correspondence and reading after his return to England, he appreciated that some types of organisms were rare on remote islands; where frogs or toads (which cannot tolerate salt water) were found on remote islands, there was evidence that they had been introduced accidentally or deliberately by human action. The distinctiveness, in all these ways, of island life confirmed in his mind, as time went on, the correctness of the evolutionary hypothesis. If one were to accept the idea of independent creation, there would be no reason for islands to be distinctive. But if one accepts that all life on remote islands has been carried there by the wind, by ocean currents, or as passengers on other organisms—through long-distance dispersal— then the low number of species, the absence of certain life forms (amphibians, freshwater fish), and the endemism occasioned by long isolation are explained. In *On the Origin of Species,* he put it as follows.

> The general absence of frogs, toads and newts on so many oceanic islands cannot be accounted for by their physical conditions; indeed it seems that islands are peculiarly well fitted for these animals; for frogs have been introduced into Madiera, the Azores and Mauritius, and have multiplied so as to become a nuisance. (*On the Origin of Species,* chapter 10)

Evolutionary theory, emphasizing that life begets life and that living things can only reach remote islands by long-distance dispersal, thus explains their absence. "But why, on the theory of creation, they should not have been created there, would be very difficult to explain."

Living quietly at Down House, Darwin, sometimes with the help of local children who collected for him, tested whether certain seeds could float or whether seeds could survive the digestive tracts of birds as part of experiments to demonstrate whether long-distance dispersal was possible. Ideas on the nature of island environments, and the thoughts about the significance of these run through the entire corpus of Darwin's work, from his notes made aboard the *Beagle* to his later evolutionary writings.